Wikipedia: The Missing Manual

John Broughton

O'REILLY®

Beijing · Cambridge · Farnham · Köln · Paris · Sebastopol · Taipei · Tokyo

Wikipedia: The Missing Manual
by John Broughton

Copyright © 2008 O'Reilly Media. All rights reserved.
Printed in the United States of America.

Published by O'Reilly Media, Inc., 1005 Gravenstein Highway North, Sebastopol, CA 95472

O'Reilly books may be purchased for educational, business, or sales promotional use. Online editions are also available for most titles (*http://safari.oreilly.com*). For more information, contact our corporate/institutional sales department: (800) 998-9938 or *corporate@oreilly.com*.

Editors: Nan Barber and Peter Meyers	**Indexer:** Dawn Frausto
Copy Editor: Sohaila Abdulali and Jill Steinberg	**Cover Designer:** David Freedman
Production Editor: Nellie McKesson	**Illustrators:** Robert Romano and Jessamyn Read
Proofreader: Nellie McKesson	

Printing History:

January 2008:   First Edition

RepKover™

This book uses RepKover™, a durable and flexible lay-flat binding.

ISBN-10: 0-596-51516-2
ISBN-13: 978-0-596-51516-4

[M]

Table of Contents

Part I.   Editing, Creating, and Maintaining Articles

Part V. Customizing Wikipedia

The Missing Credits

About the Author

 **John Broughton** John Broughton has been a registered editor at Wikipedia since August 2005, with more than 15,000 edits by the time he wrote this book. His biggest Wikipedia endeavor has been the *Editor's index to Wikipedia* (just type that in the "search" box at the left of any Wikipedia page). This index lists every important reference page on Wikipedia, as well as hundreds of off-Wikipedia Web pages with useful information and tools for Wikipedia editors.

John's first experience with programming computers was in a 1969 National Science Foundation program. Since then, he's held various computer-related management positions in the headquarters of a U.S. Army Reserve division, worked in internal audit departments as a Certified Information Systems Auditor, and was the Campus Y2K Coordinator at U.C. Berkeley.

A Certified Management Accountant, John has B.S. in Mathematical Sciences from Johns Hopkins University; an M.B.A. from Golden Gate University; an M.S. in Education from the University of Southern California; and a Masters in Public Policy from the University of California at Berkeley.

About the Creative Team

Nan Barber (editor) has worked with the Missing Manual series since its inception. She lives in Massachusetts with her husband and G4 Macintosh. Email: *nanbarber@oreilly.com*.

Dawn Frausto (editor) is assistant editor for the Missing Manual series. When not working, she rock climbs, plays soccer, and causes trouble. Email: *dawn@oreilly.com*.

Nellie McKesson (production editor) is a graduate of St. John's College in Santa Fe, New Mexico. She currently lives in Cambridge, MA, where her favorite places to eat are Punjabi Dhaba and Tacos Lupita. Email: *nellie@oreilly.com*.

Sohaila Abdulali (copy editor) is a freelance writer and editor. She has published a novel, several children's books, and numerous short stories and articles. She recently finished an ethnography of an aboriginal Indian woman. She lives in New York City with her husband Tom and their small but larger-than-life daughter, Samara. She can be reached through her Web site at *http://www.sohailaink.com*.

Jill Steinberg (copy editor) is a freelance writer and editor based in Seattle, and has produced content for O'Reilly, Intel, Microsoft, and the University of Washington. When she's not working with words, Jill takes Italian classes, practices opera singing, and helps create urban parks. Email: *saysjill@mac.com*.

Daniel Mocsny (tech reviewer) discovered Wikipedia editing in April, 2006. He edits as an ordinary user, and as of late 2007 had the second-highest edit count on the Wikipedia Help desk. In addition, he is an administrator on two other public wikis and three corporate wikis, with a real-life involvement in software development, documenting, and technical support. You can contact Daniel via his Wikipedia user talk page: *http://en.wikipedia.org/wiki/User_talk:Teratornis*.

Godmund Schick (technical reviewer) is an avid coffee drinker who periodically spends time baking, quilting, running, reading, and experiencing new things. Email: *godmschick@gmail.com*.

Acknowledgements

This book would not have been possible without the encouragement, support, and assistance of my wife Joan. I want to thank Pete Meyers, who responded so positively to my proposal for the book; Nan Barber, my editor, whose help and patience made the writing process much easier and the words in this book so much better; and the technical reviewers, Daniel Mocsny and Godmund Schick, whose comments on the first draft I found invaluable.

—*John Broughton*

The Missing Manual Series

Missing Manuals are witty, superbly written guides to computer products that don't come with printed manuals (which is just about all of them). Each book features a handcrafted index; cross-references to specific pages (not just chapters); and RepKover, a detached-spine binding that lets the book lie perfectly flat without the assistance of weights or cinder blocks. Recent and upcoming titles include:

Access 2007: The Missing Manual by Matthew MacDonald

AppleScript: The Missing Manual by Adam Goldstein

AppleWorks 6: The Missing Manual by Jim Elferdink and David Reynolds

CSS: The Missing Manual by David Sawyer McFarland

Creating Web Sites: The Missing Manual by Matthew MacDonald

Digital Photography: The Missing Manual by Chris Grover and Barbara Brundage

Dreamweaver 8: The Missing Manual by David Sawyer McFarland

Dreamweaver CS3: The Missing Manual by David Sawyer McFarland

eBay: The Missing Manual by Nancy Conner

Excel 2003: The Missing Manual by Matthew MacDonald

Excel 2007: The Missing Manual by Matthew MacDonald

Facebook: The Missing Manual by E.A. Vander Veer

FileMaker Pro 8: The Missing Manual by Geoff Coffey and Susan Prosser

FileMaker Pro 9: The Missing Manual by Geoff Coffey and Susan Prosser

Flash 8: The Missing Manual by E.A. Vander Veer

Flash CS3: The Missing Manual by E.A. Vander Veer and Chris Grover

FrontPage 2003: The Missing Manual by Jessica Mantaro

GarageBand 2: The Missing Manual by David Pogue

Google: The Missing Manual, Second Edition by Sarah Milstein, J.D. Biersdorfer, and Matthew MacDonald

The Internet: The Missing Manual by David Pogue and J.D. Biersdorfer

iMovie 6 & iDVD: The Missing Manual by David Pogue

iMovie '08 & iDVD: The Missing Manual by David Pogue

iPhone: The Missing Manual by David Pogue

iPhoto 6: The Missing Manual by David Pogue

iPhoto '08: The Missing Manual by David Pogue

iPod: The Missing Manual, Sixth Edition by J.D. Biersdorfer

JavaScript: The Missing Manual by David Sawyer McFarland

Mac OS X: The Missing Manual, Tiger Edition by David Pogue

Mac OS X: The Missing Manual, Leopard Edition by David Pogue

Microsoft Project 2007: The Missing Manual by Bonnie Biafore

Office 2004 for Macintosh: The Missing Manual by Mark H. Walker and Franklin Tessler

Office 2007: The Missing Manual by Chris Grover, Matthew MacDonald, and E.A. Vander Veer

Office 2008 for Macintosh: The Missing Manual by Jim Elferdink

PCs: The Missing Manual by Andy Rathbone

Photoshop Elements 6: The Missing Manual by Barbara Brundage

PowerPoint 2007: The Missing Manual by E.A. Vander Veer

QuickBase: The Missing Manual by Nancy Conner

QuickBooks 2008: The Missing Manual by Bonnie Biafore

Quicken 2008: The Missing Manual by Bonnie Biafore

Switching to the Mac: The Missing Manual, Leopard Edition by David Pogue

Switching to the Mac: The Missing Manual, Tiger Edition by David Pogue and Adam Goldstein

Windows 2000 Pro: The Missing Manual by Sharon Crawford

Windows XP Home Edition: The Missing Manual, Second Edition by David Pogue

Windows Vista: The Missing Manual by David Pogue

Windows XP Pro: The Missing Manual, Second Edition by David Pogue, Craig Zacker, and Linda Zacker

Word 2007: The Missing Manual by Chris Grover

The "For Starters" books contain only the most essential information from their larger counterparts—in larger type, with a more spacious layout, and none of the more advanced sidebars. Recent titles include:

Access 2003 for Starters: The Missing Manual by Kate Chase and Scott Palmer

Access 2007 for Starters: The Missing Manual by Matthew MacDonald

Excel 2003 for Starters: The Missing Manual by Matthew MacDonald

Excel 2007 for Starters: The Missing Manual by Matthew MacDonald

PowerPoint 2007 for Starters: The Missing Manual by E.A. Vander Veer

Quicken 2006 for Starters: The Missing Manual by Bonnie Biafore

Windows Vista for Starters: The Missing Manual by David Pogue

Windows XP for Starters: The Missing Manual by David Pogue

Word 2007 for Starters: The Missing Manual by Chris Grover

Introduction

Wikipedia formally began in January 2001, as a project to produce a free content encyclopedia to which anyone can contribute. Seven years later, Wikipedia pages seem to turn up near the top of almost every Google search. Wikipedia has become the first place millions of people go to get a quick fact or to launch extensive research.

Editions of Wikipedia exist in more than 250 languages, with a combined total of more than nine million articles. All the editions use the same underlying software, Media-Wiki. All are owned and supported by the Wikimedia Foundation, a nonprofit organization that also operates a number of other online collaborative projects, including Wiktionary, Wikiquote, Wikibooks, Wikisource, Wikispecies, Wikinews, and Wikiversity.

Each language edition of Wikipedia operates separately, almost entirely through the efforts of tens of thousands of unpaid volunteers. The Foundation has only about a dozen employees, including a couple of programmers. It buys hardware, designs and implements the core software, and pays for the network bandwidth that makes Wikipedia and its sister projects possible, but it doesn't have the resources to do any of the *writing* for those projects. All the writing and editing are done by people who get no money for their efforts, although plenty of intrinsic satisfaction.

Wikipedia has never lacked skeptics. Why expect quality articles if everyone—the university professor and the 12-year-old middle school student—has equal editing rights? Won't cultists and fringe theorists and partisans take control of controversial articles? Won't vandalism become rampant, driving away good editors? How can tens of thousands of people work together when there is no hierarchy to provide direction and resolve disputes?

These questions point out the inevitable disadvantages of the "anyone can edit" approach to creating an online encyclopedia. Wikipedia will always be a work in progress, not a finished product. What the skeptics overlook, however, is that letting anyone edit has proved to be an incredible *strength*. In a world where a billion or so people have access to the Internet, millions of people have contributed to Wikipedia, and their numbers are increasing every day.

As a result, the vast majority of the millions of articles in all the different Wikipedias are of at least reasonable quality although many are quite short. The Wikipedia.org domain is among the most visited on the Internet, because there's no free alternative for most of the information in Wikipedia. The critics' predictions that Wikipedia's limitations will cripple it have not come true.

What makes Wikipedia so successful? Here are some of the reasons it works:

- An overwhelming percentage of the edits to Wikipedia are done in *good faith*—that is, by people trying to improve articles, not vandalize them. When vandalism occurs, it tends to remain very briefly, because there are so many constructive editors around to fix it.
- Wikipedia has a large number of rules about its process that encourage collaboration and build consensus around what information goes into articles. When people follow these rules, quality articles are the result.
- An overwhelming percentage of editors do follow the rules, and when others point out their mistakes, they're willing to self-correct. Those editors who do find Wikipedia rules to be problematical typically leave on their own.
- Finally, there are a few editors with special authority to enforce the rules. This authority is granted by the community of users, through agreed-upon processes. So far, the enforcers have been adequate for the job, helped by increasing automation of many routine administrative tasks.

As Wikipedia grows and the number of editors, edits per day, and total articles increases, its focus has changed, and will continue to change. Wikipedia already has articles about the most important topics, so the focus is shifting away from *quantity* and towards *quality*—improving articles rather than creating new ones. As the definition for success shifts, Wikipedia's processes will adjust as well. The consensus approach has proven flexible enough, so far, to deal with problems as they arise. Emphasizing quality —in ways that affect most editors' everyday editing—will be one of Wikipedia's biggest challenges.

About This Book

This book is about the English edition of Wikipedia—the oldest, largest, and most complicated edition of Wikipedia, but not (since March 2001) the only edition. In other words, this book is about the en.wikipedia.org domain, not the entire Wikipedia.org domain. For simplicity, when you see the term "Wikipedia," it refers to the *English* edition of Wikipedia. Just remember that other language versions exist.

Why do you need a *book* about editing Wikipedia? Wikipedia certainly doesn't lack for pages that document policies, technical matters, instructions, and agreed-on processes. Wikipedia depends on volunteer editors to write and update virtually all the documentation for Wikipedia and its underlying software, and plenty of editors enjoy doing this valuable work. If printed out, Wikipedia's online reference pages would make a multivolume set of books that might be titled *Everything you might possibly want to tell million of volunteers from around the world about how to write an encyclopedia, together, including how to organize and govern themselves, and how to change the software that underlies the encyclopedia, avoid legal pitfalls, and enjoy themselves.*

What's missing, however, is structured guidance for people who want to learn the "core curriculum," the information you absolutely need to avoid running afoul of the rules, and a *structured* process for learning all about editing, including all the tips and tools that can make editing easier. Wikipedia doesn't offer anything that charts the path from novice to expert, with step by step illustrations for every topic along the way.

For example, there are dozens of pages in Wikipedia that describe the three different processes for getting an article deleted. There are no designated pages for novices and experienced editors, and there's no editorial board responsible for maintaining consistency and deciding how much duplication is appropriate. Newcomers to Wikipedia often find the large collection of massively hyperlinked online reference pages intimidating. With so many entry points, it's hard to know where to start.

This book provides a clear path to all the essentials, with numerous additions to choose among. Tens of thousands of Wikipedians have gotten off to rough starts, yet persevered, going on to become solid contributors. This book helps you learn from those mistakes without having to personally live through them.

Wikipedia: The Missing Manual is designed to accommodate editors at every level of experience. If you're just starting out, that's fine: The early chapters will make your editing experience more productive as well as enjoyable. Nor do you have to be a computer whiz. The really great editors are good at one or more of several things, including research, editing and writing, organizing, and working with other editors; technical matters are simply one realm of specializing as a Wikipedia editor.

If you've already done quite a bit of editing of Wikipedia, and learned—by trial and error as well as reading documentation—what to do and not to do, even the earlier chapters are likely to offer you useful tips and tricks. In the later chapters, you'll learn about things you've never run across before, simply because you've never had time to read through all the Wikipedia documentation. Check out the table of contents to spot unfamiliar aspects of Wikipedia, so you can turn immediately to the parts of the book most likely to help you work better and faster.

About the Outline

Wikipedia: The Missing Manual is divided into five parts, each containing several chapters.

- **Part 1, Editing, Creating, and Maintaining Articles**, covers the basics. These chapters explain the *right* way to edit, why you want to be a registered editor, how to become one, and everything you need to know about figuring out, tracking, and reversing changes to articles when appropriate. It also discusses all the things to do when creating a new article.

- **Part 2, Collaborating with Other Editors**, discusses the rules of engagement, how normal conversations occur, the standard Wikipedia processes for disagreements over content, and dealing with incivility and personal attacks. This section also covers what Wikipedia calls *WikiProjects*—groups of editors working on articles of common interest, plus the wide range of activities that go into expanding and maintaining a huge encyclopedia: answering questions, tutoring and mentoring, joint reviews of articles, and more.

- **Part 3, Formatting and Illustrating Articles**, introduces you to some parts of articles that aren't text or links: the table of contents, lists and tables, and images and other media. Much of this can be confusing when you first encounter it, but each topic has a logic that makes it easy to understand once you've worked with that it for a bit. (And you always have this book as a reference!)

- **Part 4, Building a Stronger Encyclopedia**, looks at the larger picture. It shows you that an article isn't locked in stone—you can rename it, split it up, merge it with other articles, or even ask for it to be deleted. Naming and merging are ways of getting readers to the information that they want. Another way, covered in this part, is Wikipedia's system of categories, one of several ways to find and navigate between articles.

- **Part 5, Customizing Wikipedia**, discusses every option that you have to customize Wikipedia to suit yourself, using choices you find when you click My Preferences. You'll also learn how to implement JavaScript user scripts (which you'll see mentioned in the "Power Users' Clinic" boxes in this book).

- **Part 6, Appendixes**, provides you with resources to make the most of Wikipedia, as a reader, editor, and member of the Wikipedia community. Appendix A is an explanation of every link and tab for standard Wikipedia pages (in both reading and editing mode). Appendix B, Reader's Guide to Wikipedia, provides some insider tips for those who simply want to read Wikipedia, and want to know what's available besides Wikipedia's search feature and following links in articles. Appendix C, Leaning More, provides good starting points to get you as an editor to exactly the reference page you're looking for, lists the places in Wikipedia where you can get personalized help, and shows you where you can find out about Wikipedia as a community.

The Very Basics

You'll find very little jargon or nerd terminology in this book. You will, however, encounter a few terms and concepts that you'll encounter frequently in your computing life:

- **Clicking**. This book gives you two kinds of instructions that require you to use your computer's mouse or trackpad. To *click* means to point the arrow cursor at something on the screen and then—without moving the cursor at all—to press and release the clicker button on the mouse (or laptop trackpad). To *double-click*, of course, means to click twice in rapid succession, again without moving the cursor at all.

- **Wikipedia doesn't use menus**. On Wikipedia pages, links to pages, and links that trigger a particular action (such as opening an article for editing) are found along the top and left of the screen, not in menus. These can change; what you see depends on the type of Wikipedia page, and whether or not you're logged in. In addition, the content of a page may have links, typically to content on other Wikipedia pages. Appendix A covers every single link and action at the top and left of your screen.

- **The search box on the left side of the screen** is the primary way to go to any page for which you can't see a link. For example, entering *elephant* and clicking Go (or pressing *Enter*) sends you to the Wikipedia article titled *Elephant*. If you use this book a lot, you'll probably use the search box a lot—you may find it's worth memorizing the keyboard shortcut to get to it (page 426).

- **Most of the reference pages that discuss policy, guidelines, how-to, and so on, have an abbreviation ("shortcut") that you can use to quickly get to that page**. For example, rather than type *Wikipedia:Verifiability* (23 characters; note that there's no space after the colon), you can just type the shortcut *WP:V* (only four characters), and then press Enter or click Go. In the early chapters, the search box will be explicitly mentioned; in later chapters, the book will normally just mention the shortcut name, assuming you're familiar with using the search box to get to a specified page.

- **Wikipedia uses special markup text in its MediaWiki software**. For example, to set up a link that points to another page within Wikipedia, you put paired square brackets around a word in editing—thus *[[elephant]]*, for example, entered in editing mode, would be "elephant" as a link once an edit has been saved. Chapter 1 on basic editing explains markup text.

- **Articles and pages are different things**. Readers are interested in article pages and, to a lesser extent, category pages and portal pages. Wikipedia has many other types of pages: template, image, and user pages, for example—and talk pages (page 145) for every type of page.

Mac OS, Windows, Browsers, and Keyboard Shortcuts

Wikipedia works in all modern Web browsers on both Windows and Macintosh computers. The screen may look slightly different from the illustrations in this book, depending on your browser. The screenshots in this book were taken while using Firefox and Opera, on a computer running Windows XP.

The tutorials and other instructions in this book don't use keyboard shortcuts, because shortcuts vary not only between operating systems but between browsers (Firefox 1.5

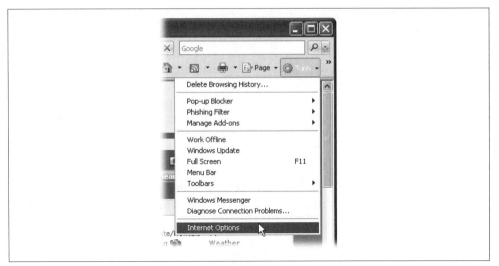

Figure 1. When you read in a Missing Manual, "Choose Tools→Internet Options," that means: "Click the Tools menu to open it. Then click Internet Options in that menu."

vs. Firefox 2.0 vs. Opera, for example, in their Windows versions). If you like using shortcut keys, see the details in Appendix A (page 426) on how to learn them.

About→These→Arrows

In this book, and throughout the Missing Manual series, you'll find sentences like this one: "Go to Tools→Preferences→Advanced tab." That's shorthand for a much longer instruction that directs you to navigate through menu commands and dialog boxes, like so: "Click to open the Tools menu; choose Preferences. In the Preferences dialog box, click the Advanced tab." This kind of arrow shorthand helps to simplify the business of choosing commands in menus, as shown in Figure 1.

Late-Breaking News

Wikipedia changes all the time. Policies and guidelines and other reference pages get reworded, merged, expanded, renamed, and updated by editors whenever editors feel that they can be improved, assuming the general Wikipedia community agrees. Developers fix bugs and add features, putting out changes every week. Administrators tweak the standard messages that all editors see, striving for clarity. Processes change because a regular editor, or the Wikimedia Foundation, or someone in between initiates a change. In short, Wikipedia today is different from what it was a month ago, and will be different a month from now.

Wikipedia's rate of change has presented a challenge in writing this book. It's as current as it can be, but if you notice that a screenshot isn't exactly the way Wikipedia appears to you on screen, then something (minor) has changed since just before this book was published. You will see mentions in a number of places in the book about where change may be just around the corner (a WYSISYG edit box, threaded discussions on talk pages, single sign-in across all Foundation projects, and more). These changes could happen just as you're reading this book, or not for a year or two.

Nevertheless, you'll find the core of Wikipedia changes very slowly—after all, it does have an established base of active editors, and a history of success that makes editors reluctant to change processes that aren't considered broken. So the changes that aren't covered by this book won't prevent you from gaining great Wikipedia editing skills. And if you find something about Wikipedia that's not in this book and should be, let us know. We'll add it to the next edition.

About MissingManuals.com

At the missingmanuals.com (*http://missingmanuals.com*) Web site, you'll find articles, tips, and updates to the book. In fact, you're invited and encouraged to submit such corrections and updates yourself. In an effort to keep the book as up-to-date and ac-curate as possible, each time we print more copies of this book, we'll make any confirmed corrections you've suggested. We'll also note such changes on the Web site, so that you can mark important corrections into your own copy of the book, if you like. (Click the book's name, and then click the Errata link, to see the changes.)

In the meantime, we'd love to hear your own suggestions for new books in the Missing Manual line. There's a place for that on the Web site, too, as well as a place to sign up for free email notification of new titles in the series.

While you're online, you can also register this book at *http://www.oreilly.com* (you can jump directly to the registration page by going here: *http://tinyurl/yo82k3*). Registering means we can send you updates about this book, and you'll be eligible for special offers like discounts on future editions of *Wikipedia: The Missing Manual*.

Safari® Books Online

When you see a Safari® Books Online icon on the cover of your favorite technology book, that means the book is available online through the O'Reilly Network Safari Bookshelf.

Safari offers a solution that's better than eBooks. It's a virtual library that lets you easily search thousands of top tech books, cut and paste code samples, download chapters, and find quick answers when you nee the most accurate, current information. Try it free at *http://safari.oreilly.com*.

PART I

Editing, Creating, and Maintaining Articles

CHAPTER 1

Editing for the First Time

Anyone can edit Wikipedia—including you. That's right. There's no fee, and you don't have to register. You don't even have to have an email account (but if you're reading this book, you probably do). As the Introduction explains, all Wikipedia articles are collaborative efforts. You can jump right in and add your own knowledge with just a few clicks and some typing.

This chapter explains what you see when you look at an article in Wikipedia's editing window and how to practice, preview, and save your edits. You'll also learn a few more basic editing skills—how to create a link from one article to another, and how to edit a section of an article rather than the whole article. Once you've got these skills under your belt, you're ready for the first step in for-real Wikipedia editing: identifying an article in need of an edit.

TIP

You can dive right in and start editing without setting up a Wikipedia account (that is, getting a user name). However, there are advantages to having a user name—increased privacy and the ability to create new articles and a personal user page, to name two. So you have an option: You can follow the chapters in the order they appear, or you can skip to Chapter 3 and get a user name first, and *then* read this chapter and Chapter 2.

The Wikipedia Way of Editing

Experienced Wikipedia editors understand one thing above all else: Wikipedia is a collaboration. There's no need to be intimidated, because you've got the support of an entire community of researchers, fact-checkers, and proofreaders. Keeping the following points in mind will get you into the right mindset for effective editing:

- **You don't need to know everything about Wikipedia to edit an article**. Wikipedia has literally hundreds of pages of policy, guidelines, and how-to information on topics such as capitalization, categorization, citations, copyrights, disclaimers, foreign language characters, headings, indentation, links, lists, neutrality, pronunciation, quotations, tags, and templates, to name just a few. *If you don't get something exactly right, don't worry—no one else gets everything right every time, either.*

- **You don't need to know everything about your subject to edit an article**. If you add something that's constructive and 90-percent right, that's far better than not doing an edit at all. As in sports, you don't need to hit a home run or score a goal on every play to be a valuable contributor. *If you don't get something exactly right, someone else is likely to come along and help by fixing or finishing it.*

- **You can contribute without editing at all**. If you see a problem in an article, but you don't (yet) know how to fix it, or you do know how to fix it, but you can't edit the article (some articles are fully protected, typically for short periods of time), you can still help by posting a constructive comment on the article's talk (discussion) page. (Chapter 8 discusses talk pages in detail.) *If you don't want to or can't edit an article directly, you can still help to improve it.*

Practicing in the Sandbox

Even if you've done a lot of writing and editing with various types of software in the past, you'll need some practice with Wikipedia's tools. Fortunately, Wikipedia has a page called the *sandbox*, where editors can practice without worrying about damaging anything. In this chapter, you'll do your work in the sandbox, rather than editing actual articles.

Remember as you go through the book (or whenever you're editing), if you encounter a feature that you don't fully understand, you can always go to the sandbox and do some testing there. You won't break anything, and you can experiment as much as you want until you figure out exactly how things work. You can even practice duplicating the actual edits that are shown throughout this book.

From any page in Wikipedia, you can get to the sandbox in one of two ways:

- In the "search" box on the left side of the screen, type *WP:SAND*, and press Return. Make sure to type it with all capital letters and no space after the colon.

TIP

WP:SAND is a shortcut, and you'll see others like it throughout the book. If you feel you need to burn a few more calories, type in the search box the full name of the page you want to go to, in this case *Wikipedia:Sandbox*. Also note that Shift+Alt+F [Shift-Control-F on a Mac] will take you directly to the search box.

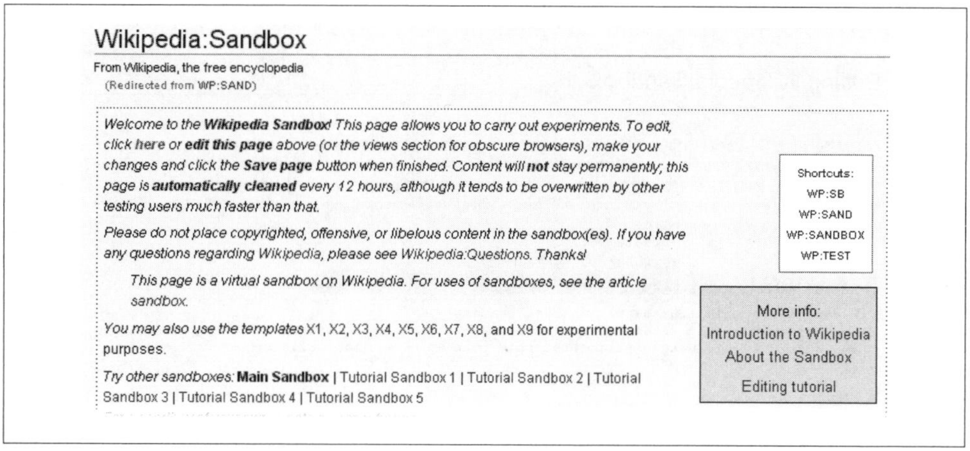

Figure 1-1. The top of the sandbox page, in normal mode. In normal mode, you can read what's on the screen, but not make any changes to it. To enter edit mode, just click the "edit this page" tab.

- Click the "edit this page" tab at the top of any page to go directly into edit mode. You'll see, toward the bottom of the screen (scroll down if necessary), "Your changes will be visible immediately." Immediately below, it says "For testing, please use the **sandbox** instead." The word "sandbox" is a bolded link—just click it.

Both ways get you to the sandbox quickly. Just use whichever method you find easier to remember. Figure 1-1 shows the sandbox before editing starts.

Starting, Previewing, and Saving Your Edit

Editing in Wikipedia is much like using a very basic text editor, with a few word-processing tools thrown in. You type text into the edit box (less commonly written *editbox*), and then click buttons to preview and finally save your work.

Adding Text

You edit Wikipedia articles in a big, white text box in the middle of the window. To get to that box, you must go into edit mode.

1. In the search box on the left side of the screen, type *WP:SAND*, and press Return to go to the sandbox.

   You'll do all your work in this chapter in the sandbox, so you won't actually change any Wikipedia articles.

2. From the sandbox page (Figure 1-1), click the "edit this page" tab.

   You're now in edit mode, complete with the edit box shown in Figure 1-2.

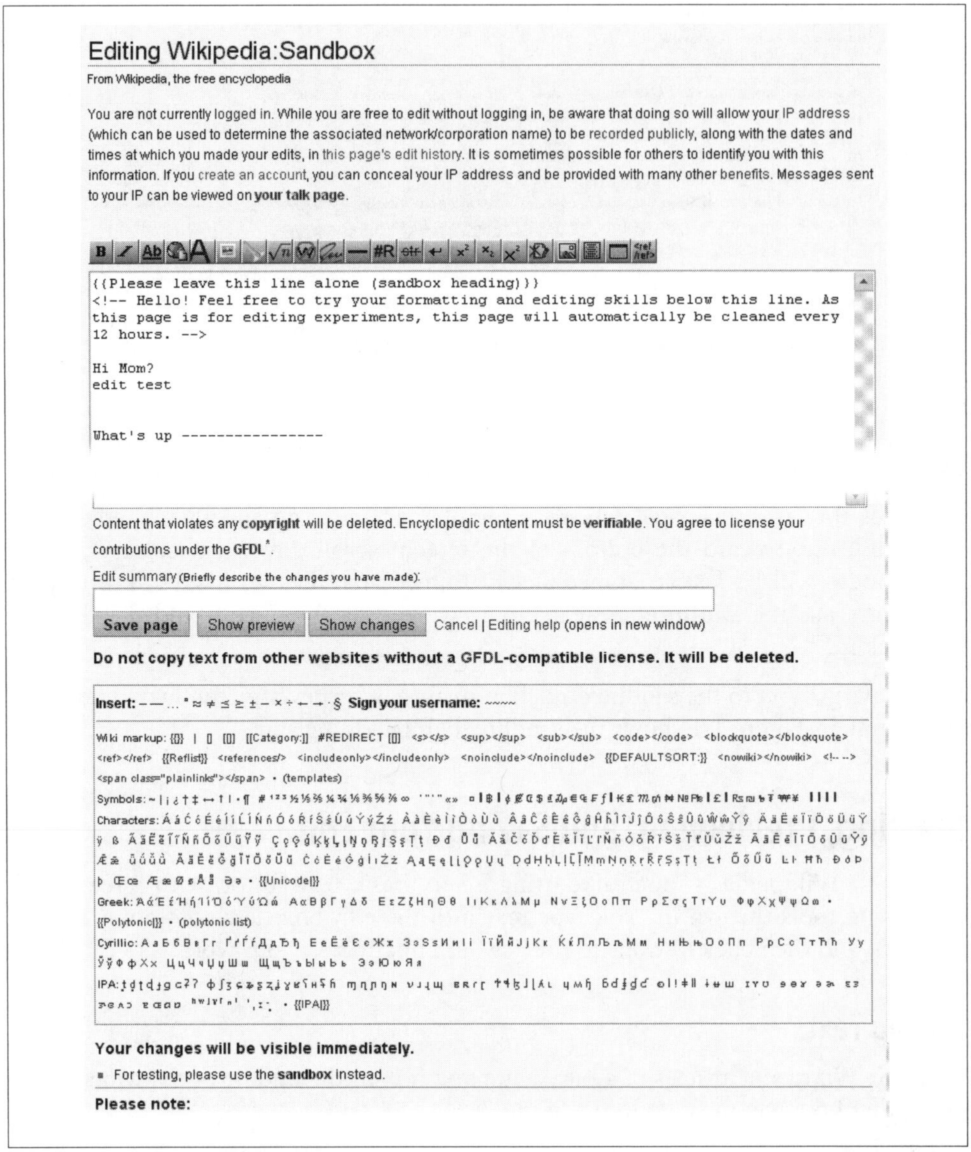

Editing Wikipedia:Sandbox

From Wikipedia, the free encyclopedia

You are not currently logged in. While you are free to edit without logging in, be aware that doing so will allow your IP address (which can be used to determine the associated network/corporation name) to be recorded publicly, along with the dates and times at which you made your edits, in this page's edit history. It is sometimes possible for others to identify you with this information. If you create an account, you can conceal your IP address and be provided with many other benefits. Messages sent to your IP can be viewed on **your talk page**.

```
{{Please leave this line alone (sandbox heading)}}
<!-- Hello! Feel free to try your formatting and editing skills below this line. As
this page is for editing experiments, this page will automatically be cleaned every
12 hours. -->

Hi Mom?
edit test


What's up ----------------
```

Content that violates any **copyright** will be deleted. Encyclopedic content must be **verifiable**. You agree to license your contributions under the **GFDL**.*

Edit summary (Briefly describe the changes you have made):

[Save page] [Show preview] [Show changes] Cancel | Editing help (opens in new window)

Do not copy text from other websites without a GFDL-compatible license. It will be deleted.

Insert: — — … ° ≈ ≠ ≤ ≥ ± − × ÷ → ← · § **Sign your username:** ~~~~

Wiki markup: {{}} | [] [[]] [[Category:]] #REDIRECT [[]] <s></s>   <code></code> <blockquote></blockquote> <ref></ref> {{Reflist}} <references/> {{DEFAULTSORT:}} <!-- --> <span class="plainlinks"></span> · (templates)

Symbols: ~ | ¡ ¿ † ‡ ↔ ↑ ↓ • ¶ # ' ¹ ² ³ ½ ⅓ ⅔ ¼ ¾ ⅛ ⅜ ⅝ ⅞ ∞ '" '' «» □ § ¢ £ € ¥ ₪ ₠ ¤ ₣ ƒ ₨ ₮ ₩ № ₧ ₱ ₡ £ ₨ ₪ ₮ ₩ ¥ ¥ IIII

Characters: Á á Ć ć É é Í í Ĺ ĺ Ń ń Ó ó Ŕ ŕ Ś ś Ú ú Ý ý Ź ź À à È è Ì ì Ò ò Ù ù Â â Ĉ ĉ Ê ê Ĝ ĝ Ĥ ĥ Î î Ĵ ĵ Ô ô Ŝ ŝ Û û Ŵ ŵ Ŷ ŷ Ä ä Ë ë Ï ï Ö ö Ü ü Ÿ ÿ ß Ã ã Ẽ ẽ Ĩ ĩ Ñ ñ Õ õ Ũ ũ Ỹ ỹ Ç ç Ģ ģ Ķ ķ Ļ ļ Ņ ņ Ŗ ŗ Ş ş Ţ ţ Ð ð Ŏ ŏ Ă ă Č č Ď ď Ě ě Ǐ ǐ Ľ ľ Ň ň Ǒ ǒ Ř ř Š š Ť ť Ǔ ǔ Ž ž Ā ā Ē ē Ī ī Ō ō Ū ū Ȳ ȳ Æ æ Ů ů Ø ø Å å Ǻ ǻ ∂ ∂ · {{Unicode}}

Greek: Ά ά Έ έ Ή ή Ί ί Ό ό Ύ ύ Ώ ώ Α α Β β Γ γ Δ δ Ε ε Ζ ζ Η η Θ θ Ι ι Κ κ Λ λ Μ μ Ν ν Ξ ξ Ο ο Π π Ρ ρ Σ σ ς Τ τ Υ υ Φ φ Χ χ Ψ ψ Ω ω · {{Polytonic}} · (polytonic list)

Cyrillic: А а Б б В в Г г Ѓ ѓ Ґ ґ Д д Ђ ђ Е е Ё ё Є є Ж ж З з С с И и І і Ї ї Й й Ј ј К к Ќ ќ Л л Љ љ М м Н н Њ њ О о П п Р р С с Т т Ћ ћ У у Ў ў Ф ф Х х Ц ц Ч ч Џ џ Ш ш Щ щ Ъ ъ Ы ы Ь ь Э э Ю ю Я я

IPA: ʧ ʤ ʈ ɖ ɟ ɡ ɢ ʔ ʔ ɸ ʃ ç ɕ ʂ ʒ ʝ ɣ χ ʁ ħ ʕ ʢ ʡ m ɱ ɲ ŋ ɳ ɴ ʋ ɹ ɻ ʀ t͡ʃ ʎ ʟ ʍ ɭ ɺ ɰ ɓ ɗ ʄ ɠ ʘ ǃ ǂ ǁ ǀ ɨ ʉ ɯ ɪ ʏ ʊ ɘ ə ɵ ɤ ɛ œ ɜ ɞ ʌ ɔ æ ɐ ɶ a ɑ ɒ ˈ ˌ ː ˑ ̩ ' ˞ ‿ ' ‖ ,̩ · {{IPA}}

Your changes will be visible immediately.

■ For testing, please use the **sandbox** instead.

Please note:

Figure 1-2. The sandbox, in edit mode. The text in the box (the edit box) is only an example—what you see will depend on what the other editors have just done to the page. The edit toolbar along the top of the edit box is standard; it provides one-click options for the most common kinds of formatting of content. Also standard is all the text between the sentences "It will be deleted" and "Your changes will be visible immediately."

```
B / Ab A ✎ √n W ✎ — #R stt ↵ x² x₂ x² 🗇 🖼 📊 ⬜ ref
((Please leave this line alone (sandbox heading)))
<!-- Hello! Feel free to try your formatting and editing skills below this line. As
this page is for editing experiments, this page will automatically be cleaned every
12 hours. -->
```

Figure 1-3. The edit box after deleting all but the top three lines. Now the edit box is ready for you to add text. Of what remains, the first line is a template (see page 17), and the second and third lines are an invisible comment—visible, that is, only when you're in edit mode.

NOTE

If the bottom of Figure 1-2 looks intimidating, don't worry: There are only about two dozen items that editors actually use, except in exceedingly rare circumstances. If you're curious, Appendix A provides a complete cross-reference to everything on the bottom of Figure 1-2, as well as all the icons on the edit toolbar.

---

3. Delete everything but the first three lines, which are instructions.

   The edit box contents should look like Figure 1-3. In this box, you'll type some text that includes bold and italic formatting, and section headings.

NOTE

If someone else has deleted part or all of the top three instructional lines in Figure 1-3, don't worry—the steps on these page will work just fine without them. But you may want to add them back to help others using the sandbox.

If you compare Figure 1-1 to Figure 1-3, you may be puzzled about a couple things: What is the purpose of the curly brackets (the first line in the edit box in Figure 1-3), and why is the text in Figure 1-1 ("Welcome to the Wikipedia Sandbox! This page allows you to carry out experiments") not the same as the underlying text in Figure 1-3?

The answer to both questions is essentially the same: The curly brackets indicate a *template*, and the purpose of templates, generally, is to add standard text to a page. Because templates are so important—you'll find them everywhere at Wikipedia—there's a separate section on them later in this chapter (see page 17).

4. Type the text shown in Figure 1-4 (except the first three lines at the top, which should already be there) into the edit box.

   For this example, you don't have to type *all* the text if you don't want to. You can even type some text of your own invention, as long as it includes each of the following:

   • **Section headings**. Type two equal signs at the beginning and two more at the end of a line of text. (If you create at least four headings, Wikipedia automatically creates a table of contents, as you'll see in a moment.)

```
B / Ab 🖊 A 📷 ✂ √n W 🔗 — #R ⊕ ← x² x₂ x✗ 🔲 🖼 🗒 🔲 ref/
                                                              ref
((Please leave this line alone (sandbox heading)))
<!-- Hello! Feel free to try your formatting and editing skills below this line. As
this page is for editing experiments, this page will automatically be cleaned every
12 hours. -->

At the very top of an article is the lead section; the '''name of the article''' is
always bolded.  Bolding is done by putting three apostrophes on each side of the
text.  Except for the article name, it is rarely used in articles.

== Section heading, level 2  ==
A "level 2" heading is one with a pair of equal signs on each side.  It's the
highest level used in articles.  If you enter a Level 1 heading, it  ''will'' work,
but you'd be wrong to do so.

=== Section heading, level 3 ===
Level 2 and level 3 headings are '''very common''' in articles.  Level 4 is less
common; levels 5 and 6 aren't used.  Level 3 and 4 headings are sometimes called
"subsection headings".

=== Another subsection ===
Next, let's ''italicize some text'' by putting two apostrophes on each side.
Italicizing text is typically used for the name of a newspaper or magazine; it's
almost never used in ''articles'' for emphasis, because emphasis isn't the neutral
point of view that Wikipedia strives for.

== Another level 2 section heading ==
```

Figure 1-4. Typing this text into the edit box is a quick lesson in the three most common types of Wikipedia formatting. Putting equal signs on both sides of text turns it into a section heading (after you save your edit). Text surrounded by three apostrophes gets bolded; text surrounded by two apostrophes gets italicized.

- **Boldface**. Type three apostrophes (') before and after the text you want to bold.
- **Italic**. Type two apostrophes (') before and after the text you want to italicize.

NOTE

Never put a blank space at the beginning of a line unless you want that line of text to stand out (which you never want in an article). With a blank space at the beginning, Wikipedia displays a line of text in a box with a light blue background. If it's a long line of text, the text goes off the screen to the right, requiring the reader to scroll to see it all.

Previewing

One of the most important things after doing an edit is to *preview* it—to see how it's going to look. For edits involving formatting, previewing is absolutely essential. But even if you've added only plain text, you should still preview it because you want to get in the habit previewing *every time*.

Experienced editors often skip previewing when making small, routine edits. Usually that's okay, but sometimes, to their embarrassment, after seeing what the page looks like after being saved, they realize they need to do another edit to fix their own mistakes. So, until you've become an experienced editor, preview your work every time.

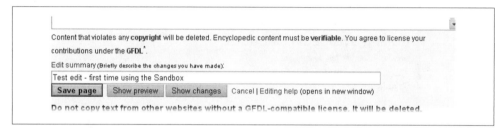

Figure 1-5. When you add an edit summary, make it descriptive but concise. (As noted in Figure 1-2, the checkboxes for "This is a minor edit" and "Watch this page" are visible only if you're a registered user who is logged in.)

Before you click the "Show preview" button, however, you should do one more thing —provide a summary of the edit you just made. You should do this *now*, rather than later, because previewing will also show you what the edit summary will look like. Think of the edit summary as a way for you to explain your edit to other editors. The explanation can be very brief ("typo," "revert vandalism") or it can be lengthy (up to 200 characters). Keep it as short as you can, and make it as long as you need to.

1. In the "Edit summary" box (Figure 1-5), type a few words to describe the purpose of your edit.

    In other words, follow the instructions in fine print: "Briefly describe the changes you have made." For example, in this case you might type *Test edit – first time using the Sandbox*. (See the box below for information about edit summaries.)

    Once you've added an edit summary, it's time to check your work.

In Summary

Filling in the "Edit summary" box, to explain your edit, takes only a few seconds but can save other editors lots of time. These summaries show up on each article's "history" tab (see page 82), on the page that lists a given editor's contributions (see page 99), and pretty much everywhere else that a list of edits appears within Wikipedia: They're important.

Edit summaries should be meaningful to all editors. If you encounter an abbreviation or other text you don't understand, check the page *Wikipedia:Edit summary legend* (shortcut: *WP:ESL*), which has a pretty comprehensive list.

Here are some common edit summaries:

- "Copyediting"
- "Removed duplicate text in section"
- "Splitting section in two with subheadings, adding new information and sources"
- "Added material, changed section heading"

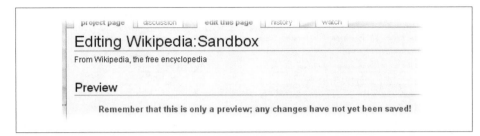

Figure 1-6. At the very top of the preview screen there's always a warning, in red, that you're looking at a preview, not something that has been saved.

If you start editing articles regularly, here's another advantage to creating your own Wikipedia account: Once you've created an account, as described in Chapter 3, you can change a setting so that you get a reminder to add an edit summary, if you've forgotten one. When logged in, click the My Preferences link (in the upper-right area of the screen), then click the "editing" tab, and at the bottom of the list of options, turn on the "Prompt me when entering a blank edit summary" checkbox. Click Save. Once you've done that, you'll never have to worry about inadvertently forgetting to fill in the "Edit summary" field.

2. Click the "Show preview" button just below the edit window (the button is shown in Figure 1-5) to see what the Wikipedia page will look like after you save your edit.

   A Wikipedia preview screen has three parts. The very top of the screen (Figure 1-6) shows a warning that you're not looking at a saved version of the page. The middle and bottom of the screen (Figure 1-7) show both what the page will look like after you save it (if you don't change it further) and the edit box and related tools.

3. Now's your chance to fix mistakes before anyone else can see them. Just make any changes you want in the edit box, and click "Show preview" again.

   When you're satisfied with what the preview shows, it's time to save the edit, which will change the version that readers see when they come to the page.

Saving

Click the "Save page" button (see Figure 1-5 for the location of this button, if you need to). At this point, one of three things happens:

- Most of the time, the page changes, incorporating your edit. That is, the page looks like what it did when you looked at it in preview mode, except now there is no preview warning on top. Your edit is complete; you're done.

- You might see a *cached* version of the page. You'll see a version of the page that looks like it did before you edited the page. In this case, you should refresh the page in your Web browser; typing Ctrl-R (⌘-R on the Mac) does the trick in most

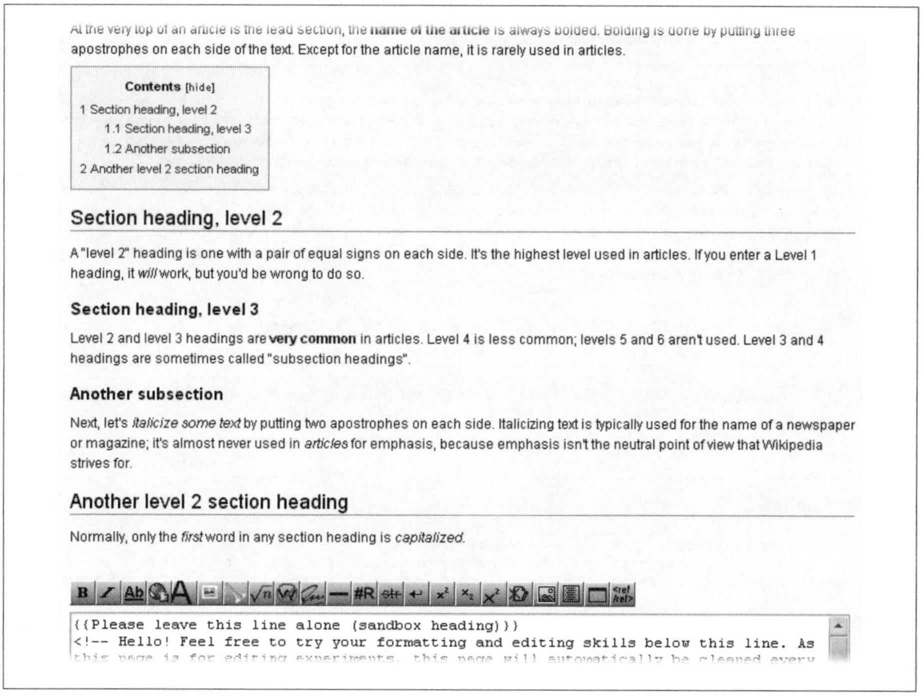

At the very top of an article is the lead section, the **name of the article** is always bolded. Bolding is done by putting three apostrophes on each side of the text. Except for the article name, it is rarely used in articles.

Contents [hide]
1 Section heading, level 2
  1.1 Section heading, level 3
  1.2 Another subsection
2 Another level 2 section heading

Section heading, level 2

A "level 2" heading is one with a pair of equal signs on each side. It's the highest level used in articles. If you enter a Level 1 heading, it *will* work, but you'd be wrong to do so.

Section heading, level 3

Level 2 and level 3 headings are **very common** in articles. Level 4 is less common; levels 5 and 6 aren't used. Level 3 and 4 headings are sometimes called "subsection headings".

Another subsection

Next, let's *italicize some text* by putting two apostrophes on each side. Italicizing text is typically used for the name of a newspaper or magazine; it's almost never used in *articles* for emphasis, because emphasis isn't the neutral point of view that Wikipedia strives for.

Another level 2 section heading

Normally, only the *first* word in any section heading is *capitalized.*

{{Please leave this line alone (sandbox heading)}}
<!-- Hello! Feel free to try your formatting and editing skills below this line. As this page is for editing experiments, this page will automatically be cleaned every

Figure 1-7. The middle and part of the bottom half of the preview screen, showing how the edit from Figure 1-4 looks after saving the page. Wikipedia automatically adds a table of contents for articles that have four or more section headings. At bottom is the now-familiar edit box, so you can make corrections or improvements to your article.

browsers. Once you see your edit has taken affect, you're done. (In the rare case where refreshing the page doesn't work, you need to tell your computer to remove old copies of *everything*. See the page *Wikipedia:Purge*; shortcut *WP:PURGE*.)

- The worst case scenario is that Wikipedia refuses to make the change because someone else changed the page while you were editing it. Figure 1-8 shows what the page will look like in case of an *edit conflict*.

Dealing with an Edit Conflict

Some articles are very (temporarily or permanently) popular with editors—perhaps the article is about a current event (say, a hurricane) or a person suddenly in the news. Such articles may be edited as frequently as once every minute or two. For such an article, if you as an editor take a while to do an edit—say, you begin editing, then do something else for five minutes, then come back to editing—your chances of an edit conflict are quite high when you attempt to save your edit.

If there is an edit conflict, the Wikipedia screen has four parts:

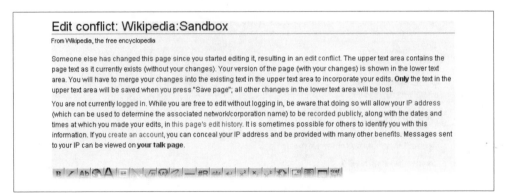

Figure 1-8. The top of a page when there's an edit conflict. If you're logged in, you see only the top paragraph of information.

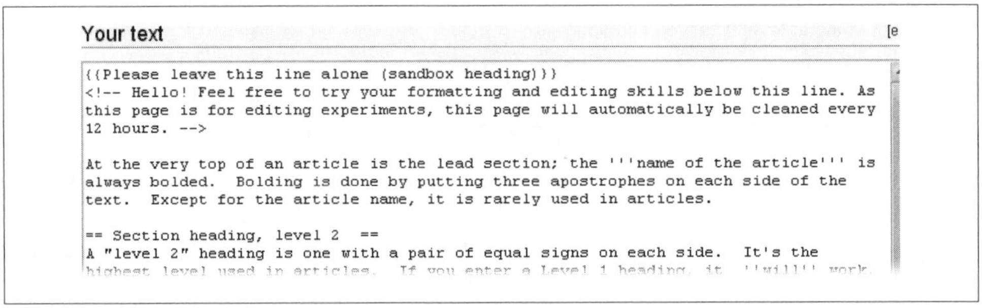

Your text   [e

```
{{Please leave this line alone (sandbox heading)}}
<!-- Hello! Feel free to try your formatting and editing skills below this line. As
this page is for editing experiments, this page will automatically be cleaned every
12 hours. -->

At the very top of an article is the lead section; the '''name of the article''' is
always bolded.  Bolding is done by putting three apostrophes on each side of the
text.  Except for the article name, it is rarely used in articles.

== Section heading, level 2  ==
A "level 2" heading is one with a pair of equal signs on each side.  It's the
highest level used in articles.  If you enter a level 1 heading, it  ''will'' work,
```

Figure 1-9. When there is an edit conflict, your screen will have an additional edit box, at the bottom of the screen, with the label "Your text." (Not all the text in Figure 1-4 is shown here, but all of it would be in the edit box.)

- The warning at the top (Figure 1-8).
- A text box with the text for the current version of the page. It's Wikipedia saying "Here's what you *can* edit—the current version," plus all the other editing stuff (edit summary box, buttons, wiki markup symbols, and so on.)
- A Differences section that shows how your version (the one you saw in "show preview") *now* differs from the existing page (the one revised by someone else while you were working on your revision).
- At the very bottom, an *additional* text edit box, with your edit in it (Figure 1-9).

The best way to handle an edit conflict depends on the circumstances. Here are two common approaches:

- If you were **adding information**, then you should copy that information from the lower text box to another place (a word processing document, Windows Notepad, or similar.). Once you have the information in a safe place, go back to the page (in reading mode) and review whether what you were adding still needs to be added.

If so, edit the section or page again (this time more quickly, if possible), do a quick preview, and save the edit.

- If you were doing a **small amount of copyediting**, just go back to the page (in reading mode), go into edit mode, and do your edit again (more quickly). Of course, before you go into edit mode, you should check that what you were trying to fix still needs to be fixed.

Basically, you haven't lost any text that you added (you can simply copy it), but if you did a lot of copyediting, you may have to do that over again, because the alternative is to overwrite what another editor or other editors just did. You absolutely don't want to do that, assuming that the other editor(s) improved the article.

Of course, the best way to settle a conflict is to avoid it in the first place. You can avoid edit conflicts entirely by using the following techniques:

- Edit a section of an article, not the entire article (editing of sections is discussed on page 18).

- Click the "history" tab to see if an article is getting a lot of edits; if so, do a series of small (quick) edits rather than trying to do a lot of changes within a single edit.

- Prepare lengthy additions offline, in a word processing document or Windows Notepad or something similar, or on a *subpage* (see page 57). After the text is ready, you can then go into edit mode for the article, copy and paste the text into the edit window, preview, and save, all in a short amount of time.

TIP

There's also a way to tip off other editors that you're working on an article. That way, they can make the choice of whether to start editing and risk an edit conflict. It's an advanced technique, explained in the box below.

POWER USERS' CLINIC

Locking Out Other Editors

In Figure 1-3, you can see (in the top line) an example of a template used to display a message on a page. You can add the *{{inuse}}* template to the top of an article to tell other editors that you are in the process of making a large edit. It asks that other editors not edit for a while; the Wikipedia page on *edit lock* recommends using this template for no more than three hours.

In practice, use of this template is very, very rare. Wikipedia etiquette says you should never use it with a popular article (one that gets a lot of edits) or an article involving a breaking news story. But you might experiment with it for articles that get relatively few edits, assuming you really do want to do a major revision. And if you do come across this template—the message at the top of the page will say "This article is actively undergoing a major edit for a short while"—you can check the article history (page 82) to see how long the template has been in place. If it's been more than three or four hours, someone's hogging the article; if so, you have every right to delete the template so other editors can feel free to make changes.

Wiki Markup: From Edit Box to Screen

Earlier in this chapter, you learned how to create section headers, and to format text as bold or italic (see Figure 1-4). Such formatting is called *wiki markup*. As you continue through this book, you'll learn about every type of markup you're likely to encounter. As a new editor, though, you need to learn three things right away: to recognize the types of markup, how templates are used, and how to create links between articles.

Types of Markup

Besides headings, bold, and italic text, you'll encounter the following types of markup as you edit articles:

- **{{pagename}} or {{pagename | info1 | info2 }} or {{pagename | this= info 1 | that= info2}}**.The double curly brackets indicate a template. An example of a template appeared in Figure 1-3 and was discussed immediately thereafter (see page 7). Templates are discussed in more detail later in this chapter (page 17).
- **[[Article name]] or [[Article name| other name]]**. Double square brackets create internal links (wikilinks), which are hyperlinks between pages in Wikipedia. They're described in the next section.
- **[http:url] or [http:url some text]**. Single square brackets around a URL create external links. This formatting is discussed in Chapter 2, "Documenting Your Sources" (page 25 to page 43).
- **<ref> text possibly with a URL </ref> and <references />**. These are footnote tags—the text between the tags is the footnote itself—plus the instruction to Wikipedia as to where to display the footnotes. Footnotes are also described in detail in Chapter 2 (page 33).
- **<blockquote> text </blockquote> and $numbers and symbols$**. In articles, you'll find a few other types of paired tags besides the *<ref>* tags for footnotes; blockquote and math tags are among the more common. Tags normally come in pairs, and the ending tag *must* have a slash character ("/") as its second character if it is to work properly.

TIP

One exception to the rule of pairs is the *
* tag that inserts a new line (for example, in a template). It's just the single <br> tag with no closing tag. If you type *
* or *</br>*, that does the same thing as *
*. (The "br" stands for "break," as in "line break.")

- **<!-- Your comment text goes here -->**. This markup turns the text inside into an invisible comment; an example appears in Figure 1-3. "Invisible" means that the text doesn't display in normal viewing mode; you can see it only in edit mode.
- **{| bunch of stuff with lots of vertical lines |}**. This formatting creates a table. Chapter 14 goes into the details.
- **One or more rows starting with an "*" or a "#"**. These characters create lists within an article (the "#" numbers the list, while the "*" just puts a bullet at the beginning of a line). Chapter 14 goes into the details.
- **[[Category:Name]]**. This markup looks like a wikilink, and it is, in a way, but it puts a category link at the bottom of a page. Chapter 19 goes into the details.

How to Create Internal Links

Linking one article to another is very easy—with good reason. Links to other articles can add a lot of value to an article because readers can follow the links whenever they come across a word they don't know a lot about. Good places to add internal links include the lead sections of articles and at the beginning of new sections within articles. A reader should always be able to get to important, related articles via a link.

In the edit box, just place paired square brackets around the name of the article you want to link to, for example: *[[Winston Churchill]]*. Figure 1-10 shows the sandbox again, in preview mode with some internal links sprinkled in.

Another kind of internal link—a piped link—is extremely useful for situations where naming varies by country. For example, you've typed the following sentence in your article: "San Francisco has an extensive public transportation system," and you want to link the words "public transportation" to the relevant article. Trouble is, there's no article in Wikipedia named "public transportation." There is, however, an article named "public transport," which was probably written by someone who speaks British English. You don't care what it's called, you just want your readers to be able to go to that article. Here's how to create the link while having the article read "public transportation": *San Francisco has an extensive [[public transport|public transportation]] system.*

UP TO SPEED

To Link or Not to Link

Wikilinks make writing on a wiki much easier than writing on paper, because you don't have to explain jargon (just link to the relevant article), and you can provide a smidgen of contextual information on people, places, and things by linking to separate articles. The resulting wiki page is easier for more people to read, since advanced readers don't have to skip explanations they don't need, and the less advanced readers can follow links as necessary to get more context.

Wikilink examples

- To insert a link to a specific article, just put two brackets on each side of the name of the article, thusly: elephant
- If you add an ending to a word, the software automatically incorporates that into the link: elephants
- You can totally change what the reader sees by using a *piped link*: In this example, although the name of the article is "United States Congress", the reader will see something slightly different: U.S. Congress

Warning

With a piped link, only the text to the *right* of the pipe symbol (the "|") is visible to the reader. It's **not** acceptable, in articles, to use piping to play tricks - so *don't* do this, for example:

- **Elephant** - *see* the article Stephen Colbert's bête noire

```
== Wikilink examples ==
*To insert a link to a specific article, just put two brackets on each side of the
name of the article, thusly: [[elephant]]
*If you add an ending to a word, the software automatically incorporates that into
the link: [[elephant]]s
*You can totally change what the reader sees by using a ''piped link'':  In this
example, although the name of the article is "United States Congress", the reader
will see something slightly different: [[United States Congress|U.S. Congress]]

=== Warning ===
With a piped link, only the text to the ''right'' of the pipe symbol (the "|") is
visible to the reader. It's '''not''' acceptable, in articles, to use piping to
play tricks - so ''don't'' do this, for example:

*'''Elephant''' - ''see'' the article [[Elephant|Stephen Colbert's bête noire]]
```

Figure 1-10. Compare what's been typed into the edit box (bottom) to what's in the preview portion of the page (top).

As helpful as links are, it's counterproductive to create internal links for a large percentage of words or phrases in an article—Wikipedians call that *overlinking*. You don't want your readers to spend more time hopping around to other articles than reading the one they came for.

To help decide whether you need to insert a link into an article, think of a link as a cross-reference in a book: "*see* such-and-such." If you wouldn't ask readers to turn to another page to read about something, don't provide a link for it either. Here's a case of excessive cross-referencing:

Mahatma Gandhi was a major (*see* "major") political (*see* "political") and spiritual (*see* "spiritual") leader (*see* "leader") of India (*see* "India") and the Indian independence movement (*see* "Indian independence movement").

Here are some general guidelines:

- Don't link plain English words or phrases; do link technical terms.
- Don't link the same word or phrase multiple times, at least not in the same section of an article.
- Avoid linking two words that are next to each other, because these will look to the reader as if they are a single link (if necessary, reword the sentence).

Understanding and Using Templates

As mentioned on page 7, if you go into edit mode and see some text surrounded by two curly brackets, like this: *{{pagename}}*, you're looking at a template. A template tells the software to get text and formatting instructions from another place and insert that formatted text into the article when the article is displayed.

Here's a common example: If you see the *{{fact}}* template in the edit box when you're editing an article, it's telling the software to go to the page *[[Template:Fact]]*, get the text there (including formatting), and insert that text into the article when the article is displayed for readers. The *{{fact}}* template, displays the following text: *[citation needed]*.

Templates are widespread for a number of reasons:

- **Consistency**. Every cleanup template looks the same, each type of infobox (page 357) looks the same, and so on. Editors don't have to constantly figure out how to present a particular type of information in an article.

- **Time savings**. You don't have to type out standard information, and you don't have to know how to format information in standard ways (such as superscript or message boxes). You just have to find out the name of the template and put it in double curly brackets. The software does the rest.

- **Automatic updating**. If the Wikipedia community decides to change a template, changing just one page—the template page itself—automatically changes what's displayed on every other page that uses the template. (High-use templates are protected from being changed by normal editors, to prevent easily-done extensive vandalism.)

- **Categorization**. Templates can include text that puts a page into a category (see Chapter 18). Then you and other editors can go to the category page to find, for example, all articles that have been categorized as needing copyediting.

Templates are everywhere in Wikipedia. In this book, you'll find discussions about templates in a number of chapters, for example:

- Formatting footnotes (smaller font size, multiple columns) (Chapter 2, page 34)
- Putting information about yourself, using userboxes, on your user page (Chapter 3, page 56)
- Marking a new article as needing categories (Chapter 4, page 77)
- Posting warnings to users about vandalism and spam, and reporting vandalism (Chapter 7, page 130 and page 135)
- Using an archive box to neatly organize links to archived talk pages (Chapter 8, page 160)
- Indicating that an article is within a topic being worked on by a group of editors (a *WikiProject*) (Chapter 9, page 171)

- Marking text as needing a source, and notifying the editor who posted the unsourced information about her mistake (Chapter 10, page 186 and page 187)
- Posting warnings about personal attacks (Chapter 11, page 198)

That's a lot of uses of templates, and that's just in the first 11 chapters. At the moment, you just need to know these two main principles of templates:

- Templates add text and formatting, which are stored on another page. To add a template to an article, you type its name between double curly brackets, at the place in the wikitext where you want the template to appear.
- If the template contains parameters, you can edit the text that has been added to those parameters just like you can edit other text in the article, without understanding any of the complexities of templates. For example, take a look at Figure 1-11, which shows a template with a lot of parameters:

In Figure 1-11, each parameter has a name that ends with an equal sign. The infobox will display only the text that follows the equal signs. You can edit text that appears after the equal signs, including adding text, but don't mess around with a parameter name. Also, be careful not to delete or add a parameter separator (the vertical bar symbol "|"), which marks the beginning of each parameter.

Editing Article Sections

Inexperienced editors often work on *entire* articles in edit mode even though they're making changes only to *one section* of that article. Not only does this make it more difficult for other editors to understand what an editor did, but it also significantly increases the chances of an edit conflict (see page 11, above). So, an important rule of editing is: *Don't edit an entire page if you're changing only one section of the page.*

Editing One Section

You'll know an article has sections if you see a table of contents near the top of the article. Even if there is no table of contents, if you see headings within an article, then the article has sections that can be edited. Figure 1-12 shows an article with no table of contents but with three headings that indicate sections that can be edited.

If you click one of the three "edit" links in Figure 1-12, then the edit box shows *only* the text in the section, not the text of the entire article. That makes it easier to edit (less text in the edit box), and it significantly lessens the likelihood of an edit conflict, because if another editor is editing a different section, your two edits can't collide.

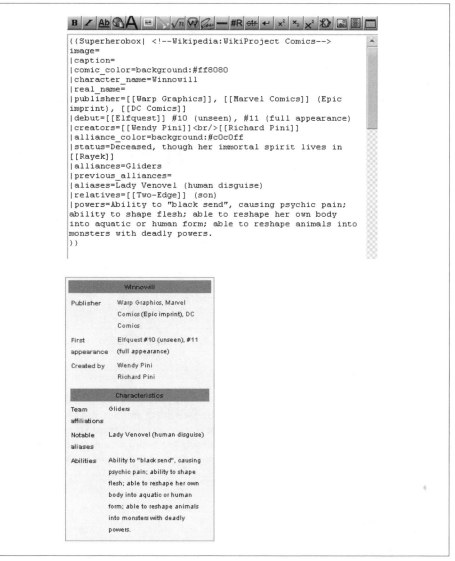

Figure 1-11. A common use for templates is infoboxes. Here's the infobox template for the article Winnowill, viewed in edit mode, on the top, and what it actually looks like in the article, on the bottom. The template has 15 parameters; the first two are for putting an image into the infobox, and are not being used here.

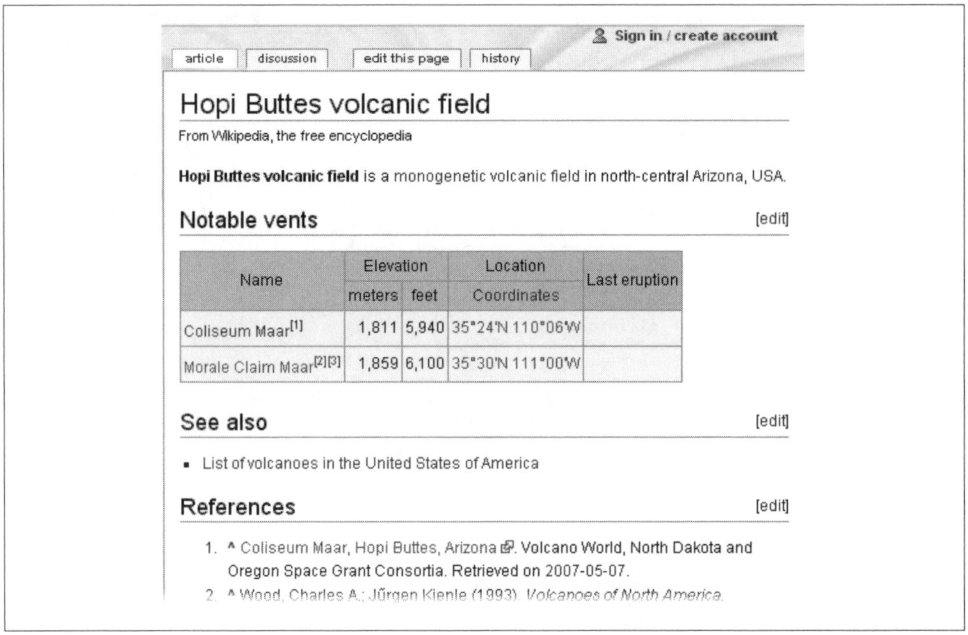

Figure 1-12. An article with three sections that can be separately edited. To edit a specific section, click an "edit" link on the right side of the page.

TIP

Sometimes editing an entire article at once is necessary—for example, if you're moving sections around, or moving text from one section to another. But often when you plan to edit two or three sections of an article, you can efficiently do these as separate edits of individual sections, rather than editing the entire article. If nothing else, it makes previewing much easier (but the preview shows only *part* of the article, not the entire article).

Editing the Lead Section

From the previous section, you know the importance of editing *only* a section rather than an entire article, whenever possible. But you may have noticed that in Figure 1-12 there was no [edit] link for the first sentence in the article, what Wikipedia calls the *lead section*. So, it appears that if you want to edit that section, you have to click the "edit this page" tab, just as if you wanted to edit the entire article.

In fact, it *is* possible to edit only the lead section of an article, though most editors don't know how. There are actually three different options:

- The manual way is to click the [edit] link for a section below the lead section, then go to the URL at the top of the screen and change the number at the end of the

---

Figure 1-13. After you've selected the option to add an edit link for the lead section on the Gadgets tab of the "My preferences" page, you see a new edit link to the right of the title of every article. Clicking that link will open the top section of the article for editing. (If you don't see such a link, make sure you bypassed your browser's cache as described at the bottom of the Gadgets tab.)

URL to "0". (The lead section of an article is always numbered section "0".) Press Enter, and you're then editing the lead section.

- The most complicated way is to add JavaScript code to your personal JavaScript page (page 402), to give you either a special tab (the "0" tab) or an "edit" link. You can find these scripts in the "Navigating to Edit page" section of the page *Wikipedia:WikiProject User scripts/Scripts* (shortcut: *WP:JS*). (Note: To do so, you must be a registered editor; see page 45.)

- The easiest way is to click the "my preferences" link on the upper right of the page (which you won't see unless you have a registered account and are logged in), go to the "Gadgets" tab. Select "Add an [edit] link for the introduction section of a page", and then click Save button. Thereafter, whenever you're editing an article, you'll see something similar to Figure 1-13.

Editing for Real

Now that you've read about the basics of editing, and (hopefully) followed the step-by-step instructions for doing a sandbox edit, you're almost ready to start editing actual articles. Before you do so, you need to understand a bit more about the rules of Wikipedia. Then you'll be prepared to find some articles that you can improve.

Wordsmithing Versus Adding Information

Taken to an extreme, there are basically two kinds of edits (other than removing vandalism, spam, and other problematic material):

- You can change the wording and/or formatting of an article, leaving the information in the article more or less intact.

- You can add new information.

But before you start adding new information, you should read Chapter 2, "Documenting Your Sources." If you want to jump right into wordsmithing, read on.

A Few Words about Content

Wikipedia has three core policies for content. Two of them, *no original research* and *verifiability*, are discussed in the next chapter. The third, *neutral point of view*, is worth mentioning now, because wordsmithing is often about a point of view.

Consider, for a moment, the goal of the people doing public relations or in a marketing department: to write about organizations, products and services, and leaders in a way that casts them in the best possible light. Or consider the wording of a press release by a political party, which tries to make the opposition look as bad as possible. In both of these situations, the writers have what Wikipedians call an extreme point of view (POV). By contrast, Wikipedia's policies require editors to follow these principles:

- Present significant viewpoints in **proportion** to the (published) prominence of each. Fringe theories, for example, deserve much less space (word count) in an article than mainstream/conventional theories.

- **Represent fairly** any differing views about a topic. *Fairly* means presenting the best case for each view, while avoiding extreme rhetoric from either side.

- Write **without bias**. The best way to do this is to write about facts, not about opinions. For example, instead of saying "X murdered Y," which is an opinion (was it self defense?), write "X was convicted of murdering Y," a documentable fact.

Wikipedia has much, much more detail that you can read about this policy (type the shortcut *WP:NPOV* in the search box on the left of the screen). Many (probably most, maybe even all) editors at Wikipedia have very strong opinions about one thing or another—cultural values, religion, politics, science, whatever. Good editors avoid problems by either focusing on making articles as factual as possible or working on articles where their potential biases aren't triggered. So if you're absolutely, positively sure you're right about a topic where many, and possibly most, other editors at Wikipedia wouldn't agree with you, it's a good idea to work on the other two million (or so) articles in Wikipedia that *aren't* about that topic. (Keep in mind that there are lots of places on the Web—blogs, personal pages, wikis other than Wikipedia, and more —where proactive opinions *are* welcome.)

Selecting a Random Page

Ready to edit? If so, you'll want to find articles that you can improve with copyediting. One way is to click the "Random article" link on the left side of the screen (see Figure 1-14).

When you click this link, there's a good chance you'll get a very short article (a *stub*), or a list, or a page that starts "XYZ may refer to ..." followed by a list of related topics (a *disambiguation* page), or a very specialized article. You can edit these, of course, but you may want to try again. When you get an article that you're not interested in editing,

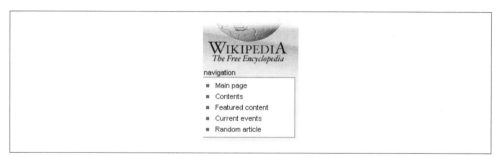

Figure 1-14. The "Random article" link. Click this to go to one of the about two million articles in Wikipedia.

just click the "Random article" link again. (Do this twenty or so times, and you get a reasonable sense of the variety in the almost two million articles in Wikipedia.)

TIP

If you encounter vandalism, you might want to look at Chapter 7 to learn your options for fixing it. Or, if you're very new at editing, there's nothing wrong with leaving the vandalism for a more experienced editor to fix.

Working on a Known Problem

An alternative to using the "Random article" link is to go to articles that other editors have identified as problematic. Several good places to find such articles are:

- Wikipedia:Pages needing attention (shortcut: *WP:PNA*)
- Wikipedia:Requests for expansion (shortcut: *WP:RFE*)
- Category:Wikipedia articles in need of updating (shortcut: *CAT:UP*)
- Category:Wikipedia maintenance (shortcut: *CAT:M*)

When you see the name of an article that seems interesting, just click the article name to go to it and start editing as described earlier in this chapter.

WORD TO THE WISE

Spelling Doesn't (Always) Count

If you find what looks like a spelling mistake, don't leap into edit mode and correct it. What you think is an error may be a perfectly legitimate spelling in context. For example, you may have stumbled upon a national variant of a word: What is "analyse" in the United Kingdom is "analyze" in the United States; neither is wrong.

Wikipedia's spelling rules are mostly based on consistency. For example, don't mix variants of the same word within a single article. If an article is about (say) a major city in Australia, then spellings used in that country are correct for the article; if an article

---

has evolved primarily with one variety of English, the whole article should conform to that variety. (For more details, use these shortcuts to get to two guideline pages: *WP:SPELLING* and *WP:ENGVAR*.)

CHAPTER 2

Documenting Your Sources

Back in high school English, you probably learned how to add footnotes and endnotes to essays and papers. If you didn't add information about your sources, your paper would get a very low grade.

Wikipedia's equivalent of a failing grade is to have another editor reverse your edit, putting the article back to exactly as it was before you changed it. If you want to add new information to articles and have it stay there, you need to understand Wikipedia's rules. This chapter explains those rules. If you follow them, you'll help ensure the accuracy and credibility of Wikipedia articles.

To add a source (what Wikipedia calls *citing* a source), you also need to learn some technical matters—how Wikipedia software handles external links, and how it creates footnotes. This chapter includes two tutorials that show you how to create links and footnotes that would make your English teacher proud.

Documentation Guidelines

Wikipedia is not the place to document the previously undocumented, to report new discoveries, to publish new theories, or to record personally observed events that may be considered newsworthy. Such content may well be true, but as far as Wikipedia's policies are concerned, true isn't enough. Information must be *verifiable*, which means it must be backed by a published source outside Wikipedia. Simply put, Wikipedia must never be the *first* place that news appears. If a tree falls in a forest and it's not reported elsewhere, then Wikipedia isn't going to report it either.

NOTE

Some places on the Web welcome original writing and reporting. You'll find a list at the page *Wikipedia:Alternative outlets*. Some, such as Wikinews, are sister projects.

Here are Wikipedia's documentation rules in brief:

- What you know is true (or, more accurately, what you *think* is true) isn't a criterion for what you can assert on Wikipedia. Information must come from a **published, reliable source**.

- Ideally, always cite your source when you add new information to Wikipedia. If you add a quotation, or if you add something that is likely to be **challenged**, you absolutely must cite a published, reliable source.

Wikipedia has three core policies for content. Chapter 1 discussed one of them—*Neutral point of view* (page 22). The other two policies are mostly about new content: *No original research* and *Verifiability*. You can (and probably should) read those two policies yourself. The shortcuts are *WP:NOR* and *WP:V*; on any Wikipedia page, just type one of those into the search box on the left, and then click Go. Misunderstandings of these policies abound. The rest of this section is devoted to clearing up some of the biggest.

Not All Sources Are Created Equal

Only reliable sources hold up to the scrutiny of the Wikipedia community. But what makes a source reliable? To quote from Wikipedia's *Reliable sources* guideline (shortcut: *WP:RS*): "Articles should rely on reliable, third-party published sources with a reputation for fact-checking and accuracy." Most international and national newspapers, magazines, and scientific journals put significant resources into avoiding mistakes, to maintain their credibility and readership (and their survival in the face of libel and other lawsuits). On the other hand, an anonymous blogger can feel pretty free to post anything on the Web without worrying about the consequences. The general rule is: "Self-published books, personal Web sites, and blogs are largely not acceptable as sources." (*Wikipedia:Verifiability*)

FREQUENTLY ASKED QUESTION

Linking to Pay Sites

I'm working on an article about the late Johnny Ray, and I've found the exact information I need about his early career. Trouble is, it's on a newspaper site that requires you to register before you read their archives. If I link to that Web page, other editors and readers will just get a notification page asking them to register. How can I cite that information?

Sometimes you'll find a source that requires registration to view its content. For example, newspapers often require registration or even payment, either one-time or via subscription, to see content. Online medical journals usually require payment as well.

First, you yourself must have access to this source; otherwise you shouldn't cite it (unless you're looking at a paper version of it). So while you must register or pay, you can't expect your readers to. Still, it's okay to link to such a source as long as you provide a full citation—which you can learn how to do on page 31—and not just a link.

Of course, if you can find a free-access online source of equal quality, use that source instead of one that restricts access. (Page 78 discusses what free resources in general

---

are available to you for writing articles.) And if there is summary or abstract of the source that's free (and has a link to the full, access-restricted content), it's okay for you to link to the shorter, free information, which all readers can view.

Some Sources Apply Only in Specific, Limited Circumstances

Now that you've got the concept of reliability drilled into you, you should know about two situations where otherwise "unreliable" information can appear in Wikipedia articles:

- Material from self-published and questionable sources may be used as sources in articles *about themselves*. You should phrase such information as an assertion. For example, say, "According to Elsbeth Wainwright's personal Web site, she was born on a mountain," not simply, "Elsbeth Wainwright was born on a mountain." The fact that a Web site says something is undisputable, and that's the fact you're asserting in this case.

- Editorial opinions in newspapers aren't the same as news articles, and you should treat them differently. For example, you can say, "The *Catfish Gazette* opposed the destruction of the historical courthouse," if you read that opinion on the *Gazette's* editorial page. But you must not use wording that makes it look like opinions are facts. You can't, for example, use an editorial opinion to put something like this into a Wikipedia article: "The destruction of local landmarks in Catfish township in the past 20 years has been a tragedy and a travesty." (Notice also the violation of *Neutral point of view*.)

You Don't Have to Provide Citations for Information Already Sourced

In four situations, you can put specific information into an article without citing a source. Mind you, the information must still be verifiable; you simply don't need to accompany it with a citation in these situations.

- **In the lead section**. The initial section of an article should be a concise overview of the article, establishing context, summarizing the most important points, and explaining why the subject is interesting and notable. Citations aren't generally appropriate in the lead section; they belong in the body of the article. (Sometimes you do have to provide citations, if other editors insist.) Figure 2-1 is a good example of a lead section. (Lead sections are discussed in more detail on page 234).

- **If a section of an article summarizes what is in another, more detailed article**. In Wikipedia, such a section is called *summary style*, and should be a couple of paragraphs long. Immediately below the heading of the section is a link to the main article, which contains all the sources. Figure 2-2 shows a section of an article that demonstrates summary style.

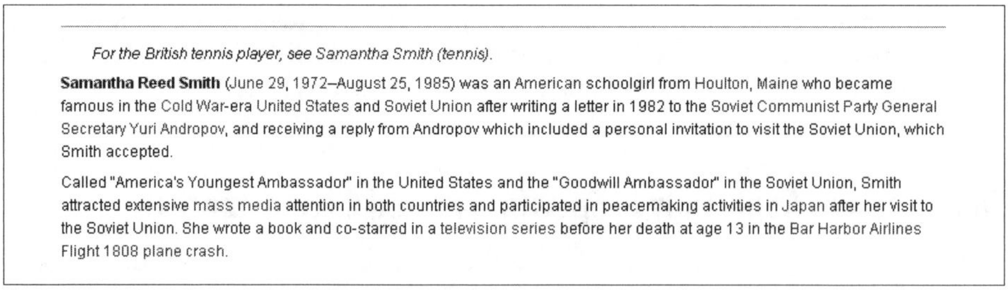

Samantha Reed Smith (June 29, 1972–August 25, 1985) was an American schoolgirl from Houlton, Maine who became famous in the Cold War-era United States and Soviet Union after writing a letter in 1982 to the Soviet Communist Party General Secretary Yuri Andropov, and receiving a reply from Andropov which included a personal invitation to visit the Soviet Union, which Smith accepted.

Called "America's Youngest Ambassador" in the United States and the "Goodwill Ambassador" in the Soviet Union, Smith attracted extensive mass media attention in both countries and participated in peacemaking activities in Japan after her visit to the Soviet Union. She wrote a book and co-starred in a television series before her death at age 13 in the Bar Harbor Airlines Flight 1808 plane crash.

Figure 2-1. This example is a good lead section. It hits the highlights, so the reader can decide whether to continue reading the article. The citations for this information come in the body of the article.

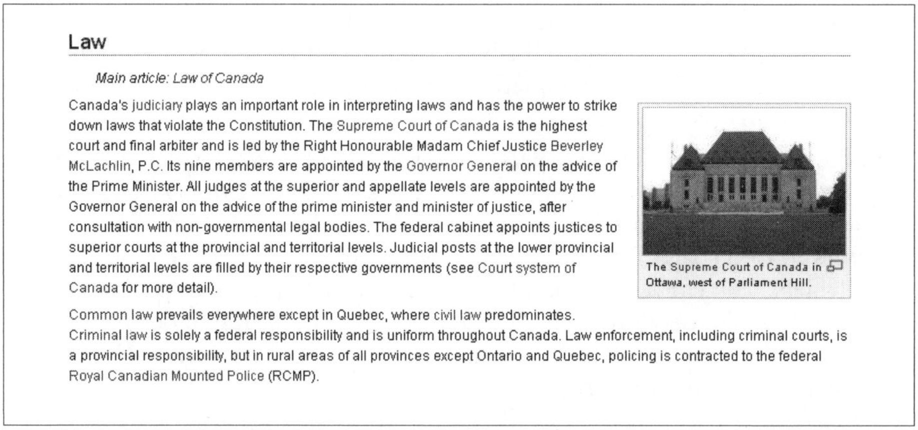

Law

Main article: Law of Canada

Canada's judiciary plays an important role in interpreting laws and has the power to strike down laws that violate the Constitution. The Supreme Court of Canada is the highest court and final arbiter and is led by the Right Honourable Madam Chief Justice Beverley McLachlin, P.C. Its nine members are appointed by the Governor General on the advice of the Prime Minister. All judges at the superior and appellate levels are appointed by the Governor General on the advice of the prime minister and minister of justice, after consultation with non-governmental legal bodies. The federal cabinet appoints justices to superior courts at the provincial and territorial levels. Judicial posts at the lower provincial and territorial levels are filled by their respective governments (see Court system of Canada for more detail).

The Supreme Court of Canada in Ottawa, west of Parliament Hill.

Common law prevails everywhere except in Quebec, where civil law predominates. Criminal law is solely a federal responsibility and is uniform throughout Canada. Law enforcement, including criminal courts, is a provincial responsibility, but in rural areas of all provinces except Ontario and Quebec, policing is contracted to the federal Royal Canadian Mounted Police (RCMP).

Figure 2-2. Shown is the "Law" section of the Wikipedia article titled Canada. *This section is a summary of a separate, more detailed article,* Law of Canada. *Citations of sources don't need to be in the "Law" section; they're in the article* Law of Canada.

- **If there's an internal link to another article**. For example, suppose you add this to an article: "**Name of person**, a historian who was written extensively about this period, said **quotation**." You don't have to document who this person is, because the reader can follow the internal link to the Wikipedia article about the person. That article, of course, should support your phrase, "a historian who has written extensively about this period." Note that you do have to add a source to document the quotation.

- **If the information in an article is documented in a section at the bottom of the article**. Consider an article that is based on primarily on books, like *George Washington in the American Revolution*. In such cases, you can document most of the information by simply listing those books in a "Bibliography" section at the end of the article (Figure 2-3).

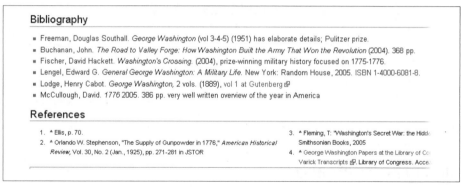

Bibliography

- Freeman, Douglas Southall. *George Washington* (vol 3-4-5) (1951) has elaborate details; Pulitzer prize.
- Buchanan, John. *The Road to Valley Forge: How Washington Built the Army That Won the Revolution* (2004). 368 pp.
- Fischer, David Hackett. *Washington's Crossing.* (2004), prize-winning military history focused on 1775-1776.
- Lengel, Edward G. *General George Washington: A Military Life.* New York: Random House, 2005. ISBN 1-4000-6081-8.
- Lodge, Henry Cabot. *George Washington,* 2 vols. (1889), vol 1 at Gutenberg
- McCullough, David. *1776* 2005. 386 pp. very well written overview of the year in America

References

1. ^ Ellis, p. 70.
2. ^ Orlando W. Stephenson, "The Supply of Gunpowder in 1776," *American Historical Review,* Vol. 30, No. 2 (Jan., 1925), pp. 271-281 in JSTOR
3. ^ Fleming, T: "Washington's Secret War: the Hidd Smithsonian Books, 2005
4. ^ George Washington Papers at the Library of C Varick Transcripts. Library of Congress. Acce

Figure 2-3. Here are the sources for the article George Washington in the American Revolution. *These two sections appear at the bottom of that article. The "Bibliography" section lists six books. By contrast, there are only four footnotes—only four cases in this article where text is footnoted to show exactly where it came from.*

You Must Provide a Source for Controversial Text

If you add potentially contentious information to an article, you absolutely must add a citation immediately following that information, so others can verify it. If you're the one who adds information to an article, the burden of proof rests on you. If another editor questions you about a specific phrase, sentence, or paragraph, the correct response is to cite your source, as a footnote, rather than say, "Find it yourself—I'm sure one of the sources in the article supports what I put in."

Wikipedia considers anything negative about a person or organization to be controversial or contentious. Editors also often challenge causal statements. ("Because the president vetoed the tax cuts, the country went into a recession.") If you add such a statement, it had better come from a reliable source, not your own opinion. When the topic of an article is controversial, other editors may interpret almost any information you add to that article as controversial. But if you always cite a good source that supports the information you're adding, then you can defend yourself if you're accused of adding original research or your personal point of view.

Citing a Source Doesn't Justify Copyright Violations

Say you've come across an online newspaper article with lots of information you want to add to a Wikipedia article. That's great, but don't just copy and paste large amounts of text—that's a copyright violation. Stick to the facts (facts can't be copyrighted), and recognize that newspapers don't object to small percentages of a story's text ending up in Wikipedia if the newspaper gets credit (via citation), particularly if you provide a link to the full story online. (For a discussion about what you *can* legally copy in large amounts, see page 68.)

```
Here's how to create an external link in Wikipedia: [http://www.slate.com/id/2654/]

Always put brackets around a URL.  Here's the URL without the brackets, so you can
see what it would look like (remember, this is '''wrong'''): http://www.slate.com/
id/2654/
```

Figure 2-4. The edit box shows the text for the external link example described on these pages. Notice the edit toolbar just above the edit box—that's a standard landmark when you're in editing mode. As discussed on page 8, the triple apostrophes around the word "wrong" are wiki markup; they make the word appear in boldface.

Adding an External Link

Much, if not most, of the information in Wikipedia is documented by online sources. In this tutorial, you'll learn how to create a link to such a source. Links to Web pages outside Wikipedia are called *external links*.

NOTE

You need to know how to create an external link if you want to do a proper citation, but the external link itself isn't enough. In the steps on page 31, you'll learn the other parts of a proper citation.

---

1. On any Wikipedia page, in the search box on the left, type *WP:SAND*.

2. You're editing in the sandbox (page 4), so you can play around without damaging anything if you make a mistake.

3. At the top of page, click the "edit this page" tab.

   You're now in edit mode. Note the edit box, the Edit summary box, and the various symbols and markup below the warning that begins "Do not copy." (To double-check whether you're in edit mode, look at Figure 2-4.)

4. Delete *all* the text in the edit box.

   At the end of this tutorial, you're not going to be saving your edit, so it's okay to delete text such as "Please leave this line alone".

5. Type the following three sentences into the edit box:

   Here's how to create an external link in Wikipedia. [http://www.slate.com/id/2654/]

   Always put brackets around a URL. Here's the URL without the brackets, so you can see what it would look like (remember, this is '''wrong'''): http://www.slate.com/id/2654/

6. Press the Tab key to go to the "Edit summary" box. (It's just above the bolded warning, "Do not copy text from other websites …") Type a few words explaining

---

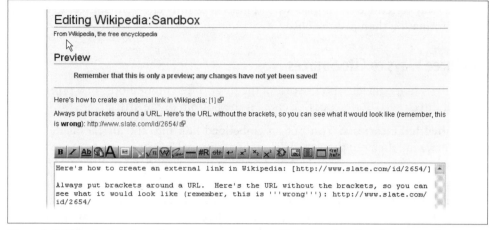

Figure 2-5. This preview shows how to create an external link in Wikipedia—by surrounding a URL with single square brackets. When you preview the page, you see the linked text but not the URL it takes you to. If you forget the brackets, then you see the whole URL when you do a preview. If you see a naked URL in preview mode, fix it.

your edit into that box. Then, just below that box, click the "Show preview" button. (See Figure 1-5 if you need a refresher.)

You see the link you just created, as shown in Figure 2-5.

Wikipedia software automatically numbers external links when they're URLs surrounded by brackets: [1], [2], and so on.

That's all there is to creating external links. If you're going to continue working in this chapter, just keep the sandbox as is; you'll use it again in the Footnotes tutorial on page 34. Otherwise, close or exit the sandbox page without saving your edit.

Citing Sources

Inserting an external link into an article to show where you got information is better than nothing, but by itself it's not the proper way to cite a source. An *embedded link* (an external link in the middle of an article) isn't a proper citation because links, like milk, have a tendency to go bad over time. Links can stop working when a Web site goes out of business, someone moves or deletes a Web page you linked to, or a URL changes for any number of reasons. When links go bad, so does any substantiation of the sentences that the links were supposed to support.

NOTE

The general problem of links going bad is called *link rot*. A non-working link without any other information is almost worthless. Page 349 discusses some ways to try to fix a bad link.

The best way to reduce the impact of bad links is to fully cite your source, to include more information than just the URL.

The Three Ways to Cite Sources

Currently, Wikipedia lets you use one of the three different methods for a proper citation. All three use a "References" section at the bottom of the article.

- **Embedded citations**. You put an embedded link into the article (as described earlier), and then put the same URL, plus additional information about the source, into the "References" section. For details on this method, go to *WP:ECITE*.

- **Footnotes**. You add all the source information into the body of the article, plus special footnote markup. When the Wikipedia software displays the article, it puts a footnote number in the body of the article and the citation information in the "References" section at the bottom. When readers click a footnote number, it takes them to the footnote information at the bottom of the article. (You can learn exactly how to create footnotes starting on page 34; also check out *WP:FOOT*.)

- **Harvard referencing**. You put the citation's cross-reference information (author, year of publication, and page number) into the body of the article, and also put that information, plus the title of the article or book, the name of the publisher and other publication information into the "References" section. If you use templates (which isn't required), then the information in the body of the article is linked to the information in the "References" section. If you use only plain text, then the two aren't tied together by the software. (For details, go to *WP:HARV* for an example.)

How do you choose among the three citation methods? If you're working on a new article, or expanding an article that uses none of these methods, that's easy. Use footnotes for the following reasons:

- The embedded citations approach can't handle *offline* sources—those for which there's no URL, even though offline sources are perfectly acceptable in Wikipedia. Don't use it.

- Harvard referencing, in the format described above, is used in only a very small percentage of Wikipedia articles—well under five percent. Moreover, there are a number of variants of Harvard citations, both for the way text shows in articles and for the underlying templates of the system, so learning this method takes more time. Plus it's often mixed with regular footnotes, as in the article *Dionysus*.

If an article already uses a method other than footnotes, you have two options:

- If the article has embedded citations, convert them to footnotes. Embedded citations are a legacy from before Wikipedia had footnotes. It's actually less work for an editor to do a regular footnote than to do an embedded citation, so if you do the work of converting to regular footnotes, other editors will be happy to do footnotes thereafter.

- If the method is Harvard referencing and you want to add information to the article, you *must* use that method. Don't get into a fight about footnotes being better—once a style is in place in an article, leave it as is.

Two Styles of Footnotes

As you'll discover as you edit Wikipedia, getting all editors to do everything the same way is like trying to herd a group of cats. It's best to take what the cats prefer to do into account. Wikipedia has policies, which everyone must follow; guidelines, which sometimes provide multiple options; and some things on which there's never been general agreement, so there aren't even guidelines. In practical terms, footnotes fall into that last category.

For example, a survey of 28 Main Page articles in October 2007 found that 12 articles used only regular footnotes, while five used only Harvard-style footnotes. The other 11 articles used a mix of the two. Even then, there wasn't just one style: eight of the 11 used two sections, but three combined the two different footnotes into a single section.

In general, you'll find footnotes appearing in two different ways in fully developed articles:

- **Regular footnotes**. A footnote number appears in the body of the article, and the full citation information for that footnote appears at the bottom the article, in a section usually (but not always) called "References."
- **Harvard-style footnotes**. A footnote number in the body of the article links to a brief citation (author plus page number, or author plus date plus page number) in a "Notes" section. Then full citation information goes in a second section called "References." There's no automated connection for the reader between text in the two sections.

Since Harvard-style footnotes are a variant of regular footnotes, once you've learned regular footnotes, you'll have no problems with the variant. Don't get into a fight over the "right" way to do footnotes. If you're creating or building an article, you can pick a style that suits you; if you're adding to an article with an established style, follow that style.

Creating Footnotes

If you've been paying attention in this chapter so far, you know that if you want to add information to a Wikipedia article, you need to have a reliable source, and you need to cite that source in the Wikipedia article. In the previous section, you also learned that footnotes are the most reliable way to provide your readers with documentation.

Wikipedia has two ways to create footnotes: freeform and citation templates. Citation templates take longer to learn upfront, but they have advantages, as discussed on page 36.

Creating a Simple Footnote

1. Open the sandbox for editing.

   If you're not there already, on any Wikipedia page, type *WP:SAND* into the search box, and then, at the top of page, click the "edit this page" tab. (And if you're in preview mode, that's fine too.)

2. In the sandbox, delete all the text, and then type the following text (see Figure 2-6):

   == Body of the article ==

   In 1997, Chrysler was more profitable, with earning of $2.8 billion, than Daimler, which earned $1.8 billion.<ref>Surowiecki, James. [http://www.slate.com/id/2654 "The Daimler-Chrysler Collision: Another Merger in Search of That Elusive Synergy"], "Slate" magazine, May 15, 1998, retrieved September 12, 2007</ref>

   == References ==

   <references/>

   As shown in Figure 2-6, Wikipedia's footnote system has two distinct parts:

   - Footnote information appears in the body of the article. It must have a *ref tag* (<ref>) in front and the companion *closing tag* (</ref>) at the end, to tell the Wikipedia software to treat it like a footnote.

TIP

You don't have to type these two tags. Instead, highlight the text to go in the footnote, then click the "ref" icon on the far right of the edit toolbar (see Figure 2-6 for example).

   - There must be a "<references/>" tag somewhere on the page to tell the software exactly where to display all the footnotes. (Notice the ending "/" that is part of this tag is necessary for the footnotes to work correctly.)

NOTE

It doesn't matter if you call the footnotes section "References" (the most common) or "Notes" or "Footnotes" or even "References and Notes." The software doesn't depend on the section name. It's the <references/> tag (or as you'll often see, a {{reflist}} template) that tells the software where to put the footnotes. The citation information you type into the body of the page (Figure 2-6) stays put, and you can still see it in edit mode; but until you add the <references/> tag, your footnotes won't be visible to readers.

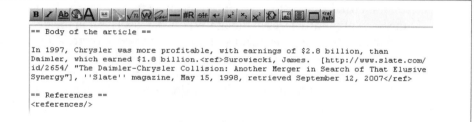

Figure 2-6. *You'll recognize some of the wiki markup that you used in the tutorial in Chapter 1, like the headings for the two sections and the italicizing of the title of the publication (the magazine Slate). The footnote begins immediately after the sentence it documents—there's no space between the period and the <ref> tag. You must both create a heading for the "References" section and add the <references/> tag to tell Wikipedia where to put the footnotes.*

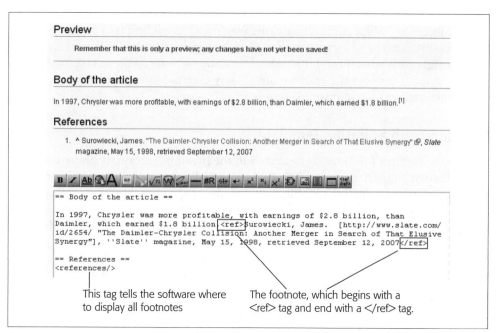

Figure 2-7. *At top, you can see how the page will look when you save it. The bottom shows the text entered into the edit box, with the two parts of the footnote system (the footnotes themselves, and where they're displayed).*

3. Type a few words explaining the edit into the Edit summary box, and click the "Show preview" button.

   If you see what's in Figure 2-7, your footnote is complete.

Now that you know how to create a footnote, remember three points before you head off to start adding citations to articles:

- When you want to edit an existing footnote, remember that the text of that footnote goes in the body of the article, even though Wikipedia displays it in the References section. So don't open the References section to edit that footnote: All you'll see is the section heading and the <references/> tag (or it's variant, the *{{reflist}}* template. To edit an existing footnote, either go into edit mode for the entire article, or preferably go into edit mode for just the section where the text for the footnote is located.

- The footnote number ([1]) and the displayed footnote are linked. If you click on the upward caret (the "^") in footnote 1, the cursor moves to the [1]. (When you do so, the page may jump around a bit; scroll so you're back to seeing the whole page.) Similarly, if you click on the [1], the cursor moves to the text for footnote 1 (and shades the whole footnote in light blue). (Try it, using either your preview or any article with footnotes.)

- In the top half of Figure 2-7, the external link (which is the title of the article) isn't numbered by Wikipedia software, the way the external link is in Figure 2-5. The reason is that the software found within the brackets both a URL and some following text. When it finds both these things, the software creates a link for the text, and doesn't number the external links. Only external links that have *only* a URL within brackets are numbered.

Footnotes with a Citation Template

Creating a freeform footnote, as described in the previous section, is pretty easy, but in articles that contain many footnotes, editors usually use one of Wikipedia's *citation templates*. Citation templates are big, ugly chunks of text that you'll run across when editing Wikipedia articles, but they have a definite purpose. They organize the internal structure of a footnote by delimiting (that is, defining) each part of the note. It's sort of as if a sentence came with descriptive markings: "This is an introductory phrase. This is the subject of the sentence. This is the verb. This is the object." A citation template defines the parts of a citation—author's name, document title, and so on, by using what Wikipedia calls *parameters*.

Figure 2-8 shows you three different ways an editor could use a citation template to create the same footnote that you created in the previous section. How an editor uses a template is entirely up to that editor, so you could see any—or all three, mixed together—in a given article. As long as what's displayed is accurate, the templates don't need to be consistent.

Not only can the same citation template look different (Figure 2-8), but there are more than a dozen footnote citation templates. Figure 2-8 shows the *cite news* template, which is perhaps the mopst common. It's designed to cite newspapers, magazines, journals, and periodicals. There are specialized templates for books, Web sites, court cases, and so on. You can see all of these—in a form that makes it easy to copy a template to a Wikipedia article you're editing, by the way—at *Wikipedia:Citation templates*

```
In 1997, Chrysler was more profitable,
with earnings of $2.8 billion, than
Daimler, which earned $1.8
billion.<ref>{{cite news
  | last = Surowiecki
  | first = James
  | coauthors =
  | title = The Daimler-Chrysler
Collision: Another Merger in Search of
That Elusive Synergy
  | work =
  | pages =
  | language =
  | publisher = ''Slate'' magazine
  | date = May 15, 1998
  | url = http://www.slate.com/id/2654/
  | accessdate = 2007-09-12
}}</ref>
```

```
In 1997, Chrysler was more profitable,
with earnings of $2.8 billion, than
Daimler, which earned $1.8
billion.<ref>{{cite news
  | last = Surowiecki
  | first = James
  | title = The Daimler-Chrysler
Collision: Another Merger in Search of
That Elusive Synergy
  | publisher = ''Slate'' magazine
  | date = May 15, 1998
  | url = http://www.slate.com/id/2654/
  | accessdate = 2007-09-12
}}</ref>
```

```
In 1997, Chrysler was more profitable, with earnings of $2.8 billion, than
Daimler, which earned $1.8 billion.<ref>{{cite news | last = Surowiecki | first =
James | title = The Daimler-Chrysler Collision: Another Merger in Search of That
Elusive Synergy | publisher = ''Slate'' magazine | date = May 15, 1998 | url =
http://www.slate.com/id/2654/ | accessdate = 2007-09-12}}</ref>
```

Figure 2-8. Here are three variations of the same citation template for the same footnote. The difference is in the spacing. Top: Each parameter (author's last name, first name, and so on) has been entered as a separate line. Middle: The four unused parameters have been deleted. Bottom: There are multiple parameters on a single line. This third variation could have been even shorter: The blank spaces before and after the vertical line ("|") symbols, and the spaces before and after the equal signs aren't required. Of course, removing those 28 blank spaces would make the template even more difficult to read.

(shortcut: *WP:CITET*). (For a quick reference guide with details about the most common templates, go to *WP:CITEQR*.)

Since you can cite any kind of source using a freeform footnote, as you learned earlier in this chapter, why use standard citations templates at all? There are a number of reasons, some of which you may find compelling:

- **A citation template is like a handy form**. Just fill it out, and the template takes care of the formatting. When you enter text into a template, you don't have to know what goes first, what goes where, and so on. The template takes care of displaying the citation for the reader.

- **Changing the template automatically updates every citation that uses it**. For example, if the Wikipedia community decided that the first name of an author should come first, followed by the last name, instead of the current approach, you could change every display of every footnote created with a particular template simply by changing the template itself. This automating updating is the true power of templates. (But to prevent tampering, high-use templates are protected so that only administrators can change them.)

- **Templates may make future automated features possible**. Citation templates make it possible (in theory) to do automated searching across articles to find, say, all the articles written by the same author, or all cited articles published on a given date. For that to be valuable, of course, there would need to be many more footnotes in Wikipedia articles—you can help!—and a much higher percentage of citation templates, as opposed to freeform templates.

NOTE

The automated tools for creating citations (see page 40) create citation templates, not freeform text. Of course, if you use these tools, you don't really have to understand templates; you just have to do a cut-and-paste of the text.

Multiple Footnotes for the Same Source

If you use the same source to support a number of statements in an article, you don't have to (nor should you) type citation information multiple times. Instead, you use a *name=* parameter to tell the Wikipedia software that multiple footnotes use the same source. Figure 2-9 shows how it works.

Multiple footnotes are marked up differently than singular ones. The second time that "Source1" is cited in Figure 2-9, it isn't between a pair of tags. Rather, this standalone tag looks like a hybrid: It had the *name=* part of a starting ref tag, with the slash ("/") of an ending tag (albeit at the end, not the beginning). When doing multiple footnotes for a single source, the format for all of the footnotes, except the one that actually has citation information in it, goes like this: *<ref name="NameYouGiveToTheSource"/>*. (For more details on what name to give to a source, see the box on page 39.)

If you forget the ending slash, the software assumes it's a *starting* tag for a footnote. It then "swallows" all the following text, stopping only when it finds either a closing </ref> tag or gets to the end of the page. That's yet another reason to always preview your changes to an article. If you add one or more footnotes and notice that a chunk of text is no longer visible in the preview, chances are you didn't include a closing slash in one of your <ref > tags or you put the slash in wrong place.

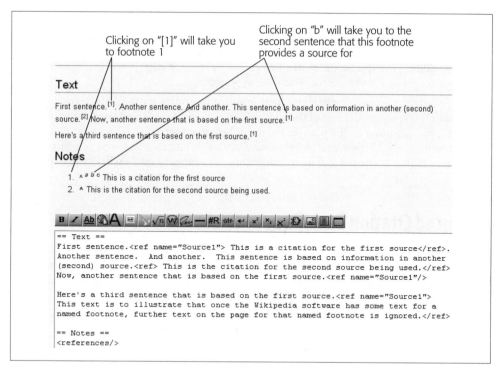

Figure 2-9. The same source is cited thrice. In the body of the text, [1] occurs thrice, as a link. Clicking any of the three takes you to the same place: the text of footnote 1, in the "Notes" section. With footnotes, linking works both ways. For example, for footnote 1, instead of clicking on the upward caret ("^") to go to the footnote, you click the "a", "b", and "c" to go to the three places in the body of the text where the footnote number ([1], in this case) is located.

The *name*= Parameter

The *name*= parameter defines the name you use to refer to a source used in an article, sort of like a nickname. When you name your sources, each one should be unique, meaningful, and fairly short. Figure 2-9 used "Source1", which is unique and short, but not very meaningful. Often you can just use the name of the author of the source you're citing (*name="JPowells"*). If you cite more than one source from the same author, you can use author and publication year (*name="Chen-1976"*). For newspaper articles, a good technique is to use an abbreviation plus the publication date (*name="NYT-2007-06-22"* or name="ST-12May2006"*). For a Web page, you might make up a brief title (*name="Congressional-bio ""*).

When you cite the same source multiple times using just one footnote, you use the *name*= parameter to refer to the source. Before you head off to try this technique in a real article, here are two tricky things you may encounter:

- Putting quotation marks around a name (in this example, "Source1") isn't required, but it's strongly recommended. If you don't use quotation marks, and you decide to use a name that has a space in it (say, *<ref name=John Smith>*, the Wikipedia software displays a glaringly red, enlarged font-size error message in the middle of the article. Hopefully, you'll see this in preview mode so you can fix it by adding the quotation marks before you save your edit. If you put quotation marks around every source, you'll never go wrong.

- Perhaps surprisingly, when you have multiple footnotes for the same source, you don't have to put the text of the citation where that source is *first* cited. If you want to, you can put it at any place in the text where you footnoted the source. The first footnote would then look like this: *<ref name="Whatever"/>*. If you're editing an article, that's why the text for a citation may not appear exactly where you expect.

Advanced Citation Techniques

With what you've learned so far, you now know how to document information in Wikipedia in just about any situation—you can create links, footnotes, and multiple footnotes, and use citation templates. The three techniques described in the rest of this chapter are completely optional. But if you spend a lot of time creating and editing citations, you may find a need for automated citation-creating tools, viewing footnotes for just a section of an article, and adding page numbers to footnotes.

Automated Citation Tools

When you want to cite a source, you usually have to cut and paste various elements—one by one—from the Web page where you found the source into the edit box where you're assembling the citation. But sometimes, computerized tools can vastly simplify your work: You can simply cut and paste the whole citation, not its individual parts. Here's an assortment of tools to check out:

- If you start a Google Scholar search with the *Wikipedia {{citation}} Assistant* at *http://www.srcf.ucam.org/~ms609/Wiki/Scholar*, you can just click the *{{Wikify}}* link that's part of each search result. That link generates a citation for you.

- For books, try *OttoBib* at *http://www.ottobib.com/*, enter an ISBN, click the Wikipedia button, and then click Get Citations.

- If you have access to and use specialized databases, and know the DrugBank ID, HGNC ID, PubMed ID, or PubChem ID of a document, you can simply enter that ID into the *Wikipedia template-filling page* at *http://diberri.dyndns.org/wikipedia/templates/*. Click "Submit" to get a complete citation, ready to copy and paste.

- If you use citation templates to create your footnotes, you might want to look at the *Reference generator*, a smarter version of the citation templates available in Wikipedia. It's at *http://tools.wikimedia.de/~magnus/makeref.php*. You specify the type of citation you want (online news Web site, journal article, book, conference report, and so on), and the form then shows you the mandatory parameters (for

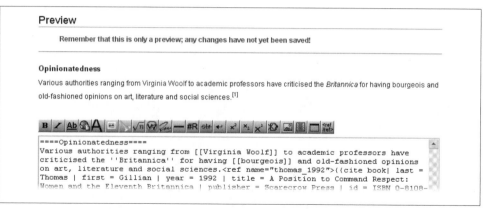

Figure 2-10. When you edit just a section of an article, the footnote numbers are visible in preview mode, but not the text of the footnotes. Some experienced editors are comfortable saving their edits without previewing what their added footnotes look like, but if not being able to preview your footnotes makes you uneasy, see Figure 2-11 for the workaround.

example, the title and URL for online news), plus other optional parameters. It also shows you examples of each parameter that you might enter, so you get the format correct.

Viewing Footnotes When Editing Only a Section of an Article

When you open only one section of an article in edit mode (which is more convenient than editing the whole article, for reasons explained on page 18), you'll find that you can't see the text of footnotes when previewing your edit. For example, suppose you're editing a section of the article *Encyclopædia Britannica* and you go into preview mode (see Figure 2-10).

The solution is to *temporarily* (note the emphasis) add a <references/> tag at the end of the section. Preview the section, and then delete the tag before saving your edit. Figure 2-11 shows another preview, this time with the *temporary* tag added.

Adding Page Numbers to Footnote Numbers

If you're using a book as a source, your may cite information from multiple locations within the book. If so, creating footnotes can be a challenge, because you seem to have three choices:

- You can create a separate citation for every page, leading to a lot of almost-duplicate entries in the "References" section. They'd be identical except for the page number cited.

- You can create a single citation with multiple occurrences, using the *name=* parameter as discussed on page 39. You can then list, in that one citation, all the pages

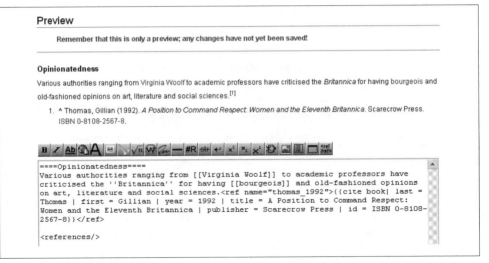

Figure 2-11. With the <references/> tag added, the footnotes are visible in preview mode. Don't forget to delete the tag before you save your edit. If you forget, the software displays all the footnotes in the article, in two different parts of the article, not once at the bottom.

numbers where you got information. (It's better than omitting the page numbers, though not by much.)

- You can use Harvard-style footnotes (page 33) instead of regular footnotes. (But you may be out of luck if the article already has a significant number of regular footnotes, because other editors may object to mixing the two styles.)

Fortunately, there's a fourth option, using a citation template called *Rp*. It lets you slot in the page number right next to the footnote number, where your readers can readily see it. Figure 2-12 shows how it works.

NOTE

In Figure 2-12, the ISBN is an internal link to a specialized Wikipedia page called *Special:Booksources*. That page in turn has links to a large number of Web sites that offer information about the linked ISBN, like online databases, general search engines, libraries throughout the world, and booksellers.

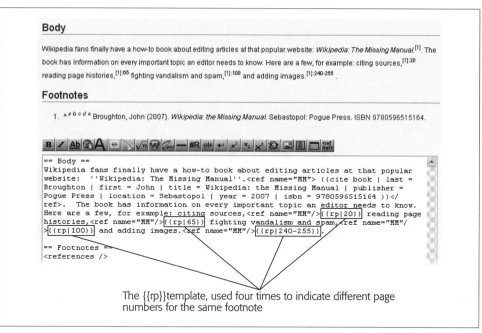

Body

Wikipedia fans finally have a how-to book about editing articles at that popular website: *Wikipedia: The Missing Manual.*[1] The book has information on every important topic an editor needs to know. Here are a few, for example: citing sources,[1]:20 reading page histories,[1]:65 fighting vandalism and spam,[1]:100 and adding images.[1]:240-255 .

Footnotes

1. ^ a b c d e Broughton, John (2007). *Wikipedia: the Missing Manual.* Sebastopol: Pogue Press. ISBN 9780596515164.

```
== Body ==
Wikipedia fans finally have a how-to book about editing articles at that popular
website: ''Wikipedia: The Missing Manual''.<ref name="MM"> {{cite book | last =
Broughton | first = John | title = Wikipedia: the Missing Manual | publisher =
Pogue Press | location = Sebastopol | year = 2007 | isbn = 9780596515164 }}</
ref>.  The book has information on every important topic an editor needs to know.
Here are a few, for example: citing sources,<ref name="MM"/>{{rp|20}} reading page
histories,<ref name="MM"/>{{rp|65}} fighting vandalism and spam,<ref name="MM"/
>{{rp|100}} and adding images.<ref name="MM"/>{{rp|240-255}}.

== Footnotes ==
<references />
```

The {{rp}}template, used four times to indicate different page numbers for the same footnote

Figure 2-12. The Rp template lets you type page numbers when you insert multiple references to a source (bottom). They appear in superscript next to footnote numbers (top). So you can cite multiple pages from the same source without any of the problems mentioned on page 41.

CHAPTER 3

Setting Up Your Account and Personal Workspace

You can edit Wikipedia articles to your heart's content—for the rest of your life even —without ever registering with Wikipedia. But the sooner you register (that is, get a user name), the sooner you'll have the benefits of a *user account*—like being able to create entirely *new* articles and to monitor changes to articles. A user account costs nothing, and you don't even have to provide any personal information. In fact, having an account actually protects your privacy *better* than editing anonymously. In this chapter, you'll learn more about these perks, get some suggestions on picking a user name, and find out about the personal user pages you can set up after you register.

Why Register?

If you sometimes feel as if every Web site, product manufacturer, and service provider wants you to register, you may be right—when you give someone your name, address, phone number, and so on, you're potentially opening yourself to junk mail, intrusive phone calls, and even the (small) possibility of identity theft. Registering with Wikipedia isn't like that at all. When you register, you don't provide any personal information except (optionally) your email address. It takes only a minute or two to get a Wikipedia user account, and it has many advantages. As you can see by the graph in Figure 3-1, you have plenty of company.

Advantages of a Registered Account

You can do a number of things as a registered (logged in) editor that anonymous IP users can't. With a registered account, you can:

- Monitor articles you've edited, or are interested in, using a *watchlist* (page 101).
- Add an external link, as described on page 48, without typing in a cryptic code —as you would if using an anonymous IP address—to prove you're a human being.

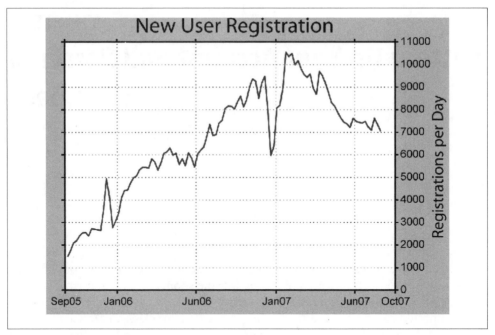

Figure 3-1. Since July 2006, the average number of newly registered accounts at Wikipedia has exceeded 7,000 per day. This graph is provided courtesy of editor Dragons Flight (Robert A. Rohde), based on a September 2007 database download of Wikipedia logs.

- Upload an image.
- Create a new page, including new articles (Chapter 4) and your personal *user page* (discussed below).
- Customize your user interface, as discussed in Part 5 and many of the "Power Users' Clinic" boxes in this book.
- Email other users, and receive email from them (see page 162).
- Mark edits as "minor" (while this isn't that useful to you, it helps other editors; see page 108 for details).
- Edit an article that is semi-protected against vandalism.
- Move (rename) an article (page 297).

NOTE

Once you have registered, you *still* have to wait 4 days before you have move/rename privileges. Similarly, you have to wait 4 days before you can edit semi-protected pages (until then, you don't see the "edit this page" tab at the top of such pages). All the other benefits kick in immediately. The 4-day waiting period is to discourage vandals from registering, since it takes away their immediate gratification. At the end of the period, you become *auto-confirmed*, which means you have all the privileges of other editors.

Disadvantages to Using Your IP Address

Not only are there benefits to having a registered account, there are disadvantages to *not* creating one. If you make an edit without registering (or without logging in, if you've registered), Wikipedia records the Internet Protocol (IP) address of the computer from which you made the edit—for example, 202.83.118.28—as your user name. And that IP address is the source of all the problems.

IP addresses are traceable

Ironically, that cryptic Internet address number provides you with *less* privacy than a registered user name. Anyone who sees your IP on Wikipedia might use a WHOIS search or other commonly available Web tools to trace it. Depending on your connection, the search may be able to trace your IP address to either your Internet service provider (ISP), or even to your school, place of business, or home. So, for example, if you edit Wikipedia from work without a login, you're leaving a permanent and public record of exactly when your particular computer was used to edit exactly which page in Wikipedia, and exactly what changes were made (presumably by you).

By contrast, when you register for an account, you don't have to provide an email address or any other personal information. Your account name can be a pseudonym—most are—and although Wikipedia's servers still record the IP address from which you edit, that address stays private, available only to a few people. All of Wikipedia's public records and pages show only your user name. If you want more privacy, register for an account.

TIP

If you want to read Wikipedia's privacy policy, a link to it appears at the very bottom of every Wikipedia page.

IP addresses change

If you're one of the not uncommon, though increasingly rare, people who dial up to connect to the Internet, you get a new IP address every time you connect. Other editors can't communicate with you via your user talk page (see page 156), and you can't build a reputation for constructive edits (because your edit history will be scattered across dozens or hundreds of different IP accounts).

Similarly, if you ever edit via a public Wi-Fi connection, a library computer, a second computer, or a smartphone, then your identity on Wikipedia is also spread across multiple IP addresses. In fact, even having a cable modem that's always connected to the Internet is no guarantee that your IP address will stay the same. You or your ISP may edit a setting, thereby changing your IP address.

A third problem is that your IP address may be *blocked*. It could be blocked because another person who did extensive vandalizing previously used it. Or an entire network (a high school, for example) may be blocked from doing editing. If you have your own user name, blocking IP addresses doesn't affect you. By contrast, without a Logon, an IP block could prevent you from doing any editing at all.

Finally, most regulars at Wikipedia tend to associate anonymous IP editing with vandalism. Roughly a quarter of all anonymous IP edits are considered unconstructive, and reversed by another editor. If you edit using a registered user name, other editors are more likely to assume good faith as they examine your edits for potential problems.

WORD TO THE WISE

Be Unique in All of Wikimedia

The English version of Wikipedia (which this book is about) is far from the only planet in the Wikimedia Foundation universe. As discussed on page xv, there are versions of Wikipedia in other languages, plus other Foundation projects (Wiktionary, Wikisource, and so on), again in a variety of languages.

The most requested (but not yet implemented) feature pertaining to all these Web sites is *single user login*. With this feature, you would need to register in only one place (for example, the English version of Wikipedia) and then use the same user name and password across all Wikimedia sites. Once this feature is implemented (if ever), conflicts will occur where two or more people have registered the same user name. In such cases, the editor whose account has the most edits will "win": Editors who have the other accounts will be forced to change user names.

Most of the common names have already been taken, so if you're registering today, you're not likely to pick a user name at the English Wikipedia that someone already uses somewhere else. Unfortunately, as this book goes to press, there's no way to be 100 percent certain.

Picking a User Name

Be prepared: Before you follow the steps in the next section to create your account, have a user name (or at least a couple of ideas) all picked out and ready to go. You may get your best ideas away from the computer screen. Read this section, then take a walk, carry a notepad, or go wherever you do your best thinking. When you come back, the registration process will go much faster.

Why spend so much time thinking about your user name? There are approximately five million registered accounts at Wikipedia. So your chances of getting an easily remembered user name of (say) six characters or less are fairly low. You could use your real name. If you don't want to do that, you should understand what types of pseudonyms are not acceptable (see page 49), and then you might want to look at some pages on Wikipedia for ideas.

Using Your Real Name

You can use your own name as the name of your Wikipedia account, assuming no one else with the same name has done so already. You won't be the only editor using a real name, but you'll certainly be part of a small minority of editors.

A real name makes it easier for you to remember your account name, and may encourage you to keep your edits polite and balanced. On the other hand, a pseudonym may make it easier for you to edit controversial topics. You should use a pseudonym if you don't necessarily want your friends and colleagues to see your name on Wikipedia.

Pseudonyms have no disadvantages. You'll probably want to use your real name only if it's important to you that the world knows that *you* are editing Wikipedia.

Other People's User Names as Examples

If you were planning to build a custom home, you'd walk through model homes to get ideas. Similarly, you may get a good idea for a user name by looking at others' user names. Here's how to browse for user names:

- You can type *Special:Listusers* into the search box (left side of screen) to look at the indexed list of all five million registered names. After you click Go or press Return, you see the Users page.

  Keep in mind that many of the names, including the ones at the beginning (consisting solely of exclamation points) have been blocked as unacceptable. (Also, if you're curious, the names in red are users who didn't create a user page for themselves.) To see more interesting names than those that appear at the beginning of the list, type some text in the "starting at" box—the first few letters of a pseudonym you have in mind, for example—and then click Go. You can also use this page to see if a name in which you're interested is already taken.

- Typing *Special:Log/newusers* into the search box takes you to a log of the more than 5,000 new names registered every day. You may see particularly clever or interesting names that spark some ideas.

- *Special:Recentchanges* takes you to a log of the most recent edits within Wikipedia. As in Figure 3-2, each line has the name of a page that was edited, followed by the editor's name. Again, you may get some useful ideas as you look at the immense flow of edits (hundreds of edits every second).

What Isn't Allowed

Wikipedia doesn't allow user names that are confusing, misleading, disruptive, promotional or offensive. Nor does it let more than one person use an account. Accounts used by two or more people in a household, an organization, or your local book club,

```
. List of typefaces; 11:27 . . (+223) . . ChristTrekker (Talk | contribs) (→Serif)
. North West England; 11:27 . . (+30) . . 213.249.162.132 (Talk) (Demographics)
. m Object file; 11:27 . . (+8) . . Tpikonen (Talk | contribs) (Fix link to Binary File Descriptor library
. User:MelicansMatkin/List of covers of U2 songs; 11:27 . . (-25) . . MelicansMatkin (Talk | contrib
R/opinion)
. m Dancing at Lughnasa; 11:27 . . (+5) . . Jonathan Cardy (Talk | contribs) (christiainty christian)
. m .hm; 11:27 . . (+16) . . Naive cynic (Talk | contribs) (cat sort)
. Apollo program; 11:27 . . (-267) . . 64.207.228.34 (Talk) (→See also)
. Bratmobile; 11:27 . . (-2) . . John (Talk | contribs) (rem redundant flag icon)
. m Pillbox Row; 11:27 . . (+54) . . Leithp (Talk | contribs) (a few links)
. m Template:Vgproj; 11:27 . . (+14) . . Jacoplane (Talk | contribs) (center)
. Talk:Khojaly Massacre; 11:27 . . (0) . . Andranikpasha (Talk | contribs) (→Who commited Mass
. Glencoe (Metra); 11:26 . . (+21) . . DanTD (Talk | contribs) (→Bus Connections - Pace Bus syste
. Britney Spears discography; 11:26 . . (+38) . . Ericorbit (Talk | contribs) (Undid revision 175943
y (talk) - rv unexplained replacement of FRA column)
. m .hk; 11:26 . . (+12) . . Naive cynic (Talk | contribs) (cat sort)
```

Figure 3-2. *You can see some editor names on this portion of the* Special:Recentchanges *log page. In each line, the name of the edited page is at the far left, followed by the time of the edit (hours:minutes on a 24-hour clock), and then the number of characters added or deleted by the edit. User names in red indicate that the user has not created a personal user page. (You'll learn how to create your user page later in this chapter.)*

are against the rules. You can set up such accounts, but if Wikipedia's administrators find out, they'll block the account.

You can read all the specific reasons for rejecting user names at the *Wikipedia:User account policy* page (type *WP:UN* into the search box). But assuming you're well intentioned, the best thing to do is simply to pick a user name and see what happens. If the user name you pick is considered borderline, you'll get a message on your user talk page (page 156) asking you to choose a new one. If Wikipedia's administrators consider your chosen user name egregiously improper, they'll permanently block your account, and you'll have to go through the registration process again and pick another name.

Sec 3.3
Registering

Now that you're well informed about why you want to create an account, and have some thoughts about your user name, it's time to register. Here are the steps:

1. When you don't have an account, or aren't logged in, you see at the upper right of every Wikipedia page (that is, every page on *en.wikipedia.org*), a link to "Sign in / create account". Click that link.

   You arrive at the screen in Figure 3-3.

2. Click the link that reads, "Create one".

   (The "E-mail new password" link makes you go through several more steps than you'd otherwise do to create an account; don't go there.) You'll see something like Figure 3-4.

Figure 3-3. Wikipedia's standard sign-in screen includes a "Create one" link for you to create an account and get yourself a user name.

3. **Type your proposed user name.**

   Consider the following points:

   - Try to keep your user name shorter than 25 characters. The shorter it is, the easier to customize your signature (page 387), and the less irritating it will be to other editors. Long names result in long signatures, which occupy a lot of space and make editing talk pages (page 145) more difficult for other editors.

   - Capitalization counts. User "fred smith" isn't the same as User "Fred Smith," so type the name *exactly* the way you want it with regard to capitalization. (This is also true of titles of articles, and in fact of *every* page in Wikipedia—except for the very first character of a page name, capitalization *does* matter.)

4. **Type your password.**

   Not all passwords are created equal. To make sure your password prevents people who aren't you from using your account, your password should *not be obvious.* Don't use your (proposed) user name as your password, or your user name spelled backwards, or the word "password."

TIP

For more information about good passwords, look below the input boxes for creating an account for two links: "Password strength" and "this essay".

---

5. **Type the email address you want to associate with your Wikipedia account.**

   You don't *have* to provide an email address, but you absolutely *should.* If you forget your password, or (even worse) your account gets compromised (someone guesses your password), having an email account is the only way that a Wikipedia

Create account

Already have an account? **Log in**.

To help protect against automated account creation, please enter the words that a|

Unable to see the image? An administrator can create an account for you.

plantgoods

Username:

Password:

Retype password:

E-mail (optional)*

- E-mail (optional): Allows us to e-mail your password to you if you forget it. If you
  by using the "E-mail this user" feature. Note that the sender's e-mail address will
  address.

☐ Remember me

[**Create account**] [by e-mail]

Figure 3-4. As explained in step 5 on page 51, providing an email address is important. After you register, you get an email message from wiki@wikimedia.org, with the subject "Wikipedia e-mail address confirmation." You must click the link in the confirmation notice if you want Wikipedia's administrators to be able to contact you. (You can change your email address anytime you want, once you've confirmed it.)

administrator can email you a new password. Otherwise, you have to register again, and get a new user name.

6. Type the words that appear in the image, and then click "Create account".

You should see a "Login successful" screen. Congratulations! You're now a registered editor in Wikipedia, albeit one without any edits under that user name.

NOTE

That abstract-looking image is called a *captcha*, which stands for "Completely Automated Public Turing test to tell Computers and Humans Apart." The theory is that it takes a human to figure out the words in the image, which prevents spammers from using automated programs to create masses of fraudulent accounts. If you get "Login error: Incorrect or missing confirmation code" in the previous step, Wikipedia thinks you typed the wrong words for the captcha; just try again with the new image on the error screen.

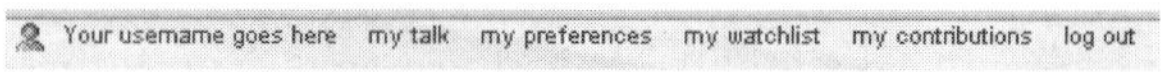

Figure 3-5. After you get a new account, six links show up at the top of the screen. The leftmost two links are red; the other four are blue (the bust-like image at the far left isn't a link). A red link means that a page doesn't exist—yet. Once you or someone else has put some content on your user page and your user talk page, two links will turn blue.

Once you see the "Login successful" screen, you see, in the screen's upper right corner, six links (Figure 3-5).

Setting Up Your User Page

One benefit of registering is that you have your own personal page in Wikipedia—your *user page*. Editors don't have to have a main user page, but the rest of this book assumes that you have one. You also can create additional pages (called *user subpages*) for things like drafts of articles, lists of helpful pages, and so on. For example, Chapter 4 has you work in your personal sandbox (page 57), as opposed to using the common Sandbox, as you did in the tutorials in Chapter 1 and Chapter 2.

Uses for Your User Page

You can use your user page for anything that you find helpful as an editor, including:

- Putting links to information pages and other pages you may want to refer to, post questions at, and so on. Figure 3-8 shows an example.

- Putting links to additional personal pages (called *subpages*) that you can create. Later in this chapter, you'll learn how to create one—a personal sandbox, which you'll use in tutorials in later chapters.

- Adding notes to yourself about what you want or might do next—articles to write or edit, WikiProjects (page 165) you might want to create, etc. (In short, a "wish list" or "to do" list.)

- Your interests and language skills (see page 56).

- Items from collaborative aspects of editing, like *barnstars* (awards for service, given by other editors), names of editors you've *adopted* (agreed to be a mentor for), and WikiProjects to which you belong.

In addition, it's okay to post *some* information about yourself that might be helpful to other editors—for example, that you have specific language skills. You *don't* want to post information such as your home address, phone number, email address, or your age (especially if you're a minor), because you don't know who's going to read the posting, or what they might do with it. Furthermore, posting personal information can be considered disruptive, if your intent is clearly to start a social interaction with other editors (if your user page resembles a page on Facebook.com, for example).

The easiest way to get a sense of the possibilities of your user page is to click the names of other editors, which will take you to their user pages. You'll find a wide variety of user pages, some minimal or utilitarian, some clearly reflecting the personality of the editor. You can find names of other, established editors in many places, including:

- The *Special:Recentchanges* page (Figure 3-2).
- Page histories (Chapter 5)
- Talk pages (Chapter 8)

How Not to Use Your User Page

Many editors aren't aware of a very important policy page about what Wikipedia is not. To distinguish yourself from the unedified, in the search box, type *WP:NOT*. This sentence is particularly relevant to user pages: "Wikipedia is not a blog, Web space provider, social networking, or memorial site."

The Wikipedia community understands that it's normal and acceptable for there to be *some* social aspects of being a Wikipedia editor. But editors who make the social aspects of Wikipedia their *main* priority, showing no particular interest in editing articles, will inevitably be asked to move on to the many other websites designed for broadcasting personal views or socially interacting with others.

Now, the bad news. An improper user page kicks off the standard process for dealing with problem editors: An editor who violates the policy gets a warning; another editor may even help by removing content. If the editor with the improper user page doesn't agree that a problem exists, an administrator removes the offending content. If the editor insists on putting that content back, he loses editing rights to his own user page, or altogether. In short, Wikipedia's purpose is to write the world's biggest and best encyclopedia. Those who want to do something else should read the page *Wikipedia:Alternative outlets* (shortcut: *WP:OUT*).

Creating Your User Page

As noted above, once you've created an account, there's a red link to your user page at the top of the screen (it's the link that shows the actual name of the new account).

1. Click the red link for your user name (upper right).

   You'll see a page that looks, at the top, similar to Figure 3-6 (your user name will appear instead of "Your username goes here"). You need to add text to this page, which you can save, thereby creating the page.

2. Click either the "edit this page" tab or on the link that begins "Start the User:".

   Both links do exactly the same thing. You see a page like Figure 3-7.

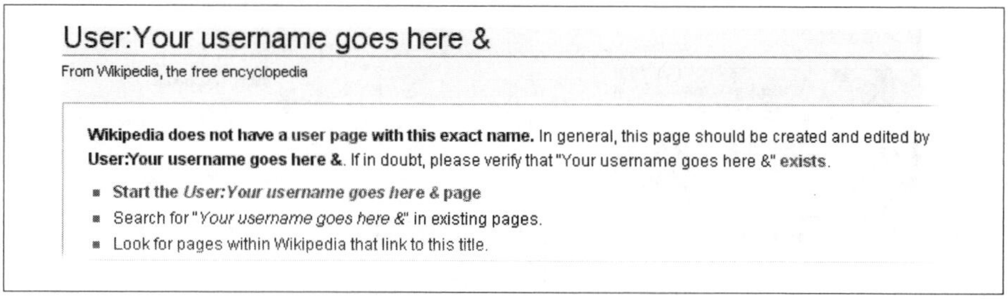

Figure 3-6. The top of a user page, when you first start to create it. It may be a bit odd to be looking at a page that seems to say it doesn't exist. This text simply means that the user page hasn't yet been created and saved.

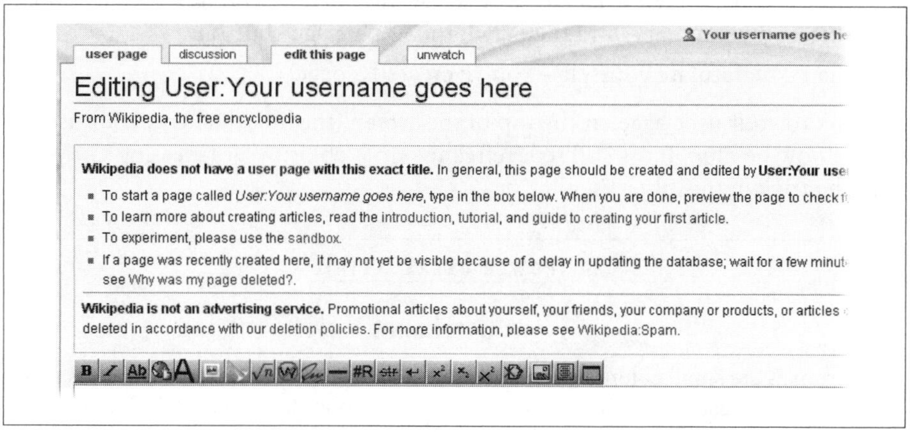

Figure 3-7. Editing your user page the first time—the top of the page, including the top of the edit box where you'll be putting some text.

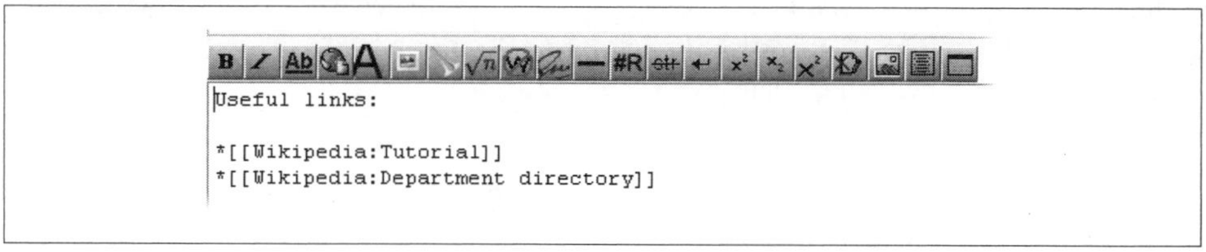

Figure 3-8. Some suggested text for you to type into the input box on your user page. If you've encountered interesting or useful pages in your travels on Wikipedia so far, here's one place to create links to those pages. For example, you type [[WP:SAND]] or [[Wikipedia:Sandbox]] to create a direct link to the sandbox for yourself.

3. In the edit box, add some text.

   Figure 3-8 gives you with a suggestion, but if you want to put "Hi Mom!" instead, feel free. You can change this page later, in any way you want, just as you can with virtually every other page in Wikipedia—all you do is click "edit this page".

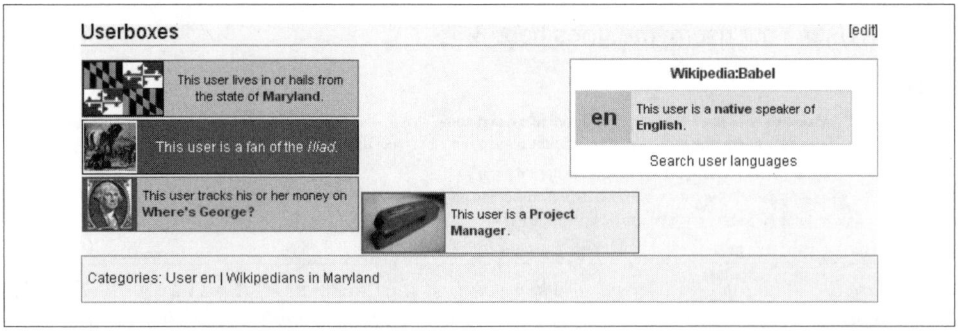

Figure 3-9. Some examples of userboxes.

4. After you've entered whatever text you want, tab to the "Edit summary" box. Add a brief edit summary, and then click the "Save page" button.

Then congratulate yourself—you've created a page!

The link to your user page, at the top of the screen (the link that says your user name) should now be blue. If it's still red, refresh your Web browser (pressing Ctrl+R [⌘-R] does the trick in most browsers).

POWER USERS' CLINIC

Userboxes

Userboxes are small colored boxes that editors can add to their user pages. As shown in Figure 3-9, userboxes can provide information about language skills, interests, profession, location, and so on. Userboxes are templates (page 17).

When you're ready to add userboxes to your page, you'll find all the information you need about the design, construction, and usage of userboxes on the *Wikipedia:Userboxes* page (into the search box, type the shortcut *WP:BOX*). Many userboxes, after being added, also put a category at the bottom of the user page. You can click on that category to see other Wikipedians who have the same userbox.

Personal Subpages

As shown in Figure 3-5, once you're registered and logged on, Wikipedia shows, in the screen's upper right, a link to your personal page (click your user name). There's also a link to your user talk page (click "my talk"), which is described in detail as described in Chapter 8 (starting on page 156). This page is for other editors to talk to you. These two standard links are in red if not yet created, or in blue, if they exist.

You're not limited to one personal page in Wikipedia (or two, if you count the user talk page, but that's really a discussion page, not a page for you to play with). You can create additional personal pages if you want. In Wikipedia, these additional pages are called *subpages*.

WARNING

Don't use the techniques in this section to create a subpage of an *article*. Although you can create such a subpage, an administrator will soon either move or delete it. Don't create such a subpage as a test—that's considered vandalism. It wastes the time of editors who monitor new page creation, and of administrators, who are the only people who can delete Wikipedia pages.

Creating Your Personal Sandbox

In Chapter 1, while editing the common sandbox, you saw the problem of an *edit conflict* (page 11). Creating your own page to practice at—that is, your own sandbox —takes care of the edit conflict problem. You also don't see any of the standard warnings or hidden text that come with the common sandbox. Plus it's good practice for creating other personal subpages that you may later decide you need.

1. In the screen's upper right corner, click your user name.

   You need to be logged in, of course, to see that link. You arrive at your personal user page.

2. Click "edit this page".

   You're now in edit mode; in the edit box, you see the existing text (as in Figure 3-8).

3. In the edit box, enter the text that'll become a link to the subpage you're going to create.

   Figure 3-10 shows you the two different ways to create a link. You can pick either one, or use both, to confirm that both links will go to the same page. If you want to call your sandbox something other than "My sandbox", feel free to do so.

WARNING

In the second link in Figure 3-10, the "/" is essential. If you omit it, you'll be starting the process of creating an *article* called "my sandbox", which you don't want to do.

---

4. Tab to the "Edit summary" box. Add a brief edit summary, and then click the "Save page" button.

   You've now modified your user page so that it has a link (or two) to a page you're going to create.

5. Click the red link to the new subpage you want to create.

   That's it—you're looking at your new, personal sandbox (Figure 3-11).

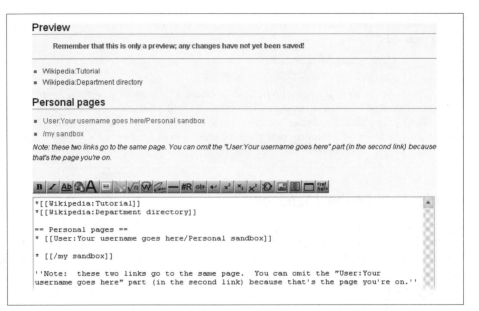

Figure 3-10. This edit box shows two different ways to create a link. In Preview mode, you can see that the links are red because the page doesn't yet exist. Also note that the page is spelled "My sandbox" in one link and "my sandbox" in the other. Those links are really to the same page because Wikipedia software always treats the first letter of the title of a page as a capital letter, even if it doesn't display it that way.

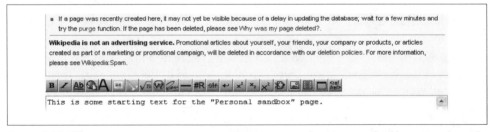

Figure 3-11. Whenever you start to create a new page, you see the same standard language above the edit toolbar. The text you enter (in this case, beginning "This is some starting text …") doesn't matter (this is, after all, your personal sandbox) but you must put some text—any text—in the edit box so you can save the page.

You can always get back to it in two steps:

1. Click your user name (upper-right part of the screen, whenever you're logged in) to go to your user page.
2. Click the link that you added to your user page.

Deleting Your Subpages

If you create a user subpage and later decide you don't want it, you can't delete it yourself because you're not an administrator. If you want it deleted, just post *{{db-userreq}}* on the subpage. That creates a notification to the Wikipedia administrators that you'd like one of them to delete the page.

CHAPTER 4

Creating a New Article

Wikipedia needs more articles. Yet of the thousands of articles that are created every day, about half end up being deleted or otherwise removed. Most of the deletions happen within a day of the article's creation. If you're thinking about adding an article to Wikipedia, this chapter will help you avoid having that article become instant roadkill. (This chapter also discusses when it's better not to write the article at all, or write it for another wiki or other Web site besides Wikipedia).

Even if you're not thinking about creating a new article, this chapter can be useful. You'll get a much better sense of what articles in Wikipedia *should be like*, which will help you when you want to improve existing articles. You'll also have some criteria to use when you come upon an existing article that you suspect might not belong in Wikipedia at all. (Chapter 19 discusses the process for getting an article deleted.)

UP TO SPEED

Does That Article Already Exist?

Before you even start thinking of writing a new article, you'll want to make absolutely, positively sure that Wikipedia doesn't already have an article on the same subject.

Wikipedia's internal search engine isn't the greatest, but it's the easiest place to start. Try searching for just part of what you think the article should be called (two or three words is plenty), and try any likely alternative names and spellings. (The page *Wikipedia:Searching*—shortcut *WP:S*—has more details. It also has a link to an alternative internal search engine, *WikEh?*)

After you've done a reasonable amount of internal searching of Wikipedia, try an external search engine. For example, to use Google to find all Wikipedia pages with the word "Wyly," type *Wyly site:en.Wikipedia.org* into the Google search box. An external search engine could turn up a page that the internal search engine missed, since external search engines can be more tolerant of misspellings than Wikipedia's.

Figure 4-1. The Articles for Creation wizard asks a series of questions to determine if your idea for an article is a good one. Registered users normally don't use this wizard to create articles, but it's still a good learning tool. To get there, go to the Wikipedia:Articles for Creation *page (shortcut:* WP:AFC*), scroll down until you see the large "Start Here," and then click that link. Then click "I would like to submit an article without registration".*

What Makes a Good Article

If you're not a registered user (see Chapter 3), you can't create new articles, at least as of January 2008. (A proposal to allow non-registered users to make new articles, in November 2007, didn't gain consensus.) Instead, you have to submit a proposed new article for review by other editors, using the Articles for Creation wizard (Figure 4-1). That wizard is a five-step online interview that questions you about three things: the proposed article's motivation, notability, and sources. This section discusses all three issues, one by one. They're important for all new articles, no matter who creates them.

TIP

Even as a registered user, it's worth your time to use the wizard to see if you can get to the final step (being allowed to submit an article) while telling the truth (starting at step 2). If you can't get all the way through the wizard by responding *honestly*, then your article will probably be deleted.

UP TO SPEED

Curb Your Enthusiasm and Expertise

If you really know (and probably really like) an area of knowledge, doing a hit-or-miss search for articles to create probably isn't the best use of your time. Consider these two options instead:

- On page 78, you'll find pointers to a number of places where other editors have identified needed (missing) articles. Many of these lists are sorted by topic area, so you can focus on needed articles in your area of interest.

- You can join (formally or informally) an existing collaboration about your area of interest—what Wikipedia calls a *WikiProject*. Chapter 9 has extensive information on these.

The Right Motivation

The ideal starting point for creating an article is when you're surprised that Wikipedia doesn't already have an article on a particular subject. If you believe that the subject is suitable for inclusion in an encyclopedia (what Wikipedia calls *notability*, as described on page 64), and that newspaper stories, magazine articles, publications in scientific journals, or public sources of information specifically focus on this topic, you have every reason to be surprised that no one's already written an article on the topic.

By contrast, if you're thinking about writing an article for one of the following reasons, then your chances of having your article deleted are high:

- **You've developed a new or unusual concept, idea, or invention;** or you know something that disproves conventional wisdom on a topic; or you have an unusual theory about the way the world works, or should work. Don't use Wikipedia to announce these things.

- **You have intense feelings about something or someone**. For example, you may have a strong dislike of something (airplane travel, wiretapping, animal abuse), or a very favorable impression of a Web site, a local band, or a cult YouTube video. Whether it's good or bad, if you have a strong feeling or opinion about something, you probably think that Wikipedia doesn't adequately cover it and could use another article or two about it. But other editors may not agree, and in any case it's going to be very hard for you to write with the required neutral point of view.

- **You see Wikipedia as a marketing opportunity** for your company, Web site, band, or product. Or worse, for a company, Web site, band, or product that you're being paid to promote. Even if the marketing or promotion is just to help a friend or relative—no money or direct involvement—it's still promotion and has no place in an encyclopedia.

It's possible, of course, that even if you have the wrong motivation, there's a legitimate need in Wikipedia for the new article you're thinking about. But if your motivation falls into one of the previous three categories, think twice. If you ignore Wikipedia's rules and write articles that are only going to get deleted, you're wasting your time and that of the editors who have to delete them.

WORD TO THE WISE

Conflicts of Interest

Conflicts of interest occur when editors add or delete information from Wikipedia articles with the intention of improving the image, interests, or visibility of the editors,

---

their family members, employers, associates, or business or personal endeavors. Reshaping articles to be more positive about such personal interests stands in direct contradiction to Wikipedia's neutral point of view policy (shortcut: *WP:NPOV*).

If you have a possible conflict of interest, you're not barred from editing articles where such a conflict may exist, but you must be careful that your work maintains a neutral point of view. (Details are at *Wikipedia:Conflict of interest*; shortcut: *WP:COI*.) To be really careful, don't delete anything but obvious vandalism from articles. When you think the article should be changed, post to the article's talk (discussion) page (see page 145), asking other editors to make the changes. (You can add the *{{request edit}}* template to make sure your request gets attention.)

Creating a new article when you have a potential conflict of interest is particularly tricky. In the tutorial on page 75 (step 9), you see how to move your article from your personal space (the draft) to *mainspace*, where actual articles reside. If there's any question of a conflict of interest, *don't move your article*. Instead, post a comment on the talk page of the most relevant WikiProject (Chapter 9) or at *Wikipedia:Editor assistance* (shortcut: *WP:EA*), asking other editors to review your draft, edit it if they want to, and—if they then consider it sufficiently neutral and meeting other criteria for Wikipedia articles—move it to mainspace themselves. Give the process a week or so. If no one moves your article, and no one objects strongly (or you feel you've addressed the objections), then move the article yourself.

Notability

Folks new to Wikipedia frequently see it as a place for information on *everything*. After all (so this mistaken impression goes), Wikipedia's the first place most people turn to for information on any possible topic, so logically it should have complete coverage of all new and interesting topics. If a topic isn't yet covered, then that's an open invitation to write a new article.

In fact, Wikipedia is by design not a publisher of initial reports. As the main notability guideline says: "A topic is presumed to be notable if it has received significant coverage in reliable secondary sources that are independent of the subject." If that sentence sounds familiar, it's because you read about *reliable sources* in Chapter 2 (page 26).

You can find specialized Wikipedia guidelines for a number of areas, including books, music, and organizations and companies, at the main *Notability* guideline page (shortcut: *WP:N*). For example, a musical band would qualify as notable if it met any of a dozen different criteria, including, "Has had a record certified gold or higher in at least one country." Or, for example, a film is notable if it's been widely distributed and received full-length reviews by two or more nationally known critics.

If you write an article that doesn't state, at the very beginning, why something is notable, you've significantly increased its roadkill potential. And if you also fail to provide any good sources, then you've backed other editors into a corner. They'll use an external search engine to do a quick search of the subject, but it's a matter of luck whether they'll find acceptable sources, such as newspaper articles, that indicate that a subject is important. If they don't, your article is probably toast.

Despite very specific guidelines for notability, many editors think notability is subjective—who's to say what's notable? Experienced editors focus on the presence or absence of reliable sources (discussed in the next section). Still, the concept of notability, as defined by Wikipedia's guidelines, helps ensure that articles are relevant and interesting to a wide audience of readers.

FREQUENTLY ASKED QUESTION

Where Original Writing Is Welcome

I know everything there is to know about custom golf clubs, a subject that's woefully neglected on Wikipedia. But since I've come up with a lot of the innovations myself, I can't provide sources that Wikipedia considers reliable. Isn't there some way I can share what I know?

Sure there is. First of all, if you have a conflict of interest (for example, you have your own custom golf club business), see the box on page 63. You can enlist other editors' help in publishing your article.

But any time Wikipedia's rules don't allow the type of new article that you have in mind, remember you don't *have* to fight the system. Instead, find a place elsewhere that's more welcoming.

Wikipedia is nothing more than a *wiki*—a collection of pages written by a group, collaboratively. But it's hardly the only wiki out there. If you've written something uniquely your own (a theory, an argument, a how-to) another wiki might be the perfect fit. Not surprisingly, Wikipedia has a page about alternatives to Wikipedia (the shortcut is *WP:NOTWP*). Another good place to check is *http://wikiindex.org/*, which has thousands of pages about wikis that aren't—let's face it—as obsessive-compulsive as Wikipedia about keeping out original writing.

Reliable Sources

Just as you must cite reliable sources when you add text to an article, as discussed in depth in Chapter 2 (and at *WP:RS*), you must fully document new articles you write. For new articles, here are the general guidelines:

- Try to cite at least couple of independent, reliable sources in your article, regardless of the article's length. If you don't, it's just your claim, as the author, that the subject is notable. While you may be the most honest and trustworthy person on the planet, other editors don't know that, and they may delete your article because they can't easily find reliable sources for it.

- Include any relevant links to Web sites created or owned by the subject of the article. For example, articles about musicians usually contain links to their own Web sites. However, although these "official" links help other editors examining the article, they don't count as independent sources.

It may seem counterintuitive, but good sources are more important than the words in your article. Yes, you want to write an article that has all the right parts (see page 73) and reads well. But if you include reliable sources in your new article, particularly online sources (in English), other editors will find it credible, no matter how poorly written. By contrast, if you write an article that doesn't cite independent sources, it doesn't matter that what you've written is elegant, thoughtful, and interesting. If other editors judge your article to be original research or about a non-notable subject, they'll just delete it.

Ideally, when you write a new Wikipedia article, you footnote every sentence (or paragraph, if the entire paragraph is from one source). It sounds like a lot of work, and it is, if you're looking for sources for an article you've already written. A better approach: Start by finding reliable sources for the article you want to write, and then write the article from those sources.

UP TO SPEED

Stubs

A *stub* is an article containing only a few sentences of text. A stub is usually long enough to serve as a quick definition, but too short to provide encyclopedic coverage of a subject (see Figure 4-2). Stubs are common. The last time someone counted, Wikipedia had roughly a hundred thousand articles with fewer than 200 characters. The most important thing to know about stubs: Don't contribute new ones. If you have a good idea, but only a little material, create a user subpage (page 56) and work on the article until it's ready for prime time.

One of the most common complaints from authors of just-deleted stubs is that they expected their article to be left in place for a while, so that other editors could contribute to it, eventually expanding it into a real article. In fact, there's no such policy of mercy for new stubs: The stubbier a new article is, the more likely it is to be deleted. If you think a topic is important enough to deserve a new article, then you should be willing to spend enough time finding information—from reliable sources—so that the article doesn't begin life as a stub. Otherwise, the article will quite possibly reach the end of its short life being a stub, and you'll have wasted your time and the time of the editors who deleted it.

What Articles Don't Belong on Wikipedia

So far, this chapter has shown you what a Wikipedia article needs: appropriate intentions on your part, notability of the subject, and reliable sources. Even with all these

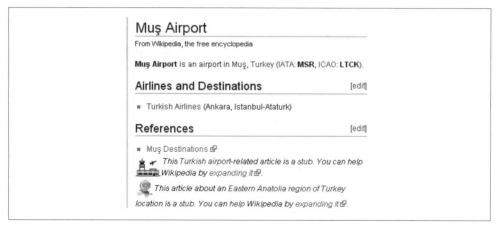

Figure 4-2. When an article is a stub, it says so, as shown at the very bottom of this example. Stubs usually have just a sentence or two about their subject, and sometimes links to related, longer articles. Wikipedia's administrators are quick to delete stubs, so work on articles in your user space until they're long enough for prime time.

factors in place, your article idea may not be right for Wikipedia. As an encyclopedia, Wikipedia is a compendium of useful information, but not *all* useful information. Some kinds of information just don't fit in.

What Wikipedia Isn't

To judge whether an article belongs in Wikipedia, take a look at what kinds of articles *don't* belong there. *Wikipedia:Not* (shortcut: *WP:NOT*) is the definitive policy on this. Much of that policy you've already heard about: "Wikipedia is not a publisher of original thought," "Wikipedia is not a soapbox," for example. But there are several more guidelines worth noting:

- **Wikipedia isn't a dictionary**. The Wikimedia Foundation does have a sister project, Wiktionary, for definitions, and there are others on the Web (for example, Urban Dictionary) that welcome your submittals.

- **Wikipedia isn't a directory**. Articles shouldn't consist of loosely associated topics such as aphorisms, people, books, unusual crimes, or geographical trivia, no matter how well referenced. Quotations belong in another sister project, Wikiquote. Similarly, radio or television station schedules, or lists of government offices and current office-holders for local governments, aren't acceptable. Product price guides don't belong on Wikipedia, either.

- **Wikipedia isn't a manual, guidebook, or textbook**. Wikipedia articles should not include instructions, advice or suggestions (legal, medical, or otherwise); how-to guides, tutorials, instruction manuals, game guides, or recipes. You can find (and submit) user-written textbooks at Wikibooks (a sister project), travel guides at Wikitravel (not related to the Wikimedia Foundation), and step-by-step guides at wikiHow (again, not related to Wikipedia).

- **Wikipedia isn't an indiscriminate collection of information**. Articles should not be constructed from, or contain, lists of frequently asked questions, lengthy plot summaries, lengthy lyrics (even when unprotected by copyright), or long and sprawling lists of statistics.

- **Wikipedia isn't a news ticker**. The fact that someone or something is newsworthy doesn't automatically justify an encyclopedia article. Newspapers and television stations report constantly on people who have been badly harmed, barely escaped disaster, done something horrible, or otherwise are unusual enough to justify 15 minutes of fame. Such stories don't make people and incidents into encyclopedic subjects. Wikipedia articles should not be voyeuristic or ongoing violations of a reasonable right to privacy.

Don't Repeat Someone Else's Words at Length

Suppose you've found a topic that isn't covered in Wikipedia—say a nonprofit group called the International Development and Improvement Organization for Theoretical Scientificality. The organization's Web site has a number of detailed pages about the history, goals, mission, and executive leadership of the organization—perfect for a detailed article. Add links to a few reliable sources, and, presto!—instant article.

This, of course, is a massive copyright violation. Even if you're the head of that organization (a conflict of interest, but that's another matter), you can't somehow waive normal copyright requirements just for Wikipedia. If the article isn't instantly deleted, it's highly likely to go into copyright lockdown (with a huge banner across the top of the page, telling editors to leave it alone until it's been fully reviewed).

With that in mind, you *can* copy, more or less verbatim, from a few places. You probably don't want to copy *lots* of text from these sources, because it's likely to be inconsistent in tone from the rest of the article, or too detailed, or quite possibly just boring. Still, if you really want to, you can copy:

- **Information from U.S. government publications and Web sites**, which are in the public domain, unless otherwise stated. (Publications of state and local governments in the U.S., on the other hand, usually *are* copyrighted.) You can find a list of resources in the public domain at *Wikipedia:Public domain resources* (shortcut: *WP:PDR*).

- **Text copyrighted with the GNU Free Documentation License (GFDL)**. That's the same type of copyright as Wikipedia uses (but see the Note on page 423). You can find research resources that use this license at *Wikipedia:GNU Free Documentation License resources* (shortcut: *WP:FDLR*).

- **Older material whose copyrights have expired**. In the U.S., any work published before January 1, 1923, anywhere in the world, is in the public domain. (For more details, see shortcut *WP:PD*.)

Preventing copyright violations, and fixing them as quickly as possible, are major concerns at Wikipedia. And you as an individual editor are liable, not Wikipedia, as long as the violation gets removed as soon as an editor detects it.

NOTE

Whether or not information is from a copyrighted source, you should always cite where you got it. That's absolutely critical if the text is a direct quotation or if the text is saying something critical of anyone or anything, particularly a living person.

Tutorial: Creating a New Article

In this tutorial, you'll see a new article created from scratch. If you want to practice creating your own new article as you follow along with the tutorial, you can do one of two things:

- Find a real topic (for example, using the information in the box on page 78, concerning articles that are needed or requested).

- Write a pretend article, and don't do the very last few steps, which involve moving the article into *mainspace*, where real Wikipedia articles exist.

  Before you start the tutorial, you might want to review Chapter 1 through Chapter 3, or take a look at *Wikipedia:Your first article* (shortcut: *WP:YFA*) to reinforce what you need to know about choosing new articles to write, and working in Wikipedia's edit window.

WORD TO THE WISE

A New Article Creator Gets It Very, Very Wrong

Zeo works at a public relations firm. One client, though quite young, is creating innovative international events. A Wikipedia article about her, Zeo thinks, would be ideal free publicity, and she would be appreciative. Creating the article is a breeze, using text from old press releases, with links to various Web sites about the client, her organization, and her events.

The next day, Zeo notices that his article is gone. Strange, but no problem—he'd saved a copy. He creates it again. Three hours later, the article is gone again, and there's a warning on Zeo's user talk page about blatant advertising.

But Zeo is persistent. He's figured out this "reliable sources" thing. He does the article again, toning down the rhetoric and adding links to a few news articles about the events and their creator. Five hours later, he logs into Wikipedia and sees a notice on his talk page that the article is up for discussion at "Articles for Deletion" (with a link).

At the AfD discussion, the regulars have already posted a lot of "Delete" recommendations. Zeo defends his article's notability, providing links to a few more newspaper articles. But he's at a disadvantage: He's new, he hasn't contributed anything else to Wikipedia, and this is the third time he's created the article. (Right or wrong, many editors see repeatedly recreating deleted articles as either fanaticism or spammer's zealotry). Of the editors commenting on the proposed deletion, almost all think that the young promoter isn't that notable: Sure, the events exist, but are they *important*? The article goes down for the count for a third time.

Zeo waits a week, and then tries again. This time, the article's deleted within an hour, the topic name is locked down (meaning an administrator needs to approve its creation), and Zeo is blocked from editing for 24 hours.

End of story? Not necessarily, but Zeo—or, better yet, Zeo, working with another, more established editor—is going to find more articles, build a new Wikipedia article solely from news stories and other reliable sources, footnote every single sentence, and then go through the deletion review process (DRV) (page 380). As long as the article, as rewritten, makes a reasonable case for notability, it's likely that DRV will approve it. But it would have been easier for everyone if Zeo had done it right the first time.

1. Choose a name for the article.

   In general, use the topic's most commonly used name. Using a search engine to compare the total number of hits for each version of the name is a good way to determine which name is the most popular. Once you have a couple of ideas, check the rules: Wikipedia has lots and lots of details about proper naming of articles. You'll find these at *Wikipedia:Naming conventions* (shortcut: *WP:NC*).

   In this tutorial, the new article is a biography, *Sam Wyly*. A search engine check shows that this is much more common than "Samuel Wyly."

2. Do a search (or several) to find out what Wikipedia already has on the topic.

   You can read about search techniques in the box on page 61. Don't search for "Sam Wyly"; that Wikipedia article was already created as an example for this book. Rather, search for the name of the real article that you want to create, or use one of the topics identified as missing in Wikipedia (see page 78).

UP TO SPEED

Biographical Information: Two Caveats

In Wikipedia articles, any controversial statement (whether positive or negative) about a living person *must* be properly sourced. If it's not, you and all other editors are authorized to—and supposed to—take it out immediately, as it's a major violation of Wikipedia policy.

When it comes to privacy violations, Wikipedia's standards are even stricter. Wikipedia biographies should not include addresses, email addresses, telephone numbers, or other contact information for living persons. If the birthday of the

---

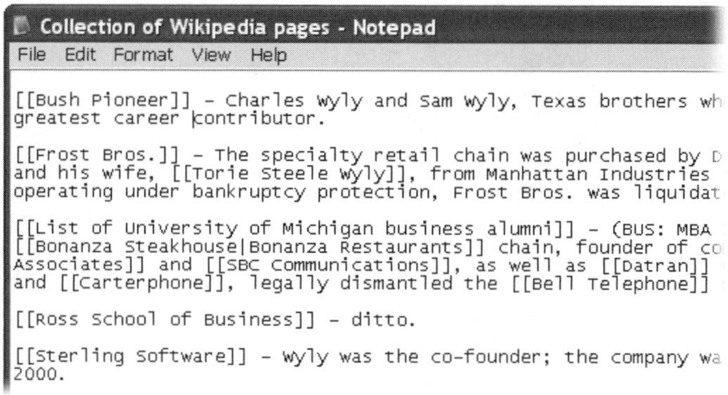

Figure 4-3. Five articles that mentioned Sam Wyly were found during the process of creating a new article about him. Information from those articles was copied (in this illustration, to the Windows Notepad) because it'll be used in the article. Part of building the web is creating outgoing links from a new article, pointing to existing Wikipedia articles.

person is not widely publicized, only the birth year should be included. These kinds of information may even be removed from prior versions of that article. (Prior versions are available via the "history" tab. You can also read about the concept in Chapter 5.) You can find full detail in the "Presumption in favor of privacy" section of *Wikipedia:Biographies of living persons* (shortcut: *WP:BLP*).

3. If you find an existing Wikipedia article that contains a mention of the topic you searched for, do two things:

   • Change that mention into an internal link (wikilink), if it's not already, by editing the page, by adding two square brackets on each side: "[[Sam Wyly]]". After you save your change to that article, you see that the link you created is a red link, since it points to an article that doesn't yet exist. Adding such wikilinks is called, in Wikipedia, *building the web*.

   • Copy the name of the page, and possibly useful details about the topic that are on the page, to a temporary place (for example, Windows Notepad). Figure 4-3 lists the Wikipedia articles that mentioned Sam Wyly *before* the Sam Wyly article was created.

4. As shown in the steps starting on page 57, create a user subpage for the article.

   Typically, you give the this user subpage the same name that the article will have. In this tutorial, though, the subpage is just called "New article."

5. Find independent, reliable sources. Add them to the subpage.

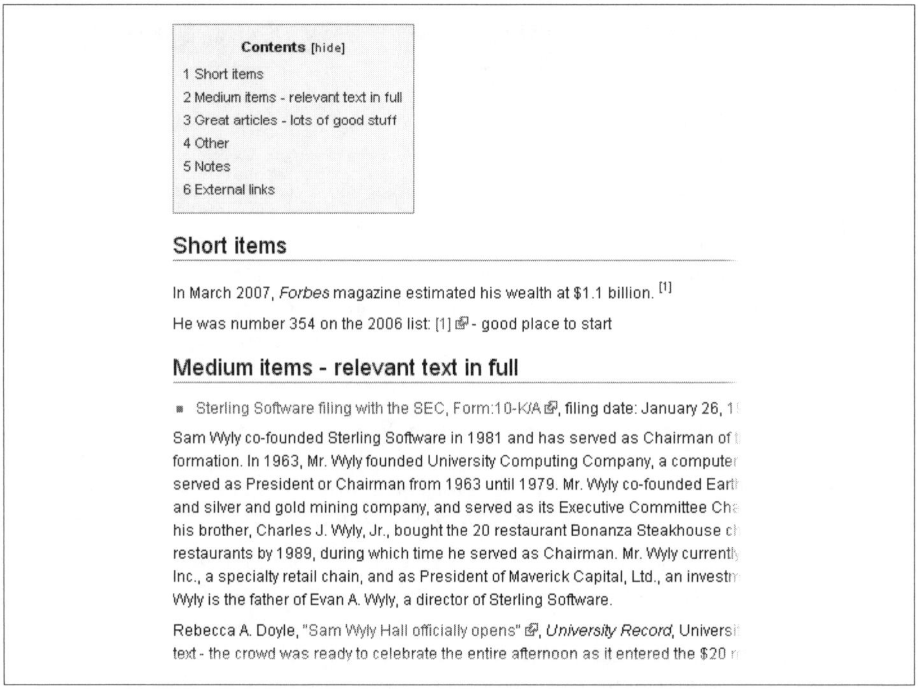

Contents [hide]

1 Short items
2 Medium items - relevant text in full
3 Great articles - lots of good stuff
4 Other
5 Notes
6 External links

Short items

In March 2007, *Forbes* magazine estimated his wealth at $1.1 billion. [1]

He was number 354 on the 2006 list: [1] ⏍ - good place to start

Medium items - relevant text in full

- Sterling Software filing with the SEC, Form:10-K/A ⏍, filing date: January 26, 1

Sam Wyly co-founded Sterling Software in 1981 and has served as Chairman of
formation. In 1963, Mr. Wyly founded University Computing Company, a computer
served as President or Chairman from 1963 until 1979. Mr. Wyly co-founded Eart
and silver and gold mining company, and served as its Executive Committee Cha
his brother, Charles J. Wyly, Jr., bought the 20 restaurant Bonanza Steakhouse cl
restaurants by 1989, during which time he served as Chairman. Mr. Wyly currently
Inc., a specialty retail chain, and as President of Maverick Capital, Ltd., an investm
Wyly is the father of Evan A. Wyly, a director of Sterling Software.

Rebecca A. Doyle, "Sam Wyly Hall officially opens" ⏍, *University Record*, Universi
text - the crowd was ready to celebrate the entire afternoon as it entered the $20 m

Figure 4-4. Here are a number of reliable sources for the planned article. There isn't any standard way to put them on the subpage (the top of which is shown here), but it's a good idea to start building the format for full citations (page 32). On the other hand, don't put the full text of long articles on the page—that's a copyright violation the moment you save the page with all the text on it, even though you're doing the work on a user subpage, rather than on an article page.

NOTE

You can read about finding copyright-free sources on page 68. Also, page 78 has a discussion about finding reliable sources from which you can take facts and limited amounts of text in accordance with fair use laws.

Figure 4-4 shows the results of searching for sources for "Sam Wyly." If you use a search engine, a lot of results are going to be links to bloggers, forums, or other unacceptable sources. Don't ignore these—they may have a link to a reliable source or ideas for keywords you can use to search for good sources.

NOTE

If you're coming up dry in Web searches for reliable sources, you may have picked a non-notable topic for a new article. Or it may mean that you need to tap into other resources (see page 78).

---

6. Create a first draft of the article, with section headings and footnotes for every sentence (or, at minimum, every paragraph, if everything in the paragraph came from a single source).

Whatever writing approach works for you, use it. Regardless of how you create the article, keep three points in mind:

- Work from the sources to the article, rather than writing the text of the article and then looking for sources.

- Don't copy and paste large chunks of text; that's a copyright violation.

- When you add text to the article, add the source of that information, right then, as a footnote.

Parts of an Article

This chapter can't describe everything that would go into a perfect article, but that's okay. A perfect article isn't your goal. Rather, you want to *start* what could at some point be a really good article. Make sure to establish notability, cite a number of reliable sources, and create something that you and other editors can use as a base to expand and improve over time.

Still, you should aim for a certain minimal number of sections in your new article:

- A lead section of a couple of sentences (see page 234 for more details).

- At least three sections in the body of the article, well footnoted. If you're having trouble figuring out how to divide the information you've found into sections, take a look at other Wikipedia articles on similar topics. If your article is a biography, look at biographies for other people in the field; if it's a company, look at larger competitors; if it's an annual event, look at larger events of a similar nature.

- A "References" section (for footnotes), and an external links section, at the bottom. The external links section should contain official Web sites related to the topic, even if already cited in footnotes. Otherwise, generally avoid duplicating links. (You'll find specific guidance via the shortcut *WP:EL*.)

For more guidance, take a look at the pages *Wikipedia:Layout* (*WP:GTL*), *Wikipedia:Writing better articles* (*WP:BETTER*), and *Wikipedia:Annotated article* (*WP:ANAR*). In Chapter 18, you'll find a comprehensive discussion of how to take a poor article and make it a much better one.

You can work offline, if you want to, writing a rough draft in your favorite word processor, with notes about where each sentence or paragraph came from. You can also do your work iteratively within Wikipedia: Edit the article draft in your user subpage, preview, edit some more, preview, and so on.

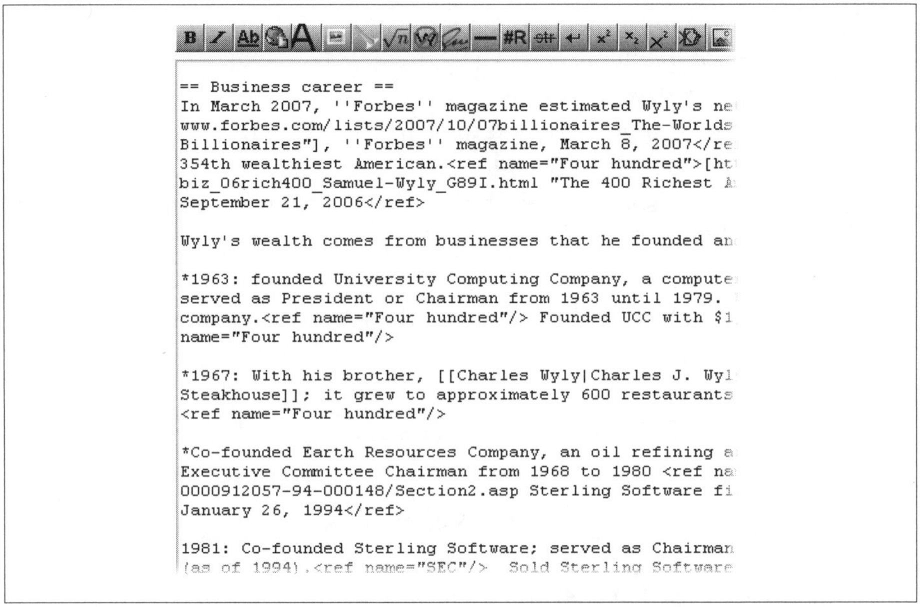

Figure 4-5. A section of the Sam Wyly *article in rough draft form. Sections in the body of articles normally consist of prose paragraphs, not bullet points or lists as shown here, but that's because the article is still in very rough form. You should at least turn the bulleted sentences into bulleted paragraphs.*

NOTE

As discussed on page 11, if you keep an article open in edit mode too long, you risk an edit conflict when you try to save it, because another editor has done and saved an edit in the meantime. You don't have to worry about this with your own user subpage, so you can be leisurely about saving your changes. Just save your work every hour or so; computers have been known to crash.

Figure 4-5 shows the wikitext for one section of the *Sam Wyly* article, partway through the process of creating a final draft. The article-building method illustrated here first starts out with less-detailed sources (typically, short articles) to construct a set of points that you or other editors can fill out later with more general sources and additional sources. Ideally, editors will replace the initial footnotes with others that better support lengthier information in each part of this section. Your approach can be different, but remember that your goal is to footnote *every* sentence (or, at the very least, every paragraph).

7. Do your final edits to the lead section.

It's okay to do a draft of the lead section early on, but it's best to wait to finalize it until the article is pretty close to done. The lead section, after all, is supposed to be a relatively brief summary that just touches on the highlights of why the topic is notable.

8. Build the web: Go through the article and create internal links (wikilinks) that point to other articles (this is part of what is called *wikification*).

Now's the time to review the list of articles you put together earlier—the ones that that'll link to the new article (see Figure 4-3). You want your new article to contain internal (wiki)links pointing *back* to those articles, whenever mentioning the topics of those articles in your new article makes sense.

Don't limit yourself, however, to this list. Almost certainly your new article should link to more than just the articles you found earlier. Add more wikilinks and check their validity (but don't overlink; see the box on page 15).

NOTE

The fastest way to check new wikilinks is to put the double brackets around the words or phrases to be linked, and then do a preview and see if the links are red or blue. Follow each blue link via a new browser tab or page. If it leads (via a redirect or disambiguation page) to an article with a different name than you thought was the case, change the wikilink to point directly to the article of interest (using a piped wikilink if you want). For each red link, either change the wording and try again, or do a search from a separate window. You can leave a red link in the article if you decide that there's no article to link to but that Wikipedia *should* have an article on that topic.

---

9. Save the subpage one last time. Now it's time for you to move the article from your personal user space (as a subpage) to Wikipedia mainspace (where the real articles are):

   - At the top of the article, click the "move" tab. (If you can't see the tab, you're not in normal/reading mode.) You'll see something like Figure 4-6.

   - In the "To new title" box, change the old name of the page (in this case, "User:Your username goes here/New article") to the new name of the page (in this case, "Sam Wyly"); enter a reason (typically, "Creating new article"); and click the "Watch this page" box (more on watching pages on page 103).

   - Click the "Move page" button.

WARNING

Don't move the page if you have a conflict of interest in publishing the article. If you do, or aren't sure whether you do, read the box on page 63 for advice on how to handle such conflicts. Basically, you should get help from non-conflicted editors to create the article.

---

10. You should now see a page that says the move was successful (Figure 4-7).

   Moving a page always leaves a *redirect* in place—that way, anyone clicking on a link to the old location of the page will end up at the new location. (Redirects are

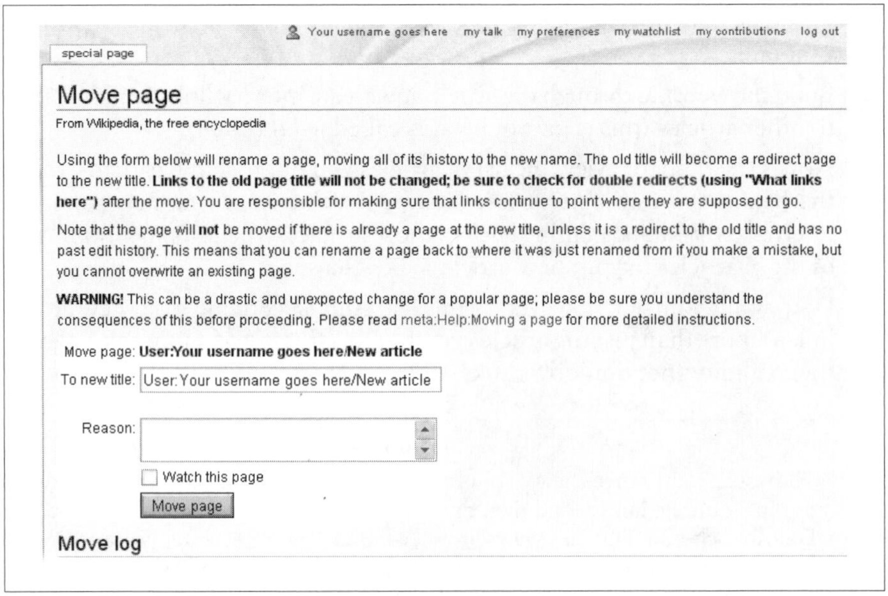

Figure 4-6. The standard page for moving (renaming) a page gives you information and warnings. Use the "Measure twice, cut once" rule: Check your spelling and capitalization carefully before you move your article to its new home. It's not the end of the world if you misspell or otherwise err with the title of your new article (you can always move the page again), but it's embarrassing.

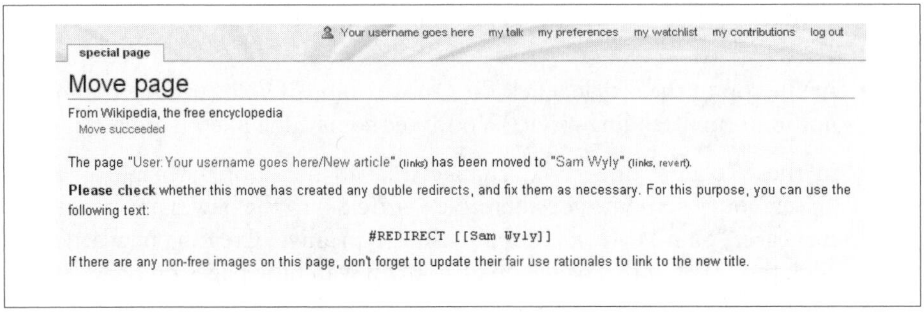

Figure 4-7. There's one more step after you've moved a page—fixing any double redirects. A double redirect is where article A has a link to page B; page B is a redirect that immediately takes the reader to page C; and page C is also a redirect that points to page D.

covered in detail in Chapter 16.) Now you just have to check for, and fix, any *double redirects*—where one redirect sends the reader to a second redirect rather than to a final destination. You'll check for these in the final step.

11. Click the bolded link that says "check" (it's in the second sentence in Figure 4-7) to see if there are any double redirects.

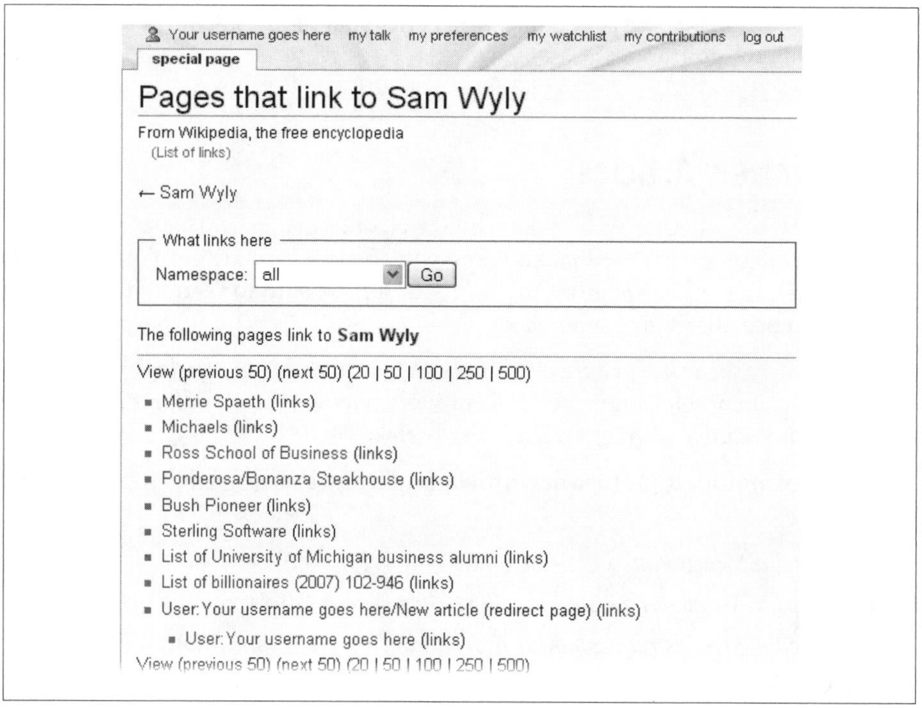

special page

Pages that link to Sam Wyly

From Wikipedia, the free encyclopedia
(List of links)

← Sam Wyly

What links here

Namespace: all ▾   [Go]

The following pages link to **Sam Wyly**

View (previous 50) (next 50) (20 | 50 | 100 | 250 | 500)

- Merrie Spaeth (links)
- Michaels (links)
- Ross School of Business (links)
- Ponderosa/Bonanza Steakhouse (links)
- Bush Pioneer (links)
- Sterling Software (links)
- List of University of Michigan business alumni (links)
- List of billionaires (2007) 102-946 (links)
- User: Your username goes here/New article (redirect page) (links)
    - User: Your username goes here (links)

View (previous 50) (next 50) (20 | 50 | 100 | 250 | 500)

Figure 4-8. There are nine direct links to the new Sam Wyly *article. The last of the nine is a redirect (which is fine). If there were any double redirects; you'd see a double indentation underneath the redirect. (For more information on redirects, including fixing them, see page 310.)*

Double redirects for new articles are exceedingly rare. Still, you want to get into the habit of checking whenever you move a page. When you click "check", the result is Figure 4-8, which shows all the pages that link to the article.

Congratulations! You now know how to create new articles, and how to do it right.

WORD TO THE WISE

Categorize with Caution

The steps in this chapter didn't say anything about adding *categories* to your new article. While adding categories isn't difficult, if you're a new editor, it's something to approach with care. If you do want to add a category or two, you can make sure you're doing so correctly by finding similar articles, and then copying any relevant categories to your newly created article. Or you can jump way, way ahead to Chapter 17 and learn about categories.

But you don't even have to add any categories yourself. Just add an *uncategorized* template to your article. That template (which looks like this: *{{uncat|date=January 2008}}*) will attract the attention of experienced editors who specialize in adding categories to new articles, and your uncategorized article won't stay that way long.

Furthermore, you're free to add more categories yourself, later, when you're more familiar with categorization.

Ideas for New Articles

If you're not sure whether Wikipedia would welcome an idea you have for a new article, consider asking for early feedback, before you spend a lot of time. You can do that at *Wikipedia:Drawing board* (shortcut: *WP:DRAW*). Be sure to read all the instructions at the top, particularly this sentence:

If you post here, you should explain (briefly) why you think an article is merited (that is, why a subject is notable), and you should provide at least a couple of links (to demonstrate that there are reliable sources for such an article).

If you're *looking* for a topic for a new article, you'll find lists of needed topics in a number of places:

- *Wikipedia:Most wanted articles* (shortcut: *WP:MWA*)
- *Wikipedia:Articles requested for more than a year* (shortcut: *WP:AR1*)
- *Wikipedia:Articles requested for more than two years* (shortcut: *WP:AR2*)
- *Wikipedia:WikiProject Missing encyclopedic articles* (shortcut: *WP:MEA*)
- *Wikipedia:Requested articles* (shortcut: *WP:RA*)
- *Category:Redirects with possibilities* (shortcut: *CAT:RWP*)

Resources for Writing Articles

It's amazing what resources are available online today, from your home computer. In addition to regular search engines, you have Google Scholar and Google Book Search. The New York Times has made its entire archives available online for free, and more and more newspapers are deciding that advertising is now more profitable than trying to collect a fee every time someone wants to read an old article.

If that's not enough, almost every town has the perfect resource for researching Wikipedia articles. That's right—a public library. That library card languishing in your wallet may even let you go online, from your home computer, and do research via the library's connections to various databases with indexes and often full-text sources. Research librarians are also happy to help you find whatever the library has to help you write a really good new article (or improve an existing one).

You'll find that the "Research" section of *Wikipedia:Article development* (shortcut: *WP:IA*) has some useful information on researching in general, including online databases to which your library might give you access. Wikipedia also has a number of pages with links to research resources. In addition to the pages for public domain and GFDL resources mentioned on page 68, these include:

- *Wikipedia:Current science and technology sources* (shortcut: *WP:CSTS*)
- *Wikipedia:News sources* (shortcut: *WP:NWSRC*)
- *Wikipedia:List of bibliographies* (shortcut: *WP:LOB*)

Wikipedia also has a central place where you can get help from other editors: *Wikipedia:WikiProject Resource Exchange* (shortcut: *WP:WRE*). That page includes a number of resources offered by other editors ("Shared Resources") and a section to ask for help getting copies of difficult-to-find things ("Resource Request"), as well as a section ("Free Online Resources") that overlaps with some of the already mentioned pages.

CHAPTER 5

Who Did What: Page Histories and Reverting

Anyone can edit Wikipedia. Most of the time that's a good thing—millions of people have made positive contributions to the largest group-writing effort in human history. Then there are the problem children: those who can't resist the urge to deface an article, or delete all its content (a practice known as *blanking a page*), and those who add incorrect information, deliberately or by mistake. Fortunately, Wikipedia has robust change-tracking built into it: Whatever one editor does, another can reverse, returning an article to precisely what it was before.

Apart from vandalism, as an editor you're likely to want to see what other editors do to articles you've edited, whether they're on your watchlist (page 101) or not. While Wikipedia's change-tracking system isn't hard to understand, you'll probably find it isn't totally intuitive. In this chapter you'll learn how to quickly read through even a convoluted page history, how to see what's happened since you last edited an article, how to restore an earlier version of an article with just a few clicks, and how to deal with a problem edit followed by other edits you don't want to delete.

Understanding Page Histories

When you're working on, say, an Excel spreadsheet, you can't turn back time and look at what the document was like last Tuesday at 10:05 a.m. Wikipedia is different—its database has a copy of *every* version of every page ever created or edited. If you click on a page history tab, you can see the text on that page at whatever date and time you pick. The page history also shows you every single edit since then (or before then, for that matter).

Why Wikipedia Keeps a Record of Everything

Keeping a copy of every revision of every page means storing a lot of data. But it's integral to Wikipedia's success. Here are the main benefits to having a record of everything:

- **Responsibility**. Page histories show who did what to a page, when, and often even *why*. Thousands of Wikipedia editors are warned, every day, for inappropriate editing. Hundreds of user accounts are blocked every day for vandalism, disruptive editing, spamming, and so on. Page histories help identify problematic edits and problem editors.

- **Reverting**. You can use page histories to easily *revert* (that is, reverse) another editor's inappropriate edit—or even your own edit, if you've made a mistake. (More on reverting on page 90.)

- **Reputation**. Because your edits will be visible to everyone, forever, you own them forever. Hopefully, you'll think twice before damaging the good work of others. That's how *most* editors behave, at least.

- **Liability**. The Wikimedia Foundation claims it isn't legally liable for any deliberately false information that an editor adds to an article, and legal cases to date have supported that position. Instead, it's the *editor* who's liable (though none have ended up in court yet). A page history, by establishing exactly who changed the article, what she changed, and when, makes it clear that the Foundation didn't create or edit a page—individual editors did.

TIP

If you inadvertently add something to a page that you later decide shouldn't be there —a home address, a complaint about your employer, or other private information —you need to do more than just edit the page again and delete that information. Anyone visiting Wikipedia can read the *previous* version of that page, where that information still exists, simply by going to the page history and opening a prior version of the page. To make something *completely* inaccessible to other editors and readers, you have to ask an administrator to help. (See *Wikipedia:Selective deletion*, shortcut *WP:SELDEL*, for details.) Even then, the problematic version of the page is still in the database, but only administrators can read it.

Reviewing a Page's Prior Versions and Edits

If you want to look at individual edits to and prior versions of a page, near the top of the window, just click the "history" tab. The list that appears shows the most recent edits/versions—up to 50, if the page has been edited that many times. The list's top row is the most recent version of the article; the bottom row is the oldest, as you see if you look at the dates and times.

You can use a page history in one of three ways:

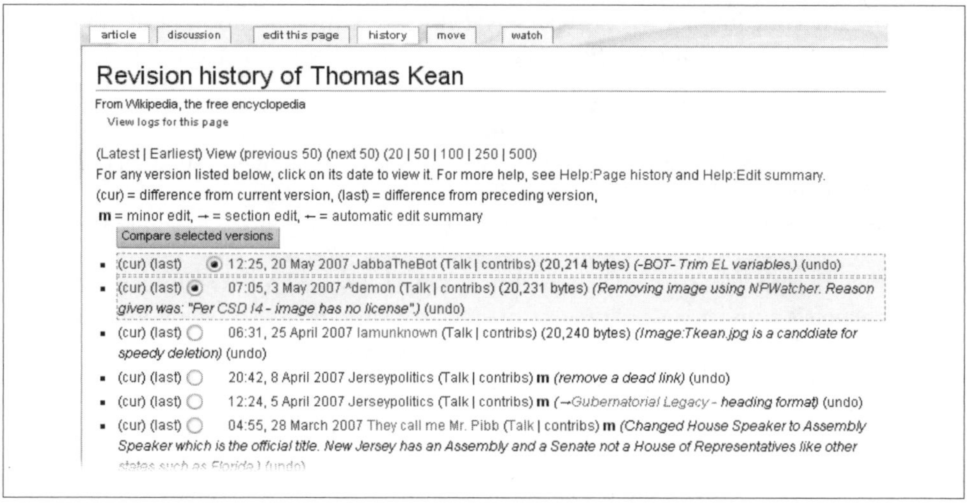

Figure 5-1. Here's a typical page history. Only six versions (edits) are shown, but a history page normally lists the first 50. Edits older than the most recent 50 are listed onto separate pages. You can specify the number of edits listed on the first page—and any subsequent pages you look at, with older edits, by clicking the 20,50, 100, 250, or 500 links near the top.

- You can simply read it to get a general sense of who did what and when.
- You can get a sense of how the text has changed by looking at individual edits, or a group of consecutive edits.
- You can click the date and time listed for a prior version of the page to read that particular version.

This section shows you how to read and interpret a page history in detail.

Reading a page history—The basics

You can learn a lot by simply reading a page history. Figure 5-1 is a snapshot of the history page for the Wikipedia article on Thomas Kean. If you've never seen a history page before, it probably looks confusing. But each of its many elements has a simple purpose.

Here's a grand tour of the page history for the Thomas Kean article in Figure 5-1:

- On the left, the first few columns—**(curr), (last)**, and the radio button—let you tell Wikipedia which versions of the article you want to compare, which you'll learn exactly how to do on page 87. If you're not comparing versions, you can ignore these columns—they're always the same.
- Next comes the **time and date** a version was created (or, in other words, the time and date an edit was saved). The time shown is Coordinated Universal Time (UTC), formerly known as Greenwich mean time. UTC is 5 hours ahead of Eastern

Standard Time in the U.S., and uses a 24-hour system of notation rather than a.m. and p.m. So, for example, 19:05 UTC is 14:05 EST, which is 2:05 p.m. EST.

NOTE

You can change the times displayed in history pages, if you want, to your local time rather than UTC. For details, see page 391.

Notice that the six versions span almost 2 months. From that you can infer that the article's subject isn't very controversial; the article doesn't get a lot of readers (because if it did, a few of them would probably edit it a bit); and there hasn't been much in the news about this person during the 2-month period of these six edits.

NOTE

The Wikipedia site gets such an incredible number of page views that the edit counters built into the software (which display the number of times a page has been viewed) have been turned off, since they were slowing down the servers. So you can't know for sure if this article was viewed a lot or only a little in the 2 months examined here—you can only speculate.

- To the right of the date is the **name of the editor**, with links to the editor's user page (click the name), the editor's user talk page, and to the "contribs" page that lists that editor's edits (called *contributions*). Sometimes when evaluating an edit, you want to see what else the editor has done. If so, you can follow the link to the user talk page (to look for warnings posted by other editors) or the link to the user contributions page (to look at the number of edits, what articles were edited, and even—via a link on that page—whether the editor has been blocked by an administrator to prevent further problems).

- The upper three rows (versions) in Figure 5-1 list the **count of bytes** (a byte is roughly one character) in those versions. Byte counts can tell you if much has changed. In this case, not much—the most recent and second-most-recent edits removed a net 17 and 9 bytes of information, respectively.

NOTE

If you're wondering why the other three rows don't list byte information, it's because the change in software that added the byte count happened in mid April 2007.

- The lower (older) three listed versions have a bold **"m"** after the editor information, indicating a *minor edit*. Generally, minor edits aren't controversial or problematical. However, since editors—not the software—decide whether an edit is marked as minor, an "m" isn't 100 percent guaranteed to be true.

- Towards the far right of each row is the **edit summary**. As discussed on page 9, this text is how the editor describes that edit. Several things are worth noting:

In the oldest edit in Figure 5-1, the editor went to some length (175 characters, to be exact) to explain the edit. The editor was probably concerned that other editors might think the edit was a mistake, and was trying to lessen the probability that the edit would be reverted (page 90).

Two of the edit summaries include wikilinks (in blue) within the edit summaries. Wikilinks in edit summaries work the same way as wikilinks in articles, and you create them the same way (with paired square brackets around the page name). The same goes for piped links (page 15).

In one edit summary, the words "Gubernatorial Legacy" are gray rather than black, with a right-pointing arrow in front of the text. As discussed on page 18, if an editor selects only one section to edit, rather than the whole article, then the software inserts the name of that section into the edit summary's beginning.

TIP

That right-pointing arrow in front of the section name is actually a link. If you click it, then you go directly to that section in the current version of the article in reading mode. Or, to be more precise, you go to that section as long as no editor has subsequently changed the section's name. (If the section name has changed, you'll go to the top of the article.)

- Finally, each row ends with an "undo" link. This link lets you revert the edit listed in that row. You'll learn how to use it later in this chapter (page 92).

Reading a page history—Making inferences

Moving from politics to movies, consider Figure 5-2, another screenshot of a page history, this time for the article on *Clark Gable*. Now that you know what all these little words and links represent, you can use them to get a sense of how the page has evolved over time. The page history gives you facts. You have to figure out what it all means.

Reading the page history for the *Clark Gable* article, you'll notice the following facts and make some related inferences:

- The top six edits were done by the same editor. Sometimes that indicates inexperience: Wikipedia veterans often do some editing of a page, click the Preview button to see the change, do more editing, preview again, and so on, before actually saving the changes to create a new version.

  Or perhaps the editor was saving changes in small increments to avoid edit conflicts (see page 11). Working in small, incremental edits is a good idea when lots of edits are happening, on popular pages and page about current events. In Figure 5-2, the information in parentheses (the edit summary) shows the editor worked on six separate sections, perhaps to make it easier for others to see what he was doing to a long-established article.

Revision history of Clark Gable

From Wikipedia, the free encyclopedia
View logs for this page

(Latest | Earliest) View (previous 50) (next 50) (20 | 50 | 100 | 250 | 500)
For any version listed below, click on its date to view it. For more help, see Help:Page history and Help:Edit summary.
(cur) = difference from current version, (last) = difference from preceding version,
m = minor edit, → = section edit, ← = automatic edit summary

Compare selected versions

- (cur) (last) ⦿ 02:56, 13 February 2007 John Broughton (Talk | contribs) *(→Death - copyediting)* (undo)
- (cur) (last) ⦿ 02:49, 13 February 2007 John Broughton (Talk | contribs) *(→After World War II - copyediting)* (undo)
- (cur) (last) ○ 02:41, 13 February 2007 John Broughton (Talk | contribs) **m** *(→Marriage to Carole Lombard and World War II - copyediting)* (undo)
- (cur) (last) ○ 02:38, 13 February 2007 John Broughton (Talk | contribs) **m** *(→Most Famous Roles - copyediting)* (undo)
- (cur) (last) ○ 02:36, 13 February 2007 John Broughton (Talk | contribs) *(→Hollywood - copyediting)* (undo)
- (cur) (last) ○ 02:29, 13 February 2007 John Broughton (Talk | contribs) *(→Early life - copyediting, including putting references into footnotes ratther than having the text in the body of the section.)* (undo)
- (cur) (last) ○ 21:15, 12 February 2007 129.82.201.96 (Talk) *(→Most Famous Roles)* (undo)
- (cur) (last) ○ 13:19, 11 February 2007 Gwernol (Talk | contribs) **m** *(Reverted edits by 131.123.48.225 (talk) to last version by 76.23.163.254)* (undo)

Figure 5-2. This page history excerpt shows only eight versions. Right away, you can see that one editor has been busily working away.

- For five of those six edits, the editor didn't offer much explanation in the edit summary (all he wrote was "copyediting"). Presumably, he thought that other editors wouldn't find the edits controversial, so there wasn't any need for lengthy explanations.

- The seventh edit was by an anonymous editor, not a registered user. For this edit, the "talk" link is red, indicating that this editor's user talk page doesn't exist yet. (If it did, the link would be blue, like the others.) User talk pages are one place where editors communicate with each other (page 156); only in very rare circumstances do established editors lack a user talk page. A red link is a red flag. It means this editor probably has very few edits, which greatly increases the likelihood that this edit is not constructive.

- The anonymous editor didn't explain what her edit was about. The edit summary has only the section name ("Most Famous Roles"). That's another indication that this person probably hasn't done much Wikipedia editing.

- You can see that the most recent editor (who did the top six edits) didn't alter the edit made by the anonymous editor, because none of that editors' six edits were to the "Most Famous Roles" section. Did that editor look at the anonymous edit and decide it wasn't vandalism, spam, or the removal of good information, and so he didn't revert it? There's no way to know for sure. In the next section, you'll look at what actually changed with this mysterious edit. If you care enough about an article to take a look at its history, you probably want to take a peek at any such potentially questionable edits you come across.

Seeing What Changed

Once you've got an overview of a page history, you can stop right there, or take it a step further—look at actual edits to see who changed what. If a glance through the page history doesn't make you suspect vandalism (for example, vandalism is unlikely if the last edit was more than a week ago, and by a registered editor with a user page and a user talk page), you can go ahead and edit the article without probing more deeply. But most of the time you're going to be curious about one or more specific (usually recent) edits, for one reason or another. In addition, when you're starting out, looking at others' edits is a good way to learn about how to edit Wikipedia.

Fortunately, you could pretty quickly go ahead and look. When you want to see what one or more editors have changed in an article, you ask the software to compare one version of the page against another version. The resulting output, the difference between versions, is the actual edit.

NOTE

The technical term for the difference between any two versions is a *diff*. You may run across it, for example, when you want to report a problem editor and page instructions, or an administrator, ask you to "provide diffs" that demonstrate the problem. One way for you to remember what this term means is that the URL of the output includes "diff=", as shown at the top of Figure 5-3.

Looking at a single edit

Any single edit of a page is the difference between one version of a page (one row in the page history) and the version immediately before it (the row below it). You have two ways to get a diff for a single edit. The slow way is to use the two columns of radio buttons, and then click "Compare selected versions" (or press Enter). The fast way is to click the "last" link, on the left side of the version you're interested in.

Time to take a closer look at that anonymous edit in Figure 5-2 to see whether it was vandalism. When you click "last" on the row for the edit of 21:15, 12 February, you get something that looks like Figure 5-3.

Here's how to read the various elements on a diff page:

- Your browser's address bar gives the output page's URL. When instructions on an administrative page say, "provide diffs," they're asking for URLs like this.

- Near the top of the output page is information about the two versions of the Wikipedia page being compared: the version just *before* the edit, and the version that *resulted* from the edit.

- The heart of the output page is the before-and-after comparison showing what text was added (nothing, in Figure 5-3), deleted (nothing), and what was changed (just one word). This side-by-side comparison is the actual edit.

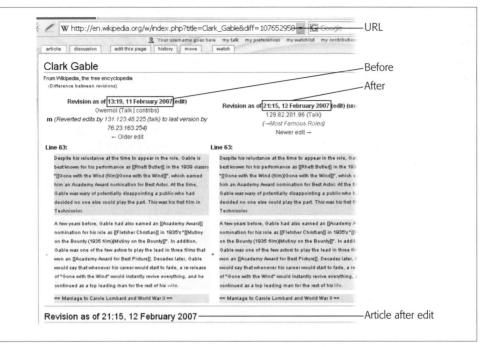

Figure 5-3. When the Wikipedia software compares two versions of a page (that is, the effects of one or more consecutive edits), you see a page like this one. Not all of this "diff" is shown—it actually includes the full version of the page after the edit listed in the right column at the top. You can turn that off— just see the top side-by-side comparison —if you want, by checking "Don't show page content below diffs" in the "Misc" tab of your My Preferences page, but most editors don't—it doesn't really save much time for the diff page to load, and sometimes having full context is helpful.

- For context, the side-by-side comparison shows a paragraph or section heading immediately above the paragraph where the change was made, then the paragraph with the change, and finally the next paragraph or the heading of section below the change.

- When a word has changed, the software shows that word in bolded red for emphasis: in this case, "wife" (before) and "life" (after). So it turns out that the edit was constructive—it fixed an incorrect word that was a typo, Freudian slip, or somewhat subtle vandalism.

- At the bottom of the diff page is the article as it appeared at 21:15, 12 February (only part is shown in Figure 5-3, to save space). You may not even need to even look at this article snapshot, but it can be helpful for figuring out things like exactly where an edit occurred within a long article.

Looking at multiple edits simultaneously

You now know how to see what changed in a single edit. But often you'll want to see what changed in a group of *consecutive* edits. For example, suppose you edited an article 2 days ago and want to see everything that's changed. If there were 10 edits since then, you would want to see, in one place, everything that's changed; you don't want to have to do 10 different diffs. Or suppose several different anonymous editors have edited an article recently. By looking only at the net affect of all the recent edits, you don't have to bother dealing with vandalism by one editor, if another editor has already fixed it.

To take Figure 5-2 as an example, suppose you want to see in a single place what editor John Broughton did in his six edits. You can view multiple edits simultaneously in one of two different ways: a quick way that works only in limited circumstances, and a slower way that works anytime. Figure 5-4 shows the tools for both options.

If the 02:56, 13 February 2007 edit was the most recent, you can quickly see what changed in the six edits of interest in Figure 5-4 when you go to the row for the 21:15, 12 February version (the one just before the edits of interest), and click "cur". That click tells the software to compare that version to the current version; the difference between the two versions, of course, is the six edits.

The quick way's limitation, of course, is you can only use it when you're comparing the *current* version to a prior version—that is, you're looking at a consecutive group of edits up to and including the most recent. The quick approach doesn't work if you want to compare one old version to another old version of the article, to see what changed between them; for example, if an edit (according to its edit summary) fixed vandalism, but you suspect it didn't completely correct the vandalism of the immediately proceeding edit. If you can't use the quick way, the slower (but universal) way to see what happened in a group of consecutive edits is to use the two columns of radio buttons. In the first column, select the "before" version; in the second column, select the "after" version (Figure 5-4). Then press Enter or click "Compare selected versions".

Looking at a Page's Prior Version

As mentioned earlier in the chapter, you can use a page history in three ways: Read it to get an overview, view and compare edits, or get to any prior version of the page. That

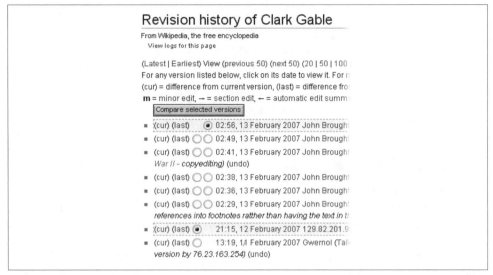

Figure 5-4. To see what editor John Broughton actually changed in his six edits, you can use the two rows of radio buttons to select a set of consecutive edits, as shown here. It's the slower way to view multiple edits, but you can use it anytime. If the edits you want to view happen to include the most recent version, a single click on the "cur" link next to the earliest edit you wanted to include would do the trick instead. Since you often focus on the most recent edits, that shortcut can be useful.

third option is the least useful, since you can better figure out what's change on a page by looking at the actual edits, but you can see what an article used to say at an earlier point in time if you really want to.

To see what text in any specific prior version of a page, on the history page, simply click its time and date. Bear in mind that Wikipedia stores the text of a page version in its database, but doesn't keep a record of any images or templates that were on the page at that time. Instead, the software recreates a prior version of a page inserting the current image and templates into it.

In other words, you're not looking at the equivalent of a snapshot of an older version of a page. But that usually doesn't matter, since it's almost always the text you're concerned about, rather than images or templates. (If you want to see what the image looked like at the time, click the image, which takes you to the history page for that image. Similarly, if you're concerned with the template, click it to go to history page of the template to see what, if anything, changed before the current version.)

Reverting Edits

If you're reading an article in Wikipedia and see vandalism, unencylopedic links to commercial or personal Web sites (*linkspam*), or some other blatant policy violation, your first impulse may be to click "edit this page" and fix the problem. Resist that urge. Manually deleting offending text is error-prone and time-consuming. And, worst of all, if the vandal or spammer deleted or overwrote text while doing the dirty deed, simply removing the problem still leaves the article damaged, since good information is now missing.

Instead, use options in the page history to *revert* the problematic edit(s). Reverting restores any content that was overwritten or deleted, *and* removes offending text, putting the article back to what it was before it was vandalized or spammed. Reverting is one of the most powerful features of wiki software. This section shows you how to do a revert in just a few easy steps.

NOTE

On the other hand, reverting isn't always the answer. If another editor adds text that you think is verbose, or is full of spelling errors, or has invalid citations (to name just a few possible problems) to an article, you should *edit*, not revert. Keep what's useful, improve what's marginal, and delete what's not useful. Restrain your reverts to bad faith edits—clear vandalism and spam, and to clear policy violations, and you'll get along well with all the other editors helping to improve Wikipedia.

Two Options: Revert to a Prior Version and Undo

Until November 2006, Wikipedia had only one way to revert a problematic edit—change the damaged page so that the current version of the page was reset to an older, good version. If the last good version was, say, as of Wednesday at 10:00 UDT, then the software would essentially copy that version, overwriting all the changes (edits) made after that time and date.

For the majority of vandalism cases, this kind of revert is sufficient, because good editors check page histories for signs of likely vandalism before editing, and because anti-vandalism activities (which you can read more about in Chapter 7) identify most vandalism shortly after it appears. But the major drawback of this approach is clear—what if one or more constructive edits came after the problem edit occurred?

The new option—*undoing* one or more consecutive edits that aren't the most recent—offers a way off the horns of that dilemma. It's now usually possible (more details below regarding "usually") to get Wikipedia software to revert *interior* edits—ones that don't include the most recent edit. Unlike a revert, an undo retains good edits that occurred after the problem edit, creating a truly new version of the article.

To revert or to undo

Say you're looking at five edits of an article, one per day starting on January 1. The edits on January 4 and 5 were constructive; you want to keep those. The edits on January 2 and 3 were vandalism. The edit on January 1 was constructive, and there's no vandalism prior to that. Using the revert approach, you'd have to revert the article to the last good version (the one on January 1), and then manually add back the good edits of January

4 and 5. That would be the only way to avoid penalizing the editors who missed the vandalism but added good information. In this case, you now can use undo to remove only the two vandal edits.

On the other hand, if you want to revert only the most recent edit, or the last few edits (say the edits from January 2 through the 5 were all vandalism), then you can use either revert to a prior version or undo. Both are four-step processes that take roughly the same amount of time. As a bonus, if you're reverting only one edit, the undo option has the advantage of automatically adding information to the edit summary.

So if undo works all the time, while reverting is useful only sometimes, why learn both processes? There's one advantage to using the classic revert: Unlike an undo, with a revert it's impossible to have an edit conflict (page 11). If you're reverting vandalism on a high-traffic page (the Main Page is the most prominent example), an edit conflict could significantly slow your fixing of some highly visible vandalism. So knowing how to revert can still be useful for relatively rare cases.

Option 1: Undo

Doing an undo is a four-step process, starting from the history page. (If you're starting from a diff page (page 87), then just skip step 1.)

1. Select the edit(s) you want to undo.

   If you're reverting only one edit, click the "undo" link (on the far right) of the problem edit's row. (This step saves you from having to click "undo" in step 2, by the way. If you clicked the "last" link, by contrast, you'd have to click "undo" in step 2.)

   If you're going to undo multiple consecutive edits, use the radio buttons (Figure 5-4) to create a diff.

   TIP

   It's best to first try to undo an entire group first (it's faster). If that doesn't work, then try to doing "undo" for smaller groups, or individual edits.

   ---

2. On the diff page, click "undo" at upper right, above the right column of text (Figure 5-3).

   The Wikipedia software tells you whether it can revert the edit(s). The more consecutive edits you're trying to undo at the same time, assuming none is the current version, the less likely that the software can actually do an undo of the whole group.

   Most of the time, you'll see the following message at the top of the page: "The edit can be undone. Please check the comparison below to verify that this is what you want to do, and then save the changes below to finish undoing the edit." If you see this message, you should take a quick glance at the comparison (two columns, just like Figure 5-3), and then skip to step 4.

3. If the top of the page reads, "The edit could not be undone due to conflicting intermediate edits", and you're looking at an edit window (don't start editing), then turn to Plan B:

- If you were trying to revert multiple edits at the same time, try doing them one by one, starting with the edit that changed the largest amount of text. You may find that you can still undo most of what was done improperly, even if you can't undo it all.

- If you were trying to revert a single edit, and the undo can't be done, then you're going to have to dive in and start editing. Click the Back arrow on your browser (or Back button on your keyboard, if you have one) to return to the diff. Then open the current version of the page (or current version of a section, if that's all that needs editing) in a different window, and use the diff as a guide to manually edit the current version.

TIP

If you're forced to do manual cleanup, you can still avoid retyping a lot of text. When you find a chunk of text that was improperly deleted, copy it where it shows in the diff—by highlighting the text, and then pressing Ctrl+C (⌘-C on a Mac)—and paste it where you're editing the current version. Clean up the pasted text if necessary.

---

4. Edit or add to the edit summary.

If you undid only a single edit, you'll see an automatically generated edit summary below the editing window like the following:

([[WP:UNDO|Undid]] revision 132832143 by [[Special:Contributions/Name Of Editor|Name Of Editor]] ([[User talk:Name Of Editor|talk]])

That intimidating text looks like the following when someone looks at the page history:

Undid revision 132832143 by *Name of Editor* (*Talk*)

Since the edit summary consists of a maximum of 200 characters, there's a limit to how many words you can add to the edit summary after the computer-added text (131 characters in this example, counting blank spaces—which do count). You have enough room to add, say, *rvv* (meaning "revert vandalism") or *rv linkspam*. If you're not reverting vandalism, however, then your undo may not be clear to other editors, and you should explain it in the edit summary. If you need more space, you can remove the link to the editor's talk page; in this example, delete *([[User talk:Name of Editor|talk]])*. (Other editors can easily get to that user talk page via the second wikilink in the edit summary, the one to the user page.)

If you undid more than one edit simultaneously, then the software doesn't put anything in the edit summary, so you need to. Be brief but clear; for example, *rv multiple vandalism by two different users on 10 May*, or *rv three edits by Name of Editor—per Arbitration Committee decision, editor is not allowed to edit this page*.

Figure 5-5. You see this standard wording of the warning when you first look at an older version of a page. Wikipedia stores only the text of old versions of pages, not images in that version. At the top of the infobox, on the right, you can see "Image:Gableautopic.JPG". If an image of that name existed in Wikipedia, you'd see it. But since the image is no longer on Wikipedia, all you see is a link to the location where the image used to be. In short, Wikipedia's copies of old versions of pages are not photographic copies, they're text stored in a database.

5. Below the editing window, click the "Save page" button.

Normally, clicking this button completes the revert. But you may get one of two error messages:

- If you've turned on "Prompt me when entering a blank edit summary" in the "editing" tab of your My Preferences page (page 393), you may see a message that the edit summary is blank, even though it's not. It's a bug: When Wikipedia's own software adds an automated edit summary, it sometimes doesn't know what it just did. If you do in fact have text in the edit summary field, just click "Save page" again, and now you're done.

- If you get a message that you have an edit conflict, then someone edited and saved a change to what was the current version, before you saved. You can either repeat this four-step procedure again (more quickly, perhaps) or do a manual edit. (See page 11 for a more detailed discussion of handling edit conflicts.)

Option 2: Revert to a prior version

Reverting to a prior version is appropriate only if, after looking at one or more edits, you decide that the most recent edit or edits should be reversed; for example, someone has just vandalized a page and the next-to-last version of the page is vandalism-free.

Doing this type of revert is a four-step process, starting from the history page:

1. Click the row for the last good version of the page.

That's the version before the vandalism or spam occurred; the version you believe is the last good one. Click the time/date link in that row. You then see that version, with a warning near the top of the window (Figure 5-5).

2. At the top of the page, click the "edit this page" tab.

Editing Clark Gable

From Wikipedia, the free encyclopedia

This is an old revision of this page, as edited by 129.82.201.96 (Talk) at 21:15, 12 February 2007. It may differ significantly from the current revision.

(diff) ← Older revision | current version (diff) | Newer revision → (diff)

You are editing an old revision of this page. If you save it, any changes made since then will be removed.

```
{{otheruses}}
{{Infobox Actor
| bgcolour = silver
| name = Clark Gable
| image = Gableautopic.JPG
| imagesize = 150px
| caption =
```

Figure 5-6. You see this warning when you're editing a version of a page other than the current one. Wikipedia wants to make sure you're fully aware that if you save this page after editing, you'll be wiping out all the edits that were made after this version was originally created, unless you manually make changes to this version that incorporate some of those edits. In this case, the last edit(s) were vandalism, not something to worry about losing.

Now you'll see a second warning, just a bit more prominent, as shown in Figure 5-6.

3. At the bottom of the edit window, add an edit summary.

   You don't need to say much:

   - The most common reason for reverting is vandalism, and the most common situation with vandalism is that you're reverting only the last edit, or only a series of edits by the same editor. If so, you need only to put *rvv* (which stands for revert vandalism) in the edit summary.

   - If you're reverting for something other than vandalism, explain a bit; for example, *rv linkspam*.

   - If you're reverting edits by more than one editor (for example, two different accounts vandalized the page, back to back), then mention which version you're reverting to—for example, *rvv, reverting to version of 10:05 15 May*.

4. Click the "Save page" button.

   That's it—you're done.

After You Fix a Page

After you've undone or reverted an edit (clicked the "Save page" button), it's a good idea to glance at the page to see if reads the way you expect. If it looks the same as before you've edited, refresh the page in your Web browser; clicking Ctrl+R (⌘-R on a Mac) does the trick in most browsers. If the problem is gone, your revert was successful. Congratulate yourself for improving Wikipedia. If you do see some vandalism that you missed, then you can fix it with another undo, if possible, or by doing a direct edit if necessary.

Advanced Techniques

Once you've mastered the steps in the previous section, you can revert or undo any edit on any Wikipedia page. You can lead a long, happy life without going any further. But if you devote yourself to lots of article repair and restoration, you may appreciate help from some power-user tools, like the three described next.

Customization

If you're an experienced editor who spends a lot of time looking at page histories, consider some customization to enhance the history display:

- The user script at *User:Stevage/EnhanceHistory.user.js* collapses consecutive edits from the same person into one. It also adds a button so that diffs show up on the history page rather than a separate page. (Chapter 21 provides details about getting a user script to work.)

- Another minor—but useful—customization often makes it much easier to locate what's been removed or added in a page change when the change involves just a period, comma, dash or other small single character. Add the following to your monobook.cs page (which you'll probably need to create, as a subpage, per the instructions on page 57):

```
.diffchange {padding: 0px 2px 0px 2px; border: 1px dashed red; margin: 0px 1px
0px 0px}
```

Automated Identification of the Editor of Specific Text

You may find yourself digging through a large number of prior versions of a page, trying to identify exactly who added a given bit of text, and when (for example, to find out if whoever added the text did anything else questionable at the same time). After scrolling through history pages and searching through a large number of versions of the page, you might think, "There has to be a better way." In fact, you have two alternatives:

- An automated tool called WikiBlame, available at *http://wikipedia.ramselehof.de/wikiblame.php*, digs through the versions for you, spotting what you're looking for.

- Another alternative is to dump up to the last 100 versions of a page into a single document which you can then search. To do so, go to the *Special:Export* page, and follow the easy instructions there. When you do paste the contents of the export into a document, do so as unformatted text; that's faster.

Counting and Sorting Edits

Sometimes you'll want to know the names of the editors who did the greatest number of edits to an article, or other statistics about edits to a particular page. Wikipedia has a number of tools to count edits, sort edits by contributor, generate statistics about contributors to a page, and so on. Three places to start are:

- **Revision counter.** *http://tools.wikimedia.de/~phroziac/revisioncounter.php*
- **Contributors.** *http://tools.wikimedia.de/~daniel/WikiSense/Contributors.php*
- *Wikipedia Page History* **Statistics.** *http://vs.aka-online.de/wppagehiststat*

CHAPTER 6

Monitoring Changes

After you edit a Wikipedia article, other editors may, in turn, change the changes you've made. As one of the notes at the bottom of the standard edit screen says, "If you don't want your writing to be edited mercilessly or redistributed for profit by others, do not submit it." *Edited mercilessly* doesn't necessarily mean your words will be ripped apart, but they could be. Once you've submitted work to Wikipedia, it's fair game.

Rather than completely abandoning your edit to its fate, you probably want to check in and see how it's faring. Most experienced editors monitor articles they've edited, both to make sure other editors treat their edits reasonably, and to learn from what other editors do. This chapter will show you a number of ways to watch articles for changes, whether or not you've edited them.

The User Contributions Page

When you're starting out, Wikipedia's list of your edits—your *User contributions page* —is a handy way to monitor changes to pages you've edited. You get to that list by clicking the "my contributions" link near the upper-right corner of your screen (assuming you're logged in). You'll see something like Figure 6-1.

> **TIP**
> If Figure 6-1 looks confusing, take a look back at Chapter 5. The User contributions page has a lot in common with page histories discussed in that chapter, though it lists only your edits.

The key to using your User contributions page as a monitoring tool is the word "top" that appears at the end of an edit. Whenever you see that, you know that you were the last to edit the article, so you don't need to worry that it's been vandalized, and you don't have to look at it to see what constructive changes other editors may have made. If the "top" is missing from an edit, then you can click the "hist" link to go to the article and see edits made since the edit you were looking at.

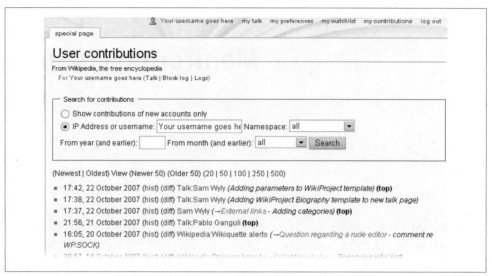

Figure 6-1. On the User contributions *page, if you've done the most recent edit of an article, you'll see "top", in bold, at the end of its row. Here you see five edits for five different pages. Only the last page has been edited subsequently by another editor, as indicated by the lack of the word "top" at the end of that row.*

However, using your User contributions page for monitoring changes has some limitations:

- If you've edited a particular article multiple times, **only the most recent edit has "top" as part of the row**. That means you have to keep a sort of mental running tally of "tops" as you read down your list, so that when you come across the same article a second (or third or fourth) time, you don't think the absence of "top" means someone else has been there last. (For example, in Figure 6-1, the page *Talk:Sam Wyly* was edited twice, but "top" appears only once, after the last edit.)
- **There isn't any way to tell when you've already checked on changes by others**. Suppose you last looked at your User contributions page on October 19. At that time, if there was no "top" after the *Wikipedia:Drawing board* entry, you probably would have checked the page history to see what happened. Are you wasting your time by checking again now? (In short, this becomes a memory test, and even if your memory is close to perfect, you can still end up wasting time.)

Still, sometimes your User contributions page is useful as a tracking device. For example, if you've done single edits to a bunch of articles, then no editing for two days, and now want to see what's happened to those articles, the User contributions page shows you which articles you need to check. (See the box on page 101 for a tip on making the page more readable.) But if you're like most active editors, you want something that monitors changes more closely, like a *watchlist*, described next.

Color-coding Your User Contributions Page

If you really like to use your User contributions page to monitor changes, you can make it so that pages you've edited last are sharply distinguished from pages where another editor was the last to edit the page. To do so, copy the script from the *User:Ais523/topcontrib.js* page (except for the top line, which is a comment), and add it to your *monobook.js* page. (See page 402 for details on this procedure, including purging your cache to see the change take effect.)

After you've implemented this script, rows where another editor was the last to edit have a light red background, meaning "most recent," or, if the same page appears multiple times, a light orange background. Those pages are the ones you may want to check. Pages where *you* were the last to edit have a blue background (for most recent) or a light blue-green background (if the page appears multiple times).

Wikipedia's Standard Watchlist

If you want to keep an eye on a limited number of articles and other pages (say a hundred or so), then the watchlist that Wikipedia provides each registered editor probably meets all your needs. Most active editors use this watchlist. You simply tell Wikipedia you want to monitor selected pages—articles, user talk pages, whatever. Then you run a report whenever you want to see if anyone has edited those pages since your last report.

NOTE

In Wikipedia, the term *watchlist* sometimes refers to the list of pages you've told Wikipedia you want to watch, and sometimes to the report that Wikipedia generates when you click the "my watchlist" link in your screen's upper right. For clarity, in this chapter "watchlist" refers to the list of watched pages, and "watchlist report" is what you get when you click the "my watchlist" link.

The Standard Watchlist Report

Wikipedia offers you three different watchlist reports: standard, expanded, and enhanced. The expanded and enhanced reports build on the standard report. But if you're like many editors, the standard watchlist report (Figure 6-2) may meet all your monitoring needs. You get to it by clicking "my watchlist" (one of the six standard links in the screen's upper right corner, when you're logged on).

Figure 6-2. The standard watchlist report starts out in the "Display watched changes" view shown here. The number of edits listed is quite short, because this editor is watching only 21 pages, and because the watchlist report is set to show only the last 3 days of edits. (But you can change that setting; see page 109.)

NOTE

If you've been following along in Wikipedia and your watchlist report comes up empty, you have few or no pages on your watchlist. See the next section to learn how to add pages, and then come back here and read on.

The rows of article-related information in the watchlist report are very similar to the rows on a page history described in Chapter 5. There's a "diff" link to show what the edit did, a "hist" link to go to the article's history page, the article or page name, the time edited, three links to pages of registered users (user page, user talk page, contributions page), and the edit summary.

What you can learn from your watchlist report

First, you can get an overview of how active your watched articles have been. In Figure 6-2, since you've told Wikipedia that you want to watch 21 pages, and only six show up in the report, you know that the other 15 pages haven't been edited in the past 3 days. So you don't have to check those 15 pages for activity.

Second, you can check out what happened in the six listed edits by simply clicking the "diff" link for each edit. If you find vandalism or other problems, then you can revert

Figure 6-3. Wikipedia gives you three ways to add a page to your watchlist. You can turn on a checkbox when you edit or move a page (top and middle), or, at the top of the page you're viewing, you can click the "watch" tab (bottom).

the edit (page 90) and take other corrective action. (Chapter 7 discusses additional steps for dealing with vandalism, beyond simply reverting it.)

Third, you can jump from this report to a history page because you want to see *all* the recent edits to a page. The watchlist report shows only the page's most recent edit. If, for example, there were three edits very close together, you wouldn't be able to see the other two; you have to click the "hist" link in a row to see the history of edits for the page that's listed in that row.

Finally, near the top of your watchlist report, you see two groups of links. One group ("View and edit watchlist", and so on) has links to related pages. The other group ("Show last 1 | 2 | 6 |12 hours", and so on) lets you tailor your watchlist report in different ways. Before looking at those links, however, it's important to understand how pages get on your watchlist in the first place.

Adding Pages to Your Watchlist

Reading a page, editing a page, or even creating a page doesn't automatically put that page on your watchlist. To monitor that page for changes, you have to put it on your watchlist yourself. You can click something in three places to add the page. Figure 6-3 shows you those three places: where you edit or create a page, where you move a page, and where you're viewing a page.

When you add a page to your watchlist, you're actually telling Wikipedia to watch *two* pages for you. That's because in Wikipedia, most pages have a corresponding talk page. For example, the *South Africa* article has a discussion page called *Talk:South Africa* associated with it; a project page such as *Wikipedia:Sandbox* is associated with the discussion page *Wikipedia talk:Sandbox*; the page *Category:Uncategorized articles* is associated with the discussion page *Category talk:Uncategorized articles*, and so on. When you pick one page of a pair (it doesn't matter which one), *both* pages show up in your watchlist report. It's normal Wikipedia behavior. You're free to ignore those extra pages when you read the report.

On the other hand, you can't add some pages to your watchlist at all; specifically, pages with the "Special" prefix, like the *Special:Contributions* page in Figure 6-1. These pages also don't have paired talk pages. "Special" pages are essentially on-the-fly reports —when you close such a page, it's gone. But then, there's no point in watching them anyway—they're not editable.

TIP

To build a quick watchlist to learn how the whole thing works (or to follow along in this chapter), at the upper-left of the window, click the "Random page" link, click the "watch" tab, and then click "Random page" again, and so on.) Don't worry about whether you really want to monitor these pages, because, as discussed next, you can easily remove pages from your watchlist.

Removing Pages from Your Watchlist

When you lose interest in watching an article, or when your watchlist gets too long and cumbersome, you can easily take one or more pages off it. You could, for example, temporarily remove part of your watchlist and save it elsewhere (to a subpage, or a non-Wikipedia document). Or you could use the removed links from your regular watchlist to create additional watchlists, as described on page 115. Or you can just delete the pages and simplify your life.

You can see three links that let you remove pages from your watchlist near the top of Figure 6-2:

- **View and edit watchlist** is the commonest choice. As shown in Figure 6-4, it takes you to a neat list of your watched pages. To remove articles from the list, simply turn on their checkboxes, and then click Remove Titles (way down at the bottom of the page).

- **Edit raw watchlist**, described next, gives you a faster way to delete titles en masse from a long watchlist.

- **Clear watchlist** is your nuclear option. If you click it, you get an "Are you sure?" warning, and if you say yes, then you get a completely empty watchlist.

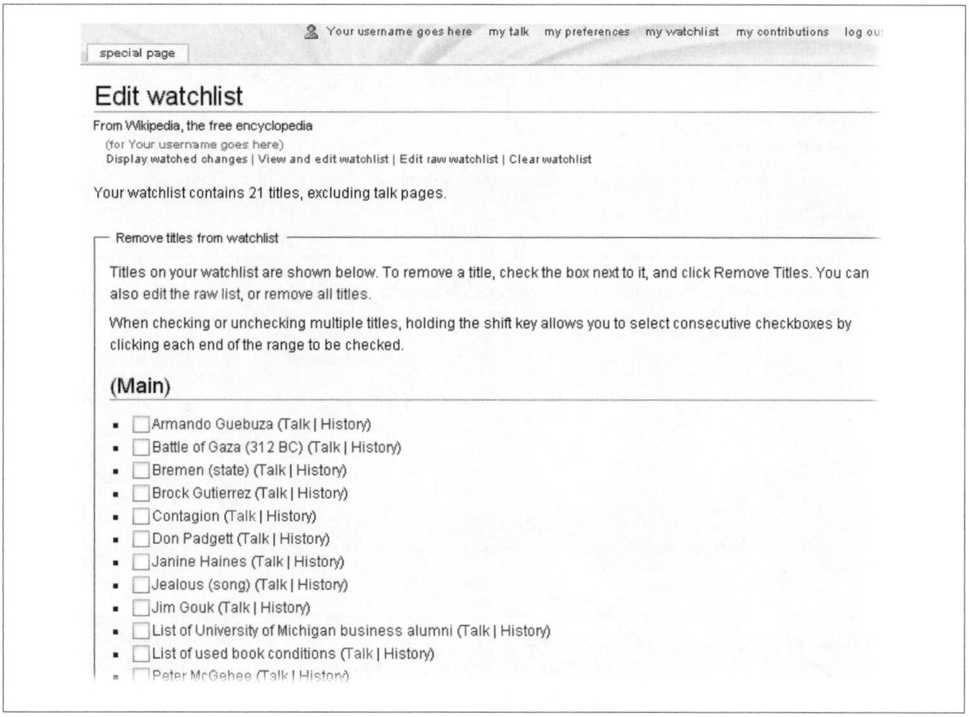

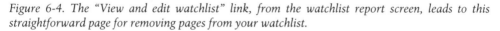

Figure 6-4. The "View and edit watchlist" link, from the watchlist report screen, leads to this straightforward page for removing pages from your watchlist.

WARNING

Wikipedia doesn't store a copy of your watchlist anywhere. Once you edit it or clear it, you can't recover or retrieve it. In case you have second thoughts about what you're deleting from your watching list, you can copy and save a list of watched pages in, say, a user subpage or a word processing document on your computer.

While the "View and edit watchlist" screen makes you click a checkbox for each page you want to remove, the "Edit raw watchlist" screen lets you select and delete wide swaths of the list as if you were editing a text document. (If you've been editing Wikipedia for a while and don't recognize this feature, that's because it's new in 2007.) As mentioned in the previous warning, you may want to save (in another place) any pages that you remove from your list. Unlike regular Wikipedia pages, your watchlist has no "history" page; you can't revert to an earlier version if you decide you've made a mistake.

Figure 6-5. One of the easiest way to do mass edits of your watchlist is via the "Edit raw watchlist" option. You can get to this screen by clicking "Edit raw watchlist" on your watchlist report, or "edit the raw list" on the "Edit watchlist" page (Figure 6-4).

TIP

If you want to stop watching just one page, you can quickly take it off your watchlist without going to a separate edit screen. See the box below to learn how to set up your watchlist report for this trick.

POWER USERS' CLINIC

Unwatching a Page Directly from Your Watchlist Report

Going to the "View and edit watchlist" page, turning on a checkbox, scrolling all the way down to the "Remove Titles" button at the bottom of the page, and returning to where you were on the watchlist report is a lot of work just to remove a single page from a list. You can modify the standard watchlist report so that you can delete a page directly from the report, with one click.

To make it so, copy the user script from *User talk:Alex Smotrov/wlunwatch.js* and add it to your *monobook.js* page. (Page 403 describes the steps to do so, including purging your cache to see the change take effect.)

When you're done, you see an "x" link in each entry on your watchlist report, immediately after the "diff" and "hist" links. Click the "x" to turn it into a "+", and the page is now no longer on your watchlist.

If you do the dynamic installation (which is recommended), you don't see this feature until you click the new "Unwatch ..." link, near the "Go" button toward the top of the page.

Modifying the Standard Watchlist Report

You can modify the standard watchlist report in a number of ways, either temporarily or permanently. If you change it temporarily, using choices on the watchlist report page itself, the changes will be gone the next time you look at your report. If you change it permanently, using your preferences page, the changes will remain in place until you go to your preferences page again and make a further change.

WORKAROUND WORKSHOP

When Pages Change (or Not)

Confusingly, not all alterations to a page show up as changes on your watchlist report. Wikipedia considers a page changed when its *wikitext* (the text in the edit box) changes. What you *see*, however, when you look at a Wikipedia page is a combination of wikitext, text added via templates (for example, the standard text at the top of the sandbox in Figure 1-1 on page 5), and images, which are stored on separate pages.

Because of this discrepancy, having an article on your watchlist doesn't guarantee that you'll see an edit appear on your watchlist report when vandalism occurs. If the article has either a template or an image, vandalizing one of them results in vandalism to the article from a viewer's perspective—but you won't know about it unless you happen to visit the article page.

Similarly, if you see vandalism while looking at an article and can't figure out where it came from by looking at the article history, consider checking the templates or images in the article.

So, if you watch a page, should you also figure out what templates are used on that page, and add those to your watchlist? Probably not. Frequently used templates are normally fully protected, which means only administrators can edit them. Nor is it worthwhile to watchlist image pages: Changing an image by uploading a new one (page 271), one type of vandalism, doesn't change the wikitext on the image page either, and thus doesn't register as a change on your watchlist report.

Temporary changes

You can change the information your watchlist report shows you without permanently editing your watchlist. Near the top of Figure 6-2, you can see links that let you make three types of temporary changes to your watchlist report. "Temporary" means that the next time you click "my watchlist", the changes are no longer in effect. However, if you just refresh the watchlist report in your browser, temporary changes remain in place. The three types of temporary changes are:

- **You can limit how far back in time the watchlist report goes**. You can tell it to show only those edits that occurred in the last hour, 2 hours, and so on, all the way up to "all" edits. ("All" in this case actually means "to the limit set in your preferences;" see page 109.)

  How far back you want to go with displayed changes depends on how much time and interest you have. The initial setting—3 days—is a pretty good choice. On the other hand, if you set the option to show more days, you're still free to ignore the older edits. To change the setting, just click 1, 3, or 7 to choose the number of days, or "all" to get the big picture.

- You can tell the software **not to display edits by bots** (automated programs that make routine corrections) or **not to display edits you've done**, or **not to display edits marked as "minor"**.

  If your watchlist report is fairly long, it's generally a good idea to shorten the report by hiding edits by bots and edits you've done yourself. Edits marked as "b", done by software bots, can be safely assumed to be boring cleanup, not anything that changes an article's meaning. And you may not need to see all your own edits, because you can remember what they are. (You probably want to leave these edits visible at first, until you have enough experience to judge whether you find them useful.)

  Whether you want to hide the edits marked that were marked as "minor" by the editors doing them, or let these edits show on your report, depends a bit on your level of paranoia: Vandalizing edits rarely are marked as "minor", but (unfortunately) some experienced vandals do know this trick.

- You can change **what type of pages are shown**, via the Namespace pop-up menu. "All" pages is the standard setting. If you change it to Main, your report shows only edits to *articles*; if you change it to Talk, it shows only changes to the discussion pages for articles, and so on.

  Changing this setting to show only changes to articles can make your life simpler, but it also hides useful information. If you put an article on your watchlist, you may learn even more about what's happening to the article by looking at postings to the article's talk page—that's where content disputes flame up. (See Chapter 10 for details.)

  In fact, if you've been concentrating elsewhere and not monitoring your watchlist for a while, setting it to Talk, and then looking at postings going back a month or so, can be a good way to find articles where interesting things are happening.

Permanent changes via your preferences page

If you find yourself continually making the same temporary tweaks to your watchlist report, or if you think that the "all" option doesn't go back far enough in time, then visit your preferences page. There, you can change nine settings for the standard

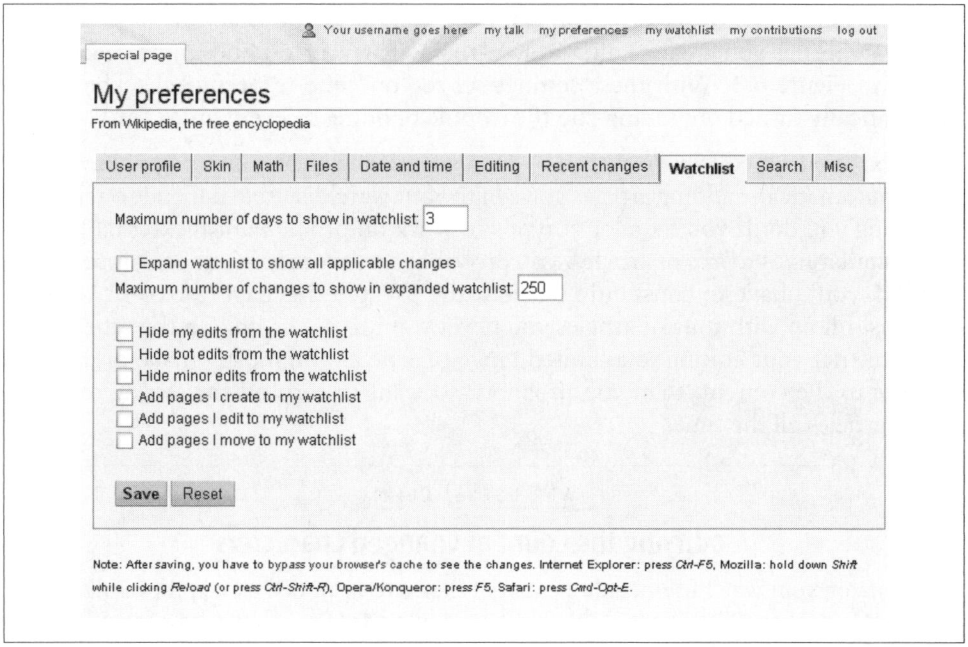

Figure 6-6. For your watchlist, there are nine different things you can change via the Watchlist tab of the My Preferences page. Whenever you open your watchlist report, Wikipedia uses these settings to decide what to show you (until you return to this tab and change them again). The "3" and the "250" are the initial settings with which every user account starts out

watchlist report, so that when it opens, it reads the way you want, not the way it automatically starts out.

To change the factory settings for your watchlist report, click the My Preferences link (at the upper-right corner of the screen), then click the Watchlist tab. You'll see the page in Figure 6-6.

Of the nine settings you can change via your My Preferences page, four are settings that you can also change temporarily, as discussed on page 108, while you're viewing the watchlist report:

- Maximum number of days to show in watchlist. This option does the same thing as the "Show last" feature on the watchlist report, as in "Show last 7 days".
- Hide my edits from the watchlist.
- Hide bot edits from the watchlist.
- Hide minor edits from the watchlist.

The next two settings, "expand watchlist to show all applicable changes", and its companion "Maximum number of changes to show in expanded watchlist", give you access to all changes ever made to an article. These options are discussed in the next section.

With the bottom three settings, you can have Wikipedia automatically add pages to your watchlist as you create, edit, or move them. They correspond to the checkboxes shown in Figure 6-3. With these settings set to "on", the respective checkboxes are automatically turned on, saving you the trouble of doing so every time.

Most experienced editors do want to watch pages they create, and pages they move. As for automatically adding articles you *edit* to your watchlist, that depends on the kind of editing you do. If you fix a lot of typos or work on problematical external links or make similar fixes to *lots* of articles, you probably don't want to turn on this setting. If you did, you'd have to constantly uncheck the "Watch this page" box—or see your watchlist fill up with tons of articles you never want to see again. On the other hand, if you restrict your editing to a limited range of articles and mostly make meaningful changes to the content, then you probably do want to turn on the setting to watch edited articles all the time.

POWER USERS' CLINIC

Modifying the Count of Changed Characters

Entries on your watchlist include a count of the increase or decrease in the number of characters on an edited page. A positive green number (+xx) shows how many characters have been added; a negative red number (-xx) shows the number of characters removed. These numbers can help you spot vandalism—for example, an anonymous IP editor removing a large amount of text is almost always vandalism.

You can modify these counts: Turn the numbers bold, or black, or remove them altogether. Doing so requires a change to a behind-the-scenes Wikipedia formatting page —your *monobook.cs.* page. You'll find details of the text you need to add to that page (which you probably need to create) at *Wikipedia:Added or removed characters* (shortcut: *WP:AORC*).

Expanded and Enhanced Watchlist Reports

The standard watchlist report (Figure 6-2), shows only information about the most recent edit to each changed page. You can find out if there were *multiple* edits to a listed page—some of which might be problematical—only when you look at the history of the page, which requires additional steps. If you'd like to see *all* the edits that have occurred during the period shown in the watchlist report, you can change your settings to either the *expanded* watchlist report, or a variant of that, the *enhanced* watchlist report. These reports do show you all the edits during a period; they differ only in presentation. With both of them, therefore, you don't have to go to a history page.

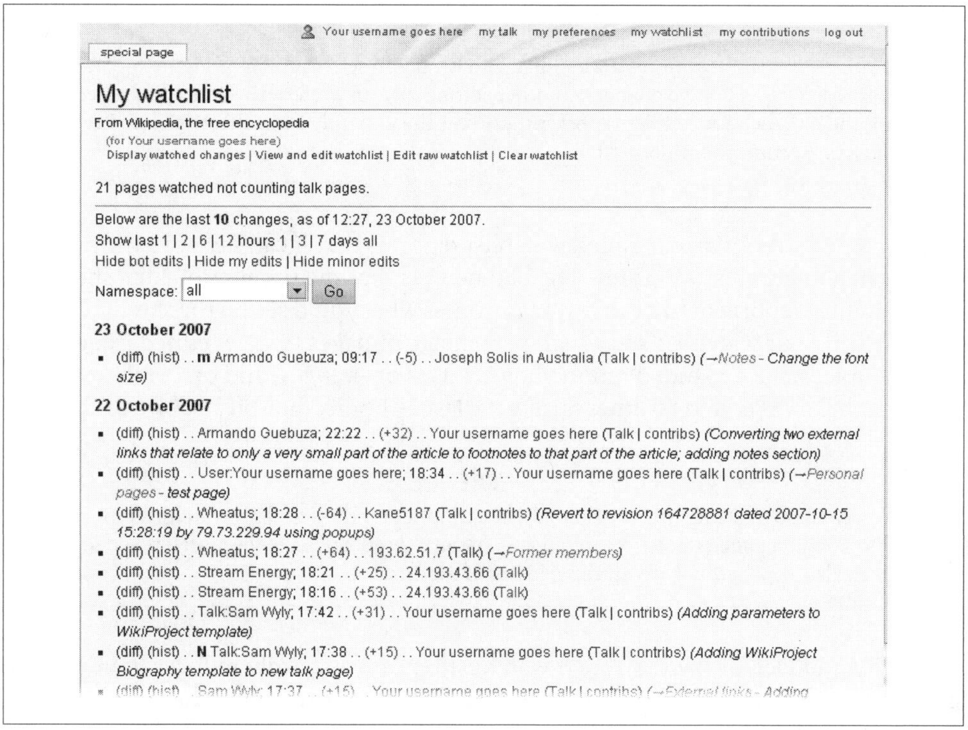

Figure 6-7. The expanded watchlist report lists all edits, not just the last edit, during a given period. You can see that report instead of the standard watchlist report shown here by turning on "Expand watchlist to show all applicable changes" in the Watchlist tab of your My Preferences page.

NOTE

If you don't have at least a couple of weeks of experience using your standard watchlist, this section may seem overwhelming. Know that your watchlist report can become more advanced, just as you will, and come back to this material later.

The expanded watchlist report

If you set your watchlist preferences to the expanded view (see the middle options in Figure 6-6), then the report automatically lists *all* changes to your watched pages during the specified period (for example, 3 days), or up to the maximum number of changes that you specify, whichever comes first. (For example, if you specify 100 changes, and there have been 125 changes in the past 24 hours, then you're not going to see 3 days of changes even if you've also specified that.)

The expanded watchlist report in Figure 6-7 has 10 entries, covering a total of six pages. By comparison, the standard watchlist report, covering exactly the same watched pages over exactly the same period, shows only six entries—one per watched page with editing activity (see Figure 6-2).

The good news about an expanded watchlist report is that it can save you the time and trouble of going to history pages. The bad news is that the number of edits shown on your watchlist report could be many, many times what you'd see on the standard report (especially if your watchlist has a high percentage of pages that get edited frequently). For example, if the expanded report shows 2 days of changes, and one of the pages on your watchlist was edited 50 times during the last 24 hours, then *all 50 changes* show up.

If you like the idea of the expanded watchlist report (it sharply reduces your need to go to history pages) but don't like the added length (one row per edit), the enhanced watchlist report might appeal to you; read on.

The enhanced watchlist report

Expanded watchlist reports can get very long. Fortunately, you can shorten the watchlist report considerably, yet still have easy access to all changes to all watched pages during a specified period, by changing to the enhanced watchlist report format. Figure 6-8 shows the same information as in Figure 6-7, but in the enhanced format.

To get this report, turn on the expanded report option in the Watchlist tab of My Preferences, if it's not already on. Then, go to the "Recent changes" tab, turn on "Enhanced recent changes (JavaScript)", and then click the Save button. Be sure to follow the instructions at the bottom of the page for bypassing your browser's cache. For example:

- **Internet Explorer for Windows**. Press Ctrl+F5.
- **Safari**. Press ⌘-Option-E.
- **Mozilla Firefox**. Shift-click the Reload button or press Ctrl+Shift+R (⌘-Shift-R on Mac).

Figure 6-8. The enhanced watchlist report. This variant of the expanded watchlist report consolidates all edits into a single expandable row for each calendar day when changes to a page occurred.

NOTE

If you change your settings, bypass your browser's cache, and still don't see the enhanced version of the watchlist report when you click "my watchlist", try shutting down your browser and starting it again. If that doesn't work, make sure that JavaScript is enabled in your browser (see page 401).

If you compare Figure 6-7 to Figure 6-8, you see that the 10 entries in the first have decreased to seven entries in the second. That's because an enhanced watchlist report has two types of lines (in addition to the header line for each day): detail lines and summary lines. If an article has been edited only once on a given day, you see a detail line. If it was edited multiple times, you see a summary line that tells you the number of edits, and the editors' names.

Figure 6-8 has three summary lines, as indicated by a right-pointing arrow on the far left. Examining these three lines more closely, here's what you can tell happened:

- The article *Wheatus* was edited twice, first by an anonymous IP editor (193.62.51.7) and then by a registered editor, Kane5187. The net result was a change of zero characters, as indicated by the "(0)", making it highly likely that this was IP vandalism that Kane5187 reverted.

Figure 6-9. When you click a summary line in an enhanced watchlist report, the right-pointing arrow changes to a down-pointing arrow, and details lines appear immediately below. Here, one of the summary lines in Figure 6-8 has been expanded.

- The article *Stream Energy* was edited twice by anonymous IP editor 193.62.51.7, who added a total of 78 characters with the two edits.

- The article talk page *Talk:Sam Wyly* was edited twice by the editor who generated this watchlist report. (Presumably he trusts himself, and doesn't need to investigate the changes.)

Say you want to see more details on the two edits of the article *Stream Energy*. Click the right-pointing arrow next to the summary line, and two detail lines appear (Figure 6-9).

The information in Figure 6-9 doesn't give you much of a clue as to whether this was a vandalizing or other problem edit—note the lack of edit summaries. To inspect the changes, either click the "last" links, which produce diffs (see page 87) or click the "Page history" link, and then, when at the history page, combine the two edits into a single diff.

Choosing Your Watchlist Report Format: Standard, Expanded, or Enhanced?

So, which watchlist report format should you use? You can easily change from the standard report to the enhanced watchlist report, or vice versa. Just change and save your preference settings, and bypass the browser cache (page 409), so you can just play around and see what you like. If you have relatively few pages on your watchlist, the expanded watchlist is great for a full overview at a glance. If your expanded reports get too long, or you prefer to have page changes grouped by page, try the enhanced watchlist report. If none of the three report versions meets your needs, then take a look at the options in the rest of this chapter: multiple checks and real-time monitoring.

GEM IN THE ROUGH

Watchlists Are Private

You can't see any other editor's watchlist, nor can any other editor see yours. Wikipedia watchlists are entirely private. That's why, if you erase yours, no one can restore it for you.

Perhaps more interestingly, there is no way for you, as a regular editor, to find out the names of other editors who are watching a given page, or even the *number* of editors who are watching that page. That's probably all to the good: Watchlists are one of the

---

main defenses against vandalism, and vandals would appreciate knowing which pages were completely unwatched.

Multiple Watchlists

When you click the "my watchlist" link, you go to your one and only "official" watchlist, and the accompanying report (standard, expanded, or enhanced). But you're not constrained to a single watchlist. For example, you could have a watchlist for articles you've created, one for editors you're watching for signs of repeated vandalism, and one for group of articles in a wikiproject you're working on, plus your "official" watchlist. Additional watchlists aren't quite as easy to create and maintain as your regular watchlist, but if you're watching a lot of pages, the extra organizational power may be worth the extra bother.

Creating Additional Watchlists

Creating a second (or third or fourth) watchlist is a two-step process: Create a subpage (see page 57); then add wikilinks for the pages of interest. You can add wikilinks in a number of ways. For example, you can add them by editing your raw watchlist (page 105).

NOTE

Additional watchlists are sometimes called "public" watchlists because other editors can view them.

Figure 6-10 shows a subpage set up for an additional watchlist. If you watch pages on additional watchlists like this one, then you can remove them from your regular watchlist. You can, for example, shorten that watchlist to the absolutely most critical pages to monitor, and use your additional watchlists to monitor less-important articles as time permits.

WORKAROUND WORKSHOP

Adding Talk Pages to Additional Watchlists

Unlike the standard watchlist report, additional watchlists don't automatically monitor *paired* pages. For example, if you have the article *Loch Ness monster* in your additional watchlist, changes to the *Talk:Loch Ness monster* page don't show up on the watchlist report. That's a problem, because, in most cases, you really do want to monitor both pages in a pair. The only solution is for you to add both a page and the related talk page. If you have already have a long list of *articles*, in wikilinks, there's a quick way to add talk pages:

User:Your username goes here/Second watchlist

From Wikipedia, the free encyclopedia

< User:Your username goes here

- Administration for Children and Families - Talk:Administration for Children and Families
- Advertising - Talk:Advertising
- Aetna - Talk:Aetna
- Aga Khan IV - Talk:Aga Khan IV
- Air Greenland - Talk:Air Greenland
- Air conditioner - Talk:Air conditioner
- Alan Cox (radio presenter) - Talk:Alan Cox (radio presenter)
- Alan Fine - Talk:Alan Fine
- Alan Sandals - Talk:Alan Sandals
- Alenia Marconi Systems - Talk:Alenia Marconi Systems
- Alexander Strategy Group - Talk:Alexander Strategy Group
- Alexander Treadwell - Talk:Alexander Treadwell
- Allegheny Institute Taxpayer Coalition - Talk:Allegheny Institute Taxpayer Coalition
- Allegheny Institute for Public Policy - Talk:Allegheny Institute for Public Policy
- Allen McCulloch - Talk:Allen McCulloch
- Allen Ravenstine - Talk:Allen Ravenstine
- Aluminum tubes - Talk:Aluminum tubes

Figure 6-10. Here's a subpage set up as a second watchlist. If you want paired talk pages, you need to be add them manually, because they're included automatically on watchlist reports that use watchlists you create yourself. See the box on page 115 for a quick way to add the talk pages.

1. Copy the list of links to a spreadsheet, or to a table in a word processing document.
2. Copy the column of the links to a second column.
3. Use find/replace on the first column to change *[[* into **[[.*
4. Use find/replace on the second column to add *, [[Talk:* to replace *[[.*
5. Merge the two columns, and then paste the merged results into your subpage.

Using Additional Watchlists

Once you've set up an additional watchlist, as in Figure 6-10, you can use it to generate a watchlist report in two short steps:

1. Go to the subpage that has the watchlist.
2. On the left side of your screen, click the "Related changes" link. (It's the second link in the "toolbox" set of links, not the "Recent changes" link in the "interaction" set of links.)

   What you see depends on the setting in the "Recent changes" tab of your My Preferences page—either an expanded report, as in Figure 6-7, or an enhanced report, as in Figure 6-8.

Real-Time Monitoring Alternatives

All the watchlist reports described so far in this chapter are snapshots of edits at a moment in time. Their information is current as of when you create the report, but they don't update themselves as edits are made. If you want to watch edits as they occur, consider receiving real-time updates for pages you want to watch. You use either standard Web feeds, or monitor changes to pages on your regular watchlist using Lupin's Anti-vandal tool (page 119).

RSS and Atom

Wikipedia supports two kinds of Web feeds: RSS and Atom. A *Web feed* is an automated way to get copies of changes to Web pages of your choice. For example, you can sign up to get new postings to a blog, saving you the trouble of checking the blog every day. You read such notifications in a *feed reader*—also called a *feed aggregator* or just an *aggregator*—a specialized application on your computer.

For RSS and Atom, you have two choices. The standard way is subscribe to individual pages. But you may also be able to use a feed to get notification of changes to your watchlist, although none of the three options for that are well-developed (see the box on page 118).

Standard RSS and Atom feeds

The most straightforward way to get a Web feed for pages you want to watch is to subscribe on a page-by-page basis to those pages. As with additional watchlists (page 115), if you want to watch *both* a page and its associated talk page, you have to subscribe to each separately. The links for the RSS and Atom feeds are available on each page's page history tab. Click the "history" tab and look for the link on the left side of the screen (see Figure 6-11).

To subscribe to the page, click either the RSS or Atom link. Your browser then gives you the option of subscribing (exactly what you see depends on your browser).

Keep in mind that Wikipedia's Web feeds include only the *changed* part of a page—in other words, the top part of a standard *diff*. That keeps the size of the text being sent via the feed to a reasonable amount, but it means that you can't see what the entire

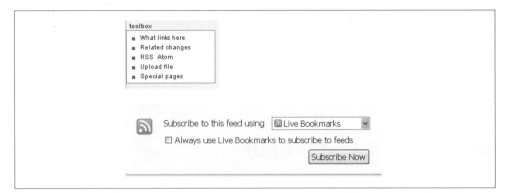

Figure 6-11. Top: To request an RSS or Atom feed for a specific article or other page, click the "history" tab for that page, and then look at the toolbox on the left side of the screen for a link to click : Bottom: Once you click either "RSS" or "Atom", what you see depends entirely on your browser. Shown here is the top of the page of what Firefox 2.0 (on Windows XP) displays.

article looks like after the edit occurred. (If you do want to see the full diff, just click the link at the bottom of the item in the feed.)

TIP

You'll find more information about RSS and Atom feeds at the page *Wikipedia:Syndication* (shortcut: *WP:XLM*).

While there's no easy way to set up a feed for your standard watchlist, any additional watchlists you create are a different matter. As of December 2007, the *Special:Recentchangeslinked* page has an RSS/Atom feed. That means it's easy to monitor changes to your additional watchlists in real time, if you want to.

POWER USERS' CLINIC

A Feed for Your Watchlist

At this writing, standard Wikipedia software doesn't support using your existing watchlist as an automated basis for specifying which pages you subscribe to. There are three currently known options, listed below. Only experienced feed users—and those with a bit of programming experience—need apply.

- *User:Adodge/WLWP* provides information about a Perl script that takes your watchlist and turns it into a single RSS feed on your local computer. You then subscribe to that page with the feed reader of your choice.

- *User:Ryos/Watchlist* provides PHP code that requires an RSS reader that can subscribe to it (as a script on a local computer). It's not clear whether Windows-compatible RSS readers exist.

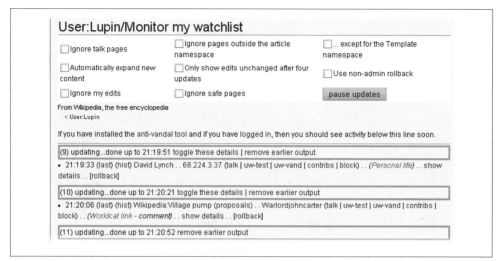

Figure 6-12. The User:Lupin/Monitor my watchlist *page has a scrolling list of edits of pages on your watchlist. At the top are a number of options. For example, you might want to turn on "Ignore talk pages" and "Ignore because pages outside the article namespace" because you're focusing solely on vandalism to articles themselves.*

- *User:Jyotirmoyb/Watchlistfeed* describes a Python script to fetch the RSS or Atom feed using an API that was in alpha at the time the script was written, and the script itself is described as alpha.

Lupin's Anti-vandal Tool

Lupin's Anti-vandal tool is the only solid real-time monitoring tool that uses your existing watchlist. This tool, described on the page *User:Lupin/Anti-vandal tool*, is a script (see Chapter 21) intended primarily for vandal-fighting, but you can also use it to identify spelling errors. More to the point, one of the vandal-fighting options is to use the tool to monitor changes to pages on your watchlist. As shown in Figure 6-12, you get a list of changes, plus checkboxes at the top that let you choose what kinds of edits you want to see.

If you don't have many pages (or many active pages) on your watchlist, you might end up scrolling for pages and pages before you see any entries for editing activity. To put it numerically, this tool reports on edit changes every 30 seconds. Let's say that your expanded watchlist report showed 24 changes in a 24-hour period—one change per hour. For that same 24-hour period, this tool would show at least 2,856 status reports with no activity, and 24 or fewer status reports with one or more edits.

Implementing this tool is very straightforward:

1. Copy the one-line script *importScript("User:Lupin/recent2.js");* to your *mono-book.js* file, and then save the change.

Figure 6-13. After you install Lupin's Anti-vandal tool and purge your cache, your "toolbox" (on the left side of the screen) has five new links. You use the "Monitor my watchlist" link to get a real-time display of changes to pages in your watchlist.

See Chapter 21 for details about implementing user scripts.

2. Purge your cache.

The keystrokes vary by browser, but Ctrl+F5 for Windows, ⌘-F5 for Mac generally works.

You should see five new items in the "toolbox" set of links on the left side of the screen (see Figure 6-13). When you click the "Monitor my watchlist" link in Figure 6-13, you go to the *User:Lupin/Monitor my watchlist* page in Figure 6-12.

NOTE

Three potential alternatives for real-time information aren't available as this book goes to press: An Internet Relay Chat (IRC) feed of page changes limited to pages on your watchlist; an Instant Message (IM) feed (of any type); and email notifications of page changes. The last of these in fact is built into Wikipedia's underlying software, but has been turned off in the English Wikipedia. (The English Wikipedia has roughly 300,000 edits *per day*, so this feature could potentially generate millions of outgoing emails every day from Wikipedia servers.)

CHAPTER 7

Dealing with Vandalism and Spam

Although vandalism and spam are constant aggravations, the ongoing efforts of thousands of editors—like you—do a surprisingly good job of minimizing these problems. This chapter explains in detail what you, a Wikipedia editor, can do in terms of spotting and fixing vandalism and spam.

For Wikipedia, the "encyclopedia that anyone can edit," *vandalism*—the destruction of content or the addition of useless or malicious content—is a constant, ongoing issue. "Anyone" includes cranks, juveniles (of any age) who don't have anything better to do, and those who hold a grudge against Wikipedia because of past blocks or bans. For readers, obvious vandalism casts doubt the accuracy of Wikipedia articles. If the vandalism is subtle, readers can be deliberately misinformed. For editors, fighting vandalism reduces the amount of time available to improve articles.

Spam, at Wikipedia, refers to improper external links added to Wikipedia articles, which is why you often see the term *linkspam*. Spam is a smaller problem than vandalism because most readers of Wikipedia articles don't follow external links. Still, as Wikipedia becomes more widely read, the temptation grows to add links in the hopes that someone will click them, generating traffic for the spamming Web site. (See the box below for more detail on the differences between vandalism and spam.)

Fighting vandalism and spam is a bit like doing detective work: In addition to figuring out who did what (Chapter 5), you investigate the extent of the problem, assess the possible underlying motives of the perpetrator (that affects things like warning levels), and then decide what to do (warn, request a block, and so on). It's important work, and many editors specialize in it.

UP TO SPEED

Vandalism and Spam Defined

Vandalism is any addition, removal, or change of content made in a deliberate attempt to compromise Wikipedia's integrity. The most common types of vandalism include the addition of obscenities to pages, page blanking, and the insertion of jokes or nonsense. (For more information, go to *WP:VAND*.)

Adding external links to an article or user page for the purpose of promoting a Web site or a product is considered *spam*, and isn't allowed. If an editor adds numerous spam links (to the same external Web site) along with a few acceptable links, the appropriate action by other editors is to remove *all* links. Over time, non-spamming editors can add back any relevant links that were mass-deleted. (For more information, see *WP:SPAM*.)

Lines of Defense

The Wikipedia community has evolved multiple lines of defense against vandalism and, to some extent, spam. They are, roughly in the order of how fast they kick in (bots being the fastest):

- **Bots**. Some vandalism is so egregious that even a computer program can recognize it. Wikipedia allows bots to revert vandalism because in the rare cases where they make a mistake, the mistake is easy to revert.

- **Recent changes patrol**. The RCP is a semi-organized group of editors who monitor changes to all the articles in Wikipedia, as the changes happen, to spot and revert vandalism immediately. Most RC patrollers use automated tools to handle the routine steps in vandal fighting.

- **Watchlists**. Although the primary focus of monitoring is often content (and thus potential content disputes, as described in Chapter 10), watchlists are an excellent way for concerned editors to spot vandalism. (Watchlists and other methods of monitoring articles are described in Chapter 6.)

- **Readers**. Readers, including editors who are just looking over an article, are in some sense the last line of defense. Most readers don't know the proper way to remove vandalism (but you do, if you've read Chapter 6). Still, even if readers bungle vandalism removal, they've still improved the page, and hopefully a more experienced editor will complete the job.

When you read a randomly picked Wikipedia article, you rarely see vandalism. That's a testimony to the effectiveness of vandal-fighting, despite evidence that the extent of vandalism is increasing (Figure 7-1).

Reverting Vandalism and Spam

If you simply revert a vandalizing or spamming edit, and then go about other business, you've missed a major opportunity to find other vandalism and spam by the same editor. Worse, you've made it less likely that other editors will check the edit history of that editor in the future, looking for vandalizing and spam, and if indeed there are such problems, you've given the problem editor more time to continue with destructive editing.

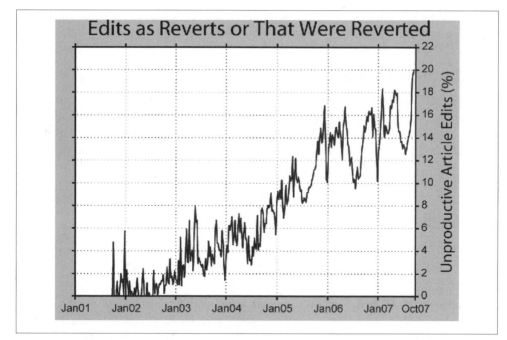

Figure 7-1. As Wikipedia has gotten more popular, the percentage of edits that are reverted—mostly, but not always, because of vandalism—has risen. This graph shows problem edits and the edits that fixed them. Assuming, for the sake of simplicity, that there is a one-to-one ratio of problem edits to corrective edits, then a point on the 20% line would mean that one of every 10 edits was a problem, and one out of every 10 edits was done to fix such problems. [Graph courtesy of editor Dragons Flight (Robert A. Rohde), based on his large September 2007 sampling of article edits.]

To handle vandalism and spam the way experienced editors do, you should do three things in addition to reverting the problem edit: determine if that editor has other problem edits, and deal with those as well; post an appropriate warning to the editor; and, in extreme cases, ask an administrator to block the problem editor. Experienced editors also know how to ask that a page be protected if it's repeatedly vandalized by a number of different (typically, anonymous IP) editors.

This chapter shows you the right way to approach what looks like vandalism. For the mechanics of identifying and reverting a problem edit, flip back to Chapter 5.

Most vandalism is obvious. But when you encounter something you're not sure about, Wikipedia's guidelines suggest that you *assume good faith* in assessing the edits of others. (Details at *WP:AGF*.) That doesn't mean that you should excuse vandalism and spam; it means that when you encounter something that's in a gray area, investigate further, as described in this section. If it isn't clearly vandalism or spam, fix the erroneous edit, and presume it was a mistake.

As a general rule, fix improper edits and remove irrelevant links, but if the editor in question has a history of constructive edits, don't label those edits as vandalism, and don't call the links linkspam unless you find a lot of problem edits. New editors can make honest mistakes.

Consider the Edit Summary

Some vandals are clever enough to add a semi-plausible edit summary to a vandalizing edit. Still, if there's an edit summary (other than a section title, added by the software), you should consider that major evidence that you're not looking at vandalism, but rather at a content dispute (Chapter 10). On the other hand, if you're looking at a questionable edit which also lacks an edit summary, it's appropriate to lean toward treating it as vandalism.

Consider the Source

Before you revert an edit, you should always think about who did that edit. Take the editor's history into account when you're estimating the likelihood that an edit is vandalism. Here are the two extremes:

- **Anonymous IP edit; link to user talk page is red**. The red link means that no one has ever posted to the editor's user talk page, which in turn indicates that there have been few or no other edits by this IP address, which means few or no constructive edits. In this case, you don't need to do any further research before reverting. If you see a questionable edit from this kind of user account, you can be virtually certain it was vandalism.

- **Experienced editor**. When you follow the link to the editor's User contributions page, you see a lot of edits with edit summaries. When you click the "oldest" link, you find that the editor has been around for years. When you check the editor's block log, you don't find anything (or anything within the past 12 months). (A user block log shows whether the user account has been blocked for vandalism or other problems. You can see the "Block log" link at the top of the *User contributions page;* see Figure 7-2.)

  In the rare case that you think there's a problem with an edit from this kind of editor, chances are you've misunderstood something. You may have clicked on the wrong line in the history page (an edit you don't want to revert), or you may be looking (again, by mistake) at an edit that *fixed* vandalism rather than created it.

The Less Clearly an Edit Is Vandalism, the More You Should Consider the Source

Suppose you notice an edit where a date has been changed – say, from "1920" to "1921," or the middle name of a person has been changed from "Smith" to "Smithers." Is it vandalism or not? When you check the page history, you see this isn't just a revert

Figure 7-2. You can get to a listing of blocks made against a user account via a link at the top of the User contributions *page. The block log shows any action taken by administrators to block the user account from editing for a hour, day, a week, or some other period, including indefinitely.*

back to the way the article had been earlier—it's a new change. You need more information.

Ideally, the article would have a citation that included an external link, so that you yourself can verify the information in the article. But if no external link provides an answer, even in the "External links" section, then information about the *editor* can help you decide what to do. Start by looking at the link to the user talk page. If it's a red link, there's no user talk page, so the user account is almost certainly new. You should then basically revert on principle, because it's more likely that the original information was correct than the change made by an editor who's apparently brand-new to Wikipedia. If the link to the user talk page is blue, follow it. If there are warnings, then again it's likely that the edit you're examining is vandalism.

If the editor in question is registered, not an anonymous IP editor, and there's no evidence that the editor is a vandal, then it's a courtesy to drop a note on the editor's user talk page, saying you've reverted the edit due to lack of an edit summary and lack of a citation, and that the editor should feel free to make the change again if an explanation is provided. Notes like that help inform new, well-intentioned editors about the right way to do things.

If the questionable edit you're examining was done by *adding* text to an article, not by deletion or changing of information, consider alternatives. You can, for example, add the *Citation needed* template (type *{{fact}}*) to the end of a sentence or paragraph that you question, rather than deleting it. You can also edit it a bit to make the language more neutral.

NOTE

If the added material is biographical information, immediate deletion may be appropriate. Wikipedia's rules regarding biographical information are different from rules for other types of information. If information is controversial—whether the information is negative *or* positive—and it's unsourced, you should remove it. But don't call it vandalism if it's at all coherent. Rather, you should note the violation of the policy *Wikipedia:Biographies of living persons* in your edit summary. Something like this will do the trick: *Removing information in violation of [[WP:BLP]].*

Explain Your Edit

When you revert vandalism and spam, it's critical to leave a clear edit summary. If you're dealing with obvious vandalism by a user account with no apparent history of constructive edits, then *rv* will suffice. That abbreviation tells experienced editors that you've reverted vandalism; it's fine that it's cryptic because communication with the editor who did the obvious vandalism is unlikely. With less clear cases, your edit summary needs to be lengthier because it may be the start of a dialog with another editor.

For example, if you suspect a subtle form of vandalism like changing a date or name but can't prove it, something like *rv edit unsupported by a citation; edit made by a user without history of constructive edits* is appropriate. Think of your edit summary as a sort of log entry; even if you're incorrect, you've still started a constructive dialog by explaining yourself.

If another editor has deleted a bunch of text but doesn't offer any explanation in the edit summary, a good edit summary for your reversion would be *rv unexplained deletion*. This summary explains why you restored the text and invites that editor to add an edit summary next time.

WORD TO THE WISE

Dealing with Vandalism When You Have a Conflict of Interest

Wikipedia's conflict of interest guideline (shortcut: *WP:COI*) says that editors generally "are strongly advised not to edit articles where they have a close personal or business connection." But it makes an exception for "non-controversial edits," which include the removal of spam and the reverting of vandalism.

If you find yourself in a conflict of interest situation, the important thing is to make sure that what you're reverting is vandalism, not something else. In particular, Wikipedia's vandalism policy (shortcut: *WP:VAND*) says that the following are *not* vandalism: edits that are not neutral in point of view, bold edits that substantially change text, and misinformation added in good faith.

If the problem is something other than vandalism, like inaccurate information, then simply post to the article talk page, citing a source (ideally providing a link) for what you want changed. (Wikipedia's conflict of interest guideline says that you don't have to volunteer that you have a conflict of interest if you don't want to, but it may help here, since other editors may wonder why you don't just fix the article yourself.)

Looking for More Vandalism and Spam

Some vandals hit only one page; some hit many. Spammers typically hit many pages, but sometimes only one (or they're caught early in a spamming spree). A good editor, upon finding one problem edit, looks for others. The place to do so is the editor's User contributions page. After you've identified the problematic edit, and are looking at a

Figure 7-3. A portion of a User contributions page, showing two edits with "top" at the end of the row of edit information. The "top" means this editor was the last person to edit that page – his edit is at the top of the revision history of that page.

history page, you can jump to the contributions page of the problem editor in one of two ways:

- For anonymous IP editors, click the IP address.
- For registered editors, clicking the "contribs" link.

At the User contributions page, focus primarily on edits done in the past couple of days. But your first concern should be those edits which have a "top" in bold at the end of the row (see Figure 7-3). If an edit was vandalism or spam, and it has a "top" at the end, that means it has *not* been reverted.

NOTE

Edits by a person to her own user talk page and (if she's a registered editor) to her user page are probably worth at least glancing at, particularly in the case of spam, but can be given much lower priority. Focus on articles and on other widely-read pages.

How you go about reviewing a specific editor's edits is a matter of personal style. Here are some tips:

- Start with "top" edits, as shown in Figure 7-3, since they clearly haven't been reverted. If they're a problem, fix them immediately, if possible. And look at all the other edits the editor did to the same page—they won't be "top" edits, but they also may be unreverted.
- Just because an edit isn't a "top" edit doesn't mean it's been fixed. It means only that the page has been subsequently edited, perhaps by someone else who completely missed vandalism or spam. Or a bot could have stopped by to fix a category or do other maintenance work, oblivious to any other problems.
- A *registered* editor who has vandalized or spammed an article represents a significant problem. Registered editors can do much more than anonymous IP addresses

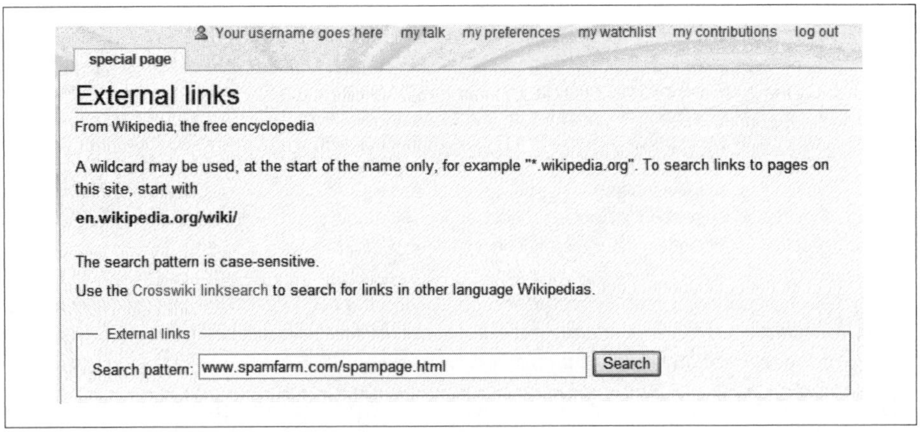

special page

External links

From Wikipedia, the free encyclopedia

A wildcard may be used, at the start of the name only, for example "*.wikipedia.org". To search links to pages on this site, start with

en.wikipedia.org/wiki/

The search pattern is case-sensitive.

Use the Crosswiki linksearch to search for links in other language Wikipedias.

┌─ External links ───
│ Search pattern: `www.spamfarm.com/spampage.html`   [Search]
└──

Figure 7-4. You can use the Special:Linksearch *page to find all Wikipedia pages with an external link to any specific URL. It even finds all Wikipedia pages with external links to a particular Web site if you use the "*" wildcard character. In this figure, a specific URL has been entered, rather than searching for links to a portion of or all of a Web site.*

(creating pages, moving pages, and so on). Vandalism-only registered accounts in particular need to be dealt with promptly.

If you find a registered editor who has done more than a couple of edits, all these edits are vandalizing, and the most recent edit is in the last 24 hours or so, then don't bother posting a warning. Instead, ask an administrator to block the account (page 134). (If the administrator reviewing the case decides not to block, she'll post a warning as an alternative.)

- Multiple people can be using the same IP address: a library or school computer; a dial-in IP address that's constantly reassigned; an Internet service provider who uses a proxy address for multiple customers; and so on. In these cases, older edits may have been done by a completely different person, so don't use them in analyzing what an IP user account did in the recent past.

- For linkspam, if the editor is posting the same link to multiple articles, you can query Wikipedia to see how many of the links still exist (that is, no one else has deleted them yet). To do so, go to the *Special:Linksearch* page, and put in the URL (see Figure 7-4 for an example).

- If you find a lot of unreverted vandalism and don't have time to deal with it, post a note at *Wikipedia:Help desk* (shortcut: *WP:HD*) so other editors can help out. For spam, post (in a new section) on the talk page of *Wikipedia:WikiProject Spam* (shortcut: *WP:WPSPAM*). (For detailed information about posting comments to talk and other discussion pages, see Chapter 8.)

Don't feel your reporting a problem is just shifting the workload to other editors. Wikipedia has power tools—including some available only to administrators—that can do mass reverts, which sharply reduces the amount of work in dealing with a problem editor. So when you post at one of these two pages, you're helping make sure that problem edits get fixed *quickly*. That's particularly true for the spamming of a large number of pages—if you don't have a lot of experience with reverting, it's really not worth your time to manually remove spam links from lots of pages, since some editors specialize in this.

- Vandals often edit the same page multiple times, so make sure you get them all. Often other editors have fixed most of the vandalizing edits, so do a diff (page 87) that includes the vandalism and its repairs (a diff on multiple edits) to make sure that the net impact of fixing vandalism was to bring the article back to its state before the vandalism. (It can be reassuring to know that others have been dealing with this problem editor.)

- When you're investigating an editor, it's normal to focus, at the User contributions page, only on edits in the past couple of days (or, if there are few edits, to look at the last dozen or so, perhaps even fewer). Reviewing older edits has much less payback; should you find one that wasn't fixed, it presumably was to a page that gets few readers, so it didn't have a great impact anyway. Plus, the older an edit, the more likely that there have been a number of subsequent edits, making it more difficult to figure out whether the vandalism got fixed (properly) or not. However, if you're checking for vandalism by a registered editor, you should review every page where that editor has a "top" edit, no matter how old that "top" edit is.

UP TO SPEED

Using an Article as a Sandbox

Despite the words "For testing, please use the sandbox instead" that appear toward the bottom of the window when in edit mode, brand-new editors often do an erroneous edit to an article, then immediately do another edit to repair the damage. This behavior is *not* considered vandalism, if this is the first time, or the editor hasn't been told to stop doing it, because vandalism requires what Wikipedia calls *bad faith*. Such edits shouldn't be ignored, but someone who cleans up after himself shouldn't be treated harshly, either.

For such cases, the best thing you can do is post a standard welcome on that editor's user talk page, assuming one isn't there already, to provide him with some useful start-

---

ing links, plus a gentle suggestion to use the sandbox for playing around. Type the following warning template on the user talk page:

{{subst:uw-test1}} ~~~~. (That may look odd, but you'll see, once you preview it, it makes sense. You'll find information on these warnings via the shortcut *WP:WARN*.)

If the editor has already been warned about not editing actual articles, use a stronger warning: use "uw-test2" or "uw-test3" instead of "uw-test1". Finally, if there have been repeated warnings, then treat the matter as pure vandalism.

Issuing Warnings

So, you've found some vandalism or spam, and researched other edits by the same user account to see if there's more. The next, and important, step is to post an appropriate warning on the editor's user talk page.

The primary purpose of a warning about vandalism or spam, perhaps counter-intuitively, is *not* to get the problem editor to change her ways. (It would be nice if they did so, but troublemakers aren't like to reform themselves just because someone asked nicely.) Rather, when you and other editors post a series of increasingly strong warnings, you're building a documented case for *blocking* a user account from further disruptive editing. If the warnings lead to the editor changing his ways before blocking is necessary, great—but don't hold your breath.

Choosing the Warning and Warning Level

Start by looking at the warnings that have already been posted on the user talk page, if any. Then take a look at the history tab for the user talk page: the editor might have deleted warnings by other editors.

NOTE
There's much confusion as to whether editors are allowed to remove warnings from their user talk pages. They are. Deletion is considered to be confirmation that the warnings have been read, and the warnings remain visible via the "history" tab. For details, see the "Removal of comments, warnings" section of the guideline *Wikipedia:User page* (shortcut: *WP:USER*). So you must check the user talk page's history to see if prior warnings were deleted, but don't revert those warnings so that other editors can see them on the user talk page.

You'll find a table of warnings at *Wikipedia:Template messages/User talk namespace* (shortcut: *WP:WARN*). Warnings to editors come in levels 1 through 4:

* **Level 1**. Assumes good faith. Generally includes *Welcome to Wikipedia* or some variant.

- **Level 2**. No faith assumption.
- **Level 3**. Assumes bad faith; cease and desist.
- **Level 4**. Assumes bad faith; strong cease and desist, last warning (this level of warning must be preceded by at least one prior warning).
- **Level 4im**. Assumes bad faith; strong cease and desist, first and only warning.

From the warning table, pick an appropriate warning at the level you've chosen. Picking the appropriate level of warning is an art, not a science. Here are some general guidelines:

- You don't have to start at level 1, nor do you have to escalate if the editor seems to have generally behaved after getting a prior warning, but you should always post *some* level of warning, or a note, when you find a recent problem.
- If you're not sure about what level of warning to post, pick one, post it (as described in the next section), and do a page preview. If the wording doesn't seem to fit, go up or down a level and see what that looks like.

  For example, assume that you found vandalism, and that a level 2 warning had already been posted for that same type of vandalism. You should post a level 3, or, if you just found a lot, perhaps even a level 4 warning.

- If there already was a level 4 (final warning), you can normally skip directly to the next step—asking an administrator to block the user account (see page 134).

  Exception: If the most recent vandalism or spam by a user account is older than 48 hours, administrators don't usually put a block in place. Blocks are preventive, not punitive. So if you find old vandalism and a prior level 4 warning, it may be helpful to post another "final warning" as a note to other editors not to give this user account any leeway in the future.

Posting the Warning

Once you've selected an appropriate warning template, posting it is a quick five-step process. (If you're not dealing with a real situation, you can still practice this procedure by posting to your own user talk page. Just don't click "Save page". Instead, in the last step, stop after doing the preview.)

1. On *Wikipedia:Template messages/User talk namespace* (shortcut: *WP:WARN*), copy the text of the template warning to the clipboard (Ctrl+C on Windows; ⌘-C on Mac).

   This step is optional, but may save you time later. Or you may want to use the clipboard for something else, like the name of the page where the problem edit occurred.

2. On the user talk page where you want to post the warning, click the "+" tab at the top to start a new topic.

3. You're in edit mode, with a new section visible for you to edit.

4. In the subject line, type *Warning* or something more specific like *Warning – your edit to [[Name of article]]*.

It's important to use neutral language here. Your primary goal is to provide information to other editors, not to chastise someone you think is a vandal. If you get personal (expressing emotion, and/or commenting on the editor as a person), you run a serious risk of either biting a newcomer (see *WP:BITE* for details) or feeding a troll (see *WP:DENY* and *WP:DIV* for details).

5. In the body of the new topic posting, paste (or type) the template, with *{{subst:* at the front and *}}* at the end, followed by tildes for your signature (for more on signing your comments, see page 143).

For example: *{{subst:uw-vandalism3}} ~~~~*

UP TO SPEED

Template Substitution

When you post a warning template, always start the template with *{{subst:*. This code tells the software to use the template page to post the standard wording, and then to *lock that wording in place*. In other words, when you save the edit, it pastes the actual text into the page's wikitext in place of the template you typed.

Reasons for including the *subst:* include the following: When an editor looks at the underlying wikitext, he sees the same text as on the page, not something like *{{uw-test1}}*, which can confuse new editors. Also, the locked text never changes, even if the wording of the warning template changes in the future, so your warning's intent remains clear. Finally, it's slightly less work for Wikipedia's servers to display the wikitext of a page rather than going to a template page to find and process the template to get that text.

---

6. Click "Show preview" to make sure everything worked as expected (see Figure 7-5).

7. If everything looks okay, then click "Save page".

When Not to Post a Warning

It's generally not worth posting a warning in these cases:

- **If a shared IP address (like that of a university or library) has been blocked at least five times within the past 6 months or so**. Instead, report the problem at *Wikipedia:Abuse reports* (shortcut: *WP:ABUSE*). The user talk page usually indicates whether an IP address is shared. Another way to tell is that with a shared IP address, the length of time for each block doesn't increase over time, or doesn't increase significantly.

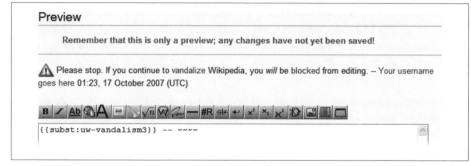

Figure 7-5. A preview of the level 3 user warning for vandalism (the uw-vandalism3 *template, using substitution). It's critical to preview user warnings, because mistyping even a single character will probably cause the template to malfunction.*

- **If you find older vandalism, and the editor's already been warned**. Adding a warning is appropriate only when a new type of problem arises, or when someone has ignored a prior warning and continued some improper behavior.

- **If the user received a level 4/4im, last/final warning, and vandalized after that**. Just request the user be blocked, as described on page 134.

- **If an anonymous IP address vandalized only a single page, on a single occasion (including consecutive edits), and has never done any other editing**. Here you're dealing with a hit-and-run vandal. It's highly unlikely the vandal will reappear with that IP address, so nobody's going to read any warning you post, and there's no point in laying down an initial warning for other editors to build on.

Wikipedia has a well-known saying: **"Don't template the regulars."** As discussed on page 124, someone who has a long history of constructive edits isn't likely to have done a vandalizing or spamming edit. If it looks like she did, you should double-check and triple-check before proceeding. And if you do conclude that her edit looks non-constructive and revert it, don't use a warning template to post a message: Write something more personal. (For example, you might post something like *I'm not sure I understood [Diff_url this edit that you did], I reverted it because it looked like a mistake; please let me know if I missed something.*)

Requesting Assistance of Administrators

In cases of vandalism and spam, administrators (there are more than a thousand of them at the English Wikipedia) can take two types of preventive measures unavailable to normal editors—protecting pages and blocking vandals.

Protecting Pages

If a page is repeatedly vandalized by a changing cast of anonymous IP editors, then temporary *semi-protection* of the page is probably appropriate. Semi-protection means that registered editors can still edit the page (starting 4 days after they register), but anonymous IP addresses can't. (Anonymous users with suggestions for changes should post them to the article talk page.) It's quite unusual to *fully protect* a page because of vandalism; full protection is normally done only for cases of major content disputes (see Chapter 10).

In the first sentence of the prior paragraph, two key words are "repeatedly" and "changing." You shouldn't request semi-protection of a page unless there have been at least a half-dozen vandalizing IP edits in the last 24 hours or so. If there are fewer, administrators may feel that it's better to simply manually revert the vandalism. And the IP addresses need to vary or otherwise be unblockable. Otherwise, administrators prefer blocking a few IP addresses.

To request semi-protection, post at *Wikipedia:Requests for page protection* (shortcut: *WP:RFPP*).

Note that semi-protection is normally only temporary: The goal is to get vandals to lose interest in the protected page. Anonymous contributions have built a significant percentage of Wikipedia, so the Wikipedia community is very reluctant to close off editing to all IP addresses for an indefinite period, even to only a single page.

NOTE

Don't ask to have a page be protected because you *anticipate* that it'll be a target for vandals in the near future. That's too subjective for administrators, no matter how well-reasoned a case you may have. You must show that vandalism is already occurring.

General Guidance on Blocking Vandals

Blocking is a *preventive* action, not a *punitive* one. If, for example, you find vandalism that's more than a day or two old (different administrators have different thresholds), it's pretty unlikely that your request to block the account will be granted.

An administrator can block an account for any amount of time between a minute and indefinitely. Registered accounts whose only edits have been vandalism are typically blocked indefinitely, but other user accounts usually get an escalating approach. For example, block for a day; if vandalism recurs, block for a week; if it recurs again, block for a month; and only then, if it recurs again, block indefinitely.

Reporting Vandalism

In this tutorial, you'll report a fictional vandal, an anonymous user who edited from IP address 127.0.0.1, and who vandalized six articles about an hour ago. You'll go through all the steps of making the report, except that on the final step, after you do a preview,

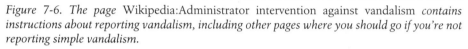

Wikipedia:Administrator intervention against vandalism

From Wikipedia, the free encyclopedia
(Redirected from WP:AIV)

Purge the cache of this page
You can subscribe to a web feed of this page in either RSS or Atom format.

Editing abuse:	**Vandalism** • 3RR • Long term • ArbCom enforcement • Usernames • Page protection
ISP/IP abuse:	Open proxy • ISP reporting • Sock puppets • Checkuser
Noticeboards:	Administrators • Incidents • Biographies • Conflict of interest • Fringe theories • Reliable sources

---

Wikipedia:Administrator intervention against vandalism

This page is intended to get administrator attention for **obvious** and **persistent** vandals and spammers only.

For other types of vandalism or problematic usernames, see the links at the top of this page. The response to a report will usually be included in the edit summary when it's removed, *not* on your talk page. **For a guide on how and when to report**, see Wikipedia:Guide to administrator intervention against vandalism.

Editors: Before listing a vandal here, ensure that:

1. The vandal is active **now**, has been sufficiently warned, and has **vandalized after a recent last warning**, except in unusual circumstances.
2. Your report **concisely** states what the vandal is doing (including an edit summary with the IP address or username).

Reports which do not adhere to the above will be declined.

Figure 7-6. The page Wikipedia:Administrator intervention against vandalism *contains instructions about reporting vandalism, including other pages where you should go if you're not reporting simple vandalism.*

you'll just close the page rather than saving your edit. (Since it's a fictional vandal, you don't want to make a real report.)

Report vandalism only when you think the problem has risen to the level where warnings are no longer appropriate. Generally, that means that either the user has already received a level 4 warning, and continued to vandalize, or that this is a vandal-only registered account, or that the account gives indication of a sophistication of edits well beyond a typical new editor. (Remember: If you decide to post a warning, do *not* also report the vandalism to administrators for their review.) In this example, IP address 127.0.0.1 has already been blocked, 2 days ago, for 24 hours, for vandalism.

1. Go to *Wikipedia:Administrator intervention against vandalism* (shortcut: *WP:AIV*).

   The top of this page is shown in Figure 7-6. It starts out with guidelines on when to report vandalism, much like you're already read in this chapter.

2. Scroll down to the section titled "User-reported", and click the "Edit" link on the left of that section title to open the section for editing.

   You'll see something like Figure 7-7. Three lines begin with an asterisk. You want to copy one of these three lines to use as the base information for your posting, which you'll do in the next step.

3. In this case, since this is an IP vandal, copy the first of the asterisked rows to the bottom of the section, and then change the characters *IP* to *127.0.0.1*.

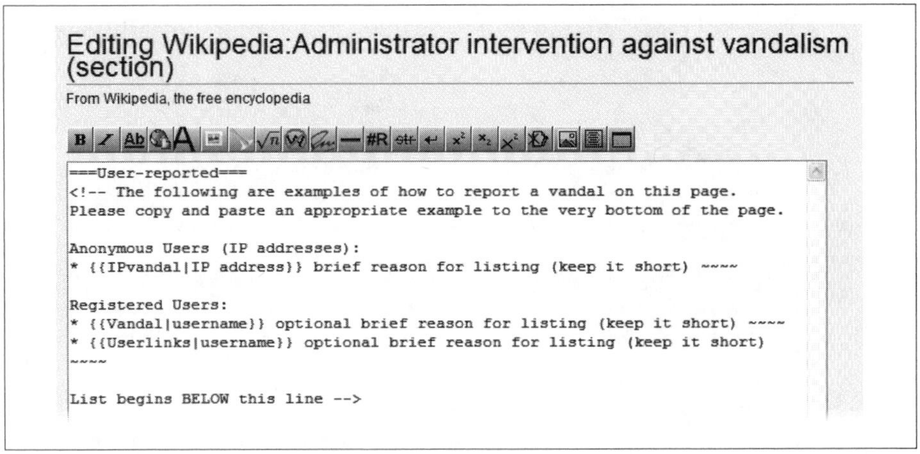

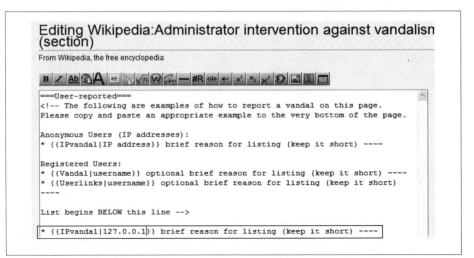

Figure 7-7. *You see this initial screen when you go into edit mode to enter information about the vandalizing account. Typically, you see a few accounts that were just reported by other editors and haven't been fully processed yet. As you see here, you use different templates for reporting IP editors and for reporting registered users.*

Figure 7-8. *Your screen looks like this after you've started your vandal report. Note that you're using the IP vandal template, not the template for registered users. The text you've copied and pasted has been highlighted.*

Your screen should now look something like Figure 7-8.

4. Replace the words *provide a reason (keep it short)* with *user was blocked for vandalism two days ago; has done it again*, and then add the edit summary *Reporting 127.0.0.1.* Click "Show preview".

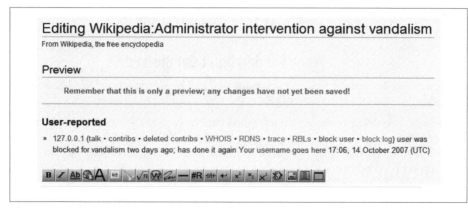

Figure 7-9. The vandalism report is complete. Here's what it looks like in preview mode.

Your screen should now look like Figure 7-9 In this example, you didn't give details about the vandalizing edits—not the number of edits, or the names of the vandalized pages, or edit diffs. Administrators checking your report will review the User contributions page and the user block log, and that should suffice. (If the editor had been repeatedly warned, but never blocked, you'd say something about the warnings.)

Your goal should be to make as convincing a case as you can in 20 words or less, remembering that the administrators who handle these cases look at hundreds every day, and don't rely particularly heavily on the reports for anything but an initial starting point.

5. Close the preview window without saving, so you don't send the administrators off on a wild goose chase.

That way, you avoid getting a polite notice on your user talk page asking you to stop submitting bogus vandalism reports.

WORKAROUND WORKSHOP

Avoid Edit Conflicts on WP: AIV

Postings to the *Wikipedia:Administrator intervention against vandalism* page are among the most likely to involve edit conflicts, because the volume of vandalism reports is so high. Here's one way to avoid the problem:

1. Write out your full posting at *WP:AIV*, in edit mode, in the edit box.

2. Copy that text to the clipboard.

3. Click your browser's Back button to go back to the WP:AIV page in read mode.

4. Click the edit button on the "User-reported" section to go back into edit mode.

5. Paste your report from the clipboard. Now you're ready to quickly add an edit summary, do a quick preview, and save your posting.

Don't Get into a Revert War

If you remove what you consider vandalism, and the same editor puts it back, don't automatically remove it again. Before reverting, you need to decide if this is a content dispute (Chapter 10) or just a persistent vandal. Here are the factors you should consider:

- **Is it clearly a case of vandalism?** If, for example, the edit again replaced good content with a string of gibberish, then you don't need to consider other factors— it's vandalism. On the other hand, if the editor simply re-deleted a paragraph, perhaps it wasn't.

- **Did the editor post anything about this matter on the article's talk page?** If so, except for cases of extremely obvious vandalism, treat the matter as a content dispute.

- **Did the other editor provide an edit summary when he reverted your edit, explaining his edit?** If so, you should treat the matter it as a content dispute, not a matter of vandalism, assuming that all the other factors don't point to vandalism. But if the editor failed to provide an edit summary (other than what Wikipedia added, such as section title), lean in the direction of repeated vandalism.

- **What's the editor's history – other vandalism or constructive edits?** As discussed in this chapter, the editor's user talk page (including its history), block log, and User contributions page provide you with a wealth of information about the editor. If they indicate that the user has at least *some* positive contributions and hasn't been recently blocked, treat the matter as a content dispute.

What if you revert an edit the second time, and the same editor (or another IP address that it appears the same editor has migrated to—say, an IP address that previously had no edits whatsoever) does the edit (or a very similar one) for a third time? Then you want to read *Wikipedia:Three-revert rule* (shortcut: *WP:3RR*) very carefully. If you're absolutely sure that any reasonable editor would agree that you're fighting vandalism, go ahead and revert again. But if there's any doubt at all, go to Chapter 10.

PART II

Collaborating with Other Editors

CHAPTER 8

Communicating with Your Fellow Editors

As a Wikipedia editor, you need to know how to use the pages where editors interact and collaborate with each other. Even if you want to focus mostly on improving articles, you'll find that discussing those improvements with other editors before, during, and after your actual article work goes a long way in making sure your changes are accurate and don't get reverted later.

Dealing with vandalism (Chapter 7) and content disputes (Chapter 10) also require you to use article and user talk pages. As a Wikipedia editor, you'll communicate with other editors on article talk pages and user talk pages—including your own. You can also, if you wish, communicate directly with other editors by email and in online chat rooms.

All these methods of communication involve standard procedures and norms of conduct. If you don't follow them, other editors are much more likely to ignore what you're saying, as valuable as it may be. This chapter spells out those processes and norms so you can make your points easily and clearly.

Identifying Yourself

When you post a comment to a talk page, you must always *sign* your comment. Other editors need to know who posted what, and when, so they can follow the thread of a conversation, post on a user talk page if appropriate, and even just know whether a posting is worth responding to. (A comment that's more than a month old is presumed to be of historical interest only if it's no longer part of an ongoing discussion.)

In Wikipedia, signing has two parts: your *signature* (sometimes called "sig"), which is a composite of one or more links (to your user page, user talk page, or user contributions page), plus the *time and date* that you save your edit. Here's an example of what signing your comment would look like: *YourUserNameGoesHere talk 22:04, 11 November 2007 (UTC)*. If you click on the first, long word, it leads to the user page; if you click "talk", it leads to the user talk page.

Signing a comment is easy: Simply put *four tildes* at the very end of your comment, without spaces between the tildes. (A tilde looks like this: "~"; on American keyboards you find it in the upper left.) If you type only three tildes by mistake, you add only your user name, not the date and time you posted your comment. If you type five tildes by mistake, you leave the date and time but not your user name or a link to your user talk page.

Don't start a new line or paragraph when you sign your comments. At the end of the body of your comment, just add a space or two, or a dash or two, or both, for separation, and then add the four tildes. (Extra lines for your signature just take up space on a page, and adding them is the mark of an inexperienced user.)

In edit mode, you can also sign by using a button on the edit toolbar (the row of icons just above the edit box). Clicking the button that has cursive writing on it inserts two hyphens and four tildes (--~~~~) in the text you're editing. (Make sure your cursor is where you want your signature to appear—the button isn't smart enough to figure that out itself.)

GEM IN THE ROUGH

SineBot and the Missing Signatures

One of the more irritating things that experienced Wikipedia editors often find themselves doing (over and over) is to add missing signatures for postings by other inexperienced editors. This gaffe would be more forgivable if talk pages and similar posting pages didn't have clear instructions at the top about signing of posts, but they *do*.

Fortunately, a software bot now takes care of most such fixes. It's not infallible, but the work of sifting through a page history to figure out who left an unsigned comment has dropped off sharply since SineBot, and its predecessor, HagermanBot, arrived on the scene.

If you chose to add a signature that SineBot missed, Chapter 5 (especially page 87) provides all the information you need to find the guilty editor's name. Once you've found the edit (or, if it's a cluster of edits, the most recent), copy both the editor's name (or IP address) and the date and time of that edit to the clipboard, return to the page that needs the signature, and then insert the information like so:

{{subst:unsigned|Name_of_user}} time & date

For example, a good edit summary would be something like this *Adding date/sig for Name_of_user*.

And if you add the following at the end of an unsigned comment: *{{subst:unsigned| 127.0.01}} 21:15 12 December 2007*, your text would look like this, after you save the edit:

—Preceding unsigned comment added by 127.0.01 (talk • contribs) 21:15 12 December 2007

Article Talk (Discussion) Pages

Wikipedia articles such as *Monty Python* have a matching talk page: *Talk:Monty Python*. On these pages, editors discuss improvements to the article, including differences of opinions about content.

Because a talk page is *conversation*, its organization is very different from that of an article, which is essay-like. The underlying page formatting is the same—the *wiki markup* for headings, bold, italics—but the rules of engagement (so to speak) are quite different. For example, italicizing words in articles, for emphasis, is simply not done, because that's not a neutral point of view. By contrast, italics are quite common on article talk pages because they can make it easier for other editors to understand what's being said. Similarly, signatures are absolutely forbidden on article pages, but you should always sign your postings on article talk pages.

NOTE

The information in this section refers to *article* talk pages. But it's also applicable (with the exception of a few aspects of archiving) to *Wikipedia talk* pages, *Template talk* pages, *Help talk* pages, *Category talk* pages, and so on. Wikipedia calls these *standard* talk pages. The information in this section is also relevant to posting at free-form discussion pages, like the Help desk (*WP:HD*) and the set of pages that make up the discussion area called the *Village Pump* (shortcut: *WP:VP*). (User talk pages are different; these are discussed on page 156.)

Posting Conventions

In addition to always signing your posts, following a few other guidelines will make you look like an experienced, knowledgeable editor right off the bat. Beside the items on this list, pay attention to what other editors are doing on talk pages. Read before you post. The more you avoid annoying or confusing other editors, the more seriously they'll take you.

- On an article talk page, when editors say, "this page" they're usually referring to the *article* page itself. If you want to refer to the talk page itself (as, for example, when asking about archiving), say *this talk page*, not *this page*.

- Piped links (page 15) and shortcuts to Wikipedia policies, guidelines, and other instructional pages are common on talk pages, typically more common than fully spelled-out wikilinks. While a shortcut like *[[WP:NPOV]]* may not have any obvious meaning to many editors, the expectation is that those interested enough to read a talk page should be interested enough to follow such links to find out what they refer to. (To an outsider, this seems like jargon; to an experienced editor, it's an efficient way of doing things.)

- Avoid text that is CAPITAL LETTERS; it's considered SHOUTING. Similarly, talk pages almost never use boldface text. Use italics (double apostrophes around text) in moderation for emphasis. You can also use underlining (place a <u> tag at the beginning and a </u> tag at the end), but again, use it sparingly. Use complete words, not text messaging abbreviations. In short, if it's wrong in email, it's wrong on a talk page.

- Talk pages don't have sections at the bottom for footnotes, "see also", external links, and so on. If you want to discuss a source, provide a URL for it (within single brackets) within the body of your comment.

UP TO SPEED

Top Templates

The majority of existing article talk pages have one or more templates at the top—and often that's *all* they have. Most templates indicate that the article is within the scope of a particular WikiProject (Chapter 9); most of the remainder are essentially notes about the article's history (nominated for deletion, assessed as being of a certain quality, and so on).

In 2007, Wikipedia introduced two templates to reduce the proliferation of templates at the top of article talk pages: *{{combines WikiProject templates}}* and *{{combines page history}}*. If you come across a talk page where you can't see the table of contents until you scroll down, adding one of these two templates might help. If one or both of these templates are already in place, consider putting *{{skiptotoctalk}}* at the very top of the page, before any other templates. This template provides an quick link for other editors to bypass the templates.

Should you bother to read the templates? If you're thinking about proposing that the article be deleted, you should definitely look at the article talk page. You might, for example, find a link to a deletion discussion about the article. But generally you won't care about the templates when you discuss improvements to an article, so a quick glance should suffice.

Posting to a Brand-new Article Talk Page

Every article is associated with an article talk page, even if the article talk page has yet to be created. If the word "discussion" in the tab at the top of an article is red, not blue, then you create that page if you post to it.

NOTE

Yes, it's confusing that the tab that goes to the *talk* page has the word *discussion* on it. That's one of Wikipedia's idiosyncrasies, which is why sometimes in this book you'll see the wording "talk (discussion) page."

When you create an article talk page by clicking the red link, you should add a section heading at the top of the edit box: On the first line, put the name of the new section, with two equal signs on each side. Talk pages don't have a lead section (a top section with text, without a heading). If you find such a lead section, you should add a heading, which can be as simple as == *Old comments from December 2006* ==.

When you've added the heading and your comment, put your signature at the end (four tildes), do a quick preview (as always), and, if things look okay, then save the page.

Posting to an Existing Article Talk Page

If the article talk page already exists, then what you do depends on whether you're commenting on an existing topic (section), or starting a discussion on a new topic. Before you make that choice, however, you check to see if there's a link at the top of the page to older, archived comments. If there is, you should follow the link to at least the most recent archive. You may find the answer to your question there, or at least get a better sense of the most sensitive aspects of the article (the ones that editors argue over).

NOTE

You'll learn how to create a talk page archive and archive old comments on page 155.

GEM IN THE ROUGH

Liquid Threads

A number of people have been doing a fair amount of work on a new discussion system called *Liquid Threads*. The model includes *channels* that commenters can attach to one or more articles; *threads* (a collection of comments about a specific subject); comments themselves (each of which has a database entry and version history); and summary pages for each channel and thread.

Exactly when (or even if) the English Wikipedia will roll out Liquid Threads, and how the new system will affect existing article talk pages, is not clear at this writing.

Adding a comment to an existing section

When you add a comment to an existing section, you should click the "edit" link for the section, not for the entire page. In general, add your comment to the bottom of the section. You may be tempted to interweave your comments into the comments of others, particularly if someone has made points 1, 2, and 3. Don't. Until Wikipedia gets specialized software for threaded discussions (see the box above), put all your comments at the bottom.

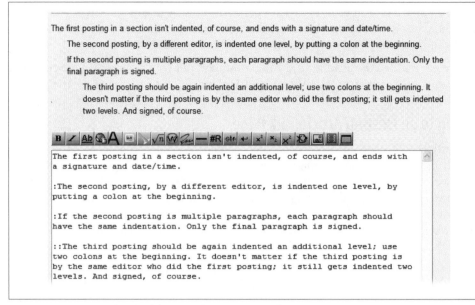

Figure 8-1. An example of indentation, done in the sandbox.

Spacing and *indentation* are critical to easy readability of discussion sections. Always put a blank line between your posting and the posting before it, and indent your comment by using one or more colons. Thus the first posting in a section is flush left; the second posting is indented by using a colon, the third indented more by using two colons, and so on. Figure 8-1 shows a detailed example.

After a section has reached five or six levels of indentation (that is, after the most recent editor has used five or six colons in front of her comment), it's acceptable to start the next comment without any indentation at all (that is, flush left on the page). Starting over on the left avoids having new text in the section being squeezed into (say) less than half the page, on the far right.

NOTE

When going from major indentation to no indentation, some editors put "(undent)" or something similar at the beginning of their first paragraph. If you do this, everyone will know that you didn't forget to indent by mistake.

Starting a new section

When you want to discuss something that isn't mentioned on the article talk page, or you want to start a discussion on a matter where discussion is quite old, start a new section. (What "quite old" means is a matter of judgment; on a page with few comments, even something 3 months old might be recent enough to continue posting to a section rather than starting a new section. On a very busy article talk page, a topic where conversation stopped just a few weeks ago may merit a new section.)

UP TO SPEED

Restarting an Old Conversation

If you're starting a new section of a talk page, and there's a previous section on the same topic, provide a link to that previous section, and a brief comment on why you're starting a new section. Here's an example:

I'd like to restart the discussion above, about [[#Removing the POV tag]]. I think...

The "#" symbol in the wikilink shows that the link is to another section on the same page (what follows the "#" symbol must be exactly the section title for the link to work). Here's another example:

Continuing a [[Article talk:Foobarness/Archive 1#What about the anti-foobar lobby?| previous discussion]] where there seemed to be no consensus, how about a compromise where...

In this example, the wikilink is to a section on the first archive page. The vertical line ("|") (sometimes called a *pipe*) hides the full name of the link from the reader. The reader sees, "Continuing a previous discussion...", where "previous discussion" is in blue, and is a clickable link.

To correctly start a new section, use the "+" tab at the top of the talk page (see Figure 8-2), rather than editing the entire page or editing the bottom-most section of the page.

When you use the "+" tab to start a new section:

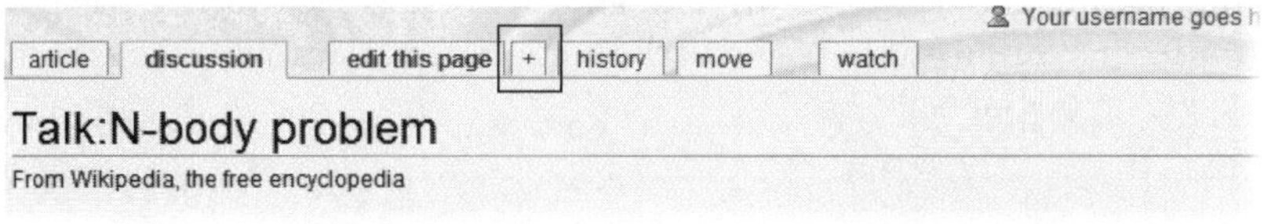

Figure 8-2. The plus ("+") tab on article talk pages lets you start a new section. Click it rather than the "edit this page" link.

- It automatically places the section (after you save your edit) below all the prior sections (which is the correct location).
- It saves you the trouble of adding equal signs to format the section heading.
- It eliminates the need for you to add a separate edit summary.
- It guarantees that you won't have an edit conflict when you save your edit.

Use a neutral heading for the section: Rather than *Article has blatant point of view*, for example, write *Issue with point of view* (or just *POV*). Don't mention any particular editor in the heading; your posting is to provide information for all editors. As always, make sure you add your signature (four tildes) at the end of your comment (but *not* on a separate line), and preview your edit before saving it.

POWER USERS' CLINIC

Highlighting Text

In your comments on article talk pages, you may want to highlight some text—for example, text from the article that you'd like other editors to review, or text you're proposing for the article.

You can place text in a light green box by adding this code (you'll find it at *WP:TP*, so you can copy and paste it from there):

```
<div class="boilerplate" style="background-color: #efe;
margin: 2em 0 0 0; padding: 0 10px 0 10px; border: 1px
dotted #aaa;">XXXXX</div>
```

(Put the text you want to highlight where the XXXXX appears, inside the *div* tags.)

Good Talk Page Practices

Used correctly, an article talk page reads like a conversation among a group of people who respect each other; who acknowledge that it's possible to have differing viewpoints yet reach agreement on the wording of content (which is about *facts*); who are constantly looking for ways to find compromises that are both correct and acceptable to the others in the discussion, and who focus exclusively on improving the articles.

As an editor, you can help move pages toward this goal by following that model. In addition, you should note the following good practices:

- **It's better to fix an article than to complain about it on the article talk page**. Per the guideline page *Wikipedia:Be bold* (shortcut: *WP:BB*), if you see a problem, the best approach is to simply fix it yourself. You don't have to fix it all at once, just start and keep chipping away at it. By contrast, putting a note on the talk page that "this article needs a lot of work" is pointless, because *most* articles in Wikipedia need a lot of work. Experienced editors already know that. Posting such a comment isn't going to magically summon legions of editors to fix things.

  The exception to being bold is where the wording of an article—typically on a controversial subject—has already been extensively debated. If an article talk page is empty, then don't hesitate to edit the article. But if the article talk page is lengthy and has dozens of archived talk pages containing older postings, being bold can be foolhardy. Except for minor copyediting or other non-controversial matters, consider posting a suggestion or question to the talk page. (Another acceptable alternative is to spend a lot of time reading comments and article versions, figure out exactly what's happening, and then edit the article.)

- **Be specific rather than general**. If you think the article has a biased point of view, and you're not going to try to fix it yourself, then cite a couple of specific sentences you find problematical, as examples, rather than making a general statement. If you don't have time to find examples, then don't post at all.

- **It's better to quote another editor you disagree with than to paraphrase that editor**. Paraphrasing someone else's words risks an argument that you improperly summarized something that you disagreed with. (The convention for talk pages, when quoting something from another editor's comments, is to make the quoted text *italic*, by placing double apostrophes on each side, which clearly distinguishes it from your opinion.)

- **Don't just name a policy, link to it**. Shortcuts don't take much time to type, but they make it easy for others to get to the relevant Wikipedia rules. If you're discussing an edit, linking to a diff (page 87) avoids any ambiguity about what you're talking about. Provide links to sources whenever the discussion is about facts (a URL is sufficient; save your full citations for articles themselves). Links also help you, when you come back to something a day or a week later, remember why you said what you did.

- **Ask for sources**. If you find unsourced non-biographical information that seems questionable (for biographical information, remove it, per page 152), moving it to the talk page can get the attention of editors who otherwise might ignore the lack of a source. But the norm is to insert a *{{fact}}* template ("citation needed") into the article at the point of question, and then give other editors a chance to respond. Only after some time (at least a week, and with useful information, perhaps as long as a couple of months), should you move the information to a talk page.

- **Use the article talk page to supplement your edit summary**. Try to fit an explanation of an edit in the edit summary. For the rare cases where you need more room, put your explanation on the talk page, and *See talk/discussion page* in the edit summary.

What Not to Post

Article talk pages are for discussing how to improve the content of articles, including the reliability of sources that have been or could be cited. Things that should *not* be on talk pages include violations of privacy, unsourced controversial biographical information, idle chat, personal attacks, and discussions about editors' behavior.

- **Personal information** (home addresses, email addresses, phone numbers, and so on) doesn't belong in Wikipedia articles, for privacy reasons. Such information also doesn't belong on article talk pages, or anywhere else for that matter, whether about the subject of the article or about a Wikipedia editor.

  External links to pages outside Wikipedia that have personal information are similarly inappropriate if the primary purpose is to lead readers and other editors to that personal information. If you see personal information or improper external links, remove that immediately. If what you removed was particularly intrusive or problematical, bring the matter to the attention of administrators (see page 163).

- **Unsourced or poorly sourced controversial biographical information** is inappropriate for article talk pages, as well as for articles. If you see this type of information, remove it. What's controversial? Although the term is subjective, think of the kind of statement to which someone is likely to say, "Prove it!"

  When you remove such postings, you should cite *WP:BLP* in your edit summary, not only to justify your edit, but also so that those unfamiliar with the policy can follow the link and edify themselves.

- **Wikichat** is text whose purpose is anything other than improving the related article —usually a comment *about* the subject an article, rather than about the wording or information in the article. Saying that a presidential candidate is inept, or that a well-known celebrity should be ashamed of herself for what she just did, belongs on a blog, discussion forum, or personal Web page. It has nothing to do with improving an article. If you see wikichat on an article talk page, regardless of its age, remove it. (In the very rare case that it's lead to a constructive posting about improving the article itself, you have to leave it.)

- **Lengthy arguments, large amounts of proposed text, or long lists of proposed or supportive sources**. If you can't make a point in two to four paragraphs, then you're either using Wikipedia as a soapbox (which is a no-no); or confused (work on what you want to say offline first); or trying to make multiple points or cover multiple subjects in a single section (in which case create separate sections, with one point per section, or one section with subsections).

NOTE

Occasionally, you may have a legitimate need to post a lot of text, if you're be proposing a major rewrite to a lengthy and controversial section of an article, or to an entire article. In that case, create a subpage (page 56). So, for example, from the *Talk:Bigfoot* page, you might create a subpage *Talk:Bigfoot/Relationship to Himalayan Yeti*, with a proposed rewrite of a controversial section of the article *Bigfoot*.

- **Incivility and personal attacks**. Article Talk pages are for discussing content, not contributors. In politics, a common tactic is to question the motives, credentials, capabilities, or other aspects of an opponent. At Wikipedia, that's completely inappropriate. If you don't think an argument is logical, or consistent with Wikipedia policies and guidelines, explain why. Don't label the editor who posted something you think is stupid or biased as *being* an idiot or *being* biased, even if he has demonstrated stupidity or extreme bias elsewhere. That's not the way to win arguments at Wikipedia. Rather, it's a good way to get warned that *you're* being disruptive. (Chapter 10 discusses the *right way* to handle disputes over content.)

Wikipedia has three overlapping guidelines regarding commenting about other editors: *Assume good faith* (shortcut: *WP:AGF*); *Civility* (shortcut: *WP:CIVIL*), and *no personal attacks* (shortcut: *WP:NPA*). Read them before you do your first response to a posting by another editor on a talk page.

NOTE

Handling incivility and personal attacks by *other editors*, particularly if directed at you, is discussed extensively in Chapter 11.

- **Discussions of behavior**. Article talk pages are the wrong place to discuss what you see as mistaken behavior by another editor. A user talk page is the right place to discuss behavior (see page 156). You don't want to derail discussions about improving the contents of articles (remember, that's the purpose of the article talk page). Equally important, you want other editors and administrators to be able to find comments about an editor's behavior *on that editor's user talk page*; not by searching through article talk pages.

If you've removed some text (see the first three items in this list), then post a note on the editor's user talk page about the matter. A link to the page *Wikipedia:Talk page* (shortcut: *WP:TP*) and/or *Wikipedia:Talk page guidelines* (shortcut: *WP:TPG*) can be helpful, if you're not citing another policy or guideline.

- **Vandalism or spam**. You can always remove vandalism or spam without discussion. Simply explain what you're doing in your edit summary (page 9).

Editing or Deleting Existing Comments

In general, the rule for editing or deleting a comment that you or another editor has posted to an article talk page is simple: Don't. That goes for fixing spelling errors, typos, run-on sentences, or any other minor wording changes, no matter how trivial. At Wikipedia, a talk page is essentially a *transcript*; no matter how well-intentioned you are in your editing, other editors aren't going to see it that way.

There are only two categories of standard exceptions to this "do not edit" rule:

- Privacy violations, violations of *WP:BLP*, and wikichat should all be deleted, as discussed in the prior section, as well as vandalism and spamming comments.

- It's okay to change indentation, or to fix the rare formatting problem that makes a comment difficult to read, since you're really not altering the *words* that were previously posted. Similarly, it's okay to insert subsection headings, or to split a section in two (for example, when an editor mistakenly starts a new topic). Just don't alter anyone's words, not even the *order* of anyone's words.

NOTE

There's a third exception when it's okay to edit comments for clarity, called *refactoring*. See the box on page 155.

Before you do any editing beyond the exceptions just listed, regardless of whether you're editing your posting or not, read the "Editing comments" section of *Wikipedia:Talk page guidelines* (shortcut: *WP:TPG*) to be absolutely certain that what you're doing is acceptable.

WARNING

Even editing your own comment when it's the last one posted to a talk page is borderline problematical, since someone else may have read it and been influenced by the posting. The more recent the posting, the less likely anyone else has seen it, so if you just posted something and immediately realized you made an error, it's okay to go into edit mode and fix it. However, if you get an edit conflict (page 11) when you try to save your change, you need to abandon the edit and read the talk page guidelines on using strikeouts to fix your own comment.

Refactoring Talk Pages

Refactoring is a form of editing to improve readability of a talk page while preserving meaning. It can include removing superfluous content, summarizing long passages, and other actions that alter the presentation of comments. It's rarely done, but it's allowed in Wikipedia. Ideally, a consensus of editors will agree that it's worth doing, and who will do it.

In theory, refactoring can make closed (completed) discussions easier for editors, in the future, to understand what's been discussed and agreed on, but most of the time, the existing discussion is fine as is. Moreover, editors generally prefer to concentrate on current matters, and have no interest in refactoring work. Also, if a talk page has open discussions that need resolving, refactoring can lead to arguments as to whether the refactoring was done fairly.

However, if you're willing to take the time to improve an existing talk page by refactoring, consider one of these two methods:

- Do conservative refactoring. That is, add subheadings and reorganize comments within individual sections, but don't create new sections or move contents between sections. Adding section summaries can also be part of conservative refactoring.

- Instead of rewriting a page, write a new page, organizing the outstanding issues and identifying the points that have been made for each issue. Then archive the sections on the current talk page so that they're out of the way, but still available without having to go to a historical version of the page.

For full details, see *Wikipedia:Refactoring talk pages* (shortcut: *WP:RTP*).

Archiving

Archiving a talk page means moving one or more sections of the page to a subpage. For example, sections of the page *Talk:Sherlock Holmes* might be moved to *Talk:Sherlock Holmes/Archive 1*. The goal of archiving is to clear out the talk page so editors new to the page can quickly see current discussion.

Any editor can archive. If you choose to do so, be sure to archive entire sections, not parts of sections, and archive only sections that are no longer in use. Avoid archiving a section where a discussion is still ongoing (where there's a recent posting within the past week or so).

There are no hard-and-fast rules for deciding when a section can or should be archived. In general, talk pages with a lot of postings should be archived frequently to keep their length down; low-volume talk pages should be archived rarely or not at all. If a talk page is relatively short (for example, less than 10 sections, none of them long), then don't waste your time archiving parts of it. The older sections may be irrelevant, but editors can easily ignore them.

The mechanics of creating an archive of an article talk page are essentially the same as creating an archive for one's own talk page, as described in the steps on page 159. Just be sure to place a link to the archive pages at the top of the talk page, so any editor can quickly get to the archives.

NOTE

If you archive a section, and another editor puts it back onto the talk page (which is extremely rare), don't bother to contest the matter. Let other editors (if they care) deal with the matter, if it needs dealing with, which would be only if an editor appears to be deliberately disruptive.

At some point, an archive page can get too long, so an editor creates a new archive page. Since archive pages are infrequently read, it's not worth fussing over whether an archive page is too long or not long enough to start a new one. Here's a rough guideline: Never start a new archive page unless the old one is at least the equivalent of three printed pages, and always start a new archive page (rather than adding sections to the current one) when the current archive has reached the equivalent of five or six printed pages.

WORD TO THE WISE

Editing Archive Pages

Archives are, in a sense, historical documents. *Don't edit them.* Except for adding new sections to the most recent archive page, it's bad form to add, delete, or change text on an archive page. There's also no point changing or deleting something embarrassing, since anything that was on the page is still visible via the page history. And virtually no one reads the archives anyway, so there's no point to adding something.

If you absolutely must comment on a matter discussed in the archive, then make a *copy* of the text in the section where that matter is discussed, and create a new section on the article talk page that begins with that copied text, followed by your comment. Make sure that you clearly indicate, in both your edit summary and in the new section you're creating on the article talk page, that you've copied text from the archive.

User Talk Page Postings

As noted above, Wikipedia has two types of user talk pages—standard talk pages, such as article talk pages, and user talk pages. The two have similar formatting, but very different purposes.

Why post a message on another editor's user talk page? One common reason is to issue a warning for vandalism or spam (page 130). But you can also use user talk pages to ask a question ("How did you do that?"), to thank someone, to ask someone for help with an article, to make a suggestion, to point out an interesting page or posting to

Figure 8-3. You see this "You have new messages (last change)" alert after someone edits your user talk page. If you're a registered editor, you need to be logged in to see this alert. You see it only when you open a new page or refresh a page you're viewing.

someone you've worked with before, and so on. The more involved an editor is with Wikipedia, the more likely it is that her user talk page has a lot of different postings.

User Talk Page Basics

When you post to a user talk page, you have the same two basic options discussed earlier in this chapter: Post to an existing section, or start a new section. Almost always, unless you've posted very recently, you'll post to a new section, using the "+" tab. There's often only one post per section, either because no reply is needed, or because of the way Wikipedia editors normally interact via user talk pages, as discussed in the next section.

Just as with article talk pages, you should use indentation to make it easier for other editors to see who said what, if the conversation goes beyond a single post. And while you can split sections or change headings for clarity, those types of thing are rare on user talk pages (as on article talk pages).

When you post to a user talk page, it generates an alert for that user, as shown in Figure 8-3.

The alert isn't instantaneous: For a registered user, the user must be logged in and must change or refresh a Wikipedia page. Editors using an IP address don't have to log in, of course, to see such a message, but they have to visit a new page or refresh a page to see it.

Extended Conversations

Contrary to what you might expect, if a user (let's say AvId) posts to a user page (let's say *User talk:BeYonC*), Wikipedia etiquette dictates that BeYonC should *not* reply on the same page. Rather, BeYonC should post her reply on the *User talk:AvId* page. The rationale is that her reply will result in an alert to AvId, who will then post on BeYonC's user talk page; that will alert BeYonC that there's something new on her user talk page. If she needs to reply, she'll post again on AvId's user talk page (creating a new alert), and so on.

One odd result of this scheme is that half of a two-way conversation occurs on one user talk page with the other half on the other user talk page. In the case of a running conversation, a third editor, viewing only one side of the conversation, can get confused. (But that's not normally a problem, since most user talk pages are boring to anyone other than the editor herself.)

Some editors (typically administrators, who get a lot of messages) don't follow this norm. You should always take a quick look at the top of a user talk page before posting there, to see if there's a note saying that the editor will respond on *his own* user talk page, and similarly that if the editor posted to your user talk page, you should reply *there*. This approach has the advantage of keeping the conversation all in one place, and the disadvantage that only one of the two editors involved gets the automated alert about a change to his user talk page. You may need to figure out a way to check back periodically to see if the conversation has been continued. (Chapter 6, on monitoring pages, discusses Wikipedia-based alternatives for monitoring pages. Or you can, of course, just put a sticky note on your monitor. A proposed new talk page system, Liquid Threads, discussed on page 147, may solve this problem.)

Article Content

Occasionally a discussion on a user talk page turns into a conversation about what should or shouldn't be the content of a specific article. Such discussion belongs on an *article* talk page, not a user page. If this happens on your user talk page, move the discussion to the corresponding article talk page.

There's a fairly standard process for moving text from one discussion page to another:

1. In edit mode, copy the section heading and all text in the section to the clipboard.
2. On the target page (in this case, the article talk page), go into edit mode (generally in a new section, via the "+" tab) and paste the information from the clipboard. Make any deletions you want (in this case, some of the initial comments may not pertain to the article).
3. Just below the heading, add a note at the top of the section, such as *Moved from [[User talk:Name of User]]* (in italics). Save the edit.
4. On the originating talk page, delete all the text that you just pasted to the article talk page. Add a note with a link to where the discussion was moved to, like: *Moved discussion to [[Talk: Elephantiasis#Do elephants get this disease?]]*. (This wikilink goes directly to a talk page section, because of the "#" sign and the section title following it.)
5. Add an edit summary saying the same thing as the note, including the wikilink, and save the user talk page.

Editing or Deleting Existing Comments

In some ways you *own* your user talk page; in some ways you don't. On the one hand, you don't have the right to prevent others from posting to it, and you should never modify comments by others, except for indentation and the addition of a section heading. On the other hand, you can delete comments by others at will, as well as to delete entire sections of the page. (Archiving, discussed in the next section, is the preferred way to remove comments from your user talk page, but it's not mandated.)

You should still avoid editing your own comments except as described at *Wikipedia:Talk page guidelines* (shortcut: *WP:TPG*).

Editing any existing comments on another editor's user talk page is absolutely inappropriate. (Even editing your own comments is normally inappropriate, unless you do it very quickly after you initially post.) The only clear exceptions are vandalism involving deletion of content, privacy violations (posting of personal information), and violations of the policy on biographical information (*WP:BLP*)—feel free to revert those. Otherwise, if you see something that you think is a serious problem—for example, an extreme personal attack—either let the editor handle the matter herself, or bring it to the attention of administrators at *Wikipedia:Administrators' noticeboard/Incidents* (shortcut: *WP:AN/I*), especially if it's a recurring problem.

NOTE

Some editors consider personal attacks (say, from a frustrated vandal) a badge of honor—it shows they're having an impact on problem editors. They therefore keep (and archive) such postings. That's another reason why you shouldn't remove content from another editor's user talk page that you, personally, wouldn't find acceptable.

Archiving Postings on Your Own User Talk Page

Except for vandalism, newsletters, and possibly personal attacks, the recommended approach for removing text from your user talk page is to *archive* it, not delete it. Usually, you archive a talk page by moving complete sections of comments to subpages. When a subpage starts getting long, start a new archive page.

NOTE

The standard way to number *article* talk page archives is simple: *Archive 1, Archive 2*, and so on. With your user talk page, you can be more flexible if you want. For example, you can call October-December archived sections *Archive Q4 2007*. Still, there's little reason not to stick to the basic numbering and save your creativity for other things.

You archive a talk page in two phases: First create the archive page, and then move one or more sections of comments to the archive page. (Once you've mastered the technique, you can create an archive page at the same time as you do the archiving.)

Creating an archive page for your user talk page

1. On your user talk page, click "edit this page".

   You can go to your user talk page quickly via the "my talk" link, which is at your screen's upper right, when you're logged in.

Figure 8-4. The archive box template creates a neat list of archive pages. You can create archive links without using the archive box template, but the box is a handy way—particularly on article talk pages—to show other editors that older postings have been archived.

2. At the top of the page, *below* any other templates at the top of the page, add an archive box template: *{{archive box| [[/Archive 1]] }}*.

   If the archive box template already existed, and you were adding a second archive page, the template would look like this: *{{archive box| [[/Archive 1]] [[/Archive 2]]}}*.

NOTE

Everything after the vertical bar ("|") symbol is free-form, so you could be fancier and do something like the following, which would put each archive page on a separate line:

```
{{archive box |
* [[Archive 1]] January, 2008
* [[Archive 2]] February, 2008
}}
```

---

3. Add a brief edit summary, do a quick preview, and then save the page.

   You now have a red link to your archive page, with an archive box to set it apart from the rest of the page, as illustrated in Figure 8-4.

Archiving user talk page content

In the previous section, you created an archive box on your user talk page. The box you created includes a link to the *Archive 1* page. Now it's time for you to move a section from your user talk page, putting it in storage on that archive page. (If you don't have an old section on your user talk page that you can archive, then use the "+" tab to create and save a new section—call it, say, *Archive test*—so that you do have something to archive.)

1. Open the archive page for editing. If it's a red link, then simply click that link; if it's a blue link (meaning that the page exists), then click the link, and then click "edit this page".

If you're editing this page for the first time, add the *{{talkarchive}}* template to the top of the page. This template adds a notice explaining that the page is an archive, and links back to the main talk page.

2. On your user talk page, click the "edit this page" tab to open the page for editing.

   You see the edit box, containing all your talk page's text, ripe for cutting.

3. In the edit box, highlight one or more consecutive sections that you want to archive. Cut the sections' heading and body text.

   On Windows or Linux, press Ctrl+X (or right-click, and then choose Cut); on Mac, press ⌘-X (or Control-click, and then choose Cut).

4. Switch to the archive page; paste the removed sections into the edit box of the archive page (below any other archived sections, if any).

   Don't worry about strict chronological order (for example, sorting sections by when they were first created). The rule is simply that the most recently archived sections are at the bottom.

   Repeat steps 3 and 4 as needed.

5. Add a brief edit summary to each of the two pages, do a quick preview of each, and then save both.

POWER USERS' CLINIC

Automated archiving

Wikipedia has several bots that editors can use to archive talk pages. They're most commonly used, however, for pages like the Wikipedia Help desk, which gets a lot of postings every day. If you have a page handled by an archive bot on your watchlist, or check the revision history of such a page, you can see the edits of such bots. Otherwise, you'll probably never encounter such a bot, or need to.

- Archiving most article talk pages is best done by hand. It's nice to leave up a section or two, even if they're old, rather than present editors with a page without any visible comments. Another reason is that human editors can apply discretion: Is a month-old comment still useful? Should a week-old comment be archived because the page is getting too long and the matter is closed?

- Unless you're an administrator or an active user who gets a lot of postings on your *user* talk page, it's not a lot of work to archive sections once every month or two, and it's good practice for archiving article talk pages.

If you do decide that an article talk page would benefit from an archiving bot like MiaBot or ClueBot III, make sure you post something about your intent to set up a bot for archiving, and that you get consensus from other editors on both the concept and the details (in particular, how old the most recent comment in a section must be before archiving that section).

Figure 8-5. The toolbox set of links is on the left of the Wikipedia screen. You don't see "E-mail this user" unless you have a confirmed email address in your profile, and, in your preferences, you've turned on "Enable e-mail from other users" (see page 384).

Communicating via Email and IRC

Besides posting to a talk page, you have two other options—email and Internet Relay Chat (IRC)—to interact with other editors. In such cases, you're taking the conversation outside Wikipedia and communicating with fellow editors just like your friends and coworkers. All the warnings about contacting strangers via the Internet apply.

Email

Wikipedia has no policy or guideline about when it's appropriate to email another editor. In Wikipedia—like other wikis—the culture dictates that conversations about articles, behavior, policies and processes, selections of administrators and other functionaries, and so on, be done on wiki pages, so that everyone can see who said what. Still, email may be better sometimes: a friendly suggestion about behavior to a long-time contributor, an invitation to meet face to face, or perhaps a query as to whether an editor would be interested in being nominated to be an administrator.

To email another editor, both you and the other editor must have turned on email in Wikipedia. If you didn't enter an email address and turn on email when you registered, (page 51), or want to change your email address, see the instructions on page 384 on how to change your preferences so that you can email other editors.

To find out if the other editor has also enabled email, you need to go to his user page or user talk page, and, in the "toolbox" set of links on the left side, find the "E-mail this user" link (Figure 8-5).

Click that link to start the email process. You then see one of two things – a page with the heading, "No e-mail address", that says, "This user has not specified a valid e-mail address, or has chosen not to receive e-mail from other users", or a screen to compose the email (Figure 8-6).

If you get an email from another editor via Wikipedia, you're not obligated to reply via email (and thereby divulge your email address to that editor). If you're not interested in an email conversation with that editor, post some sort of reply (even if just a polite

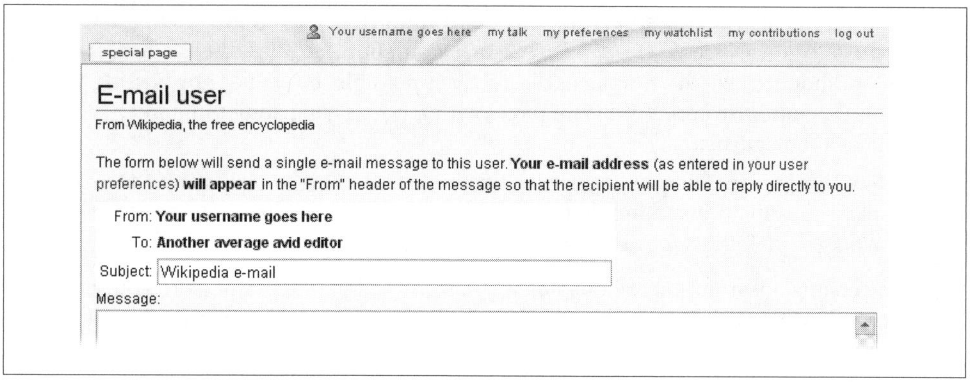

Figure 8-6. Clicking "E-mail this user" on someone's user page or user talk page opens this "E-mail user" form. When you send email to another editor, it originates from a Wikipedia server, though the email will show your email address as the "from" address when the recipient gets it.

variant of "sorry, not interested") on the editor's user talk page, as a courtesy to let the editor know that you got his email.

NOTE

In the rare instance that you get spam, vandalism, or some other problematical email from another editor, report it at *Wikipedia:Administrators' noticeboard/Incidents* (shortcut: *WP:AN/I*).

WORD TO THE WISE

Privacy for editors

You can find Wikipedia's privacy policy at *http://wikimediafoundation.org/wiki/Priva cy_policy*. It's supplemented by the Wikimedia Foundation's Access to nonpublic data policy, at *http://wikimediafoundation.org/wiki/Access_to_nonpublic_data_policy*. Basically, the Foundation (which runs Wikipedia) won't sell, rent, trade, or otherwise divulge any information about your identity, including your email address, unless you get yourself in enough trouble to personally come to the attention of the Foundation, law enforcement, or someone who can convince a judge to issue a subpoena.

Wikipedia has several Ombudsmen to receive complaints about violations of the privacy policy; more information is at *http://meta.wikimedia.org/wiki/Ombudsman_com mission*.

If you do make a mistake and post personal information to a Wikipedia page, or see personal information posted by another user, delete it immediately, to get it off the current version of the page. (The most common mistake is posting one's own email address.) If the disclosure of information is significant enough (for example, a street address, home phone number, or date of birth of an editor), you should do one of two things:

- Contact an administrator, who can remove history pages from the view of normal editors. The pages are still visible to other administrators, but that's a limited, very trusted group. (See *Wikipedia:Selective deletion*, shortcut *WP:SELDEL*, for details.) You should make the contact as discreetly as possible: by email or by posting a diff on the administrator's user talk page, with a note saying something like, "Please take a look at this.").

- Request that the history pages with this information be blocked from the view of all editors, including administrators. To do so, follow the instructions at the page *Wikipedia:Requests for oversight* (shortcut: *WP:RFO*).

If the personal information about a person was posted by different person, you should do both these things, to ensure that Wikipedia isn't being used as a platform to violate anyone's privacy.

IRC

The Freenode IRC network (*http://freenode.net/*) has chat rooms dedicated to Wikipedia 24 hours a day, where editors can have real-time discussions. Many Wikipedians have an IRC window open for chatting, and hop back and forth between it and other windows in which they're working on Wikipedia. If you're familiar and comfortable with IRC, this may be the best way to get help whenever you encounter something about which you'd like advice.

You'll find full information about IRC at Wikipedia on the page *Wikipedia:IRC channels* (shortcut: *WP:IRC*). There are more details at the page *Wikipedia:IRC tutorial* (shortcut: *WP:IRCT*). You can log in to Freenode's Wikipedia IRC Help Channel at *http://tools.wikimedia.de/~bjelleklang/pjirc/index.php*.

NOTE

If you're familiar with user scripts (Chapter 21), you might want to take a look at the "IRC channel scripts" section of the page *Wikipedia:Scripts* (shortcut: *WP:SCRIPTS*).

CHAPTER 9

WikiProjects and Other Group Efforts

Everything so far in this book has been about you as an individual editor, working on your own, interacting with others only to discuss problems or changes to articles. But editors at Wikipedia also work together in groups, formal or informal. Not only is there strength in numbers, there's energy and fun. Such group work is one of the things that make Wikipedia as much an online community as it is an encyclopedia.

Most editors edit articles that particularly interest them: articles about television comedy shows; the region where they live; sports; areas of science or technology; history; multiplayer video games; and so on. If you're one of them, the next natural step is joining a topical area *WikiProject*—a group of editors working on a collection of articles related to the same topic. Or you may take pleasure in a specific kind of editing: fixing footnotes; improving lead paragraphs; or adding geographical coordinates to articles. There are also WikiProjects for editors with such interests.

Although working in WikiProjects is the most common kind of group effort in Wikipedia, there are others: *Collaborations* are where a group of editors works on a single article for a week, fortnight, or month, and then turns to the next article they choose, often within a broad topical area. *Organizations* are less formal and less numerous than WikiProjects. *One-time initiatives* form and end whenever editors see the need and other editors agree to help.

This chapter describes each of these group efforts, and shows you where to get more information about the groups that already exist. And if you don't find a group that covers something you're interested in, this chapter also tells you how to create a group focused on your interest.

WikiProjects

There are basically two types of WikiProjects—topical ones that focus on a subset of articles in a particular area (like *WikiProject Poker*), and cross-cutting ones that could theoretically work on *any* article in Wikipedia (like *WikiProject League of Copyeditors*).

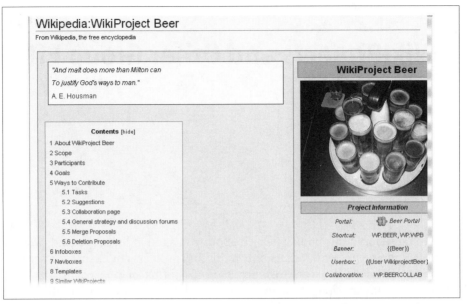

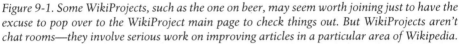

Figure 9-1. Some WikiProjects, such as the one on beer, may seem worth joining just to have the excuse to pop over to the WikiProject main page to check things out. But WikiProjects aren't chat rooms—they involve serious work on improving articles in a particular area of Wikipedia.

In all, there are over a thousand WikiProjects (there's no official count), of which about a third are labeled inactive. Over 80 percent of all WikiProjects are topical; the rest are cross-cutting.

Topic-specific WikiProjects

WikiProjects that focus on a subset of Wikipedia articles are listed in the main directory, which you'll find at the page *Wikipedia:WikiProject Council/Directory* (shortcut: *WP:PROJDIR*). Four major subdirectories are linked to from there:

- Culture and the arts (for example, *WikiProject Beer*, *WikiProject Discworld*) (See Figure 9-1)

- Geographical (for example, *WikiProject British and Irish hills*, *WikiProject California*)

- History and society (for example, *WikiProject Military history*, *WikiProject Universities*)

- Science, technology, and engineering (for example, *WikiProject Space exploration*, *WikiProject Linux*)

Each of the four major groupings has hundreds of different WikiProjects in it, but there are definitely gaps—that is, *opportunities* for additional WikiProjects. That's because there isn't any person or group at Wikipedia responsible for top-down organizing:

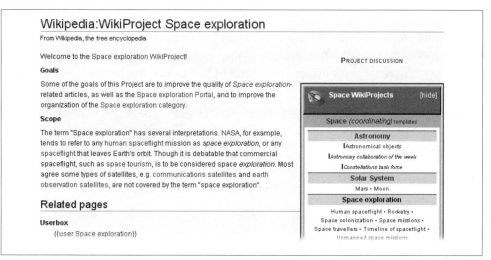

Figure 9-2. WikiProject Space exploration *is one of three WikiProjects concerned with the larger topic of Space. To coordinate efforts with two other related WikiProjects, the three have created a common template that summarizes the scope of each.*

Every WikiProject that exists is the result of individual editors deciding that they wanted to create it.

Often topical WikiProjects are coordinated with each other when there's potential overlap. Figure 9-2 shows an example.

Cross-cutting WikiProjects

The 150 or so cross-cutting WikiProjects focus on Wikipedia-wide issues, rather than on a subset of articles in a particular topical area. Most of these fit into two general categories:

- **Article focused**. Deal with things like categories, citation cleanup, counter-vandalism, illustrations, image monitoring, lists, maps, neutrality in articles, and spam fighting, to list just a few. Such tasks are often described as maintenance, though much of their work is focused on enhancing articles rather than fixing mistakes.

- **Process and editor focused**. Devoted to awards to editors, the closing of deletion discussions, improving database analysis, improving user pages, and so on.

And then there are the more or less one-of-a-kind WikiProjects, such as:

- *Wikipedia:WikiProject Classroom coordination*. Covers "all formal educational assignments to edit Wikipedia articles including primary, secondary, and university level classes" (to quote from the project's main page).

- *Wikipedia:Scientific peer review*. Its goal is to "offer a high-calibre, content-oriented critique of articles on scientific subjects."

- *Wikipedia:WikiProject Usability*. Promotes "the application of standards related to usability and/or Web usability."
- *Wikipedia:WikiProject Wikipedians against censorship*. Coordinates efforts to oppose what members consider censorship of Wikipedia articles.

Cross-cutting WikiProjects are not just places to do types of work you enjoy, but they're also excellent places to discuss the finer nuances of article construction and how to get the most out of Wikipedia's powerful software tools. If you find a chapter of this book particularly interesting, and want to improve Wikipedia by working in that area, you'll probably find a matching WikiProject. (If not, consider creating one, as described on page 174.)

WikiProjects are Everywhere

An August 2007 survey of random 100 articles found that more than half had a related WikiProject noted on their article talk page. Thirteen of those article talk pages had two or three associated WikiProjects, not just one. The good news: WikiProjects are important. More than half of articles in Wikipedia have at least one WikiProject interested in improving them. The bad news: Almost half of all articles in Wikipedia are WikiProject orphans—either outside of any existing WikiProject's scope, or undiscovered by the relevant WikiProject.

There's more evidence of the pervasiveness of WikiProjects: Statistics on all Wikipedia articles, as of October 2007, showed that 900,000 had been assessed for quality by WikiProjects (assessments range from stub to featured article), with another 300,000 or so still to be assessed.

What WikiProjects Do

Looking at the examples on page 167, it's clear that a WikiProject can aim to improve just about anything on Wikipedia. But the vast majority of WikiProjects focus on articles, and the majority of those focus on articles within a particular topical area. Understanding such WikiProjects will give you a good idea of WikiProjects as a whole.

Goals and roles

The first and foremost goal of topical WikiProjects is to improve Wikipedia's coverage of articles within that topic. Most of that effort is aimed at existing articles, but WikiProjects are also involved in creating new articles where needed.

WikiProjects are no more than the sum of the work of participating editors, so a certain amount of effort must be put into recruiting editors and retaining the interest of participating editors. ("Finding Other Participants and Encouraging Participation" on page page 170 goes into more detail.)

A second role of WikiProjects is to maintain *portals*, mini-Main Pages which are entry points for particular topics. For example, WikiProject Indonesia maintains the page *Portal:Indonesia* (shortcut: *P:ID*) and WikiProject Books and WikiProject Novels jointly maintain the page *Portal:Literature*.

NOTE

If you want to search for text or information on a portal page, you need to modify your search to include the namespace Portal, because the normal Wikipedia search is only for information on article pages (pages in the Main namespace). You can do this by modifying your search on the Wikipedia search page by checking the box for the Portal namespace, after doing an initial search to get to the main search page. Another is to change your preferences (page 396) so that your searches automatically include both mainspace and portalspace.

A third WikiProjects role is to assess the quality of articles within their projects. As of October 2007, an estimated 800 WikiProjects had done assessments (quality of articles, importance of articles, and so on) within their topics. The *Version 1.0 Editorial Team* (shortcut: *WP:1.0*) uses these assessments to select articles, and in April 2007 released a collection of about 2,000 articles as Wikipedia version 0.5, on a set of CDs.

Activities

A WikiProject's size significantly affects a given project's activities. Some projects have hundreds of members and cover tens of thousands of articles; some have only a handful of members and less than a hundred articles. Task forces (or similar subgroupings) are critical for large projects, while small projects need to minimize administrative housekeeping, instead focusing on working on articles. Still, here are a few things that most projects can or should do:

- **Recruit editors to the project**. Finding and retaining capable editors is necessary for any WikiProject to stay afloat.

- **Peer reviews, where an editor can submit an article for review by others**. Peer reviews should be limited to articles that are reasonably well developed, since the primary problems with short articles—the lack of information and lack of sources —don't require a peer review to point out.

- **Tagging articles that are within the project's scope**. Tagging—placing a WikiProject banner on article talk pages—can be done manually, but bots can help. Bots can use categories (Chapter 17) and keywords to tag articles talk pages, and they can create article lists for human review.

- **Picking a single article to improve enough for it to become a featured article**, and maybe even appear on Wikipedia's Main Page for a day. (There's more detail on featured articles at *WP:FA*.) A featured article campaign is an excitement-generating way to kick off a WikiProject, though the process can take a month or

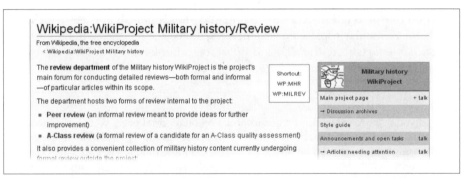

Figure 9-3. WikiProject Military history is among the largest WikiProjects at Wikipedia. Its review department gives a good indication that it has a large number of active participants.

two. And it's important to pick an article for which sufficient sources exist so that it *can* achieve featured article quality.

- **Creating a list of needed articles within the project scope**. (Page 78 lists some starting places to find articles identified as missing.)

- **Running a collaboration (weekly, monthly, or whenever) to try to focus the group on at least one article at a time**. There's more detail on collaborations on page 175.

If you're a member of a WikiProject and hear of something interesting that your project isn't doing, don't be shy about suggesting it on the main talk page of that WikiProject or on another, more relevant talk page within that project. You may end up doing most of the initial work yourself, so avoid suggesting something you don't have the time to work on alone or with one or two others. (If no one else is interested, it's not a crime to drop the idea.)

Joining a WikiProject

One way to find a WikiProject you'd be interested in joining is to go to an article of personal interest and check the article's talk page. If the article has a WikiProject banner, follow the link to that WikiProject, and see if you want to join.

The other way to find a WikiProject of interest is to use the page *Wikipedia:WikiProject Council/Directory* (shortcut: *WP:PROJDIR*). Start with one of the subdirectories, and drill down until you find something that looks interesting. Or if you see a gap where the WikiProject you'd like to join would be, consider starting a WikiProject yourself (page 174).

Finding Other Participants and Encouraging Participation

Keeping a WikiProject going can be a challenge. After all, Wikipedia editors are unpaid volunteers whose interests and free time can change, so attrition is normal. Successful

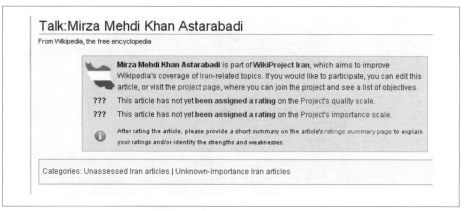

Figure 9-4. This template for WikiProject Iran *includes parameters (which would be visible in edit mode) for quality and importance. Because neither has yet been assessed, they show as "???" in the message box the template creates. Article assessments are important for a number of reasons, including identifying articles that might be included in published DVDs, and measuring Wikipedia's progress.*

WikiProjects need to both recruit new members and retain the interest of existing members. If you're in a WikiProject, it's in your best interest to help with both of these.

You might think that recruitment and retention are the responsibility of whoever is in charge of a WikiProject. But the whole point of WikiProjects—and Wikipedia—is that no one's in charge. The Wikipedia community strongly discourages voting, elected positions, and hierarchy; *Wikipedia:What Wikipedia is not* (shortcut: *WP:NOT*) clearly states that Wikipedia is neither a democracy nor a bureaucracy. (Some large WikiProjects have coordinators, but they're primarily responsible for administrative house-keeping.)

So if, for example, your WikiProject doesn't have a newsletter, and you want to write one, all you need to do is post to a talk page, saying that you're thinking about doing so, asking if anyone has an objection—or wants to help. If no one objects, then you're now the newsletter editor (or co-editor, if others are interested).

Recruitment

There are two standard ways to recruit new members for an ongoing WikiProject:

- **Putting WikiProject templates on article talk pages**. Templates that mark articles as belonging to a given WikiProject always include a link to that project. Interested editors can click the link. Figure 9-4 shows an example.

- **Creating a userbox template** (page 56) for posting on member editors' user pages. While user pages get fewer visits than article pages, an editor with similar interests may follow the userbox to the WikiProject page.

Less common methods include:

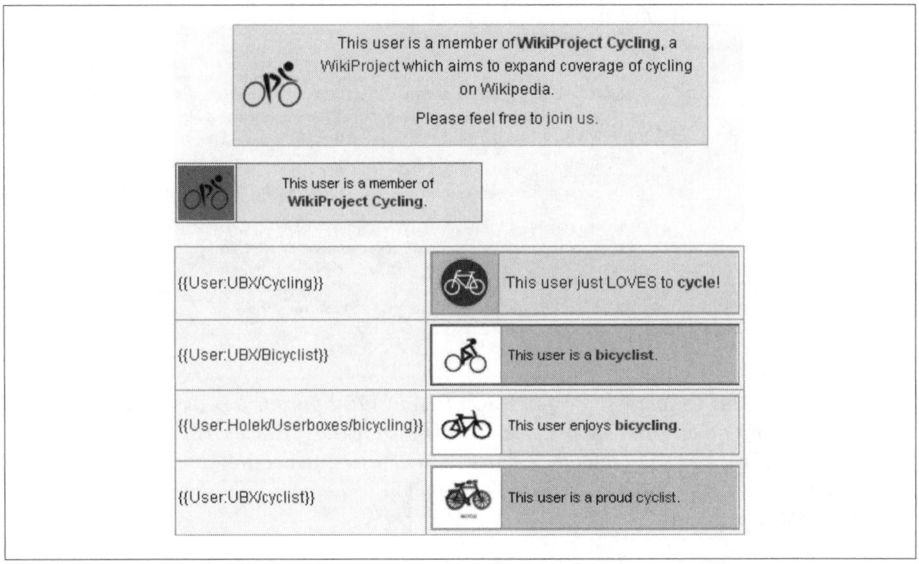

This user is a member of **WikiProject Cycling**, a WikiProject which aims to expand coverage of cycling on Wikipedia.
Please feel free to join us.

This user is a member of
WikiProject Cycling.

{{User:UBX/Cycling}}	This user just LOVES to **cycle**!
{{User:UBX/Bicyclist}}	This user is a **bicyclist**.
{{User:Holek/Userboxes/bicycling}}	This user enjoys **bicycling**.
{{User:UBX/cyclist}}	This user is a proud cyclist.

Figure 9-5. WikiProject Cycling *has created two userboxes that participants can pick from, for posting on the user page. But they've also created or collected four userboxes for cycling enthusiasts who aren't participants, perhaps a subtle way of encouraging editors to work on cycling articles, even if they're not formal WikiProject members.*

- **Posting a note on the article talk page of WikiProject articles**. For example, say your group has worked formally on a particular article—more than the work of a single editor or a quick brush-up. Then you can write something like, "This article has just been substantially edited as part of the work of WikiProject Sea Monsters. If you have any questions about these edits, please contact us."

- **Advertising**. Yes, Wikipedia has advertising, at least internally, for WikiProjects and other good causes. To get your WikiProject into the loop of ads, see *Template:Wikipedia ads/doc* (shortcut: *WP:BANNER*).

TIP

To view the ads for yourself, put the template *{{wikipedia ads}}* onto your user page, or simply check out that template on a sandbox page.

- **Looking at the history of articles within a WikiProject to find non-members contributing something significant to an article**. Then drop them a note on their user talk pages, inviting them to join the WikiProject. (This kind of note is a perfectly legitimate use of a user talk page.)

- **Making sure that your project's entry in the WikiProject directory (shortcut:** *WP:PROJDIR***) is complete**. The brief description in the last column is particularly important for attracting potential editors.

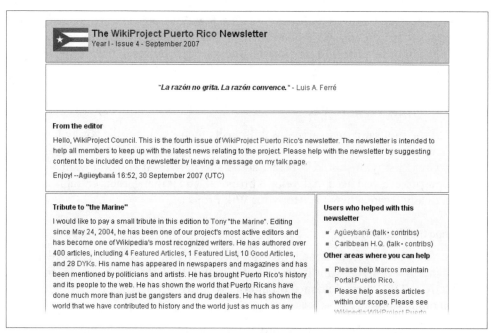

Figure 9-6. The September 2007 newsletter for WikiProject Puerto Rico *prominently mentions some editors who have contributed significantly to the WikiProject.*

Retention

Many WikiProjects have their own welcome template, which is ideal to post to the user talk pages of editors who sign up. If there's no template, you can post a personal note. Making the new editor feel welcome helps encourage active participation.

A monthly newsletter updating editors on progress and plans can encourage editors to spend some time on the WikiProject. Mentioning new members by name is a great way to increase the enthusiasm level. If you want something more than a plain text newsletter, check out sample newsletters from a number of WikiProjects, collected at *Wikipedia:WikiProject Council/Newsletters*. (One sample is shown in Figure 9-6.)

TIP

A number of bots automate the work of posting newsletters on individual user pages, including Anibot, COBot, EnewsBot, GrooveBot, and R Delivery Bot. Simply post a request on one of the bot talk pages (*User talk:Anibot*, *User talk:COBot*, or whatever).

An announcements page within the WikiProject can be a good way to encourage members to check in frequently. Just don't hide the page away somewhere without putting up clear links to it.

Finally, while it may sound a bit hokey, at least a few WikiProjects have created awards for high participation editors. Having such an award posted on the editor's user talk page is a pleasant surprise and provides reassurance that others in the group recognize the editor's efforts.

Creating a New WikiProject

If none of the thousand or so active WikiProjects focuses on a topic you're interested in, you can take the initiative and start a new WikiProject. But you have a few steps in front of you. First, you should consider some alternatives. If you still want to start a whole new project, you need to develop a proposal, and if that gathers enough support, you can finally create a new page for your WikiProject.

Considering the alternatives

Starting a new project from scratch may not be the only way to collaborate with others on the kind of work you want to do. *Wikipedia:WikiProject Council/Guide* (shortcut: *WP:PROJGUIDE*) offers guidance on alternatives to starting your own WikiProject. Here's a quick summary:

- Check to see if someone else has proposed a similar project in the past few months (the shortcut to the proposals page is *WP:COUNCIL/P*). If so, you can contact that editor and find out what's happening.

- If your topic is narrow enough, you can coordinate other editors via the talk (discussion) page of the main article of interest; for example, the page *Talk:Tulip*. Simply list (on that article talk page) the articles that need improving and ask other editors to work on them, or to let you know that they're interested in doing so.

- If the topic falls within an existing WikiProject, you can create a task force or work group *within* that WikiProject. This approach is easiest if the WikiProject already has a structure for and history of such smaller groups. Even if it doesn't, the other editors may well be willing to try a pilot project.

- If the topic falls partly in several existing WikiProjects, perhaps a parent/coordinating WikiProject might be the answer. This arrangement requires agreement by the existing WikiProjects, which may not be easy to get, but it's worth a try.

Proposal

If after considering the alternatives you decide that a separate WikiProject is still the right way to go, the next step is to post a proposal at *Wikipedia:WikiProject Council/ Proposals* (shortcut: *WP:COUNCIL/P*). The proposal will stay up for 4 months, and then be archived if there isn't sufficient support—a minimum of five to 10 active editors.

Don't count on other editors just stumbling across the WikiProject. If it's a cross-cutting project, it's fine to post a note on the talk page of any relevant instructional pages (ones with a *Wikipedia:* prefix), and put a note at the proposals page of the Village Pump (shortcut: *WP:VP/PR*). If the proposed WikiProject is a subset of an existing WikiProject, then you also post something on the main talk page of that WikiProject.

Also, don't be shy about posting notes on at least a few user talk pages, if you come across edits by others that indicate an interest in the topic (check their User contributions page). However, don't post to dozens of random pages; that's considered internal spamming.

Creating the WikiProject page

If and when you've got sufficient indications of interest by other editors, go to *Wikipedia:WikiProject Council/Guide/WikiProject* for detailed instructions on starting a base page to launch your WikiProject. That page spells out all the steps for making the project a success: creating a template for article talk pages and a userbox for user pages, creating task lists, issuing newsletters, and so on.

Collaborations

A *collaboration* involves a single article, chosen by editors working in the group doing the collaboration, where editors work on that article for a week, fortnight, or month, and then turn to the next chosen article.

Existing Collaborations

You can see the list of existing collaborations at *Wikipedia:Collaborations* (shortcut: *WP:CO*), as shown in Figure 9-7.

Some collaborations involve several WikiProjects, and some are separate entities unconnected to any WikiProject. But most collaborations occur within an existing WikiProject. One reason is that recruiting new members to a collaboration can be difficult, since collaborations don't post templates on large numbers of article talk pages, as WikiProjects do.

Another factor in favor of single-WikiProject collaborations is the process for selecting a new article to collaborate on: Editors whose articles aren't chosen for collaboration may give up, while editors who do continue to push for a particular article to be the subject of the collaboration may find that when it's chosen, hardly anyone else wants to work on it. Drawing participation from a single WikiProject can minimize or compensate for such problems, since project members have a high interest level, and new members are always joining.

Figure 9-7. Here's the top of the list of collaborations as of mid-October 2007. At the time, about 40 collaborations were considered active.

Creating a New Collaboration

The process for starting a new collaboration is basically to create a new page with details about what you have in mind, and then advertise it. You'll find full details in the "Creating a new collaboration" section at *WP:CO*.

Given the challenges of keeping the interest of editors, think twice before creating a collaboration *outside* a WikiProject. Rather, if you're a member of a WikiProject, test out the waters by posting a note on the talk page of that project. If you get only one or two other editors who show interest, perhaps you can collaborate informally, and try again in a few months, when you can point to a couple of successes.

You might want to start a new collaboration as a monthly thing, rather than weekly. That gives you and the other editors more time to make progress. Also, you might want to focus on articles that are relatively short, and not the subject of any ongoing editing battles. That increases the chances of substantial results.

Less Formal Working Groups

If you've been reading your way steadily through this book, you probably already have a good sense that there are no absolute rules in a lot of Wikipedia areas. Groups of editors working together is one of those areas. Such activities can be much less formal than WikiProjects and ongoing, listed collaborations.

Organizations

Wikipedia has a small number of *organizations*, several of which are mentioned in later chapters of this book. You can see the complete list via the shortcut *CAT:ORG*. For example, the *Wikipedia Typo Department* (shortcuts: *WP:Typo* and *WP:Tyop*), which began in November 2003, "aims to make Wikipedia look more professional by correcting typos and misspellings." That organization has no formal members. Instead, a section of the organization's main page contains pledges by a number of editors; for example, to fix all typos immediately.

One-time Initiatives

Temporary, one-time, initiatives by a group of editors are even more informal than organizations. For example, in late August 2007, a proposal was posted at the Village Pump proposals page (shortcut: *WP:VP/PR*) to standardize the template messages that appear at the top of article pages. (These are templates indicating that the article needs cleanup, needs to be wikified, has its neutrality disputed, and so.) Within about a month, interested editors had agreed on and implemented changes to all the top-of-page article message templates (sometimes called *amboxes*), and the initiative was basically over. A remnant of it continues on in the form of the guideline *Wikipedia:Article message boxes* (shortcut *WP:AMB*), simply for maintenance and minor tweaks.

Creating Your Own

If you're inclined to propose a new initiative, task force, working group, or similar project, whether a new organization or a temporary initiative, the Village Pump proposals page is a good place to start. Read the information at the top of the page, and then follow the link to the page of perennial proposals (shortcut: *WP:PEREN*); you won't get much traction if you bring up something that experienced editors have seen several times before, or if you post to the wrong page. And also post to the talk pages of related instructional pages. For example, a discussion about template standardization occurred at a subpage of *Wikipedia talk:Template messages* before the first posting about the subject appeared at the Village Pump.

Finally, you can always create a subpage within your user space to start working on an initiative and trying to find other interested editors. In such a case, again, you can post to the talk (discussion) page of the relevant instructional page such as the page *Wikipedia talk:Manual of Style*, to see if anyone else is interested.

> **NOTE**
>
> Often, only a few editors read instructional talk pages, and a lot of ideas about change are floating around Wikipedia. Don't take a lack of response as something personal. You can still find plenty of other things to do on Wikipedia.

CHAPTER 10

Resolving Content Disputes

Wikipedia's core is its articles' content. With so many editors collaborating on Wikipedia, disagreements over content are inevitable. Most of the time, editors resolve these matters on their own, after a reasonable discussion. If you find yourself involved in a content dispute, follow the guidelines in this chapter to engage the other editor in a helpful discussion. If push comes to shove, this chapter also shows you how to use Wikipedia's formal processes for important disagreements that can't be resolved informally.

Why Editors Disagree

If it's true that there's strength in diversity, then Wikipedia has the strongest volunteer corps possible. More than a billion people worldwide have Internet access, and a very large percentage of those speak English as a primary or additional language. They're all potential editors of the English Wikipedia. The diversity of editors is one reason why editors disagree about article content. Another is a lack of knowledge of Wikipedia's rules, which aren't all intuitively obvious.

Diversity of Backgrounds

Only about half the editors of the English Wikipedia live in the United States (population 300 million). The rest come from an incredibly wide range of countries, cultures, and continents. English is the primary language of most inhabitants of the United Kingdom (60 million people), Canada (33 million), Australia (21 million), Ireland (6 million), New Zealand (4 million), and numerous Caribbean islands like Jamaica (population 3 million). English is also spoken as an additional language by hundreds of millions of adults in Europe, India, the Philippines, and other countries. United primarily by a common language, differences of opinion are inevitable when people work collaboratively on an encyclopedia that intends to offer definitive information to the world.

Wikipedia has no age requirement for editors; there are certainly many pre-teenagers and teenagers who contribute constructively, as well as a number of adults who do not.

Nor are there requirements for expertise (in anything, let alone in what's being edited), a point on which Wikipedia has been criticized by many people. (People often overlook the fact that the lack of such barriers made Wikipedia what it is today.)

Finally, people's beliefs differ. This goes beyond whether Elvis is alive or not; Wikipedia's articles cover politics, religion, sexuality, culture, geography, and numerous other areas where people *know* they are right and others are wrong. Wikipedia's rules emphasize that facts and sources matter, and that personal beliefs and opinions don't, but that's not the norm on the Internet, at places like discussion boards and blogs. Wikipedia's rules are thus often a major shock to newcomers.

Differing Motivations

Other editors may not only come from a different background, but may also have different reasons for editing at Wikipedia. Those reasons can make a big difference in how determined they are to defend their edits.

A number of studies have looked at why people edit at Wikipedia. From the perspective of content disagreements, the level of emotional engagement an editor has with an article he's editing is important. Not surprisingly, emotional engagement runs the gamut: negative concern (a vandal), just passing by (a casual reader), relatively disinterested (not the same as uninterested), personally involved (a conflict of interest problem), expert (a plus, but not an unmitigated one), passionate (a plus if the passion can be kept in check), fanatic (a big problem), and kook (someone usually shut down pretty quickly).

Not Knowing Wikipedia Policies

As discussed in Part 1, Wikipedia has three core content policies: neutral point of view, no original research, and verifiability. These three policies are at the heart of a majority of content mistakes, so checking for their violation should be the first step in examining an article's edits (page 184). Editors also frequently violate two other policies, simply because they're not familiar with them:

- *Wikipedia:Ownership of articles* (shortcut: *WP:OWN*) states that no editor owns the content of an article. It doesn't matter if she created it, or if she has been the main contributor to it for the past year, or if she is the acknowledged world's best expert in the subject; she doesn't have the right to revert other editors' edits simply because she doesn't like them.

  The only way that an editor can properly prevent her words from being changed is not to put them in a Wikipedia article in the first place. And no editor has any special power or authority over any other editor when articles are edited.

- *What Wikipedia is not* (shortcut: *WP:NOT*) makes it clear that certain types of information aren't in accordance with Wikipedia's purposes. Content that doesn't belong in Wikipedia includes: usage guides or slang and idiom guides; presentation of original thought; routine news coverage, including first-hand news reports on breaking stories; advocacy, recruitment, opinion pieces, self-promotion, or advertising; directories of external links; collections of public domain or other source materials; tributes to departed friends and relatives; instruction manuals, and how-to instructions; FAQs; plot summaries and song lyrics; and other matters lacking encyclopedic substance, such as announcements, sports, and gossip.

In short, if the text in question is not the sort that you'd find in the Encyclopædia Britannica, then there's a pretty good chance that Wikipedia doesn't want that text either. Wikipedia is, like EB, an encyclopedia.

Avoiding Content Disputes

You can avoid a lot of content disputes by doing just a bit of checking before you make major changes to articles, by doing as few reverts as possible (and not getting into edit wars), and, above all, by focusing on content rather than commenting on editors. *Wikipedia:Dispute resolution* (shortcut: *WP:DR*) includes the following tip: "The best way to resolve a dispute is to avoid it in the first place."

Don't Charge in Blindly

If you're adding just a little well-sourced information to a page, or if you're doing minor copyediting of a section of a page, then go ahead and do the edit; only rarely will someone object. But if you're planning to add a lot of information, change a lot of wording, or reorganize an article, you can minimize content disputes if you do just a little bit of checking first: Read the article's talk (discussion) page. If you see a gnarled mass of recent arguments, you stand a significant chance of getting caught up in an edit war. Even if you aren't interested in joining whatever argument's going on, other editors may interpret what you did as supporting one side or the other.

NOTE

Chapter 18 (page 343) discusses making major changes to an article when you can reasonably expect some opposition.

Secondly, you should routinely do a quick check in the article history tab. If you see a lot of recent edits, make sure you're not updating a vandalized version.

Explain Your Edits

Provide a good *edit summary* when making significant changes to which other users might object. If you can cite a relevant policy or guideline, do so. Wikilinks in edit summaries *do* work, as in this example:

Removing information that appears to be added from personal knowledge (see [[WP:NOR]]) and copyediting.

If you can't fit your explanation into an edit summary, then put a brief summary and conclude it with *See talk/discussion page*. Explain further on the article talk page. (Chapter 8 covers the use of article talk pages—see page 145.)

Minimize Your Reverts

Reverts (Chapter 5) are powerful things. Use them only when there are clear policy violations. Experienced editors often consider being reverted an insult. (Consider how you'd feel if an edit you did that you thought improved an article was entirely removed.) If you revert an edit by an experienced editor, you'd better be justified.

It's much better if you can salvage part of the content from an edit that you disagree with. And don't use the *rv* expression or standard (software-supplied) undo text (page 93) in an edit summary unless you're absolutely sure that you're right. To quote directly from *WP:DR*: "When someone makes an edit you consider biased or inaccurate, improve the edit if you can, rather than reverting it, or if you do not see it as improvable, discuss it on the talk page." (For more details on dealing with content added by others, see "Reviewing Content Changes: A General Plan of Action" on page 184.)

Wikipedia forbids edit wars—two or more editors reverting each other continuously. (For details, see *Wikipedia:Edit war*, shortcut *WP:EW*.) To prevent edit wars, the *Wikipedia:Three-revert rule* (shortcut: *WP:3RR*) states that editors who revert a page in whole or in part *more than three times in 24 hours*, except in certain special circumstances, are likely to be blocked from editing. Those exceptions include simple and obvious vandalism, copyright violations, spam, copyrighted images that lack a free content license, and unsourced or poorly sourced controversial material about living persons, particularly negative information, which could be libelous.

If you run into an editor who's unaware of this policy, warn him after he's done two or three reverts within a day to the same article, on the same content. You can find the standard warning at the page *Template:uw-3rr*. Simply post this warning text on the user talk page of the editor who's approaching the 3RR limit (or has even gone over, but not yet been warned). If you want to use your own words, make sure to provide a wikilink to the policy *Wikipedia:Three-revert rule*, because you can't expect new editors to find the policy without such a link.

NOTE

If you see a valid 3RR warning (one linking to the policy) on the user talk page, *don't* post another one. Some editors regard that as harassment. Similarly, if the user's been blocked one or more times for a 3RR violation, there's no need to post a new warning. You can assume he's quite familiar with the policy.

Once you've posted the warning, don't worry if the editor deletes it from his talk page. If an editor deletes the warning, that means he's read it. The warning remains in the history of his user talk page. (Users have every right to delete postings from their own user talk page. Don't make the mistake of taking it as an insult.)

The 3RR rule does not convey an entitlement to revert thrice each day, nor is it intended to encourage reverting as an editing technique. Rather, the rule acts as a sort of electric fence that gives a little leeway to revert but prevents an intense edit war. An administrator may still block an editor if her pattern of ongoing reverts is found to be disruptive, even if she's following the 24-hour rule. The policy aims to get editors to work together; administrators consider it a violation when editors treat the rule like a challenge.

NOTE

An academic study of Wikipedia found that double-reverts—when one revert is immediately followed by another—dropped by half due to the 3RR rule, comparing the periods before and after the implementation of the rule in November 2004. The number of double-reverts then stayed roughly the same for the next year, the ending point of the study.

Discuss Edits, Not Editors

When disagreement about content spills over into incivility and personal attacks, it gets much harder to resolve the content dispute. Chapter 11 shows you how to deal with incivility and personal attacks directed against you, and also has advice on what to do if you get irritated (or worse) with another editor, or if you've posted something that you realize you shouldn't have (page 210). If you're involved in a disagreement over content that's becoming uncivil, take a look at Chapter 11: If you can get the focus back to content, the chances are much better that you and other editors can find an acceptable compromise.

NOTE

One of the best ways to keep matters focused on edits is to provide links to specific sections of specific guidelines and policies. Wikipedia has a large number of policies and guidelines related to content, so there's a good chance that one of them pertains to your situation. Often a disagreement evaporates when everyone has a chance to review the rules. (If you're unsure where to start looking, one good place is the Editor's index, *WP:EIW*.)

It's a good idea, every now and then, to review the guideline at *Wikipedia:Assume good faith* (shortcut: *WP:AGF*). If you start out with the attitude that a particular editor is a problem, there's a good chance that she will be one. On the other hand, if you assume that the editor is well-intentioned, but perhaps uninformed, and does have something to contribute, then you're following the "assume good faith" guideline. You may be incorrect, but you won't make the problem any worse.

Finally, it's important to use article talk pages correctly. Keep discussions about editor behavior off article talk pages. Discussions about editors belong on *user* talk pages, not *article* talk pages. If someone else starts something on an article talk page, don't take the bait.

NOTE

The *Bold, revert, discuss (WP:BRD)* approach is the one exception to using article talk pages to discuss differences. Said to be a cross between the Harmonious Editing Club and an "Ignore all rules" policy, it's appropriate only in very limited circumstances, and best left to experienced editors. (See *WP:BRD* for details.)

Reviewing Content Changes: A General Plan of Action

If you're an experienced Wikipedia editor, you probably have a pretty good idea of what you shouldn't do when editing, and you can identify problems in others' edits without going through a step-by-step review. While you're still gaining experience, however, a systematic approach is a good way to figure out what not to do yourself, what you should revert and what you shouldn't, and how to handle edits by others that aren't bad enough to revert but aren't good enough to stay as is.

The approach laid out in the following sections will help you improve articles and reduce the number of content disputes you're in. For example, policy violations come first, since they're easy to define and no one disputes the need to revert them. Then you'll turn to more subtle points like sourcing and wording.

Policy Violations

If you see any of the following, revert them (page 90), and cite the applicable policy in your edit summary:

- Simple and obvious vandalism (*WP:VAND*); for more information, see page 121.
- Linkspam (*WP:SPAM*); see page 122.
- Copyright violations (*WP:COPYVIO*); see page 361.
- Unsourced or poorly sourced controversial material about living persons (*WP:BLP*); see page 152.
- Privacy violations (*WP:BLP*); page 152.

Proper Weight and Balance

Most editors probably think of the policy *Wikipedia:Neutral point of view* (shortcut: *WP:NPOV*) as being about *wording*. For example, the following text wouldn't pass the POV test, since it's hopelessly biased (as well as unverifiable, and quite possibly a copyright violation):

> *The committee has become a significant force in enhancing relations between Somewheristan and Nowhereistan. With an in-depth understanding of both countries, the committee deepens the ties of friendship and addresses the concerns of all who are interested in the wellbeing of both countries.*

But Wikipedia also defines "neutral point of view" to include the *amount* of text about different aspects of a topic. An article that goes into detail about extreme fringe views on a topic is violating the NPOV policy, as is an article that lists *all* the good legislation that an elected official has voted for. (The latter also is a violation of *WP:NOT*, since it's a collection of indiscriminate information.) So while a chunk of text may have a neutral point of view, inserting it into an article could well unbalance the article, and unbalanced articles aren't neutral.

To apply the "weight and balance" part of the NPOV policy, evaluate the importance of added information to a particular aspect of a topic. When a particular aspect or view is getting way too much coverage (usually because it includes a level of detail that isn't appropriate for the entire article), the proper action is to remove the excess, leaving an appropriate amount of text, plus cited sources that readers can pursue if they're interested in more information.

On the other hand, if an article is short, the addition of a lot of information about a particular aspect of the topic may seem to make the article unbalanced, particularly where that text is negative (say, about the problems of a politician, businessperson, or company). In fact, the article is *not* unbalanced—it's simply too short. The real problem is the lack of information about other aspects of the topic, not the new addition. Someone who adds information to a short article isn't required to simultaneously expand all parts of the article. The solution is for other editors to expand the rest of the article, not to remove valuable information.

WARNING

Removing detailed, sourced information from a short article for balance is usually an honest mistake. Removing it after discussion has clarified NPOV requirements is borderline vandalism.

Proper Sourcing

If editors provided sources for everything they added to Wikipedia, the number of content disputes would drop sharply. When content is controversial, editors have an extra responsibility to cite a source, in accordance with the core policies of verifiability

(*WP:V*) and no original research (*WP:NOR*). If you add information to Wikipedia only when you have the source in hand (or onscreen), other editors are much less likely to find problems with what you add to articles. Unfortunately, not everyone has read this book or understands the importance of sourcing as well as you do. You're going to have to deal with editors who don't provide sources, or who provide inappropriate ones. This section describes what to do in such cases.

When no source is given

Unsourced content falls into several types. How you handle unsourced information depends what kind of information it is:

- **Non-controversial and plausible**. Leave as is. It's not absolutely against the rules to mark such statements as needing a source, but if every unsourced statement and section in Wikipedia articles were marked as such, it would make articles far less readable. It definitely won't bring a rush of editors to fix things. Editors know when information is unsourced; you don't need to mark it just to identify that you know this too.

- **Controversial or contentious, but not negative**. Any controversial statement needs a source. You can request one by placing a *{{fact}}* template immediately after the unsourced sentence or paragraph, which tags the text with "citation needed". If the problem is with an entire section, use *{{Unreferencedsection}}* immediately after the section heading.

    If you doubt that a reliable source will turn up (perhaps the wording has an obvious point of view), move the information to the article talk (discussion) page, noting in your edit summary that you're doing so, and comment on the talk page about your doubts.

    For biographical information, check *WP:BLP* and *WP:3RR* about removing controversial but not negative information. As of late 2007, such removals were allowed, but the matter isn't set in stone. So check the policy before you remove any information, and cite the policy when you do.

- **Implausible**. If you have the time and interest, consider using a search engine to see if you can find a source. If you don't find a source, or don't have time, remove the information, but don't cite vandalism in the edit summary. Instead, say that the editor is free to add back the information if a source is provided.

- **Controversial and negative**. Generally, you can remove information like this on sight. It's potentially libelous, and a clear violation of *WP:BLP* if it concerns a living person. In the edit summary, note that the editor's free to add it back if a source is provided.

Ideally, whenever you decide not to revert an edit that added unsourced material to an article, letting some or all of the material stay in the article (because it's not a serious problem), you should take a moment to post a note regarding the problem on the user talk page of the editor who added the material. The *Needsource* template makes it easy.

Add a new section to the talk page with the heading *[[Articlename]]* and the text: *{{subst:Needsource|Articlename}} ~~~~*.

NOTE

Many editors don't know about Wikipedia's requirements for providing a source. It's a chicken and egg problem—so much information is unsourced that it's not obvious that adding more is wrong. If more editors posted *Needsource* notes, then the problem of unsourced information would start to shrink.

When the source isn't reliable

A *reliable source* is a published work regarded as trustworthy or authoritative in relation to the subject at hand. Self-published works, particularly personal Internet blogs, discussion forums, and personal and social Web pages are almost always considered unreliable. *Wikipedia:Reliable sources* (shortcut: *WP:RS*) goes into more detail about the requirements of Wikipedia's policy on verifiability (*WP:V*).

NOTE

An exception to the general rule about self-published information is if it's published by an established expert on the topic. An expert is someone whose work in the relevant field has previously been published by reliable third-party publications. These self-published sources are acceptable, but Wikipedia still discourages their use in favor of more standard sources. If nothing else, that policy eliminates arguments about whether a specific person is an acknowledged expert and whether the self-published information is relevant to her expertise.

You can often determine that a source is unreliable just by the URL, or by the citation information. If it's not obvious, and the source is online, follow the link and make a determination.

If you find information that's supported by an unreliable source, do the following:

- If the cited source is online, be sure to follow the link. Sometimes an unreliable source, like a blog, has a link to a newspaper story or other source that *is* reliable. If you find a reliable source, edit the article to change the source.
- If you can't find a reliable source as a substitute (using a search engine is another option, if you have time), then evaluate the information as if it were unsourced (as described in the previous section), and take appropriate action.
- If you decide to remove unreliably sourced information based on the previous section (treating it as if it had no source), make sure your edit summary includes an explanation, like *source provided was not [[WP:RS|reliable]]*.
- If you decide to leave the added information in the article, even though it's essentially unsourced, edit the article to delete the unreliable source and put *{{fact}}* in

its place. That action, and, ideally, a note on the editor's user talk page, alerts the editor who added the information that it needs a reliable source.

Correct Wording

If you've made it this far in the process, and have taken care of any policy and sourcing issues, it's time to shift your focus to the *wording* of the information added to an article. In "Proper Weight and Balance" on page 185, you saw how to evaluate information added to an article for neutrality and balance. Now you need to see whether these issues exist in the wording itself.

Even when information is taken verbatim from a reliable source, it can be problematical. Omitting key phrases like "Some critics in the opposition party have charged that" can shift an article's point of view to one side of an arguments or the other. Also, as mentioned above, the added text may include excessive detail on certain points.

NOTE

Verbatim copying not only isn't a solution to the issue of weight and balance, it also create raises copyright issues, particularly where a large percentage of the text in a source has been copied into a Wikipedia article. Don't copy text except for direct quotes from a person, or when the source supports a controversial point (as in, for example, "*The Washington Post* reported that Fernandes 'would like to see the institution become more inclusive of people who might not have grown up using sign language.'")

Editing a Wikipedia article to get exactly the right wording is an art, not a science. It's impossible to come up with a comprehensive checklist, because the English language is so diffuse and flexible. Fortunately, you're not required to get the wording perfect, just to try to improve it when you see problems. If you do that, and other editors do the same, then the wording will improve with every edit.

Here are three pages to consult when wording is at issue. Each has a lot of good examples:

- *Wikipedia:Guidelines for controversial articles* (shortcut: *GFCA*)
- *Wikipedia:Avoid weasel words* (shortcut: *WP:AWW*)
- *Wikipedia:Words to avoid* (shortcut: *WP:WTA*)

Resolving Content Disputes Informally

The first part of this chapter focused on ways to decrease the probability of getting into a content dispute. But if you're editing articles, such disputes are almost inevitable, unless no one else cares enough to edit the same articles. This section shows you what to do if someone disputes one of your edits, or disagrees with how you responded to one of *his* edits. When you're in a content dispute, your goal should be to resolve the matter *informally*. You usually try to reach an informal resolution by discussing the matter on the article talk page, as discussed on page 145.

With any luck, both you and the other editors who get involved in the discussion about content are reasonable, respectful of the other editors (who are also unpaid volunteers), and focused solely on what's best for Wikipedia. Taking that approach improves the chances of a successful outcome. If you find yourself disagreeing with another editor about content, start with the following suggestions. You'll be much less likely to need to use more formal methods to resolve matters.

Avoid Incivility and Personal Attacks

"Discuss Edits, Not Editors" (page 183) stressed the importance of avoiding incivility, and assuming good faith. Those objectives hold even more true once a dispute is underway. Don't make disagreements a personal matter if you want to easily resolve content disagreements.

Look for Compromises

Remember that your goal is improve an article, not to win an argument. As the guideline *Wikipedia:Etiquette* (shortcut: *WP:EQ*) puts it, "Concede a point when you have no response to it, or admit when you disagree based on *intuition or taste*." Ski instructors tell new students, "If you're not falling, you're not learning." In Wikipedia, when you edit articles, you should consider your errors (when pointed out) as an indication that *you're learning*. There's absolutely nothing wrong if your changes to an article weren't perfect. What's absolutely wrong is defending something because you did it and another editor didn't like it, and you think that somehow you have to defend the edit simply because it's yours.

An example of a compromise, where information posted by another editor seems plausible and there's no problem with wording, is to put a "citation needed" template (like *{{fact | date=December 2007}}* into the article, rather than removing the information for lack of a source.

If your goal, even for controversial content, is to get *everything* that you think belongs in an article into that article, and to have the wording exactly as you *want* it, then you're just asking for more arguments. You're not going to reach those goals without a grinding battle that consumes time much better spent editing (or doing just about anything else). Here are three goals that are far more achievable than getting exactly what you want:

- Get enough information into an article so that readers have at least a *basic* sense of why a topic is interesting and important, and what that topic is.
- Keep incorrect information out of an article, so that readers aren't misled.

- Keep good links and sources in an article, so that interested readers can follow the links and read the sources for more information.

Remember also that a bitter, protracted battle over content can play a large part in a decision by an editor to quit Wikipedia. (If you're not enjoying editing, why do it?) When you know that the other editors involved in a discussion are valuable contributors to Wikipedia, be especially certain that discussion about content is a constructive, pleasant one. By contrast, if you battle over every point and refuse to concede anything, you hurt Wikipedia in many ways.

WORD TO THE WISE

Pick your Fights

Some things are worth trying to get right in a Wikipedia article; for example, the facts about a group that some consider a cult. Other things aren't worth battling over; for example, the absolutely correct phrase to describe the underlying concept engine of a role-playing computer game. (In the latter case, just use the wording in the best available source, even if it's slightly wrong. Good enough is good enough.)

When you edit at Wikipedia, you'll eventually run into an editor who cares way more about an article than you do. If you get into a disagreement with someone like that, balance the amount of time you'd have to struggle with that editor over content with the time you could spend working on other things at Wikipedia instead. And you also have to consider the satisfaction and enjoyment factor. There's no point burning yourself out fighting a battle, and then quitting Wikipedia altogether.

On the other hand, you don't have to abandon an article at the first sign of a dispute. Just keep the following points in mind:

- Wikipedia has lots of editors. You're not personally responsible for any particular article.

- If you're disputing with only one or two other editors, that's a sign that the article may not be that important.

- If you're making progress in a discussion, stick with it. If you're not, get others involved as soon as you can (see "Resolving Disputes with Assistance" on page 191).

- When you make your points on an article talk page, you leave valuable information for other editors, in the future, to restart the discussion. So if you leave the article, your efforts have still been useful. (That's one reason why succinct arguments, with links to relevant policies and guidelines, are so important.)

Disengage for a While

A very experienced editor once said that the most effective tactic he knew was to post, on a user talk page, the message, "It's getting late, let's continue this tomorrow or the day after that." Waiting a day or two gives everyone's inner caveman (who always wants to fight back) a chance to settle down. Then you can look at the discussion with better perspective.

In *WP:DR*, disengagement is the second step in the dispute resolution process. The policy says that the simplest way to resolve a dispute is to simply stop having it. You can just stop editing the article or you can ask another editor to join in, and defer to that editor's suggestions. Work on other articles instead. By the time you return to the disputed article, it'll have evolved, other editors will have worked on the problem, and the disagreement may no longer exist.

Disengagement is also good because it gives you a chance to do a reality check. The following two essays may help get you into an effective frame of mind:

- *Wikipedia:Don't be a fanatic* (shortcut: *WP:DBF*)
- *Wikipedia:Uphill Battles* (shortcut: *WP:UHB*)

Resolving Disputes with Assistance

It may be clear, after some discussion, that you and other editors involved in a content dispute aren't making much progress in resolving a dispute. Sometimes no one's aware of a particularly relevant policy or guideline; sometimes one side or the other can't state clearly what they object to or why; and sometimes editors have different opinions about what's acceptable at Wikipedia. Regardless of the reason, some informal discussions just aren't particularly productive.

Wikipedia has a number of ways editors in a dispute can get assistance. Don't hesitate to use them when progress slows or stops. These resources exist because editors do need help, even when everyone's being reasonable. (And, unfortunately, sometimes editors *aren't* reasonable, so getting help is even more important.)

As mentioned earlier, *Wikipedia:Dispute resolution* (shortcut: *WP:DR*) lays out the recommended process for resolving content disputes. Which processes you use, and in what order, depends on the nature of the dispute. But in general, try following the order listed in this section, starting with editor assistance. And take it slow: The Wikipedia community doesn't like what it calls *forum shopping*, where the same question is posted on multiple pages without waiting to see if the first posting gets satisfactory answers.

NOTE

With the exception of the first of these six options—editor assistance—any time there's a content discussion somewhere *other than* the article talk page, someone should add a note to the article talk page that links to that outside discussion.

Editor Assistance

Wikipedia:Editor assistance (shortcut: *WP:EA*) is an informal way of getting one-to-one advice, feedback, and counseling from another, more experienced editor. You can get this advice in two ways: You can post something on the Requests page, or you can contact one of the editors listed on the primary page.

If you ask at the editor assistance page, it should be about processes and policy, not to get a tie-breaking vote regarding content. Or, put differently, you should be looking for a way to restart or improve the informal discussion, if possible, not trying to get someone else to join in the discussion among you and other editors. (If you want to get other editors to join an existing discussion, you can ask at a WikiProject or use the RfC process, below.)

NOTE

If you decide to go the route of asking an editor directly for advice, be sure to check the User Contributions page of the editor you're thinking of asking. You want to pick someone who has edited in the last day or so, not someone who has largely stopped editing but has forgotten to remove his name from the list.

Subject Specific Pages

If the matter involves some specialized knowledge, like terminology for Canadian football, then a good place to ask for comments is at a WikiProject (Chapter 9). For example, *Wikipedia talk:WikiProject Canadian football*. You can find the directory of WikiProjects—over a thousand exist—at *Wikipedia:WikiProject Council/Directory* (shortcut: *WP:PROJDIR*).

If the matter concerns the interpretation of a policy or guideline, try posting a question at the talk page of the policy or guideline. For example, suppose editors disagree on whether combining statistics from a report is a synthesis of information that's not allowed by the "no original research" policy. In that case, posting at the page *Wikipedia talk:No original research* might get a good answer from an editor who is particularly interested in how the policy has been interpreted in the past, or should be interpreted. (If you don't get much of a response in 3 or 4 days, try another approach.)

NOTE

It's courteous to discuss, with the other editors involved n a content dispute, the wording of a query before you post it. In fact, the process of agreeing on wording may clarify matters. Don't try to bias the wording to favor your side of the argument, and if you get some proposed wording from the other side that seems biased, don't comment about the perceived bias, just propose a change. User talk pages are good places to discuss such wording, since it's about *process*, not about content changes to the article.

Third Opinions

Wikipedia:Third opinion (shortcut: *WP:3O*) is a place to request a third-party mediator to review the arguments presented and offer an opinion. Only two editors can be involved; if there are more, you have to use another alternative. After you post the request, a mediator (from a group of editors who have volunteered to help) will read the discussion and post her opinion. Hopefully that editor's opinion will help resolve things. (The chances are better that it will if the other editor has agreed to the *WP:3O* process, though agreement's not mandatory).

Informal Mediation

The *Wikipedia:Mediation Cabal* (shortcut: *WP:MEDCAB*) provides informal mediation for disputes on Wikipedia. The page states, "Mediation is purely voluntary. All interested parties must be willing to accept mediation. If any interested party does not accept mediation, we cannot help."

This informal mediation is only as good as the mediators who handle each case, who are other editors (unscreened volunteers) with limited time. If your mediator vanishes, don't be shy about posting a request for a new one. And don't expect an instant response, since the service may have a backlog. Some mediators here are very good, but they can only make progress if both sides are willing to try for an acceptable compromise. If the mediator proposes something that you can live with, but isn't perfect, give strong consideration to accepting that proposal. (Good wording is, "That's okay with me if it's okay with the others.")

Requests for Comments

On *Wikipedia:Requests for comment* (shortcut: *WP:RFC*), you'll find a link at the top of the page to the section "Request comment on articles". Article RfCs are split out by general topic; pick whichever area seems appropriate.

RfCs aim to get a number of other editors to join in a discussion, thereby (hopefully) getting something approaching (rough) consensus. Splitting RfCS into a number of general topics is intended to encourage editors to pick an area and comment on a number of RfCs in that area.

Although RfCs are the first step in the Wikipedia's formal dispute resolution process, an RfC does not result in a formal decision or in any enforcement action by administrators. Rather, the intent is that the involved editors, in view of comments by others that are posted via the RfC, change their minds sufficiently to be able to reach an agreement on changes to the article.

Formal Mediation

Getting a case listed at *Requests for Mediation* (shortcut: *WP:RFM*) is the second step in Wikipedia's formal dispute resolution process. Formal mediation is carried out by members of the Mediation Committee, whose members are experienced editors who have demonstrated sufficient skills to be selected for that committee. The Mediation Committee considers requests to open new cases only where all parties to the dispute indicate willingness to take part in mediation, and, most of the time, have attempted informal resolution first. Parties are given 7 days from the time of the initial request to indicate that they're willing to participate.

Disputes that can't be resolved through mediation, or where editors are unwilling to take part in voluntary dispute resolution, may be referred by the Mediation Committee to the Arbitration Committee for binding resolution, including sanctions.

NOTE

The Arbitration Committee does not rule on content disputes. The focus of arbitration is on behavior. If one or more editors are referred to the Arbitration Committee after, or in lieu of mediation, it would be because editors refused to seek compromise or otherwise behaved improperly. (For more on the Arbitration Committee, see page 208).

CHAPTER 11

Handling Incivility and Personal Attacks

In an ideal world, Wikipedia editors would discuss only content and would post only well reasoned, informative comments. They would assume, unless faced with overwhelming evidence, that other editors were also editing and commenting in good faith. Personal attacks would never occur.

Unfortunately it's not an ideal world. Bad things do happen to good people. This chapter shows you helpful ways to respond to incivility and personal attacks directed against you or other editors. It also discusses what you should do if you slip up and use uncivil words, or worse, attack someone personally.

NOTE

If you've *just* experienced severe incivility or a personal attack, flip to "Initial Responses" on page 200.

Enforcing Norms of Conduct

This chapter lays out some step-by-step processes for dealing with problematical editors. First, you need an understanding of Wikipedia's rules regarding its editors' behavior, and how those are enforced. With that understanding, you'll find it easier to understand the step-by-step process.

The Norms

Wikipedia's rules for behavior center around two policies and a guideline. Experienced editors often mention the trio all in one breath: *WP:CIVIL, WP:NPA, WP:AGF*, or even just *CIVIL, NPA, AGF*.

- *Wikipedia:Civility* (shortcut: *WP:CIVIL*). Being rude, insensitive, or petty makes people upset and prevents Wikipedia from working well. Be careful to avoid offending people unintentionally. For example, an edit summary of "Making content compliant with [[WP:NPOV]]" is less likely to upset an editor than "Removing garbage and biased personal opinions."

- *Wikipedia:No personal attacks* (shortcut: *WP:NPA*). Do not make personal attacks anywhere in Wikipedia. Comment on content, not on the contributor. Personal attacks damage the community and deter users. Nobody likes abuse.
- *Wikipedia:Assume good faith* (shortcut: *WP:AGF*). Unless there's strong evidence to the contrary, assume that people who work on the project are trying to help it, not hurt it.

Of the three, violations of NPA are considered the most serious, by far. Extreme or repeated violations will lead to an editor being *blocked* (prevented from editing) for a while, in the hopes that he comes to his senses. The administrator doing the blocking decides how long the blocked period lasts. If the editor doesn't mend his ways, he'll be blocked indefinitely.

Violations of AGF, on the other hand, don't lead to blocking. The purpose of the AGF policy is to remind editors that underlying almost all incivility and, occasionally, personal attacks, is a lack of respect for other editors. It's the incivility and personal attacks —the *consequences* of failing to assume good faith—that get an editor into trouble.

Violations of CIVIL but not of NPA can lead to blocking, but an editor must truly persist in uncivil behavior to get banned or blocked indefinitely. Some editors, nevertheless, have succeeded at this dubious accomplishment.

FREQUENTLY ASKED QUESTION

Incivility and Attacks

What's the difference between incivility and a personal attack on Wikipedia? Aren't all attacks uncivil?

Incivility and personal attacks do overlap some. As a general rule, a personal attack is directly saying, "You're stupid" (or racist, incompetent, ugly, and so on). Incivility is less overt; it *implies* something negative about an editor without actually saying it.

Examples of incivility:

- An article talk page comment that starts, "The text you keep adding to the article is really difficult to read, so why don't you edit at the version of Wikipedia in your native language?"
- An edit summary that says, "removed poorly worded garbage"
- Posting a note on another editor's user talk page that says, "If you're going to create a pointless article, could you at least spell check it?"

Enforcing the Rules

The entire Wikipedia community bears the responsibility of enforcing policies and guidelines. If you see incivility or personal attacks against another editor, you ought to help out, just as other editors should help out if they see incivility and personal attacks directed at you.

Normal editors can issue warnings, but they can't prevent a problem editor from continuing to post to Wikipedia. That's where *administrators* come in. Administrators are editors who have special authority, chosen by a rough consensus of editors. They can block editors from further edits, as a preventive measure against further abusive editing.

UP TO SPEED

How Administrators are Selected

Any registered editor can nominate herself, or be nominated by other editor, as a candidate for adminship, in a process called Request for Adminship (see Figure 11-1). Then other registered editors ask questions of the candidate, express their opinion (support, oppose, or neutral), and explain their reasoning if they want (which is expected for opposing and neutral opinions). An RfA stays open for 7 days, unless a candidate withdraws or the RfA has absolutely no chance for success. (That's a snowball case; see *WP:SNOWBALL.*)

After a week, a Wikipedia bureaucrat reviews the RfA, judges it successful or unsuccessful, and closes it. The threshold for success is around 80 percent support votes (not counting neutrals), but bureaucrats have discretion to close an RfA as successful or unsuccessful regardless of the actual percentage of support. (Such deviations are rare and usually controversial, but they do happen.)

Unsuccessful candidates typically fail to reach the 80 percent support level for one of three reasons: lack of general editing experience, lack of edits that demonstrate knowledge of Wikipedia policies and processes, and past problems like unproductive disputes with other editors. For more information, see *Wikipedia:Guide to requests for adminship* (shortcut: *WP:GRFA*).

Actions by the community

When one editor attacks another, she may think that any response by the attacked editor is defensiveness. A third editor entering the discussion can be quite a shock, particularly a third editor who civilly points out exactly what was done wrong and issues a warning.

Warnings serve a very important role in Wikipedia, in that they point out problems. As warnings accumulate on an editor's talk page, they provide the basis for more severe warnings and, when all else fails, a block on the account. If you see a problem and post a warning, you're not only informing an editor about problems with his edits, but you're

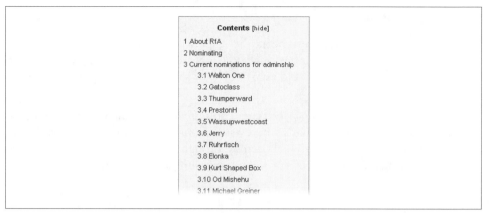

Figure 11-1. On December 10, 2007,Wikipedia:Requests for adminship (shortcut: WP:RFA) listed 19 open candidacies for adminship. Editors are expected to read the answers given by candidates to questions posed to them, and the opinions of others editors about the candidates, and research the information provided to ascertain whether the candidate seems trustworthy and capable of handling administrator responsibilities.

also building a case against that editor. Hopefully, the case will end quickly with the editor seeing reason, but, if not, it may end with the editor getting removed from Wikipedia.

Interestingly, standard user warnings found on the page *Wikipedia:Template messages/ User talk namespace* (shortcut: *WP:WARN*) (see Figure 11-2) do *not* include any warnings about incivility (as of this writing). Presumably, either warnings for AGF or warnings for NPA cover incivility. For example, here's the level 3 NPA warning: "Please assume good faith in your dealings with other editors. Please stop being uncivil to your fellow editors; instead, assume that they are here to improve Wikipedia."

NOTE

There is no level 4, final warning for an AGF violation. Presumably that's because there would be associated violations of the *no personal attacks* rule, and those would lead to a level 4 warning and then, if necessary, to a block.

As with vandalism and spam warnings (page 130), you need to look at prior warnings to determine what level of warning to issue. Sometimes you shouldn't issue a warning at all; for example, when a level 4 warning has already been issued, and there's yet another personal attack. (In this case, you'd post at *WP:AN/I*, as discussed on page 206.)

Should you *remove* personal attacks against other editors? The general answer is that personal attacks on article talk pages, where the posting has at least some relevance to the topic, should be left as is. But Wikipedia's NPA policy specifies that serious personal attacks—those that reveal an editor's personal information or "go beyond the level of

Description	Level 1	Level 2	Level 3	Level 4	Level 4im
deletion}} templates	speedy1}}	speedy2}}	speedy3}}	speedy4}}	{{N/A}}
Behavior towards editors and articles					
Personal attack directed at a specific editor	{{subst:uw-npa1}}	{{subst:uw-npa2}}	{{subst:uw-npa3}}	{{subst:uw-npa4}}	{{subst:uw-npa4im}}
Not assuming good faith	{{subst:uw-agf1}}	{{subst:uw-agf2}}	{{subst:uw-agf3}}	{{N/A}}	
Ownership of articles	{{subst:uw-own1}}	{{subst:uw-own2}}	{{subst:uw-own3}}	{{N/A}}	

Figure 11-2. As of late 2007, there was no formal warning template for incivility. Warnings regarding failure to assume good faith only went to level 3, meaning that it's inappropriate to request that an editor be blocked for this problem (blocks require ignoring a level 4 warning). Wikipedia uses a catch-all "personal attacks" label for improper behavior toward other editors, and that can be the basis for blocking editors, whether or not they get level 4 warnings.

mere invective"—should be deleted. Any attack that threatens an individual, the project, or the general community should be removed immediately. (For more on editing comments of other editors on talk pages, and other pages within Wikipedia where discussions occur, see page 154.)

Actions by administrators

Many editors think of Wikipedia administrators as *judges*: They analyze the facts, weigh the arguments, and mete out punishments (blocking people from editing, or at least harshly threatening the miscreants). But that's *not* the role of administrators. Administrators mostly do administrative tasks involving egregious cases of vandalism, deleting pages, protecting pages involved in edit wars, and so on. Furthermore, as the *Wikipedia blocking policy* (shortcut: *WP:BP*) says, blocks are for preventing damage to pages, not punishing users afterwards.

The difference may be difficult to grasp, but it's important. It's why warnings are so critical to fighting vandals and dealing with poor behavior. As well as giving an editor a chance to change his behavior, warnings—if ignored—demonstrate that the editor is unlikely to change his behavior in the future, and a block is the next step to protecting the project. Blocks typically start out being for short durations, and only escalate in length if an editor continues to show that he can't restrain himself from repeating problematic behavior.

Wikipedia has only a small number of administrators—roughly a thousand—who are unpaid volunteers like all Wikipedia editors. Their number has not increased as quickly as Wikipedia has grown (see Figure 11-3), making their limited time a valuable resource that Wikipedia needs to protect. That's why, in the processes described next, there's so much emphasis on ways that editors can solve problems themselves, or get the assistance of other editors, rather than asking administrators for help.

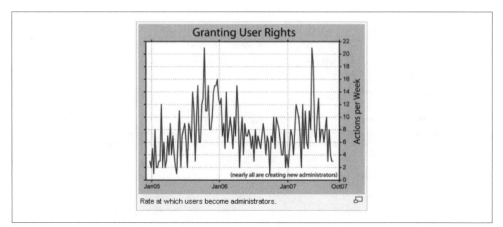

Figure 11-3. The greatest number of editors became administrators per week around late 2005, when Wikipedia was much smaller than it is today. The number of active Wikipedia administrators has grown more slowly than Wikipedia as a whole. The graph shows "User Rights" granted, not "Admin Rights" granted, but almost all rights granted are for new admins. [This graph is courtesy of editor Dragons Flight (Robert A. Rohde), based on a log analysis.]

Dealing with Incivility and Personal Attacks

The processes described in this section may seem like bureaucracy run amok, but in fact they're an efficient, logical way to escalate a matter until it's solved, whether that's because an editor changes his ways, quits Wikipedia, or gets blocked.

If you're the subject of a personal attack or significant incivility, both you and the other editor determine what will succeed in stopping recurrences of the problems. If you fan the flames by attacking back, that's a violation of rules in its own right, and will probably get you your own warnings. In that case, the matter may not get resolved until it goes to the highest level of community decision-making in English Wikipedia—the Arbitration Committee (page 208). If both you and the other editor are reasonable people (and you'll certainly encounter editors who aren't), you may be able to solve the problem by simply talking it out on user talk pages.

What happens after your first response depends on what kind of person you're dealing with. So circumstances decide which of the following measures to choose. You're certainly not required to use them all.

Initial Responses

Personal attacks almost always occur on your own user talk page or on an article talk page. There may be some obvious lead-in (you and another editor have reverted each other's edits in a content dispute, for example) or the attack may come out the blue (from someone whose edit you've reverted as part of vandal-fighting, for example). Regardless, there it is, staring you in the face. It may be a graphic insult, or a passive-aggressive jab. The first thing you should do is nothing. That's right. Don't respond at all until your emotional reaction has passed. Then you can consider your options.

Don't respond until you can respond unemotionally

The standard human response to an attack is hardwired into your brain—fight or flight. When you're in danger, your emotions tell you to act immediately. Your emotional system is much faster than your logical system. Quick decisions are emotionally driven, not the product of rational thinking. So before your typing fingers fly into action, say to yourself: *Those are just words on a computer screen. I don't have to do anything right now. I have all the time I need, to think this through and do the right thing. I don't need to do the first thing that comes to mind.*

Wikipedia doesn't operate at real-world speeds. Take a break, come back in an hour or a day, work on something else, breathe deeply, have a nice cup of tea—there isn't any rush.

Don't attack back

In the real world, responding to an attack is considered standing up for yourself. In Wikipedia, editors who attack back are considered part of the problem. Attacking an editor whom you think attacked you turns Wikipedia into a personal battleground, which is against policy. As *WP:NOT* puts it: "If a user acts uncivilly, uncalmly, uncooperatively, insultingly, harassingly, or intimidatingly toward you, this does not give you an excuse to do the same in retaliation."

Your goal in dealing with this type of problem is to get the other editor to change her behavior, and if she doesn't, have her removed from Wikipedia. If you succeed in the first, or are efficient in doing the second, that's what standing up for yourself in Wikipedia is all about.

Decide if you even need to respond

An editor who resorts to uncivil comments and personal attacks loses credibility at Wikipedia. If the editor's arguments were sound and logical, why would he need to get personal and emotional? You can gain credibility, assuming that what occurred wasn't a clear and convincing personal attack, if you simply ignore it. An editor may just be having a bad day. Don't reinforce snarky behavior by responding to it.

How you ignore incivility depends on where it occurs. If it's a posting on your user talk page, you can delete it or archive it (see page 158). If it's a posting on an article talk page, you can see whether someone else responds to it (with a comment or a warning), or if another editor ignores it and discusses the non-personal aspects of the posting.

If you're not sure whether or not to respond, wait a full day or so, and see whether anything else happens.

Don't comment about problematical behavior on article talk pages

As discussed in Chapter 8 (page 153), article talk pages are for discussing articles, not editors or their behavior. That said, if you've decided to post a warning or request that the editor be blocked (see page 198), it's helpful to leave a response to that effect on an article talk page. That way, other editors know the problematical posting is being dealt with. A comment like this is appropriate:

This violates [[WP:NPA]]; I've posted a warning at [[User talk:Name of problem editor]].
~~~~

Or this:

I've reported this violation of [[WP:NPA]] at [[WP:AN/I]]; repeat problem. ~~~~

If you respond, be factual, not emotional

If you respond at all, stick to the facts. If particular wording wasn't in accordance with a Wikipedia policy, that's a fact. If you speculate on the editor's motives for writing something, that's your opinion. The guideline *Wikipedia:Etiquette* (shortcut: *WP:EQ*) stresses that text on a screen may comes across as rude, when you can't hear the voice or see the facial expressions of a person sitting in front of you. An ironic joke may come across as a full-on insult. Again, assume good faith. Don't assume someone's out to get you. Similarly, be sure your own writing is brief, clear, and to the point. Avoid saying things that someone could take the wrong way.

Your goal isn't to hammer the other editor into submission (which rarely works, anyway), it's to get her to realize that her actions have consequences. If the other editor has improved articles and shown reason in other edits, that's all the more reason to assume good faith. You're not helping Wikipedia by making things unnecessarily unpleasant and driving her away.

Your response should depend on the editor

The correct approach to warning an editor about behavioral violations is somewhat similar to warnings about vandalism, as discussed on page 130. Start by looking at the warnings that others have posted on the user talk page, if any. Then take a look at the user talk page's history—the user may have deleted warnings. Next, take a look at the User contributions page: Is this a regular contributor or someone with very few edits? (It's harder to tell with anonymous IP accounts; just look at the last week or two of postings.)

Here are some types of editors you might encounter, and the appropriate responses:

- **An anonymous IP editor with no other postings**. If you get a single drive-by attack, it's best to just drop the matter. Your warning probably isn't going to do any good. If the posting is part of an ongoing series, post something at *Wikipedia:Administrators' noticeboard/Incidents* (shortcut: *WP:AN/I*).

- **Relatively new editor, lots of warnings**. Post a standard warning template from the *WP:WARN* page, following the procedure laid out in Chapter 7 (page 131). If the editor has already hit level 4, and then attacked you, take the matter to *WP:AN/I* rather than posting a warning.

- **Regular editor, lots of contributions, very few problems**. Depending on how egregious the attacking post was, tailor your posting from nothing at all to a measured response. Reasonable wording is, "Maybe I'm misunderstanding your post, but it seemed to me that saying I need to repeat the third grade crossed the boundary of *[[WP:CIVIL]]*."

TIP

Before you post any kind of response, double-check to make sure you're posting to the correct user page. Don't use a template on an editor who has been a regular contributor for a long time.

Don't argue about warnings

If you post a warning and the other editor comments that it's not justified, don't argue. If what the other editor says seems to have merit, it's fine to reconsider your warning (and, if you change your mind, do a strike-through, as described on page 210). If the other editor says your warning is uncivil, or amounts to a personal attack, or violates AGF, ignore it. Those allegations are considered *wikilawyering*, and it doesn't impress administrators. Ultimately, the matter comes down to the future behavior of the other editor, future warnings he gets, and what administrators decide when they read the edits that caused the warnings. You've made your contribution to reducing future problems by posting a warning, and that's what counts.

Read other editors' essays about civility

If you're still struggling with some of the underlying concepts of the advice above, reading a couple of these essays may help:

- *Wikipedia:Avoid personal remarks* (shortcut: *WP:APR*)
- *Wikipedia:No angry mastodons* (shortcut: *WP:NAM*)
- *Wikipedia:Staying cool when the editing gets hot* (shortcut: *WP:COOL*)

Explore Less Formal Solutions

Most of the time, incivility or a personal attack is a one-time occurrence. But if it's repeated, and you think you need help dealing with it, you have a number of informal options. Use one or more of these options before turning to the formal process for dealing with problem editors.

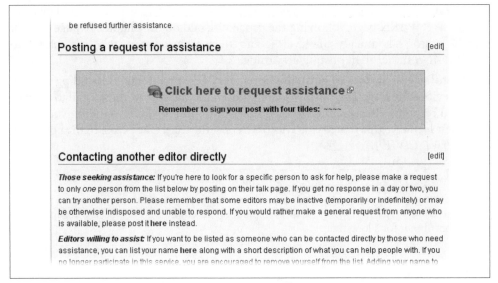

be refused further assistance.

Posting a request for assistance   [edit]

🐱 **Click here to request assistance** ⮐

Remember to sign your post with four tildes: ~~~~

Contacting another editor directly   [edit]

Those seeking assistance: If you're here to look for a specific person to ask for help, please make a request to only *one* person from the list below by posting on their talk page. If you get no response in a day or two, you can try another person. Please remember that some editors may be inactive (temporarily or indefinitely) or may be otherwise indisposed and unable to respond. If you would rather make a general request from anyone who is available, please post it **here** instead.

Editors willing to assist: If you want to be listed as someone who can be contacted directly by those who need assistance, you can list your name **here** along with a short description of what you can help people with. If you no longer participate in this service, you are encouraged to remove yourself from the list. Adding your name to

Figure 11-4. At the Editor assistance *page, you can post an open request for any editor who wants to assist you, or you can pick an editor from a list (lower down on the page than shown here). In either case, you can get a personal consultation about any editing situation.*

You'll find instructions at the top of the main page of each option listed in this section. Read them. Other editors appreciate it when you read and follow instructions for asking for help.

Editor assistance

Wikipedia:Editor assistance (shortcut: *WP:EA*) is an informal way of getting one-to-one advice, feedback, and counseling from another, more experienced, editor. You can actually get advice in two ways: Post something on the Requests page, or contact one of the listed editors on the primary page (Figure 11-4).

You may think that asking another editor for assistance is an intrusion on her time. It is, in some sense, but for many editors, offering advice to a sane, reasonable person can be a welcome change of pace from what they normally do, particularly if they're administrators.

NOTE

If you decide to go the route of asking an editor directly for advice, be sure to check his User Contributions page. You want to pick someone who has edited in the last day or so, not someone who has largely stopped editing but has forgotten to remove his name from the list.

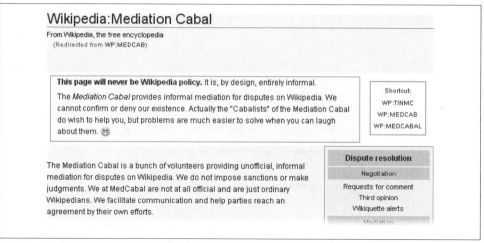

Figure 11-5. The Mediation Cabal is an unofficial group of editors who offer informal mediation. The "cabal" aims to help with disputes in a way that minimizes administrative procedures. If you ask for help, you get help, but all the editors involved in a dispute must agree to participate.

Wikiquette

Wikipedia:Wikiquette alerts (shortcut: *WP:WQA*) is "where users can report impolite, uncivil or other difficult communications with editors, to seek perspective, advice, informal mediation, or a referral to a more appropriate forum." If you post here, you may get advice from just one editor, or from several.

You can certainly try "Editor assistance" first, then "Wikiquette alerts," though the two actually overlap. Just don't post in both places simultaneously. That's *forum shopping*, and most editors consider it bad form. If you're debating which to choose, know that EA is faster, but WQA has more activist editors who do things like post warnings themselves.

Informal mediation

The *Wikipedia:Mediation Cabal* (shortcut: *WP:MEDCAB*) provides informal mediation for disputes on Wikipedia. (See Figure 11-5.) Their page states, "You must already be having a discussion. We cannot start a discussion for you." In other words, both you and the other editor must be willing to participate in such informal mediation. It never hurts for you to offer the other editor this option. It's a demonstration that you're trying to assume good faith; just don't expect instant agreement. (The catch-22 here is that if you and the other editor are both willing to go into mediation, most of the time you'd be able to work out a reasonable solution without needing mediation.)

People use this type of informal mediation more frequently for content disputes, as discussed in Chapter 10 (page 179). If a mediator suggests that both you and the other editor agree to do (or not to do) certain things in the future, don't protest that the other editor is at fault, not you. If what the mediator proposed isn't onerous, and getting the

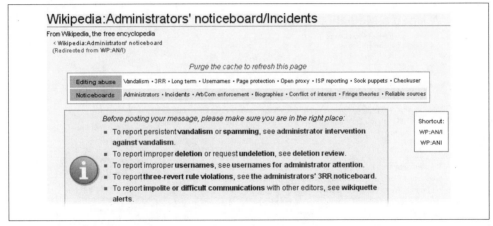

Figure 11-6. The page Wikipedia:Administrators' noticeboard/Incidents *is for reporting and discussing incidents on the English Wikipedia that require administrators' intervention. But if you can use a more specialized noticeboard (listed at top, in small print), you should post there, not here. Similarly, if a specialized page exists to report editing abuse, then you should post there, not here.*

other editor to agree hinges on whether you agree, then agree. You won't help yourself by arguing. Your goal is to get the other editor to change her ways, not to have a mediator declare who's at fault.

Community enforceable mediation

Wikipedia:Community enforceable mediation (shortcut: *WP:CEM*) was an experimental alternative where editors could resolve disputes by negotiating and agreeing to binding agreements that mimic arbitration remedies. Like informal (Cabal) mediation, above, it required all parties to agree to participate in mediation. Unlike less formal mediation, however, if agreement is reached, administrators would enforce it.

The process was opened for cases in March 2007 and shut down (marked as inactive/historical) in December 2007. Five cases were submitted; none resulted in enforceable agreements.

AN/I

Wikipedia:Administrators' noticeboard/Incidents (shortcut: *WP:AN/I*) is for only serious, repeat attacks where the editor has received clear warnings and is ignoring them (Figure 11-6). You go here if an editor has engaged in a personal attack after receiving a level 4 warning, or if you've posted a warning and then a higher level of warning, and the editor persists in violating the NPA policy. (You could, in theory, continue to escalate your warnings, but two is enough.)

If you're unsure that the problem is serious enough for AN/I, don't go there—the page gets enough traffic as is. If you do post to the noticeboard, be sure to include a succinct description of the problem, together with roughly a half-dozen diffs (page 87) showing problem edits.

NOTE

Report any cases of aggressive harassment (see *WP:HAR*) or attack pages (*WP:ATP*) to this noticeboard without waiting to see if warnings are useful. If behavior is egregious, deal with it promptly.

Use Formal Processes

If the problem continues, and you've exhausted your informal options, Wikipedia has two formal processes for dealing with problem editors: a Request for Comments regarding user conduct; and binding decisions by the Arbitration Committee, the highest level of community decision-making within the English Wikipedia.

Both of these processes are time-consuming: Each can take several months to play out, and the evidence presented and arguments made can be voluminous. Fortunately, only a small percentage of disputes are so entangled that they go to arbitration; RfCs are much more common.

NOTE

Chapter 10 (page 194) described a third formal process, action by the Mediation Committee. Requests for mediation (shortcut: *WP:RFM*) are limited to *content disputes*, so they're not included in this discussion of personal attacks and incivility.

User conduct RfCs

The cases opened at *Requests for comments – User conduct* (shortcut: *WP:RFCC*) require that at least two editors have contacted the editor whose conduct is being questioned, on that editor's user talk page or the talk pages involved in the dispute, and tried but failed to resolve the problem. The two (or more) editors certifying the dispute must be among those who attempted to resolve the matter. Filing an RfC is not a step to be taken lightly or in haste. Informal ways of resolving disputes (like talking it out) are preferable, but if they don't work, then an RfC provides the last chance for an editor to come to his senses.

There are aspects of a court case to an RfC, although it's by no means a legal matter. Editors present evidence (diffs), make statements, and endorse viewpoints. If you're doing a user conduct RfC against another editor, be clear and succinct, and present compelling details about who said what, when, and where. Figure 11-7 shows a table of contents for a typical RfC user conduct case.

Editors named in an RfC are expected to respond to it. If the matter goes to the Arbitration Committee (see page 208), failure to respond is a factor that arbitrators take

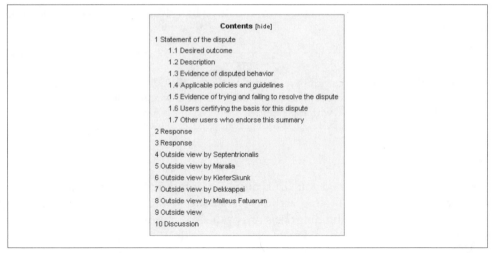

Figure 11-7. A Request for Comment on user conduct is a cross between a legal case and a public hearing, with evidence, responses, and statements of view from uninvolved editors. Here's the table of contents of an RfC that's been open for about 6 weeks.

into consideration. Within an RfC case, though, there's no way to compel an editor to comment, and no penalty for failing to do so. But as in real life, failure to respond tends to be seen as an admission that the editor has no good explanation or defense for her actions.

An RfC will not result in any enforcement action by administrators. The ideal outcome is that the involved editors, in view of comments by others that are posted in the RfC, find a way to agree to what they will and won't do in the future. An RfC may even result in apologies offered for past behavior. So even if an RfC shows an overwhelming consensus of opinion by uninvolved editors who comment in the RfC, resolution depends on the problem editors accepting that such a consensus is valid, and that they need to change. If an RfC doesn't result in voluntary changes, the final step (if the problem continues) is the Arbitration Committee.

The Arbitration Committee

A Request for Arbitration (shortcut: *WP:AFAR*) is the last step of dispute resolution on Wikipedia. The Arbitration Committee (see Figure 11-8) makes *binding* decisions. In most ArbCom cases, at least one editor gets banned from editing Wikipedia for at least a year, and rulings against multiple editors are common.

The Arbitration Committee consists of volunteer editors. Committee members are appointed by Jimmy Wales, who owned Wikipedia before giving it to the Wikimedia Foundation, which he created. The appointments are based on the results of advisory elections held annually, where registered editors at Wikipedia express support and opposition to the candidates. Wales does not consider himself bound by the results of

Members

The number of active Committee members affects the number of Arbitrators needed to reach a ruling. For example, if seven Arbitrators are active on a given case, then four votes are needed to reach a majority decision. If ten are active, then six votes are needed, etc. (In general, if an even number of members vote on a proposal and there is a tie vote, the proposal is not adopted. In this circumstance, the Arbitrators may ask Jimbo Wales to cast a tie-breaking vote, but this has yet to occur.)

The Committee has also decided against having a chairperson.

Status of members is either Active or Inactive (no Arbitration activity in the last two weeks, or a statement indicating inactivity).

As of 5 December 2007:

Active

- FloNight (talk · contribs · email)
- Fred Bauder (talk · contribs · email)
- Jdforrester (talk · contribs · email) (James Forrester aka "James F.", jdforrester@gmail.com)
- Jpgordon (talk · contribs · email) (Josh Gordon, user.jpgordon@gmail.com)
- Kirill Lokshin (talk · contribs · email)
- Mackensen (talk · contribs · email)
- Morven (talk · contribs · email) (Matthew Brown, morven@gmail.com)
- Paul August (talk · contribs · email)
- Raul654 (talk · contribs · email) (Mark Pellegrini)
- UninvitedCompany (talk · contribs · email)

Figure 11-8. The Arbitration Committee consists of volunteer editors; the English Wikipedia is essentially a self-governing community. Committee members are appointed by Jimmy Wales, based on the results of annual elections. The fifth annual elections were held in December 2007; roughly a third of the Committee is elected each year, for 3-year terms.

the elections, but he's generally appointed arbitrators from among the candidates with the highest percentage of positive votes.

Except for a few cases involving serious problem actions by one or more administrators, the Arbitration Committee requires that cases must first have gone through the RfC process. The Request for Arbitration policy states that "The Committee considers community input from the RFC process both in determining whether to accept a case and also in formulating its decisions."

The likelihood that you'll ever be involved in a case before the Arbitration Committee is small, unless you're an active editor of articles whose basic subjects are controversial. In 2006 the committee handled 116 cases. This book doesn't cover the intricate details of filing and arguing a case. For now, know that this final resort is there for extreme cases. If editors don't voluntarily agree to behave properly, and if their behavior is not so egregious that an administrator blocks them, then the Arbitration Committee process is the final step that the Wikipedia community can take to prevent an editor from disrupting Wikipedia.

When You Get Irritated (or Worse)

This chapter is primarily for situations where you're the target of incivility or personal attacks. But, sadly, you may be the one committing—or thinking about committing—mayhem against another editor. You know you shouldn't, but sometimes telling yourself that you shouldn't do something isn't enough. If it's not, this section can help.

If You *Haven't* Yet Posted Something You'll Regret

If you're just *thinking* about posting something snippy, subtly insulting, or otherwise critical of another editor, take yourself promptly to one or more of the following pages:

- *Wikipedia:Truce* (shortcut: *WP:TRUCE*).
- *Wikipedia:A nice cup of tea and a sit down* (shortcut: *WP:TEA*).
- Or take a look at some of the essays mentioned earlier in the chapter: *WP:COOL*, *WP:NAM*, and *WP:APR*.

If You *Have* Posted Something You Realize You Shouldn't Have

Say you've indulged in a little biting criticism of another edit. And, quite possibly, the editor deserved to be criticized. Nevertheless, you've committed a violation of Wikipedia policy, and (as good as it may have felt when you were doing it) done nothing to further the goal of building the world's best online encyclopedia.

First, rest assured that you won't get booted off Wikipedia for a single mistake, or even for a couple. You *will* get into trouble by ignoring justified warnings and continuing your behavior. As discussed earlier in the chapter, Wikipedia administrators don't block editors to *punish* them, they block editors to *prevent* future problems.

Second, do what you can to mitigate the damage. At minimum, do the following:

- For anything relatively recent (say, in the past week), go back and strikethrough inappropriate wording. To change text from normal to strikethrough, use a pair of tags: Put a *<s>* at the beginning and a *</s>* at the end. If you replace inappropriate words with neutral words, underline the added text using *<u>* at the beginning and *</u>* at the end. Make sure your edit summary includes something like *my prior comments*, so other editors understand that you're not editing someone else's words, which isn't allowed.

- Post an apology on the user talk page of the editor who you attacked. If you can't bring yourself to actually say *I apologize*, then say something like *I have realized that my postings were a violation of [[WP:CIVIL]], and I'll do my best not to do that again.*

Third, try really, really hard not to do it again. In the future, when you're irritated (or worse), get up and walk away from the computer, or at least switch to doing something else. And if you decide you can't tolerate whatever's pushing your emotional buttons on a particular page or area, *go to a different page*. Wikipedia is a huge project (as this book should make clear), with an amazing variety of things to do, and whatever you do, you should *enjoy* doing it.

CHAPTER 12

Lending Other Editors a Hand

Most of this book is about articles—creating, improving, arguing over, deleting. But Wikipedia is more than just a large number of articles. It's a community of people—the editors. Wikipedia has a number of pages and activities to assist editors: to answer specific questions, to help editors learn more about good editing, to help resolve differences of opinion, and even just to show appreciation. As with everything else at Wikipedia, the people who run these pages and activities are also editors—volunteers just like you. This chapter shows you all the places and ways you can lend other editors a hand.

If you're not an experienced editor, you may feel that it's too soon to read this chapter. But many of the pages and activities described below don't require a lot of experience. More importantly, you can pick and choose where you want to help. For example, if you're looking at a page of questions by editors, you can just skip any questions that you don't understand. Furthermore, you have one advantage that many other editors don't—you have this book.

Answering Questions

One of the easiest ways you can help other editors is by answering their questions. If you don't know an answer, or don't have the time to research an answer, you can simply leave the question for other editors to answer.

TIP

You may find answers to other editors' questions in this book. But there's another general resource for researching questions—the *Editor's Index to Wikipedia* (shortcut: *WP:EIW*). With more than 2,000 entries, this index probably has a link to the page or pages you need to answer most questions. You must understand the subject matter well enough to get to the right section of the index, and you may have to click through several pages to find exactly the information you need.

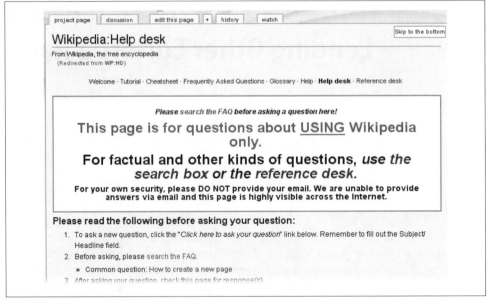

Figure 12-1. The phrase "For factual and other kinds of questions" means that the Help desk is not the place to look for information contained in encyclopedia articles. For a question like, "How long do butterflies live?" use the search box to find the article Butterfly, *which probably contains the answer.*

General Questions

The main place for editors to ask general questions is the page *Wikipedia:Help desk* (shortcut: *WP:HD*). On a typical day, editors ask and answer 50 to 100 questions. This section shows you how to answer Help desk questions. You can also answer questions on other Wikipedia pages, listed at the end of this section.

Helping at the Help desk

To get started answering questions at the Help desk, first read the top of that page (Figure 12-1). The Help desk page starts out with a number of, er, emphatic announcements. As you can guess, a lot of folks have misunderstood the Help desk's purpose. It's for help using the online encyclopedia, not for help finding articles. People who are very new to Wikipedia should check the FAQ first, since the answers to their questions are probably already there. Self-help, however, doesn't come easily to people who are completely new.

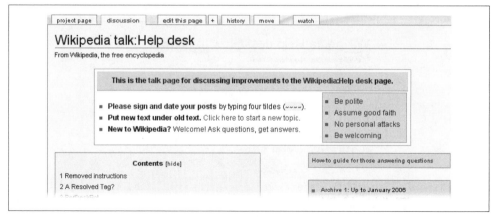

Figure 12-2. The top of the Help desk's talk page has instructions to help you get started using the page. The links at right ("Be polite", "Assume good faith", and so on) link to guideline pages. These norms of conduct (page 195) apply throughout Wikipedia, as well as to editors working the Help desk and posting on the talk page.

TIP

Some questions aren't answered in articles because they're not really encyclopedic, like, "What's a good camera to buy for someone who wants to be a professional photographer?" Take those questions to the *Reference desk* (shortcut: *WP:RD*), which is similar to a librarian service (and another place to put your question-answering expertise to good use). See the box on page 216 for more detail.

The top of the Help desk page contains two links to different collections of frequently asked questions (FAQs). The "Frequently Asked Questions" link near the top of Figure 12-1 goes to a set of FAQs on Wikipedia pages. The link "search the FAQ" (which appears twice) goes to an alternative, searchable compilation of FAQs called Nubio at *http://tools.wikimedia.de/~tangotango/nubio/*.

The Help desk also has its own talk (discussion) page (Figure 12-2). If you want to lend a hand answering questions, read the talk page to get a feel for what other volunteers have been doing and thinking for the past couple of months. If you have a question about answering questions, or you think of a way to improve the help process, bring up the issue on this talk page.

The most important link for a helpful editor like you who wants to answer questions is hidden on the talk page, in small print at that. Look on the right, just below the first box of instructions in Figure 12-2, for the box that reads, "How-to guide for those answering questions". That page walks you through the process of answering questions from other editors (Figure 12-3): being concise, avoiding edit conflicts with other editors who are answering questions, providing links to relevant policies and guidelines, finding answers to questions about Wikipedia, and handling general knowledge questions that really belong at the Reference desk.

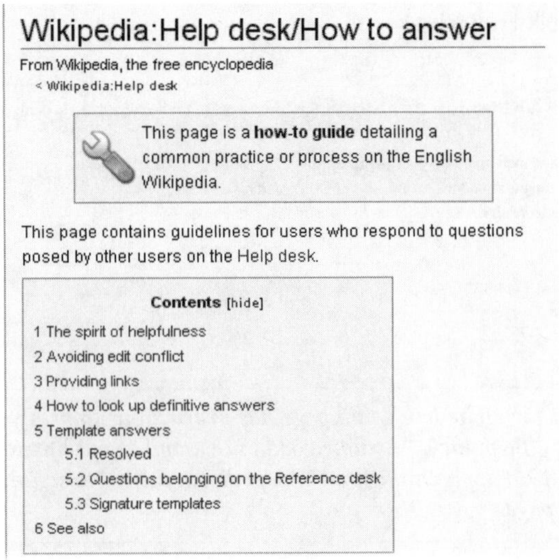

Wikipedia:Help desk/How to answer

From Wikipedia, the free encyclopedia
< Wikipedia:Help desk

This page is a **how-to guide** detailing a common practice or process on the English Wikipedia.

This page contains guidelines for users who respond to questions posed by other users on the Help desk.

Contents [hide]

1 The spirit of helpfulness
2 Avoiding edit conflict
3 Providing links
4 How to look up definitive answers
5 Template answers
    5.1 Resolved
    5.2 Questions belonging on the Reference desk
    5.3 Signature templates
6 See also

Figure 12-3. This "how-to" guide helps you become a better question-answerer. For example, it has templates that you can paste in for common questions: how to create a new article, how to link from an article to another Wikipedia article, how to report vandalism, how to upload an image, and so on.

UP TO SPEED

The Reference Desk

The Wikipedia Reference desk (shortcut: *WP:RD*) is like the reference desk at your local public library, except volunteer editors take the role of all-knowing librarian. Visitors post questions about things *other than editing Wikipedia*, and volunteers post answers or suggestions (Figure 12-4). Here's a condensed sampling of questions from a number of Reference desk categories:

- I'm looking for a data structure that's sort of a queue with hash-table-like properties. (Computing)

- If you have a protein kinase C (PKC) inhibitor, and want to inhibit pkc, how would you use it? (Science)

- How does one calculate the Euler angles for a roll-less rotation? (Mathematics)

- Was the Holy Roman Empire not the first attempt at a 'universal state'? If so what went wrong? (Humanities)

- Are prepositions ending a sentence really so bad? (Language)

- Why are new releases of DVDs, CDs, and books always released on Tuesdays? (Entertainment)

- Why do dogs howl at the moon? (Miscellaneous)

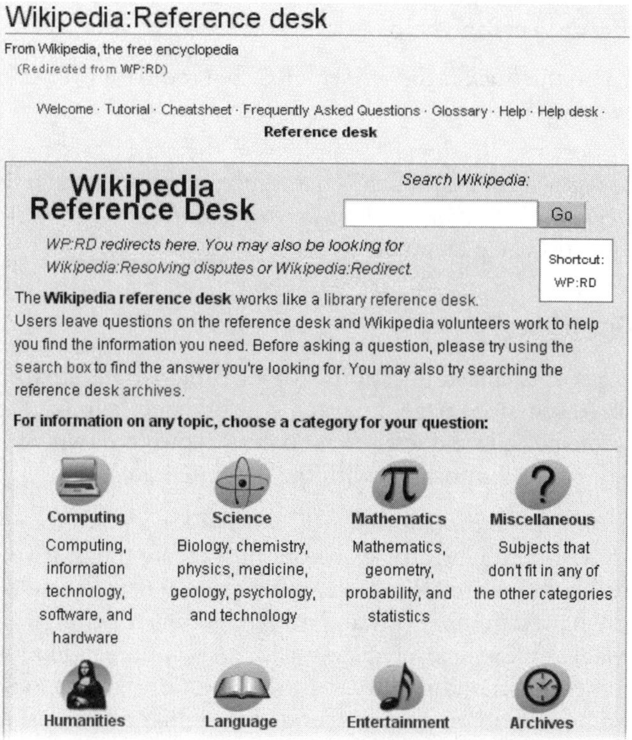

Figure 12-4. When you click a Reference desk category, you go to a page of instructions for asking questions, plus a list of previous asked (and answered) questions archived by date. Click the question to see volunteers' answers on a discussion page.

> If you have some specialized or eclectic knowledge, or like researching possibly obscure questions, you might consider lending a hand. If so, read *Wikipedia:Reference desk/ guidelines* first.

Other places where general questions appear

The Help desk gets a wide range of questions about editing every day. You can learn a lot there just by reading answers, or by researching questions yourself in order to provide answers. But it's not the only place folks go to ask questions. If you're looking for quieter territory—with fewer questions and fewer editors answering questions—check out the following pages:

- *New contributors' help page* (shortcut: *WP:NCHP*)
- *Village pump (assistance)* (shortcut: *WP:VPA*)
- *Village pump (miscellaneous)* (shortcut: *WP:VPM*)

And if that's not enough, editors can ask questions in two more ways—two more ways that you can offer answers and help:

- Editors can join the *#wikipedia-en-help* IRC chat room for live assistance. For more on IRC, see page 164.
- Editors can post the *{{Helpme}}* template on their user talk pages, along with a question or request for assistance. That template automatically lists the user talk page at *Category:Wikipedians looking for help* (shortcut: *CAT:HELP*). It also sends a notice to the IRC help channel.

Specialized Questions

Editors tend to ask specialized questions (for example, about a particular policy) on the relevant talk (discussion) page, not on a consolidated help page. Still, Wikipedia has a few places for specialized questions, and thus a few places where you can consider offering advice if you're comfortable with the particular area:

- *Wikipedia:Drawing board* (shortcut: *WP:DRAW*) is a place for editors to discuss ideas they have about new articles before they create them. If you've read Chapter 4 of this book, you're already qualified to help here. Some editors who post answers here have a number of standard paragraphs (opening welcome, showing notability via reliable sources, registering for an account, and links to instructional pages) that they select and modify to fit the question. Take a look at the archives to see how different editors have responded to similar questions. Don't hesitate to borrow the wording of other editors when you see something you like.
- *Wikipedia:Media copyright questions* (shortcut: *WP:MCQ*) is a place to get help with image tagging, or questions about specific images. If you want to join in answering, read Chapter 15.
- *Wikipedia:Village pump (technical)* (shortcut: *WP:VPT*) is for discussing technical Wikipedia issues. More often than not, those questions are about problems, or how to do something. It's also the Wikipedia page that developers of the Media-Wiki software—which runs Wikipedia and all the other wikis of the Wikimedia Foundation (page xv)—are most likely to read.
- *Wikipedia:Graphic Lab* (shortcut: *WP:GL*) takes existing images created by other editors and improves them as requested. If you're experienced in image manipulation and creation, this could be a fun gig to help out with.

Showing Appreciation for Other Editors

Wikipedia gets better every day, because of the efforts of thousands of editors every day. There are many ways you can help other editors by recognizing the time and effort that they give to Wikipedia.

Figure 12-5. If you'd like to give accolades to an editor who made tremendous improvements to a number of articles or a huge contribution to a project, check out one of these pages with information on awards.

For brand-new editors, Wikipedia has a *Welcoming Committee* (the shortcut to its main page is *WP:WC*). Committee members mainly post welcome notices (in the form of templates) on the user talk pages of newly registered editors. They also suggest to anonymous (IP address) new editors that they register and get user names. The committee also maintains pages specifically for helping new editors get started. You can see a list of such pages—including the *New Contributor's help page* and the *Help desk*—at *WP:WC*.

For appreciation of more established editors, the *Kindness Campaign* main page (shortcut: *WP:KC*) provides a good starting point. The most common way of recognition, by far, is to post an *award*—a template—on the editor's user talk page, with a signature identifying who gave the award. You'll find more information at *Wikipedia:Awards* (shortcut: *WP:Award*), including the box of links shown in Figure 12-5.

Reviewing Articles and Images

The best way you can help improve articles and other content is by editing articles: improving the wording, removing improper content, and adding new information and sources. But Wikipedia has many places where editors ask for opinions about the quality of what's already in place. Editors have various reasons for requesting review: They're not sure what to work on next, they're looking for recognition, or they're hoping that other editors will see the article and join in. No matter the reason, your job as a reviewer is not to change or add content but to provide suggestions and opinions on quality.

Reviewing Articles

You don't have to be an ultra-experienced editor to make good suggestions for improving an article, but you should understand what a really good article looks like. If

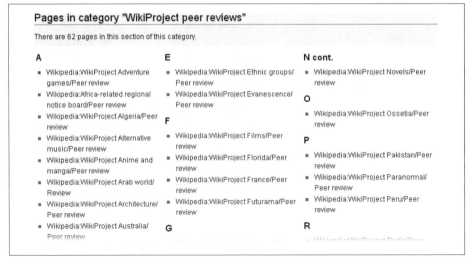

Figure 12-6. Many WikiProjects set up pages where editors can nominate a project article for review by other editors. All these reviews are open to any editor who wants to help.

you're just gaining experience, be sure to read Chapter 18 before adding your opinion to any of the review pages listed here.

Basic to fairly good articles

Article reviews have a hierarchy. In the next section, you'll find places to discuss articles that are among the best at Wikipedia. Here are some places where you can review articles of lesser quality and development:

- *Requests for feedback* (shortcut *WP:RFF*) is where editors who have created an article, or substantially improved one, can get "comments and constructive criticism." If you're just starting a career as an article critic, RFF a good place to begin.

- *WikiProject peer review*. More than 50 WikiProjects (Chapter 9) have set up specific pages for peer reviews of articles within their purviews.

  Even if you're not a member of a WikiProject that has such a page (the full list, partly shown in Figure 12-6, is available via the shortcut *CAT:WPPR*), you can always contribute your opinion if the topic is of particular interest to you.

- *Peer review* (shortcut: *WP:PR*) is for high-quality articles that have already undergone extensive work. It's often used to prepare an article for candidacy as a Good or Featured article, as described next.

Going for the gold: better and best article candidates

Wikipedia has two classifications for high-quality articles that have been through an assessment nomination process: *Good* and *Featured*. Below are five places where assessments take place, and you may be able to contribute.

NOTE

If you're an academic, scientist, or engineer, or an expert in a particular field, then the articles at the pages listed in this section could particularly benefit from your comments, even if you're relatively new to Wikipedia.

Candidates for Good and even Featured classification may be a long way from perfect. You may find the checklist approach to improving articles described in Chapter 18 a big help here. As always, when you're looking over listed articles, you can pick and choose. You don't have to comment on articles you're not interested in, or where you don't see obvious opportunities for improvement.

- *Wikipedia:Good article nominations* (shortcut: *WP:GAN*). At any given time, you'll probably find several hundred articles undergoing review, nicely organized into topical categories.

- *Wikipedia:Good article reassessment* (shortcut: *WP:GAR*). Good articles occasionally go bad, or turn out never to have been that good. This page is where Good article ratings are reassessed. Typically you see only a handful of articles here at any time. Most reviewers probably visit because of a notice on an article talk page.

- *Wikipedia:Featured article candidates* (shortcut: *WP:FAC*). Nominees for Wikipedia's highest quality category are on this page—usually 50 to 100 articles at a time. Articles are often up for a month or two while undergoing review, so checking in every 3 or 4 weeks to see what's up is frequent enough.

  As with Good article nominations, Featured article candidates have almost always been nominated by the editors who created or significantly improved those articles. These editors are available, motivated, and capable of fixing just about anything that other editors identify as needing attention. If you make detailed suggestions, you may be gratified by quick responses to your comments.

NOTE

Not all Featured articles become "Today's featured article" on Wikipedia's Main Page. As of late 2007, more than a dozen articles a week were successful candidates for FA status, but there are only seven opportunities per week to become a Main Page article.

- *Wikipedia:Featured article review* (shortcut: *WP:FAR*) is similar to good article reassessment. FAs do acquire problems and errors after they've passed their candidacy.

  These reviews take place in two stages: First, a basic review with the goal of improving the article. Second, when improvements are inadequate, the article is declared a removal candidate, and editors declare whether they support keeping or removing the article's FA status; this stage is also an opportunity for editors to overcome deficiencies. Each stage typically lasts 2 to 3 weeks. Typically, a dozen or so articles are in each stage at any given time.

- *Wikipedia:Featured list candidates* (shortcut: *FLC*). Lists are a specialized type of article (page 256). Much of the discussion on this page is about formatting, particularly tables (Chapter 14).

Reviewing Other Content

Other types of content besides articles can achieve Featured status. As with articles, they gain that status via editor review. Those reviews take place on the pages listed in this section. You can contribute to the evaluations and suggest potential improvements.

Portals

Portals serve as main pages for specific article topics or areas. For example, *Portal:Africa* has an introduction to Africa, a table of contents of Wikipedia articles on Africa, an African news feed, and so on. (For more information on portals, see page 169.) You can contribute to portal review in two places:

- *Wikipedia:Portal peer review* (shortcut *WP:PPREV*) is for high-quality portals that have already undergone extensive work.

- *Wikipedia:Featured portal candidates* (shortcut: *WP:FPOC*) is where good portals are nominated for Featured status.

There are only about 500 portals on Wikipedia, so only a handful of portals are normally under review at each of these pages at any given time.

Pictures

There are two places for reviewing pictures. In a two-stage process, picture can attain Wikipedia's highest quality rating—Featured. If you're a skilled or aspiring photographer, you may find the critiques interesting and want to join in the discussion.

- *Wikipedia:Picture peer review* (shortcut: *WP:PPR*) is a staging area for potential Featured pictures before full nomination on *Wikipedia:Featured picture candidates* (described next). It's also a working area for photographers to request help with pictures that need editing, or finding an article to which to add their images.

- *Wikipedia:Featured picture candidates* (shortcut: *WP:FPC*) are pictures that significantly enhance the articles they illustrate. Given the vast number of pictures uploaded every week, it's interesting that only about 10 pictures per week achieve FP status.

If you're not a skilled or aspiring photographer, you may still want to take a look at these pages to learn about the challenges of taking high-quality pictures for Wikipedia.

Coaching Other Editors

As mentioned in Appendix C (page 453), Wikipedia has three pages where an editor can get personal advice from another editor. Two—*Adopt-a-User* and *Admin coaching* —are primarily for experienced editors; you can learn about them later in this chapter (page 227). The third is *Wikipedia:Editor review* (shortcut: *WP:ER*), which lets editors have their edits evaluated by several peers, who provide tips and pointers on areas for improvement. There's often a backlog of reviews here, so this can be a great place to jump in and provide much-needed help. You need to be able to spot flaws (and strengths) of other editors, and have a bit of time to provide them with feedback.

Helping Resolve Disputes

Chapter 10 and Chapter 11 discussed a number of different places you can go for help resolving a disagreement over content or behavior. This chapter shows you how to get involved helping out with disputes at Wikipedia.

Effective Dispute Assistance

This book can't give you a full course in negotiation and mediation skills. There are entire college degrees in that topic. Instead, here are a few Wikipedia-specific principles to keep in mind when you're helping in a situation where two or more editors disagree:

- You use your time better when you focus on one particular dispute instead of spending a little time each on a lot of disputes. Spending more time on one situation helps you learn the system, come up with good suggestions, and write a clear and non-inflammatory response.

- Wording counts. People normally get a lot of context from body language and tone of voice—context that isn't available on a computer screen. Be extremely careful to avoid commenting about a person, rather than about her edits. There's a big difference between "You don't seem to understand the policy about original re-search", and "Your last few changes to the article are against the rules in the 'No original research' policy [[WP:NOR]]."

- If an editor argues over the validity of a policy or guideline, don't defend it—that's not your job. Tell the editor that he has a choice: Try to change the policy or guideline, or leave Wikipedia. Not following the rules because he disagrees with them isn't acceptable. For editors who don't like the constraints of Wikipedia, there are other places (personal Web pages, blogs, discussion forums) with fewer rules. (Mention WikiIndex.org (*http://wikiindex.org*) and *WP:TRY*.)

- In content disputes, try to find something resembling middle ground, even if it's very close to the position of one side or the other. Or, if there are multiple points being discussed, and one side seems clearly correct, look for minor points where you can expect that side to yield (at least grudgingly). Still, the goal is to help improve the article. If your compromise leaves a problem in the article's content, other editors will only raise the issue again.

- There's usually some validity, if only a bit, to both sides in a content dispute. You should take a look at an editor's contributions only when you can't see anything valid in what he's saying. (Is the editor totally inexperienced? Does the account seem intended only for a single article or narrow range of articles? Is the editor newly registered, but a little *too* capable? These factors help you understand the editor's motivations.) Also look at history of postings to that editor's user talk page. (Do you see repeated warnings or other indications of an inability to work with others?)

- If you're helping on a content issue, you don't have to ignore behavioral misdeeds. But put comments about behavior on user talk pages—don't inject them into the middle of a discussion about improving an article.

- One editor's violation of behavioral policies or guidelines isn't an excuse for another editor to violate the rules. Evaluate each editor's behavior separately. Regarding fighting fire with fire, be sympathetic but firm: Wikipedia policies don't allow exceptions if "the other guy started it."

- When you're commenting about behavior, be as factually neutral as possible. Instead of paraphrasing editors, quote exact words and point to the policy or guideline that the words violated. The big two are Civility (*WP:CIVIL*) and No personal attacks (*WP:NPA*), but it helps to be familiar with all the behavioral policies (see *WP:LOP*) and behavioral guidelines (see *WP:LOGL*).

Where the Action Is

If you're game for helping with content and behavioral disputes, you can get involved in a number of areas. Your options range from offering your opinion on content disputes to helping editors reform uncivil behavior.

Discussions about content

- *Wikipedia:Third opinion* (shortcut: *WP:3O*). Here's a great place to start practicing the art of working with others (in this case, two others). You'll figure out the root causes of a disagreement and the extent to which the two editors' arguments are valid. While the page implies that you can write your opinion and then walk away,

Issues by topic area

Biographies	*(watch 🔗)*	{{RFCbio}}
Economy, trade, and companies	*(watch 🔗)*	{{RFCecon}}
History and geography	*(watch 🔗)*	{{RFChist}}
Language and linguistics	*(watch 🔗)*	{{RFClang}}
Maths, science, and technology	*(watch 🔗)*	{{RFCsci}}
Art, architecture, literature and media	*(watch 🔗)*	{{RFCmedia}}
Politics	*(watch 🔗)*	{{RFCpol}}
Religion and philosophy	*(watch 🔗)*	{{RFCreli}}
Society, sports, law, and sex	*(watch 🔗)*	{{RFCsoc}}

Figure 12-7. Requests for Comment regarding articles are divided into major topical areas. However, disputes may be more about applying a particular policy or guideline than a particular subject matter.

General policy and convention issues

Wikipedia style, referencing, layout and WikiProjects	*(watch 🔗)*	{{RFCstyle}}
Wikipedia policies, guidelines and proposals	*(watch 🔗)*	{{RFCpolicy}}

Figure 12-8. Requests for Comments for policy and conventions are also split out, but into fewer groups than for articles, probably because Wikipedia has considerably fewer RFCs of this type.

an acceptable resolution is more likely if you stick around and see if either editor has further comments. A quick read and a brief, dashed-off comment aren't what's needed here.

- *Wikipedia:Requests for comment—articles* (shortcut: *WP:RFC*). Article RfCs are split by general topic (see Figure 12-7), so you can, in theory, focus on articles that interest you more. However, most RfCs are about the application of guidelines and policies: merging, emphasis and balance, whether something can be considered a reliable source, and so on. If you want to be constructive in your comments, be prepared to spend a bit of time studying the applicable policies and guidelines.

- *Wikipedia:Requests for comment—policy and conventions* (shortcut: *WP:RFC*). There isn't a clear line between policy RfCs and article RfCs. Often RfCs in this area (Figure 12-8) are about *applying* a policy or guideline or convention to a particular article, rather than about *changing* a policy, guideline, or convention. If you want to help out here, it's a good chance to see Wikipedia's rules in use, up close.

Discussions about behavior

If you want to participate at the pages listed below, which involve disputes between editors about behavior, you *must* be willing to spend time gaining a thorough understanding of the issues and writing a good response, plus any necessary follow-up responses. Doing a half-baked job (for example, misreading what an editor did, or misreading a guideline) just makes things worse. It's fine if you look into a case and decide it's too complicated, given your available time. In such cases, leave the matter to other editors.

- *Requests for comments—User conduct* (shortcut: *WP:RFCC*). This page is a good place for relatively new editors to start getting involved in discussions of user behavior. In these RfCs, the editors bringing up a matter have to prepare a complete statement about it: what happened, what policies or guidelines are involved, what they've done to date to try to resolve it, and what they'd like to see done. So there's much less detective work required by editors commenting on the problem.

  You probably should wait until the editor who's at the center of the RfC (the defendant, if you will) has had a chance to comment, which gives you more information about the dispute. Sometimes an editor doesn't respond, so after the RfC has been up for at least a week, you can figure that the chances of a response are fairly low, and go ahead with your own comment.

NOTE

If you decide you can only do a minimum amount of participation, simply endorse a statement or view posted by another editor. Before you even read other editors' views, however, you should do your own analysis and jot down a few notes. If what you come up with matches what someone else said, then go ahead and endorse that statement or view. And yes, it does make a difference—the more editors endorsing a particular view, the more weight a reasonable participant in the dispute would give that view.

- *Wikipedia:Wikiquette alerts* (shortcut: *WP:WQA*) is "where users can report impolite, uncivil or other difficult communications with editors, to seek perspective, advice, informal mediation, or a referral to a more appropriate forum." If you want to help here, be prepared for a wide-ranging cast of characters, from well-meaning but inexperienced editors to argumentative editors who have posted the same complaint in multiple Wikipedia forums.

  If you're thinking about responding to an alert, first read the section "Instructions for editors responding to alerts" (which is primarily about using templates to mark the status of a posted problem). Then take a deep breath and start reading what the editor with a problem posted, and look at the actual edits that caused the problem. At minimum, you'll learn a lot about what *not* to do as a Wikipedia editor: Edit articles in a way that shows a strong point of view; tendentious editing and evasion of consensus; incivility; and repeated improper reverts, to name a few.

Grab bag

Finally, here are two places where you find requests on just about anything, including both content disputes and behavioral issues:

- *Wikipedia:Editor assistance* (shortcut: *WP:EA*) offers an informal way to request one-to-one advice, feedback, and counseling from another editor. Editors can either post something on the Requests page, or contact one of the listed editors on the primary page. If you want to offer assistance and don't have lots of experience, don't list your name—just look at the open requests.

- *Wikipedia:Mediation Cabal* (shortcut: *WP:MEDCAB*) provides informal mediation for disputes on Wikipedia. (No, it really isn't a secret group of conspirators—that's just Wikipedia humor. Anyone's welcome to participate.) The good thing about helping out here is that all parties to a dispute (usually two) must agree to such informal mediation. Given such agreements, resolution is usually possible.

If you're interested, follow the link from the *WP:MEDCAB* page to the page with suggestions for volunteers. Read the instructions, as well as the other pages linked to from the *WP:MEDCAB* page, to get a feel for what's involved before you volunteer to take a case. Remember that you can always ask other editors for help if you get stuck on something. If there's not already a clear statement of the situation, start by stating exactly what you see as the issues. If you can clearly define those, you're halfway home. If editors disagree on what's really the problem, then do a rewrite; keep listening and rewriting till you get agreement. Get agreement on the issues *before* you start offering suggestions. And keep in mind that people who believe they've been heard, and fairly treated, often don't feel they have to "win" (or win completely) in order to be satisfied with the process.

NOTE

Experience is less a factor than a willingness to listen carefully; a commitment to taking the time to read what editors have done and said, and to read relevant policies and guidelines; and a methodical approach in working toward clarifying issues and exploring options. The most important factor is a belief that when reasonable people work together, you can achieve acceptable outcomes.

For Experienced Editors

The previous sections discussed pages where extensive experience at Wikipedia isn't a requirement for helping out (although more experience is always better). In the two places described in this section, which involve mentoring, experience matters a lot.

If you haven't spent at least 6 to 12 months doing editing at Wikipedia, and if you haven't accumulated a couple of thousand edits, then refrain from offering your help at these two places until you have more experience:

- *Wikipedia:Adopt-a-User* (shortcut: *WP:ADOPT*). A program where experienced editors take new, inexperienced editors under their wings and help as requested. The two editors decide what that help entails. For example, the adoptee may ask questions on the adopter's user talk page. Or they come up with a more elaborate arrangement—the adopter may suggest working on a new area of editing every week, or do a weekly review of the adoptee's edits.

- *Wikipedia:Admin coaching* (shortcut: *WP:ADCO*). A program for editors who know the basics of editing articles, but need help in learning new roles, such as vandal-fighting. The requesting editor can specify the type of help he wants, or the coaching editor can review the requesting editor's experience to date and suggest areas to broaden that experience.

If you're an experienced editor, you may find these two programs a change of pace from editing or vandal-fighting or whatever most occupies your time at Wikipedia.

Choosing Where You Want to Help

As an editor at Wikipedia, virtually *every* page where a discussion is going on is open for you to add comments. Even with Arbitration Committee cases, the most formal process within Wikipedia, outside comments are accepted at certain points. Thus, you can interact with and help other editors just about anywhere you want: talk pages for guideline and help pages; discussion areas like the Village Pump (see below); or pages like RfCs (page 225)where editors come specifically for assistance.

More Hot Spots

The pages mentioned in this chapter have probably given you at least one option that fits your skills and desire to help. But if you're still looking for more places where lots of discussion's going on, where editors are asking questions and requesting input, here are more pages that might interest you:

- *Wikipedia:Village pump (policy)* (shortcut: *WP:VPP*). Discussion of existing and proposed policies and guidelines.

- *Wikipedia:Village pump (proposals)* (shortcut: *WP:VP/PR*). Discussion of new ideas and proposals that are not policy related.

- *Wikipedia:Administrators' noticeboard/Incidents* (shortcut: *WP:AN/I*). Reporting and discussing incidents on English Wikipedia that require administrator intervention.

    Non-administrators are welcome to comment, but don't post something here simply to see your words in print. You must move the discussion forward by bringing new information.

- *Wikipedia:Conflict of interest/Noticeboard* (shortcut: *WP:COI/N*). Discussions of Wikipedia's conflict-of-interest guideline and its application to incidents and situations where editors may have close personal or business connections with article topics.

What to Consider When Deciding Where to Help

As with editing articles, it's up to you to decide where your time—for reading, researching, analyzing, and composing a reply—is best spent. Here are some points to consider:

- If you absolutely know the answer, or can find it quickly, go ahead and answer, so that other editors who aren't as knowledgeable can work on other things.

- If requests for help on one page are being answered promptly and correctly by other editors, look around for other places with a backlog. That way, you can be assured that you're not getting into a game of musical chairs with other editors helping out. Similarly, if you can help with an older, unclosed case or question, others who assist at that page will be appreciative.

- It's better to be *slow* in responding and *correct* when you do respond than to be the first to provide an answer and to be partly wrong. And if you can't figure out a good answer, don't answer at all. If you've promised to answer and can't, just apologize and withdraw gracefully.

- Helping others can be a stress-reducer. Editing articles often involves changing other people's work, and having your own work changed by others. But for relatively stress-free advice-giving, remember that your job is to offer good suggestions, not to assume responsibility for their being accepted. Nor should you expect that you'll always be thanked for what you did, but if you're civil and constructive in your comments, your help will be appreciated.

- Most importantly, if you find you're doing things at Wikipedia that you don't enjoy, stop. Do something else that you *do* enjoy and let other editors take over what you were previously doing. As the t-shirt says, life is too short to drink bad wine. You can see from this book's table of contents that Wikipedia is a big place. No matter what you work on, you're making a difference, and you might as well enjoy it. If you can help editors seeking assistance, great. But if you start feeling overwhelmed, irritated, or bored, that's a sign that you should spend your time and effort on other things.

PART III

Formatting and Illustrating Articles

CHAPTER 13

Article Sections and Tables of Contents

Wikipedia has two features to make readers' lives easier—sections and tables of contents. Without these, most Wikipedia articles would be a mass of text, unbroken except for images and infoboxes. Getting a quick overview could cause eyestrain as well as mouse cramp.

A well-done table of contents is a godsend. It appears high on the page, giving readers a quick overview of the article, as well as a quick route to an interesting part of the article. Best of all, Wikipedia's software generates the table of contents automatically from the section headings (page 11). If you get those right, then the TOC is going to be in good shape.

This chapter starts out showing you how to effectively use sections in an article. From there, you can tweak the automatic table of contents to make it even better.

Getting Sections Right

Much like magazine and newspaper feature articles, Wikipedia articles have three different kinds of sections.

- **Lead**. The lead section introduces the article's topic. Like the introductory paragraph of a newspaper article or a term paper, it tells readers exactly what they'll learn in the rest of the article.

- **Body sections**. Even relatively short articles are easier to read when the main body is broken up into sections, one for each subtopic. Sections are so important that you learned to create them in Chapter 1 (page 7).

- **Bottom**. Since Wikipedia articles should always be based on research from reliable sources, most articles have sections for footnotes, external links, and so on. These items always come at the bottom.

Lead Section

The *lead* section is always the first section in the article (which is why you may hear it called the *top* section). To help editors write strong leads, Wikipedia provides a guideline at *Wikipedia:Lead section* (shortcut: *WP:LS*). Unlike a tabloid magazine article lead, a Wikipedia article lead doesn't tease or tantalize the reader into reading further. Instead, it provides a brief summary of what the article covers, and, equally important, why the article's subject is important or notable.

The following four points can save you from committing the *Lead section* guideline to memory:

- When an article is very short, a lead section isn't necessary. The body of the article is one section and starts with an introductory sentence or introductory short paragraph. *WP:LS* has more detail on how to craft the first sentence of a lead section.

- If an article's in poor condition, focus most of your efforts on fixing the body (Chapter 18), and *then*, if you have time, do a thorough rewrite of the lead section. (You don't have to do it all in one session, and other editors will probably pitch in.)

- If the article's long enough to have several sections in the body, but still less than roughly 32,000 characters in length (see Figure 13-1), aim for a lead section of about two paragraphs. For very long articles, the lead should be no more than four paragraphs, and the paragraphs should be no more than four or five sentences each.

- A lead section generally doesn't contain citations. A lead is a *summary*, and supporting information comes in the body of the article. However, if the summary contains a controversial statement, a footnote in the lead improves its credibility. If the consensus of editors working on the article is that certain statements need citations, don't fight it, even if you disagree. An extra footnote isn't a big issue.

    Footnotes are always required in lead sections for contentious information about living persons, regardless of the generality of the statement or the supporting information in the body of the article.

TIP

You'll also find some detailed advice about wording in the "Lead section" portion of the guideline *Wikipedia:Writing better articles* (shortcut: *WP:BETTER*).

UP TO SPEED

Leads and Accessibility

For fully sighted readers, the arrangement of items in the wikitext of the lead section —the stuff you see when you go into edit mode—doesn't matter much, because the software figures out what to display first. But the sequence *does* matter to physically impaired readers using special software to read the page. Make sure items in the lead section are in the following sequence, so that page-reading programs work properly:

1. Disambiguation templates like *{{otheruses}}* (see page 319)
2. Maintenance tags/templates like *{{unreferenced}}*
3. Infobox templates such as *{{Taxobox}}*
4. Links to image pages [[Image:Imagepagename]] (see Chapter 15)
5. Lead section text (the other five items are optional; this one isn't)
6. *{{TOCleft}}*, which creates a floating table of contents. (Or you can use *{{TOC-right}}*, in which case place it between any maintenance templates and the infobox template, if any.)

If you make sure this sequence is in place, as specified by the guideline *Wikipedia:Accessibility* (shortcut: *WP:ACCESS*), you'll help make Wikipedia accessible to everyone.

Body of the Article

Breaking the body text of an article into sections makes it easier for readers to scan and follow, and makes for a more useful table of contents. Sections with more than 12 or so paragraphs could benefit from subsections, which provide additional headings for readers. On the other hand, sometimes you end up with a section of just one or two paragraphs. That's okay if the subsection fits within the section, and the information can't logically fit into another subsection.

TIP

Chapter 18 discusses at length how to improve the body of an article. This chapter, in contrast, focuses on the length of sections, and when to add subsection headings, since they affect the table of contents.

Here are some tips for paragraphs and subsections:

- Aim to have few or no single-sentence paragraphs. At the other extreme, paragraphs beyond 1,000 characters (roughly 12 lines of typed text) are hard to read. In that case, there are probably multiple thoughts that would be better revealed if they were separated. In other words, make paragraphs short enough for readability, but long enough to develop an idea.

- When creating subsections, your most important goal is to preserve the hierarchy of the article. For example, in an article about a movie, it makes sense to have a section called "Reception" (or perhaps "Reviews"), with subsections "Critical", "Commercial", and "Nominations and Awards". On the other hand, adding a "Sequels" subsection to "Reception" could be questioned. "Sequels" should probably be its own section, even if it's only a paragraph or two.

- A chronological approach for subsections is also logical. For example, an article about a military battle might start with a section or two about events leading up to the battle; then a section about the battle itself, with subsections being the chronological phases of the battle; and finally one or more sections describing the immediate aftermath of the battle, and its longer-term consequences.

Section Headings—Under the Hood

If you look at the wikitext of Featured articles (from the Main Page, you can get to these easily), you see differences in the formatting of and around headings. Some of these matter; others have no effect on the way that the reader sees headings.

Putting a blank line below a heading is completely optional. It makes the wikitext more readable but doesn't affect what the reader sees. Also optional (and the norm) is a single blank line *above* a heading—it makes no difference to the reader.

But *multiple* blank lines do make a difference—a negative one. They add blank lines to a displayed page. If you see two blank lines together when you're in edit mode, remove one.

Spaces between the equal signs in a heading and the text of the heading make no difference. The software that powers Wikipedia renders the page exactly the same, no matter what the number of spaces.

But a blank space at the *beginning* of a heading, just like a blank space at the start of any line with text, is always wrong. It puts a blue dotted box around that heading, just as it would around the text on any line that started with a blank space.

When an article gets too long

Even when you've gotten the sections exactly right, there may be too many of them—that is, the article may be too long. How long is "too long?" One hint is when Wikipedia starts *telling* you the size of the article, which will start happening at around 6,000 words. Next, at around 12,000 words, it starts *advising* you to consider splitting the article (see Figure 13-1).

Anything over 100K (roughly 20,000 words) almost always need to be split. This general rule has several exceptions: lists, articles summarizing certain fields, and controversial subjects where an article is heavily documented. That last group includes examples like *USA PATRIOT Act*, at 224K; *chronic fatigue syndrome*, at 187K, and *Franco-Mongol alliance*, at 172K. These sizes are as of this writing. You can see more examples at *Special:Longpages*. (For more on lengthy articles, see the guideline *Wikipedia:Article size*, shortcut : *WP:SIZE*.)

When there's an editorial consensus to shorten an exceptionally long article, you can do it in several ways. For example, you can split up long lists somewhat arbitrarily (for details, see page 262). The standard solution when dealing with a long article, or even a too-long section, is to *spin off* part of that article—creating what Wikipedia calls a *daughter article*. The details are in the guideline *Wikipedia:Summary style* (shortcut:

---

236 | Chapter 13: Article Sections and Tables of Contents

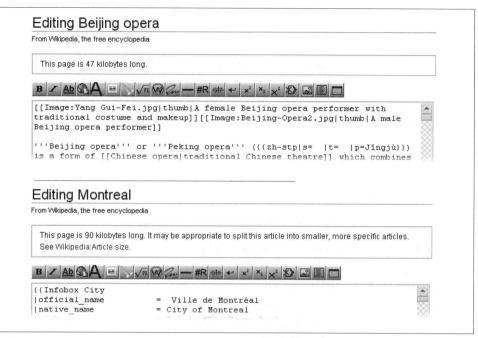

Figure 13-1. When you click "edit this page", Wikipedia tells you if the page exceeds 32 kilobytes (a kilobyte is roughly 1,000 characters). If the size exceeds 64K, you see a link to the guideline on article size. Consider that a strong suggestion to look closely at whether one or more sections can be spun off as separate articles.

WP:SS), but the concept is straightforward. Two things get left in the original article: a link to the new daughter article, and a summary of the contents of that daughter article.

Creating daughter articles is a matter of judgment. Don't start spinning off content as soon as article exceeds 32K or 64K or even 100K. Instead, discuss the matter with other editors on the article talk page, to determine whether to treat the topic as a whole as several shorter articles or to just create daughter articles for one or two sections.

Thus, you can either leave a too-long article as is, split it into multiple articles, or spin off a daughter article. But there's a fourth alternative—you can *remove content*. You'll probably only do so as a last resort when an article violates *WP:NOT* by including too much detail. If you can't see a way to spin off that excess detail into its own article, advise other editors via the article talk page *before* you start chopping.

Creating a daughter article

Creating a daughter article isn't hard, but it requires a lot of steps. The following example uses the article *Dallas Independent School District* as a case study. In late 2007, this 170K behemoth was number 50 on the list of biggest articles in Wikipedia.

1. Scan the article to determine why it's so long.

   In this case, it's obvious: Section 6, list of schools, is made up of a number of very long tables. That's perfect for a daughter article.

2. Decide on the name for the new daughter article.

   Generally that's a variant of the title of the existing section. In this case, the title of the section is "List of schools". The daughter article will become *List of schools of the Dallas Independent School District*.

3. Open a second browser window (or tab) that shows any Wikipedia page.

   You're opening a second window because you want to continue to have a window open to the article you're going to shorten. It doesn't matter what page, because you're going to be there only momentarily.

4. In the second window, in the search box, type the new title. Or type the name elsewhere, and then paste it into the search box. Click Go.

   Presumably, the daughter article doesn't already exist. You see something like Figure 13-2.

5. Click "create this page".

   That click puts you into edit mode at the new page, the one for the daughter article. The page for the new article is now ready to receive content from the parent article.

6. In the original article, click the "edit" link for the section you're moving. Select all the text in the section except for the heading. Right-click the selected text, and then, from the shortcut menu, choose Cut, or use the keyboard shortcut Ctrl+X (Windows) or ⌘-X (Mac).

   If cutting all this text feels scary, don't worry—you can't really damage the article. Remember, as discussed in page 81, that Wikipedia software keeps a copy of every version of the article. If anything goes wrong, you can always go to the history page and revert back to an undamaged version.

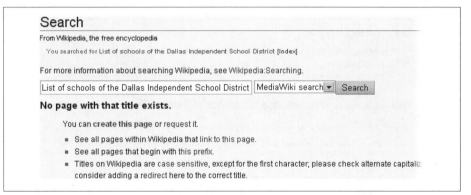

Figure 13-2. *When you're creating a new page for a daughter article, you first search for the name of new article you intend to create. The search fails, leaving you with a link on the search page that you want to click: "create this page".*

TIP

To easily select a large chunk of text in a section, click at the beginning of the text you want to select, use the scroll bar to get to the end of the section, and then Shift-click at the very end. That sequence selects everything between where you click and the final Shift-click point.

7. In the edit window of the new article, paste everything into the edit box. Add an edit summary, something like: *Creating daughter article from content of [[Article name]], per [[WP:SS]]*. Do a page preview, and then click "Save page".

   If you want to see what happens to the new article after you create it, turn on the "Watch this page" box below the edit summary before you save the page.

8. Now back to the original article. In the section still open for editing, which now has only a heading, add a *{{main|Daughter article name}}* template just below the heading, and a paragraph or two to summarize the daughter article.

   In an ideal world, the daughter article's first paragraph is already a summary that you can use; if not, usually much of it is usable for a summary. Figure 13-3 shows what the section of the DISD article looks like (both the reader's version and the underlying wikitext) after a template and summary have been added.

9. Add an edit summary, something like: *Creating daughter article at [[Name of daughter article]], per [[WP:SS]]*.

   As usual, do a page preview, check the "Watch this page" box below the edit summary, if you wish, and then click "Save page".

10. Finally, go back and polish the daughter article, adding some things that were in the original article but are now missing or need editing.

    You'll probably need to do most of the following:

    • Add or revise the lead section so it meets the criteria discussed earlier in this chapter (page 234) and the specifications of *WP:LEAD*.

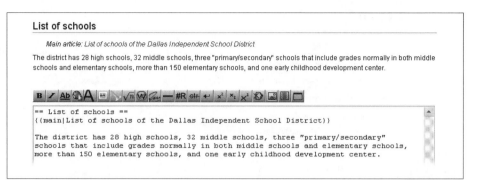

Figure 13-3. The critical thing when spinning off a daughter article is to put the {{main}} template into the section from which the daughter article's content was taken. If you do that, and prepare at least a brief summary, then other editors can easily improve that summary.

- Change the section headings to fit the new article (that generally means removing one equal sign from each side of every heading).

- Add one or more categories to the article (you'll want to use most, if not all of the categories on the parent article; you'll see the wikitext when you edit the final section of the parent article). (For more on categories, see Chapter 17.)

- If the text you moved contained any footnotes (<ref> tags), copy (don't move) the "References" section (sometimes called "Notes") from the original article.

- Start a talk page for the daughter article (page 146), and paste in any WikiProject templates from the talk page of the parent article. (If there are article assessments of quality or importance, change those to be blank. Assessments of the parent article aren't valid for the daughter article.)

Bottom

Certain optional sections always go at the bottom of an article. Although they're technically optional, all properly sourced articles have sections for footnotes and external links.

NOTE

Empty sections look unprofessional, just like "Under construction" signage on Web pages. If you don't have anything to put in a section, don't create that section. If you see an empty section, delete the heading. If you find an article that doesn't cite its sources, don't add a section for footnotes just in case.

The sections that can appear at the bottom of an article, in the preferred order, are:

See also

- Alternative propulsion
- Automotive design terminology
- Cleanova, a derivative of the Kangoo
- Efficient energy use
- FreedomCAR
- Low-energy vehicle
- Mitigation of global warming
- Net metering
- Plug In America

Figure 13-4. The "See Also" section from the article Plug-in hybrid. One of the links has a few words of explanation ("a derivative of the Kangoo"), which is optional, and somewhat unusual.

Further reading

- Nunn, J.D. (ed.) 2002. *Marine Biodiversity in Ireland and Adjacent Waters.* Proceedings of a Conference 26 - 27 April 2001. Ulster Museum publication no. 8.
- Hackney, P. Ed. 1992. Stewart and Corry's Flora of the North-east of Ireland. Institute of Irish Studies, The Queen's University, Belfast. ISBN 0 85 389 4469.
- Haigh, A. and Lawton, C. 2007. Wild mammals of an Irish urban forest. *Ir Nat. J.* **28**: 395 - 403.

Figure 13-5. The "Further reading" section of the article Ireland. *None of the links are to an online source; those go in the "External links" section instead.*

- **See also**. A bulleted list of internal links and, optionally, a short explanation for any link whose purpose isn't obvious. Figure 13-4 is an example. (If the link is already in the article, don't add it to the "See also" section.)

- **References, Notes, Footnotes**, or **Notes and footnotes**. Whatever you find, don't change any of these four section headings when you find them in an article (unless you're an experienced editor). But if the section is (incorrectly) called "Citations", change it to "References" or "Notes", whichever isn't already being used.

  If you're adding footnotes for the first time to an article, set up a "References" section for that, as described in Chapter 2 (page 34).

- **Further reading** or **Bibliography**. This section contains sources that weren't used in writing the article, but that provide material that could eventually be used. It's unusual to find this section, mostly because if a potential source is online, it should be listed under "External links", not in "Further reading". Figure 13-5 shows an example.

- **External links**. Lists a small number of high-quality sites that most readers will find useful and that were generally not cited as sources. Figure 13-6 gives an example. Most experienced editors find links to prune from these sections. The external links section is where you're most likely to find *linkspam*. And even when links to blogs, personal Web pages, and so on are well-intentioned, they normally

External links [edit]

- Polishing the Jewel: An Administrative History of Grand Canyon National Park ⧉, U.S. National Park Service
- Grand Canyon Railway ⧉ official website
- Diane Grua, "Saving the Life Work of Two Daring Grand Canyon Photographers: The Emery Kolb Collection at Northern Arizona University's Cline Library" ⧉, *Annotation*, December 1998
- Grand Canyon North Rim ⧉

Listen to this article (2 parts) · (info)
Part 1 · Part 2

This audio file was created from an article revision dated 2005-07-22, and may not reflect subsequent edits to the article. (Audio help)

More spoken articles

Figure 13-6. The external links section of the article History of the Grand Canyon *area.*

don't belong in an article. The guideline *Wikipedia:External links* (shortcut: *WP:EL*) has details.

NOTE

An exception is blogs and other pages maintained by the subject of the article. For example, an article about a band *should* include the band's MySpace page, official Web site, or blog among the external links.

Getting Headings Right

As discussed in Chapter 1, headings are easy to create and format—just add the right number of equal signs on either side (page 7). This section focuses on what to put *between* the equal signs.

Sometimes headings violate one of Wikipedia's rules. You may not get a warning on your user talk page if you make an error, but by following a few simple rules, you can create excellent headings every time.

Wording and Capitalization

Many of the guidelines for headings are the same as for article titles, as discussed on page 295. The top seven rules are the most important (and the most common opportunities for error):

- **Capitalize only the first letter of the first word, letters in acronyms, and the first letter of proper nouns**. All other letters are in lower case. Thus: "Funding of projects," not "Funding of Projects."

- **Don't restate the article title or a higher level heading**. For example, the article *Greta Garbo* has a section called "Later career". "Her later career" or "Garbo's later career" would be wrong.

- **Keep headings short**. You can sum up almost any subject in 10 words. Thus: "Housing boom in the early 1990s", not "Housing boom in the early 1990s lasts for only a few years". Long headings, as in this example, tend to reveal the storyline. The goal of a heading is to invite readers to read the section and find out what happened.

Long headings are also a problem when a different article links to that section heading. Not only is the link longer, but the likelihood of the heading being changed—damaging the link—is much higher because of the length.

- **Stick with nouns or noun phrases**. "Effects of the wild" is a good heading. "About the effects of the wild" or "Effects of the wild can be serious" are not. (This principle ties back to the goal of shorter headings.)
- **Don't use "a", "an" or "the" as the first word in a section title** (unless it's part of a proper noun). Thus, "Condition of the frescos," not "The condition of the frescos."
- **Don't use boldface or italic text for emphasis**. The only time you can use italics is for the rare occasions when a book, magazine, or similar title occurs within a heading.

NOTE

Don't use boldface and italics for emphasis in the body of articles as well. They're not consistent with Wikipedia's neutral point of view.

- **Avoid "loaded" or controversial wording**. For example, if the term "terrorist" is disputed in a given setting, don't use "Terrorist attacks" as a heading. Content within a section can be used to explain, fairly, the controversy over a word or phrase, but a heading lacks necessary nuance.
- **Don't have two sections or subsections with the same heading**. Though this won't bother the software that handles the links that make up the table of contents, it *will* confuse editors looking at edit summaries, which include the section name being edited. Matching headings also make it problematical to link from another article to the second (same-named) section or subsection.

Links and Footnotes

Links and footnotes have no place in headings, but some editors put them there anyway. If you see these problems, fix them:

- **Links never go inside headings**. Even if the heading is (or contains) the title of another Wikipedia article, don't wikilink it. Instead, the first paragraph of the section should mention—and link to—that article. (Links in headings also cause accessibility problems for visually impaired readers using special software to read Wikipedia articles.)
- **Don't put a footnote into a section heading**. It looks ugly, and since a heading should be a noun clause, not a sentence, it shouldn't require a source. If you're

using a single source for an entire section, add a footnote at the end of each paragraph in the section, not in the section heading.

Single Subsections

Just as your English teacher told you, if section 2 has a subsection 2.1, there'd better be a section 2.2 as well. If you see a section with a single subsection, you have three choices:

- If there's a lot of text in the section, followed by the subsection, you ought to be able to carve out a good subsection from the initial material, or even two, to create multiple subsections.
- If most of the section's material is in the subsection, you may not need a subsection. Just combine the two.
- If the content of at the top of the section is short and substantially different from what's in the subsection, you might be able to *promote* the subsection (for example, change the heading from level 3 to level 4). On other hand, if the subsection covers something relatively unimportant, then don't promote it to a level 2 (top-level) heading.

Incoming Links to Article Sections

If you find errors in section headings, like those just described, fix them. But occasionally fixing a section heading (changing or even deleting it) can cause a problem—when another article links to that section heading. Wikilinks from one article to another are very common; wikilinks from an article to a *section* of another article are rare. When they do occur, these links are also very *brittle*, meaning that if a single character of a section heading is changed, the link breaks. (When that happens, Wikipedia sends the reader to the top of the article page, rather than displaying an error message, so a damaged link isn't fatal, just irritating.)

The guideline *Wikipedia:Manual of Style* (shortcut *WP:MOS*) suggests that you "change a heading only after careful consideration, because this will break section links to it from the same and other articles. If changing a heading, try to locate and fix broken links." In this case, the guideline is giving you questionable advice. First, since incoming links to article sections are rare, changing a heading isn't as dangerous as *WP:MOS* would have you believe. Second, trying to "locate and fix broken links" can be a wild goose chase. Unless a section heading is unusually worded, a search for that phrase could yield hundreds of Wikipedia articles. You can try "What links here", but if there are more than a couple of articles linking to the one you're looking at, you're still facing a lot of effort that's unlikely to pay off.

Instead, tell other editors when *you* create a link to section in an article. That way, they know to avoid changing the heading (or adjust the link if they do). By the same token, check whether there's such an indication on a section heading you're changing or deleting, so you can keep the link functional. Here's how to do these things:

After you create a link to a section in an article, leave an *editor's note* (a comment that's visible only in edit mode) to tell other editors what you've done. Let's say you're linking to a section called "Evolutionary implications", and that you're linking from the article *Richard Dawkins*. Here's what the section heading should look like after you've posted your note:

==Evolutionary implications== <!-- The article [[Richard Dawkins]] links to this heading -->

Coming from the other direction, suppose you want to change the section heading "Evolutionary implications" to "Evolutionary and other implications". You see the editor's note, and realize that changing the heading will damage the wikilink in the *Richard Dawkins* article. Go ahead and change the section heading, and then go to the Dawkins article and find the wikilink, which will include the following text:

Somearticlename#Evolutionary implications

The "#" indicates the start of a section heading. Edit that wikilink so it reads:

Somearticlename#Evolutionary and other implications

Now the link will continue to take the reader directly to the desired section.

Improving the Table of Contents

Getting section headings right, as described above, makes the article's table of contents —generated automatically from those headings—concise and readable. You can take further steps to improve a TOC by reducing its length, or changing where it's located and how text flows around it.

Reducing the Length of the TOC

Long tables of contents defeat the whole purpose of a table of contents, which is to provide a quick understanding of what the article is about. When TOCs get really long, readers may even have to scroll down to read the whole thing. Some readers won't realize that they can either click the small Hide link to shrink the TOC, or click the first link to jump to the top of the article's body.

A quick sampling in late 2007 of four weeks of articles featured on the Main Page found that the average number of lines in the table of contents was a succinct 16. Only four featured articles had TOCs with more than 24 lines. Since featured articles are those judged to be the best by editors, a 16-line TOC is a good goal to shoot for.

You have two approaches to getting excess lines out of a TOC—reduce the number of sections and subsections, or use one of Wikipedia's technical gizmos. Cutting down

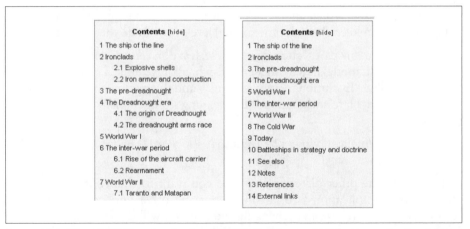

Figure 13-7. The table of contents for the article Battleship: *on the left side are the first 15 lines of the TOC before the template* {{TOClimit | limit=2}} *was added to the article; on the right is the TOC after the template was added. A 38-line TOC is now 14 lines.*

on headings is the sure-fire way to succeed, although using one of the gizmos, if applicable, may be faster.

Fewer sections and subsections

If you have sections or subsections that are very short, you can combine them. To eliminate subsections, remove subheadings and revise the text as needed. For sections, create a single section heading for the contents of two sections, and revise the transitional text. (If you haven't already done so, see the advice earlier in this chapter, starting on page 235, about the proper length of sections and subsections.)

Another way to get fewer subsections is to spin off the content of a section that has lots of subsections into a separate article, as discussed on page 236. That leaves you with just the one remaining section heading in the TOC.

If neither of these work, then your only other option is to see if Wikipedia has a technical gizmo that can help.

Technical Solutions for Long TOCs

Wikipedia offers three technical solutions to shorten lengthy TOCs.

- **Keep lower-level subsections out of the TOC**. Add the template *{{TOClimit}}*, which lets you specify which level (and above) you want the TOC to include. Figure 13-7 shows an example.

   Using the *{{TOClimit}}* template has advantages and disadvantages. It reduces the white space to the right of the TOC, and shows only the most important headings, for a quicker understanding of the article. On the minus side, the reader doesn't get as good a feel for the details of the article, and can't click a link to get to a

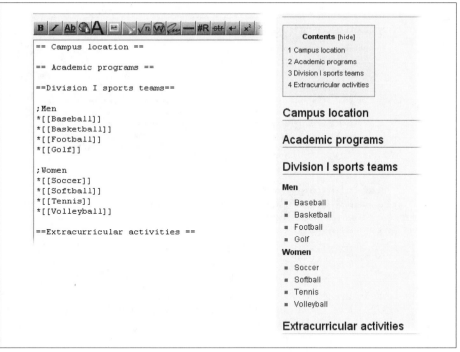

Figure 13-8. When a line starts with a semicolon (left), the line is bolded and looks like a subsection heading, but it doesn't show up in the table of contents. This technique is particularly handy for lists, to separate items in the body but mention only the full list in the TOC (right).

subsection that isn't shown. Another option in Figure 13-7 would be to use *limit=3* instead of *limit=2* as the parameter. That would reduce the TOC length to 30 lines, which is a compromise between the original length of 38 lines and the dramatically shortened 14 lines.

- **Use semicolons as pseudo-headings**. When an article covers a long list of items, it makes sense to organize them under subheadings. Yet from a reader's viewpoint, such subheadings aren't very useful when scanning the table of contents. Consider a list of towns within a county: It would be nice to split the list into several groups by subheading (east, west, north, and south), yet "Towns in the county" is all you need for the TOC. In Wikipedia, you can use a *semicolon* at the beginning of a line to create a heading that *doesn't* appear in the TOC. It's not quite having your cake and eating it too, but pretty close. Figure 13-8 shows the semicolon in use.

- **Compact TOC**. These are pre-made, specialized tables of contents where multiple links to sections are on one line. Figure 13-9 shows one of the most common compact TOCs, for the 50 U.S. states.

Compact TOCs take up very little space, so if your article's sections match up well with an existing compact TOC, it's an excellent choice. (Typically, such articles

Template:TOCUSStates

From Wikipedia, the free encyclopedia

Contents	[hide]

before

Alabama | Alaska | Arizona | Arkansas | California | Colorado | Connecticut | Delaware | Florida | Georgia | Hawaii | Idaho | Illinois | Indiana | Iowa | Kansas | Kentucky | Louisiana | Maine | Maryland | Massachusetts | Michigan | Minnesota | Mississippi | Missouri | Montana | Nebraska | Nevada | New Hampshire | New Jersey | New Mexico | New York | North Carolina | North Dakota | Ohio | Oklahoma | Oregon | Pennsylvania | Rhode Island | South Carolina | South Dakota | Tennessee | Texas | Utah | Vermont | Virginia | Washington | West Virginia | Wisconsin | Wyoming

after

`{{TOCStates|before=before|after=after}}`

- noendlinks=yes (adds "see also" and "external links", and only those)
- DC=yes (adds District of Columbia)
- PR=yes (adds Puerto Rico)

Category: TOC templates

Figure 13-9. Shown here is the entire page for the template {{TOCUSStates}}. This compact TOC, for U.S. states, can be tailored by adding links (which point to sections of the page) both above and below the standard list (links). In this documentation, the words "before" and "after" are inserted as (non-link) placeholders.

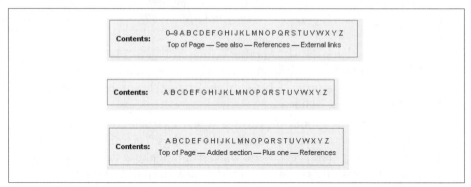

Figure 13-10. At the top of this figure is the standard version of the A-to-Z TOC ({{AlphanumericTOC}}). You can tailor most compact tables of contents, including this one, to add or subtract sections. In the middle is a variant with only the 26 letters displayed; and at the bottom is another variant, with editor-specified additional sections.

are lists.) Figure 13-10 shows another common compact TOC, the Alphanumeric TOC.

You'll find a full list of compact TOCs on the page *Wikipedia:Template messages/Compact tables of contents* (shortcut: *WP:CTOC*).

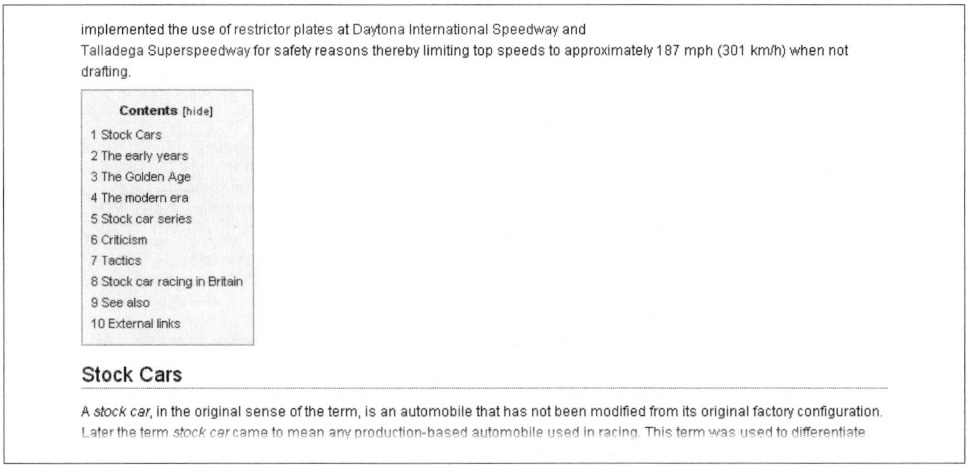

Figure 13-11. The standard table of contents for the article Stock car racing *appears on the left side of the page, immediately below the lead section. With all the white space on the right, the layout isn't particularly attractive, and the main article text can't begin until after the TOC.*

Floating the Table of Contents

If you don't specify otherwise, the TOC of a Wikipedia page appears just below the lead section, on the left, with no text to its right. If the TOC is long, the reader may have to scroll quite a bit before seeing any of the body text. In many cases, you can improve the layout of articles by telling the software exactly where to put the TOC. This technique, called *floating* the table of contents, also wraps text around the TOC.

Figure 13-11 shows the TOC of the article *Stock car racing* with the standard TOC, and Figure 14-12 shows the same article, with a *{{TOCleft}}* template. The template tells the software exactly where to put the TOC, and makes the text wrap around the TOC.

Figure 13-13 shows the wikitext that creates the left-floating TOC in Figure 13-12. The standard location for *{{TOCleft}}* templates is the bottom of the lead section, to avoid accessibility problems for impaired readers. In general, a floating TOC should never be put into the middle of a section.

A less common alternative is placing the table of contents on the right, using the template *{{TOCright}}*. If you look at the wikitext for Figure 13-14, you see the *{{TOCright}}* template at the top of the edit box. No text should ever be in the lead section above this template.

for safety reasons thereby limiting top speeds to approximately 187 mph (301 km/h) when not drafting.

Contents [hide]	Stock Cars [edit]
1 Stock Cars 2 The early years 3 The Golden Age 4 The modern era 5 Stock car series 6 Criticism 7 Tactics 8 Stock car racing in Britain 9 See also 10 External links	A *stock car*, in the original sense of the term, is an automobile that has not been modified from its original factory configuration. Later the term *stock car* came to mean any production-based automobile used in racing. This term was used to differentiate such a car from a *race car*, a special, custom-built car designed only for racing purposes with no intent of its ever being used as regular transportation. When NASCAR was first formed by Bill France Sr. in 1948 to regulate stock car racing, there was a requirement that any car entered be made entirely of parts available to the general public through automobile dealers, and that all cars must be from a model run of which at least 500 cars of that model were sold to the general public. This is referred to as "homologation". In NASCAR's early years, the cars were so "stock" that it was commonplace for the drivers to drive themselves to the competitions in the car that they were going to run in the race. While automobile engine technology had remained fairly stagnant in World War II, advanced aircraft piston engine development had provided a great deal of available data, and NASCAR was

formed just as some the improved technology was about to become available in production cars[citation needed]. Until the advent of the Trans-Am series in 1967, NASCAR homologation cars were the closest thing that the public could buy that was actually

Figure 13-12. *Here's how the table of contents for the article* Stock car racing *looks with a* {{TOCleft}} *template inserted. Note how the text wraps neatly around the TOC, unlike the previous figure.*

```
[[Lowe's Motor Speedway]].  NASCAR has implemented the use of [[restrictor
plates]] at [[Daytona International Speedway]] and [[Talladega Superspeedway]] for
safety reasons thereby limiting top speeds to approximately 187 mph (301 km/h)
when not [[drafting_(racing)|drafting]].

{{TOCleft}}
==Stock Cars==
A ''stock car'', in the original sense of the term, is an automobile that has not
been modified from its original factory configuration.  Later the term ''stock
car'' came to mean any production-based automobile used in racing.  This term was
used to differentiate such a car from a [[Racing cars|''race car'']], a special,
custom-built car designed only for racing purposes with no intent of its ever
```

The TOCleft templatehas been placed at the end of the lead section

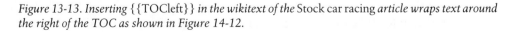

Figure 13-13. *Inserting* {{TOCleft}} *in the wikitext of the* Stock car racing *article wraps text around the right of the TOC as shown in Figure 14-12.*

NOTE

The page *Help:Section* (shortcut: *WP:SEC*) offers specific suggestions on floating the TOC. In particular, be aware that floating a wide TOC can squeeze the article text into a very narrow column on low-resolution monitors. (Yet another reason why short section headings are better.) Still, even with a narrow TOC on one side, a wide, deep image can cause problems for readers with older, smaller monitors. So if you don't have at least 50 percent of your screen still available for text to flow between the TOC on one side and images on the other, think twice about floating the TOC.

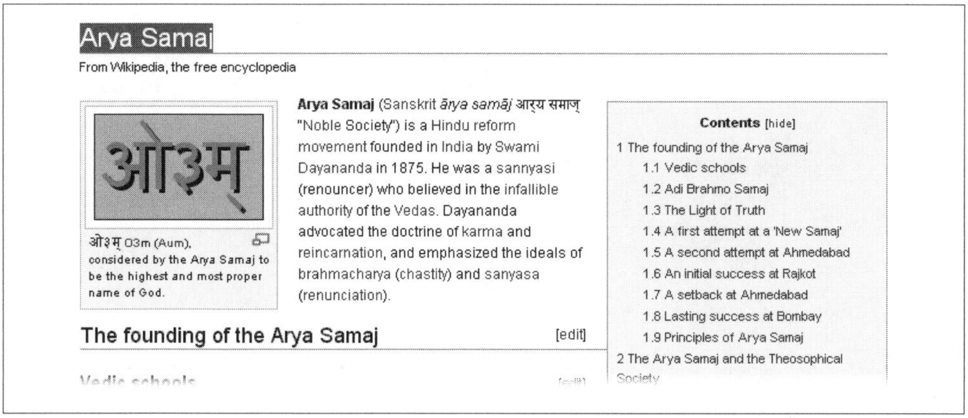

Arya Samaj

From Wikipedia, the free encyclopedia

Arya Samaj (Sanskrit *ārya samāj* आर्य समाज़ "Noble Society") is a Hindu reform movement founded in India by Swami Dayananda in 1875. He was a sannyasi (renouncer) who believed in the infallible authority of the Vedas. Dayananda advocated the doctrine of karma and reincarnation, and emphasized the ideals of brahmacharya (chastity) and sanyasa (renunciation).

ओ३म् O3m (Aum), considered by the Arya Samaj to be the highest and most proper name of God.

Contents [hide]

1 The founding of the Arya Samaj
   1.1 Vedic schools
   1.2 Adi Brahmo Samaj
   1.3 The Light of Truth
   1.4 A first attempt at a 'New Samaj'
   1.5 A second attempt at Ahmedabad
   1.6 An initial success at Rajkot
   1.7 A setback at Ahmedabad
   1.8 Lasting success at Bombay
   1.9 Principles of Arya Samaj
2 The Arya Samaj and the Theosophical Society

The founding of the Arya Samaj [edit]

Vedic schools [edit]

Figure 13-14. *This article has the table of contents on the right. The image at the top of the article is on the left instead of the right, since the TOC is on the right. The layout makes efficient use of space —the entire TOC is visible on one screen, yet the reader has the option of simply reading the article and ignoring the TOC.*

CHAPTER 14

Creating Lists and Tables

Lists and tables are two different ways to format multiple, similar items on a page. Lists and HTML tables go back to Wikipedia's early days. The current wikicode tables (page 262), which you can edit more easily and even sort, came later.

You'll find many more lists than tables on Wikipedia. For example, the *External links* sections that appear in almost every Wikipedia article are lists. Tables are less common, but they're making up ground fast. You'll probably have occasion to edit a table, if not make one. This chapter shows you how to create and edit both lists and tables.

Creating and Editing Lists

Wikipedia has two kinds of lists: embedded lists (a list within a larger article), and standalone lists (an article that's only a list). An example of the latter is the article *List of colors*. Embedded lists are easier to grasp, both conceptually and in terms of formatting, although you won't have trouble understanding articles that are lists.

Bulleted and Numbered Lists Within Articles

Lists are easy to create, but sometimes you really shouldn't. Before you make a list, read the first part of this section and think about whether you could present the information in narrative form. When you're ready to make a list, flip to page 255 to see how to create the underlying wikitext.

Presenting information: list, narrative, or neither?

Wikipedia articles are intended to be narratives, not guides or places for stockpiling information, as explained at *What Wikipedia is not* (shortcut: *WP:NOT*). So first ask yourself, when you see a list in an article, or when you're considering adding a list to an article, whether that list even belongs in an article. Some cases are very clear: A list of links in the *External links* section of an article absolutely needs to be there, in list

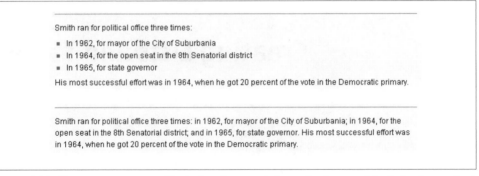

Smith ran for political office three times:

- In 1962, for mayor of the City of Suburbania
- In 1964, for the open seat in the 8th Senatorial district
- In 1965, for state governor

His most successful effort was in 1964, when he got 20 percent of the vote in the Democratic primary.

Smith ran for political office three times: in 1962, for mayor of the City of Suburbania; in 1964, for the open seat in the 8th Senatorial district; and in 1965, for state governor. His most successful effort was in 1964, when he got 20 percent of the vote in the Democratic primary.

Figure 14-1. Shown are two ways of including the same information in an article: in list format (top) and narrative format (bottom). In this case, narrative is better. It maintains the article's flow and takes up less space.

format. But in an article about a nonprofit organization, a full list of the 45 members of its advisory board would be a violation of *WP:NOT*.

Some editors feel that the more information an article contains, the better. Long lists tend to prove the opposite: They take up valuable editing time to create and maintain, and they're distracting. In the nonprofit organization example, readers who are really interested in who's on the advisory board can find out by going to the organization's Web site. If there are a few notable board members, you can simply mention them in a quick sentence. ("The advisory board includes Michael Dell, Al Gore, and David Hasselhoff.")

If you decide that some or all the items in a list belong in a Wikipedia article, your next decision is whether to use a *formal* list; that is, one using wiki markup. For example, Figure 14-1 shows two ways of presenting the same information, with a list and without.

Popular opinion at Wikipedia is against lists in articles, particularly numbered lists, if narrative is an alternative. But sometimes a bulleted list can break up what would otherwise be an overly large, gray mass of text, particularly if the topic is dry or complex. (Put differently, sometimes bulleted narrative makes sense.) You'll find a nuanced discussion of bulleted lists versus fully narrative text at the guideline *Wikipedia:Embedded list* (shortcut *WP:EMBED*).

NOTE

Sometimes the term "list" refers to something more complicated—a presentation of similar, multiple items in a multi-column format. That's actually a *table*, and you can read about them on page 262.

How to create a list

To create a list in Wikipedia, you add special characters to the text of the list items. The special characters tell the software how to format the list onscreen. The

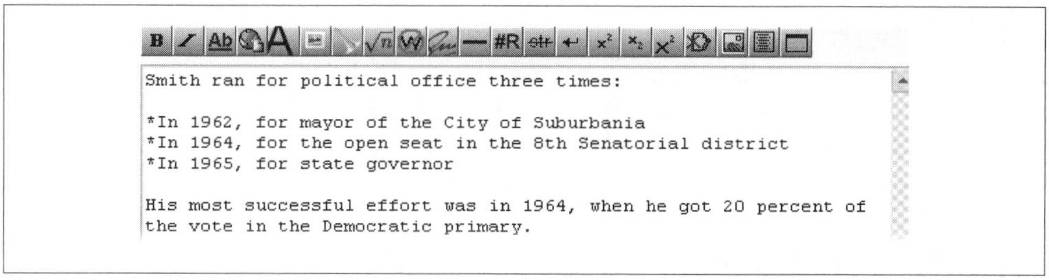

Figure 14-2. The wikitext for the bulleted list in Figure 14-1 is very simple—an asterisk at the beginning of each item in the list.

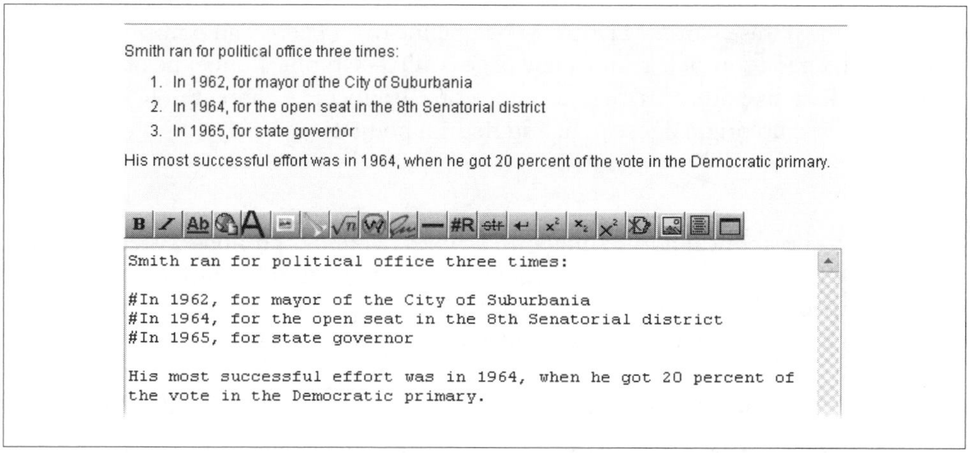

Figure 14-3. Putting pound (#) signs at the beginning of a line of text will number that line. Numbering is rare in articles, but it's handy (and common) on discussion pages. Typos can wreak havoc in wikitext numbered lists. For example, if you put a blank line between items, the numbering starts over.

combination of text and formatting characters is called *wikitext*. In Figure 14-2, you can see the underlying wikitext that creates the bulleted list in Figure 14-1.

To create a list, simply go into edit mode, type or paste the list items (each on a separate line), and then type an asterisk (*) at the beginning of each list item for a bulleted list or a pound sign (#) to create a numbered list. Figure 14-3 shows the same list used in previous examples, this time as a numbered list.

TIP

The technical page *Help:List* describes more than a dozen ways to modify lists: indentation, splitting lists, Roman numerals, extra indentation, a specified starting value for a numbered list, multicolumn bulleted lists, and more. You don't need to know any of them for editing articles. You might see the more fancy options on discussion pages, but rarely even there.

Long lists within articles

Lists often begin as sections of an article, and then expand. At some point, a list can become too long to be part of an article, and needs to be spun off as a separate "List of" article. On page 238, you can find step by step instructions for spinning off a section into an article of its own (in fact, the example in that section is a list).

Lists as Separate Articles

Standalone lists are Wikipedia articles that are basically one big list, usually consisting of links to articles in a particular subject area; for example, North American mammals, or economists, or events listed chronologically. The titles of these articles almost always begin with the phrase words "List of" or "Timeline of". (There's an occasional "Glossary of", which is a sort of list, and a few pages called "Graphical timeline of", as well.) Standalone lists, like other articles, are subject to Wikipedia's content policies, including verifiability, no original research, and neutral point of view.

Bad lists

Lists need to be about notable things. Red links (wikilinks to non-existent articles, which show as red instead of blue) are allowed in lists, but only in small amounts. A preponderance of red links probably means that the subject isn't notable enough to be on Wikipedia. For example, an article called *List of high school science teachers in New York City*, with entries that include only a couple of blue links, would make the article at best a guide and at worst a vanity article, both of which are disallowed by *WP:NOT*.

Lists that are too general or too broad in scope have little value. For example, a list of brand names would be far too long to be useful (it would also require Herculean efforts by a fairly large number of editors to properly maintain it). Lists that are too specific are also a problem. For example, an article *List of one-eyed horse thieves from Montana* would be of little interest to anyone except the person making the list.

Lists are prone to suffering from unclear criteria or a non-neutral point of view, which may actually be the same problem. Examples include *List of exploitative companies*, *List of authoritarian leaders*, and even *List of famous Brazilian people*. (Change "famous" in the last example to "notable," and the problem goes away, since Wikipedia has notability criteria for articles about people, for the purposes of determining if they're entitled to a separate article in Wikipedia.) A related problem—of point of view—occurs when an article consists of lists of arguments for and against some particular contention or position. Such articles are not acceptable per the guideline *Wikipedia:Pro and con lists* (shortcut: *WP:PACL*).

As with everything else at Wikipedia, there isn't universal agreement about exactly what's acceptable as the subject of a list. One argument, mentioned in the essay *Wikipedia:Listcruft* (shortcut: *WP:LC*), states that the only legitimate "List of" articles start

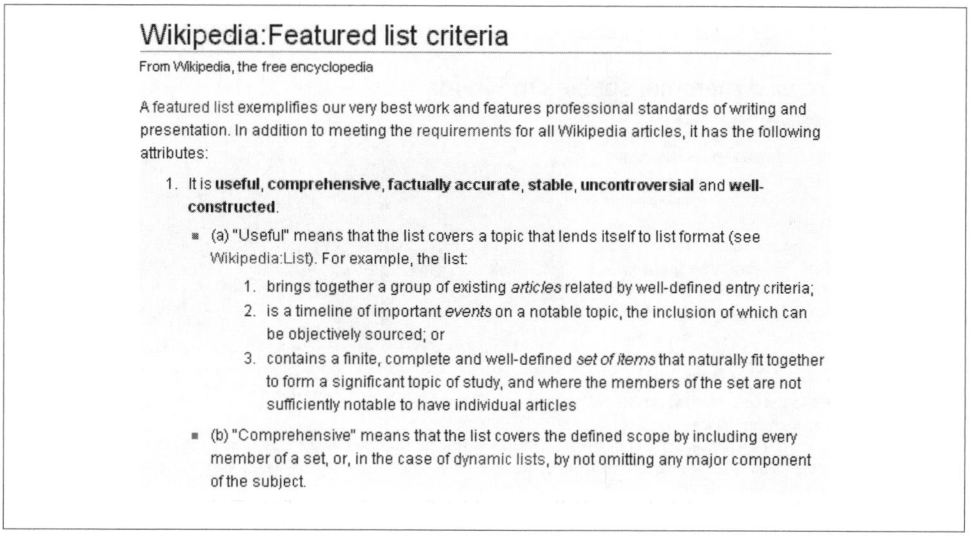

Wikipedia:Featured list criteria

From Wikipedia, the free encyclopedia

A featured list exemplifies our very best work and features professional standards of writing and presentation. In addition to meeting the requirements for all Wikipedia articles, it has the following attributes:

1. It is **useful, comprehensive, factually accurate, stable, uncontroversial** and **well-constructed**.
   - (a) "Useful" means that the list covers a topic that lends itself to list format (see Wikipedia:List). For example, the list:
     1. brings together a group of existing *articles* related by well-defined entry criteria;
     2. is a timeline of important *events* on a notable topic, the inclusion of which can be objectively sourced; or
     3. contains a finite, complete and well-defined *set of items* that naturally fit together to form a significant topic of study, and where the members of the set are not sufficiently notable to have individual articles
   - (b) "Comprehensive" means that the list covers the defined scope by including every member of a set, or, in the case of dynamic lists, by not omitting any major component of the subject.

Figure 14-4. The criteria for evaluating whether an article gets to be a Featured list is at Wikipedia:Featured list criteria *(shortcut:* WP:WIAFL*). You can use the criteria as a checklist to improve a list that interests you. When you think your list is good enough, you can submit it to a review to see if it earns the Featured list designation.*

out as sections of existing narrative articles, and are only broken out when they become disproportionately long for the original article. (Essays are opinions, not policy.)

NOTE

As an editor, treat problematical lists exactly like other problem articles, as described in Chapter 18. If you see what looks like a bad list, you might want to post a question on the talk page of the guideline *Wikipedia:Lists (stand-alone lists)* (shortcut: *WP:SAL*) before formally proposing the list for deletion.

Good lists

As of late 2007, roughly 500 articles had earned the honor of being designated Featured lists, with roughly 20 to 40 more lists being so designated each month. Figure 14-4 shows some of the criteria. The full criteria include complying with the Manual of Style (*WP:MOS*) and standards of any relevant WikiProject, and making sure any images are appropriately captioned and not copyright violations.

Looking at articles designated as Featured lists can show you the variety of formats used for lists, and the astounding quality achieved by some. Figure 14-5 shows one example.

Figure 14-5. The article List of wild mammal species in Florida *has been designated as a Featured list. It's an amazing collection of sortable lists, with pictures and well over a hundred footnotes for those interested in more information. The star in the upper-right corner indicates that it's a Wikipedia featured page. The same star appears on Featured Articles and Featured Portals.*

Lists versus categories

A list article in its simplest form consists of an introductory sentence or two, followed by an alphabetized bullet list of links to (mostly) existing Wikipedia articles. It resembles a category page.

NOTE

Wikipedia:Categories, lists, and series boxes (shortcut: *WP:CLS*) discusses the differences between list articles and category pages. Chapter 18 (page 336) goes into detail about the advantages and disadvantages of the two approaches.

Formatting alternatives

If you look at the wikicode for articles that are lists, you find a number of different things:

- **Narrative**. The initial section of an article that's a list explains what the list is about, in the usual narrative format. Narrative can also appear in other places—the article in Figure 14-5 has not only a long lead section but also a number of

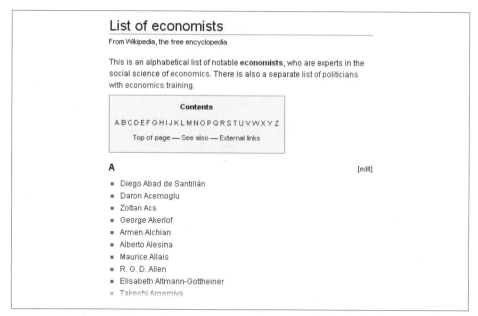

List of economists

From Wikipedia, the free encyclopedia

This is an alphabetical list of notable **economists**, who are experts in the social science of economics. There is also a separate list of politicians with economics training.

Contents

A B C D E F G H I J K L M N O P Q R S T U V W X Y Z

Top of page — See also — External links

A   [edit]

- Diego Abad de Santillán
- Daron Acemoglu
- Zoltan Acs
- George Akerlof
- Armen Alchian
- Alberto Alesina
- Maurice Allais
- R. G. D. Allen
- Elisabeth Altmann-Gottheiner
- Takeshi Amemiya

Figure 14-6. The article List of economists *is a simple bulleted list of wikilinks. It resembles a category page (Chapter 17) so much that pages like this one have been the subject of fights between proponents of categories (who want to delete lists like this) and those arguing that lists are just as good, if not superior. For more information, see page 336.*

narrative paragraphs at the beginning of sections. Some articles that have a name beginning with "List of", such as *List of Pokémon (481-493)* are a collection of information that might at some later point become individual articles, and are entirely narrative. (On the other hand, the article could be renamed *Pokémon species 481 to 493*.)

- **Bulleted lists using asterisks**. You saw an example of bulleted lists at the top of Figure 14-1, with wikitext in Figure 14-2. That's an embedded list, but the code is exactly the same for standalone lists. That kind of bulleted list created with asterisks is the oldest form of Wikipedia list, and it's still the most common for standalone lists, since it's so easy to use. You can see an example in Figure 14-6.

The bulleted list has a couple of variants. One, called an annotated list, adds a bit of information after each link. If Figure 14-6 were an annotated list, for example, the entry for Diego Abad de Santillán might have "(1897–1983), Spain" after the wikilink. A second variant is a bulleted list with some items indented, as a sort of subcategorization. Figure 14-7 shows an example of a bulleted list with indented items.

The formatting for the indented, bulleted paragraphs in Figure 14-7 is straightforward, as shown in Figure 14-8.

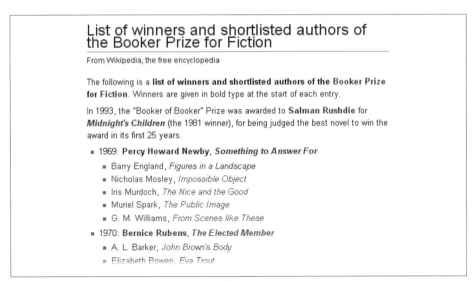

List of winners and shortlisted authors of the Booker Prize for Fiction

From Wikipedia, the free encyclopedia

The following is a **list of winners and shortlisted authors of the Booker Prize for Fiction**. Winners are given in bold type at the start of each entry.

In 1993, the "Booker of Booker" Prize was awarded to **Salman Rushdie** for *Midnight's Children* (the 1981 winner), for being judged the best novel to win the award in its first 25 years.

- 1969: **Percy Howard Newby, *Something to Answer For***
  - Barry England, *Figures in a Landscape*
  - Nicholas Mosley, *Impossible Object*
  - Iris Murdoch, *The Nice and the Good*
  - Muriel Spark, *The Public Image*
  - G. M. Williams, *From Scenes like These*
- 1970: **Bernice Rubens, *The Elected Member***
  - A. L. Barker, *John Brown's Body*
  - Elizabeth Bowen, *Eva Trout*

Figure 14-7. Here's the beginning of the article List of winners and shortlisted authors of the Booker Prize for Fiction. *It's an example of indented bulleted paragraphs within articles.*

```
The following is a '''list of winners and shortlisted authors of the [[Booker
Prize]] for [[Fiction]]'''. Winners are given in bold type at the start of each
entry.

In 1993, the "Booker of Booker" Prize was awarded to '''[[Salman Rushdie]]'''
for '''''[[Midnight's Children]]''''' (the 1981 winner), for being judged the
best novel to win the award in its first 25 years.

*1969: '''[[PH Newby|Percy Howard Newby]]''', '''''[[Something to Answer
For]]'''''
**[[Barry England]], ''[[Figures in a Landscape]]''
**[[Nicholas Mosley]], ''[[Impossible Object (fiction)|Impossible Object]]''
**[[Iris Murdoch]], ''[[The Nice and the Good]]''
**[[Muriel Spark]], ''[[The Public Image]]''
**[[G. M. Williams]], ''[[From Scenes like These]]''

*1970: '''[[Bernice Rubens]]''', '''''[[The Elected Member]]'''''
**[[A. L. Barker]], ''[[John Brown's Body (novel)|John Brown's Body]]''
```

Figure 14-8. You indent bulleted paragraphs simply by putting two asterisks at the beginning of a line, rather than one. This arrangement looks nicer than colon indenting, but it's more fragile. If you make a mistake and have a blank line just above the double asterisks, then the viewable version of the page shows two bullets at the beginning of the line, not one indented bullet.

The bulleted list in Figure 14-6 is alphabetical; the one in Figure 14-7 is chronological. (Lists whose titles begin "Timeline of" are, of course, always chronological.) Bulleted lists can also be hierarchical, as in Figure 14-9.

- A *table* is a third kind of wikitext (besides narrative and bulleting) used for lists. Figure 14-10 shows an example. Tables can be the bulk of a list article or just part

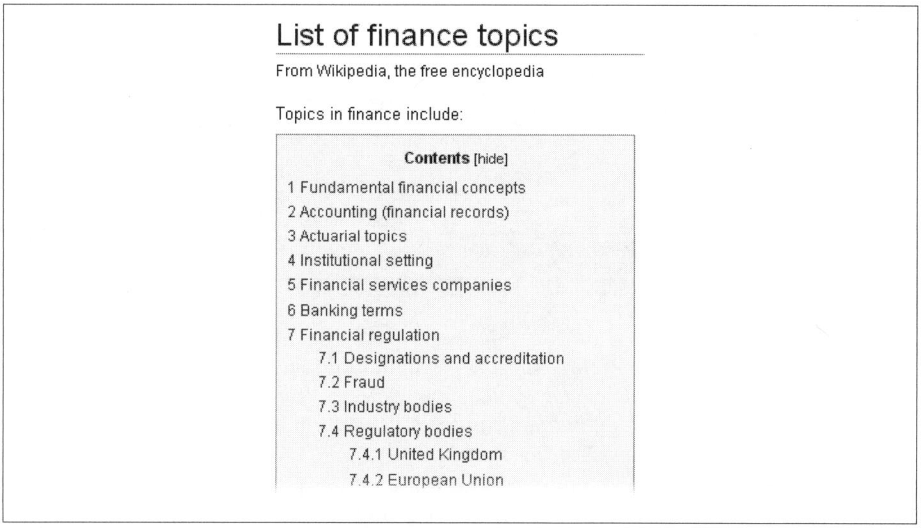

List of finance topics

From Wikipedia, the free encyclopedia

Topics in finance include:

Contents [hide]

1 Fundamental financial concepts
2 Accounting (financial records)
3 Actuarial topics
4 Institutional setting
5 Financial services companies
6 Banking terms
7 Financial regulation
    7.1 Designations and accreditation
    7.2 Fraud
    7.3 Industry bodies
    7.4 Regulatory bodies
        7.4.1 United Kingdom
        7.4.2 European Union

Figure 14-9. The article List of finance topics *is arranged hierarchically. This scheme is a bit more challenging for editors, but it helps readers comprehend what otherwise might be a long alphabetized list. It also helps readers find related articles that wouldn't be obvious in an alphabetical list.*

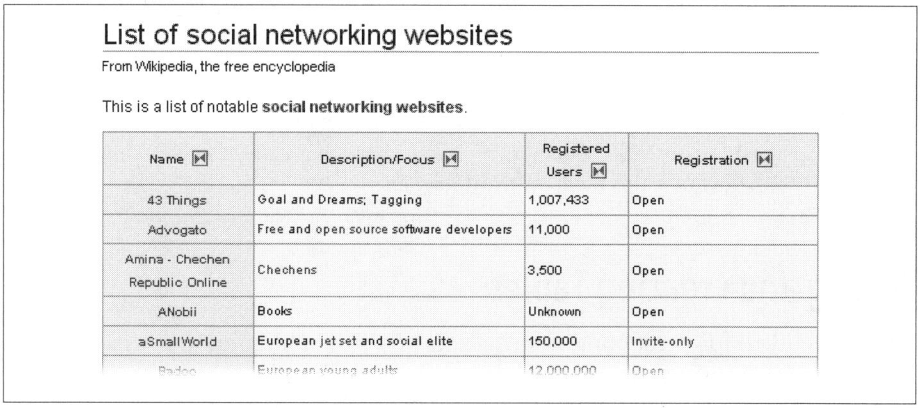

List of social networking websites

From Wikipedia, the free encyclopedia

This is a list of notable **social networking websites**.

Name	Description/Focus	Registered Users	Registration
43 Things	Goal and Dreams; Tagging	1,007,433	Open
Advogato	Free and open source software developers	11,000	Open
Amina - Chechen Republic Online	Chechens	3,500	Open
ANobii	Books	Unknown	Open
aSmallWorld	European jet set and social elite	150,000	Invite-only
Badoo	European young adults	12,000,000	Open

Figure 14-10. The article List of social networking websites *consists primarily of a sortable table, which lets readers reorganize the table to better find what they want. (For more on sorting tables, see page 268.)*

of a narrative article. ("Editing and Creating Tables" on page 262 has the full story.)

- A fourth kind of formatting for lists uses a graphical timeline. Such lists are usually named "Timeline of X," or "Graphical timeline of X". Figure 14-11 has an example of a graphical timeline that functions as a list.

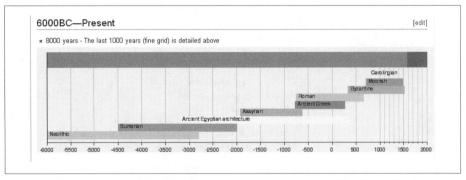

Figure 14-11. Here's one of three timelines that make up the article Timeline of architectural styles. *It uses the <timeline> tag syntax, sometimes called EasyTimeline syntax. Graphical timelines are relatively rare, but you can read about them at* Wikipedia:Timeline *(shortcut: WP:TIMEL) and Help:EasyTimeline syntax.*

NOTE

Timelines also appear in non-list articles, often as navigation templates. (Some of these timelines actually are templates, with a different syntax from the newer <timeline> tag syntax.)

- Finally, you can split long lists using a navigational template that lets readers know that though they're looking at just one article, that's part of the a set of related articles that together make up a full list. Figure 14-12 gives an example.

NOTE

Figure 14-12 is another example of a list that's basically a table. Unlike Figure 14-10, however, this table isn't sortable.

Editing and Creating Tables

Tables are ideal for presenting information in a row-and-column format. You create Wikipedia tables using wiki markup, which begins with "{|" and ends with "|}". Since you'll edit tables much more often than create them, this section begins with editing. (To see how to create a wikicode table, flip to page 265.)

Editing Tables

Even if you never create a table from scratch, you still need to understand the basic structure to edit a table. Figure 14-13 shows the wikicode underlying a simple table.

Here are the elements of the wikicode that makes up a table:

List of places in Alabama: D-H

From Wikipedia, the free encyclopedia

This **list** of current cities, towns, unincorporated communities, counties, and other recognized **places** in the U.S. state of **Alabama** also includes information on the number of counties in which the place lies, the name of its principal county, and its lower and upper zip code bounds, if applicable.

Places in Alabama starting with the letter A-C **D-H** I-K L-N O-R S-Z

References   [edit]

- USGS Fips55 database

See also:

- Alabama
- List of cities in Alabama
- List of counties in Alabama

Name of place	Number of counties	Principal county	Lower zip code	Upper zip code
Dadeville	1	Tallapoosa County	36853	
Daisey City	1	Jefferson County		
Daisy	1	Butler County		

Figure 14-12. The article List of places in Alabama: D-H. *The box near the top of the article, with text that begins "Places in Alabama", is there because the underlying wikitext includes the template {{List of places in Alabama}}. That template also appears at the top of the other five lists (A-C, I-K, L-N, O-R, and S-Z) that comprise a single list. This navigational template makes it easy for the reader to get to any of these six parts, although they're separate articles.*

- **1**. A table always begins with "{|". In this case, an optional parameter, *class="wikitable"*, has been added. That parameter tells the software to do standard table formatting, such as shading the top row.
- **2**. This line adds an optional caption (starting with "|+").
- **3** through **6**. Each row of a table, including column headings (if any) consists of two or more lines, with the first line essentially saying, "A new row starts here!"
- **3, 4, 5** and **6** illustrate four different ways that cells in a table can look in wikitext. Each cell must be separated from the previous cell in its row by either inserting two vertical lines between the cells, if the cells are placed on the same line, or putting the second cell on a new line, with one vertical line ("|") at the beginning.

  In **3, 4,** and **5**, one or more of the "|" symbols have been replaced by the "!" symbol, which tells Wikipedia to format that cell as a heading. Exactly how that heading appears to the viewer depends on the viewer's browser.

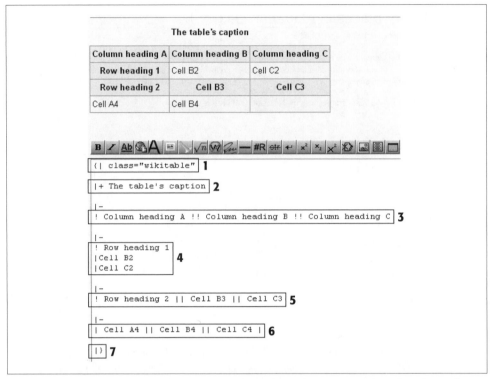

Figure 14-13. Here's a table (top) and its underlying wikicode (bottom). The wikicode is split into seven chunks by six blank lines, for ease of understanding. You don't usually find blank lines in the wikicode between rows of a table, as is the case here. (These blank lines make no difference in what the reader sees.)

Comparing **4** to **5**, the reason that cells B3 and B4 are bolded (treated like headings) is because they're on the same line as row heading 2, which has an "!" in front of it. Row 4 is correct; row 5 is wrong.

- **7**. A table must end with "|}" on its own line

When editing a table, you generally want to do one of three things: Change the content of an existing cell, add a row, or delete a row. The first is fairly straightforward: In editing mode, find where the cell starts, and add or change text. Adding a row isn't difficult either: In editing mode, find the row above or below where you want to add a row; copy that row and paste it into the table. Now you have two identical rows; edit one of them with the information you're adding. (Deleting a row is even easier than adding one; just select the lines that make up that row, and delete away.)

To test your understanding of editing tables, see if you can answer the following question: In Figure 14-13, look at the last three rows in the table. How many lines of wikicode are there for each of these three rows? (Do count the first line of each row, the line that begins "|-"; don't count any of the six blank lines inserted in the wikicode to make it easier to read.) The answer: 4 lines, 2 lines, and 2 lines, respectively. If you got that, then you're ready to copy, insert, and even delete rows from any table you find.

Creating Tables

In your career as a Wikipedia editor, you'll make lists, as described at the beginning of this chapter, much more often then tables. First off, lists are much easier to create—for most, you just type an asterisk before each list item. Tables involve much more complex wikicode.

You probably don't want to create a table unless your information needs three or more columns. If there's only one column, you can simply display the information in a list, which is much easier to edit than a table. If there are two columns, it's still better to present information as a list (either annotated or indented, as discussed on page 259) unless it would be useful to sort the information by the second column. (Tables can be sorted, lists can't.) For a fuller discussion of when to create a table instead of list, check out the guideline *Wikipedia:When to use tables* (shortcut: *WP:TABLE*), which is part of Wikipedia's *Manual of Style*. If you're still sure you want to create a table, read on.

Basics of creating tables

For the most basic table, you can use the edit toolbar's table icon to generate some starter wikicode (Figure 14-14). Then you can expand it and add your information.

You can also use a table to format a multicolumn list. To do so, use the simplified wikicode shown in Figure 14-15.

If neither of the previous two examples meets your needs, you need to create a table from scratch. Here's a quick three-step plan for creating a table:

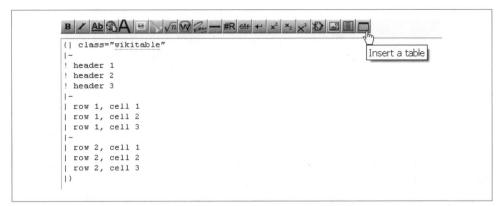

Figure 14-14. On the edit toolbar, if you click the "table" icon, in editing mode, the software generates a basic table for you. It may not be much, but it's a start if you're creating a table from scratch.

1. Read the page *Help:Table*; which has lots of detailed information and examples.

2. Read the tutorial *User:Smurrayinchester/Tutorial/Tables* and slightly more advanced *User:Dcljr/Tables*.

3. Find a table in an existing article that's pretty close to what you want, and copy it. Then you only have to tinker with the formatting, add or subtract rows, and edit the contents of the cells in the table, replacing them with whatever you want in your table.

POWER USERS' CLINIC

Table Classes

Specifying a class for a table, such as *class="wikitable"*, tells Wikipedia to use predefined formatting for the table. An extreme example would be putting *class="wikitable sortable collapsible collapsed"* into the first line of a table. That makes it a standard wikitable (governing things like how headings are formatted); sortable by clicking on a column heading; collapsible to a single row, with just a click, if a reader wants to get it out of the way; and initially displayed as a single row (collapsed) rather than fully visible when the page first opens. The collapsed option is the least common. If a table's worth adding to an article, why hide it?

You can learn more about sorting tables on page 268. Collapsing is less common. If you really want to learn how to do it, see *Help:Collapsing*.

Making tables more usable and accessible

You can make tables more usable to everyone, not just normally sighted people with high resolution monitors, by doing several things:

- **Don't set fixed column widths**, unless you're trying to slim down a column where only a few cells have lengthy text. Setting a lot of fixed width columns, even if the

---

This is the caption		
▪ Left column, top item ▪ Left column, second item ▪ Left, third	▪ Center column, very first item at top ▪ Center column, second ▪ Center, 3rd ▪ Center, 4th	▪ Right column, top ▪ Right column, this time a very, very long (well, much longer) item ▪ Right column, end

```
{| class="wikitable"
|+ This is the caption
|
*Left column, top item
*Left column, second item
*Left, third
|
*Center column, very first item at top
*Center column, second
*Center, 3rd
*Center, 4th
|
*Right column, top
*Right column, this time a very, very long (well, much longer)
item
*Right column, end
|}
```

Figure 14-15. This table arranges a list of information into three columns. In some sense, this isn't a true table because it doesn't have rows (or, to be exact, it's formatted as if it had only one row), and the information in one column doesn't necessarily line up with information in the other columns. (Notice that the center column has four entries, versus three entries for the left and right columns.) Still, it can be useful for getting a long list to fit into much less space.

total is less than 800 pixels, can cause problems for users with narrow viewports (mobile devices) or those using large text sizes. If you need to, specify a percentage to allow a degree of flexibility. Even then, you may still be better off simply trusting the software to deliver an acceptably viewable table.

- **Put a summary in the top line of the table**. The format is simple: *summary="..."* (you don't need a comma, or any other separator, before or after). A summary (which isn't displayed visually) provides a description of the table's purpose and structure for non-visual browsers, which read the page aloud. For example, a summary might say, "The table is organized with the oldest model of the automobile first, and the latest model last."

- **Use exclamation points ("!") for row and column headings**, as shown in Figure 14-13, Figure 14-14, and Figure 14-15, rather than specifying specific formatting for headings (bold, larger font size, or whatever). When you let the software do the work, it can adjust for different browsers and screen sizes and resolution. Also, omitting your own personalized formatting for headings simplifies the table.

When voice browsers read a table aloud, they repeat the appropriate column headings when reading a cell. If they can't figure out the column heading, they just read cell information without the context of a column heading.

- **Add an abbreviation for voice browsers** if column headings are more than a word or so. For example, if a column heading is *Number of edits*, change that to *abbr="Edits" | Number of edits*. The heading stills visually displays "Number of edits", but the voice browser just says, "Edits."

- **Don't code information into the table using only colors or colored symbols**. For example, in a table about U.S. politicians, if you color rows about Republicans in one way, and Democrat rows in another way, you should also include text in the rows that specifies party affiliation. Similarly, in a table about subway stations, it's okay to indicate the subway lines that stop at a station by using colored boxes, but you also need to put text in those boxes.

Coloring and bolding are good things, not problems, since they provide immediate visual cues. But make the same information available in text form as well, at least subtly: "(R)" for Republican, "(D)" for Democratic, for example, or by putting a "B" or a "BL" inside the blue box that indicates that the Blue Line stops at that station.

Sortable tables

Being able to sort a table—especially a long table—makes it much more valuable to readers. For example, some people may want to look at a list of U.S. presidents in chronological order; others want to see it alphabetically. Whenever you create or edit a table, consider whether you can make it sortable.

Sortable tables have arrows in the cells of the top row that you can click to sort by that column, as shown in Figure 14-10 (page 260). The code to make a table sortable is straightforward: Instead of *class="wikitable"*, in the first line of the table, use *class="wikitable sortable"*.

NOTE

If you've never seen a sortable table in Wikipedia, go to *Help:Sorting* and check some of the examples there. If you can't get any tables there to sort themselves, then you don't have JavaScript turned on in your browser. (See page 401 for how to do so.)

In a sortable table, when you click an arrow, the table sorts itself based on the selected column, in ascending order. The arrow's a toggle switch: If you click it again, the table sorts itself in descending order rather than ascending order.

NOTE

Just because a table is sortable is no reason for you to just add new rows at the bottom of the table. Some readers won't understand the table is sortable, and folks viewing via a mobile device, or via a screen reader, or on a printed page, won't be able to. Sorting should always be an option for a reader who wants to see a table in a different way, not a requirement to see it in the correct sequence.

If you create a sortable table or change one to be sortable, you need to understand the software's logic when sorting. First, the software decides which of four types of data is in that column: dates, currency, numbers, or text (what Wikipedia calls *strings*). Looking down the column, the software finds the first non-blank cell and assumes that everything else in the column is in the same format. But a number of things can go wrong:

- **Mixed types of data in a column don't sort right**. For example, in a column that's for calendar dates, don't put "Unknown" where a date isn't known. Just leave the cell blank.

- **Numbers aren't displayed correctly**. The sorting algorithm isn't thrown off by commas or decimal places, but it doesn't insert missing commas, or align a column of numbers on the decimal point (rather, columns are aligned left or right, or centered). So make sure to format numbers consistently. Don't put commas in some figures and leave them out of others. Similarly, when you have figures with decimal places, try to have the same number of digits to the right of the decimal point.

- **Dates aren't formatted correctly**. The correct format for Wikipedia purposes is "14 June 2007", not "June 14, 2007". If you use the latter, the software thinks you're using text, and alphabetizes the column.

TIP

Avoid using a format like "05-01-2007"; in some countries that date would be May 1, 2007, in others it would be January 5, 2007.

GEM IN THE ROUGH

Importing Tables from Microsoft Word and Excel

Three tools let you transfer non-wiki text into wiki code without knowing wiki code. The first two preserve the formatting of tables and their contents, but you should use them only if you're well-versed in Word or Excel or if you have a large number of offline documents that you plan to convert into Wikipedia content.

(If you do have a lot of documents to add to Wikipedia en masse, make sure that they follow Wikipedia's rules about content being notable, verifiable, and not original research, as discussed in Chapter 4.)

- *Word2MediaWikiPlus*, described at *http://www.mediawiki.org/wiki/Word2Media WikiPlus*, converts Microsoft Word tables to wikitables, using a set of Visual Basic macros. Setting up the converter requires downloading a compressed folder from www.sourceforge.org (*http://www.sourceforge.org*), and then copying a number of components to Word's normal.dot template.

- *VBA-Macro for EXCEL tableconversion*, described at *http://de.wikipedia.org/wiki/ Wikipedia:Helferlein/VBA-Macro_for_EXCEL_tableconversion*, converts a selected cell range in an Excel workbook into a wiki table format with all essential formatting information. Setting up the Visual Basic for Applications (VBA) module is straightforward if you're familiar with VBA. You just copy some lengthy VBA code to your spreadsheet.

- The third tool is much simpler, but moves only content – not formatting—from an Excel spreadsheet. You'll find the details at *http://de.wikipedia.org/wiki/Benut zer:Duesentrieb/csv2wp_(en)*.

CHAPTER 15

Adding Images

One of the most striking changes in Wikipedia in the last few years is that most articles now include at least one image. Editors have added those images, one by one, and now an article without at least one illustration seems incomplete.

This chapter shows you how to upload an image for use in a Wikipedia article. Until you get an image off your computer and onto a server that Wikipedia uses, you can't use that image in an article. This chapter also shows you how to place an image in an article, after you or someone else has uploaded it.

NOTE

In Wikipedia (and in this chapter), the word "image" doesn't just mean a photo; it can be a map, a drawing, a chart, or even an animated gif. "Photo" refers only to an image taken by a camera.

Uploading Images

When it comes to images, less is usually more. A glut of images in an article may make it worse, not better. Don't overwhelm a medium-sized or small article by adding lots of images to it. Focus on uploading images that can support and illustrate the text of an article, not replace that text.

If you do have a bunch of images that you could use for an article, but that you don't intend to use unless the article becomes much larger, you can still upload them. Instead of uploading them to the English Wikipedia (where every uploaded image needs to have a home in an article), you'll upload such images to the Wikimedia Commons, the place where all the 250-plus different language Wikipedias can use it. In fact, this chapter recommends uploading all your images to the Commons, whether you immediately put them into articles or not.

Wikimedia Commons holds uploaded media files like photos, diagrams, animations, music, spoken text, and video clips, but no text documents. You can think of it as a stock media site for Wikipedia and other Wikimedia Foundation projects.

Before You Upload

Before getting to the tutorial on uploading, you need to go through a short checklist. While this list talks about photos, a similar policy applies to other types of images.

- Is the photo you want to upload something you took and thus own? Is it in the public domain, or already licensed as free content by its owner? If it's not any of the above, you can't upload it to the Commons. For details, see "Uploading a Non-Free Image" on page 288.

- Are you willing to give up certain rights for a photo you took yourself, when you upload it? You must agree that, once you upload the photo, anyone can use it for any purpose, including commercially, and you won't get paid. Basically, you must agree to license your photo for use by anyone. All you can ask is that they attribute the photo to you.

- Is the photo of acceptable quality? Is it a file type that Wikipedia can use? (See the box below.)

- Do you have a user account at the Commons? If not, get one as described in the next section.

Once the answer to all four questions is "yes," you're ready to upload your image, following the steps on page 275.

UP TO SPEED

Acceptable Types of Photos

Wikipedia and the Wikimedia Commons aren't file-sharing storage sites. If you upload a photo, it must be of the quality and type that would be suitable in an encyclopedia. That means no tiny photos, no blurry photos, and no sets of 47 poses by your dog.

The recommended format for photos is JPEG. Other acceptable formats are SVG, PNG, JPEG, XCF (GIMP), and SXD (OpenOffice.org (*http://OpenOffice.org*) 1.x). This list is notable for its omission—no TIFF files.

Most images on Wikipedia are JPEGs, which is the default setting on most digital cameras.

Creating a User Account at the Commons

Images at Wikimedia Commons are available to all Wikipedias, not just the English one. Images in the Commons don't have to actually be used in an article. They are there because they *could* be used in an article. You can take useful photos, upload them, and come back later to use them. Or not—they're still available to every other editor at the different language Wikipedias.

To upload images to the Commons, you need an account. Creating one is a quick three-step process.

1. Go to *http://commons.wikimedia.org/*. Click the "create account" link (in the upper-right corner), click the bolded "Create an account" link, and then fill in the requested information (see Figure 15-1).

   As when you're creating a Wikipedia account (page 50), providing an email address is highly recommended.

   #### NOTE
   If you're asking yourself why you can't use your Wikipedia account for the Commons, you're not alone. A single sign-on has been under discussion for years (see the box on page 48). For now, you should create your Commons account using your Wikipedia user name, if that's available.

   ---

2. When you're done filling in the form in Figure 15-1, click "Create account".

   If you included an email address, as recommended, then you'll get a confirmation email (Figure 15-2). Reply to that, and your email is set up.

As with the English Wikipedia, you have the option of creating user pages. If you have an account only for the purpose of uploading images, you probably won't want to bother. But if you do want to, the process is exactly the same as at Wikipedia; the Commons runs on the same MediaWiki software.

The standard setting in your user preferences at the Commons is "E-mail me when my user talk page is changed" (Figure 15-3). Keep it turned on. That way, you don't have to log in periodically to check for notifications—for example, that there was a problem with an image you uploaded. Instead, you can just assume that no news in your email inbox is good news.

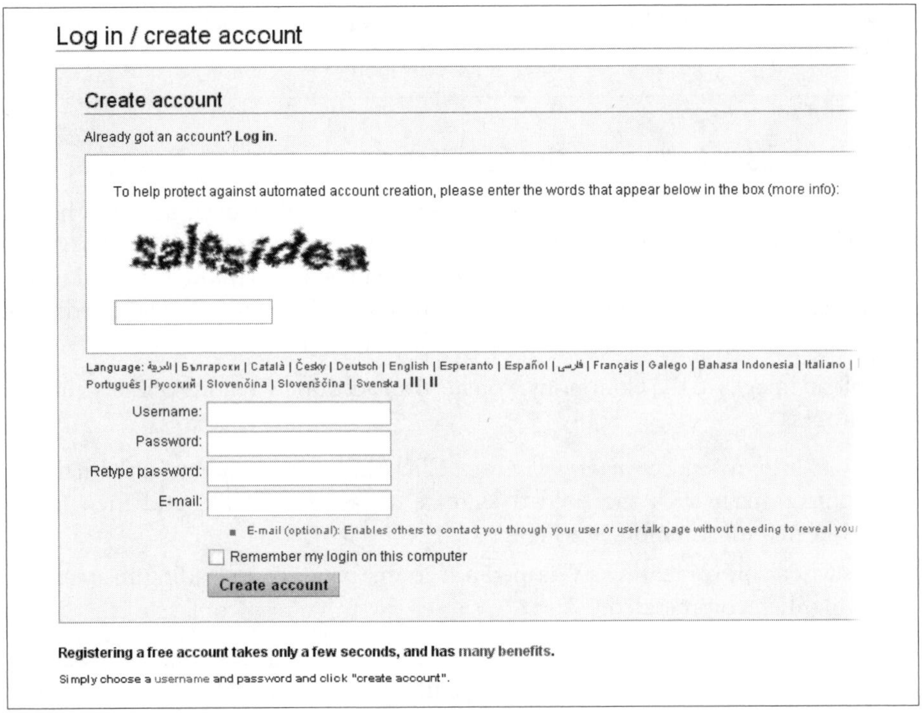

Log in / create account

Create account

Already got an account? **Log in**.

To help protect against automated account creation, please enter the words that appear below in the box (more info):

salesidea

Language: العربية | Български | Català | Česky | Deutsch | English | Esperanto | Español | فارسی | Français | Galego | Bahasa Indonesia | Italiano | Português | Русский | Slovenčina | Slovenščina | Svenska | ‖ | ‖

Username: _____

Password: _____

Retype password: _____

E-mail: _____

- E-mail (optional): Enables others to contact you through your user or user talk page without needing to reveal your

☐ Remember my login on this computer

Create account

Registering a free account takes only a few seconds, and has many benefits.
Simply choose a username and password and click "create account".

Figure 15-1. Not surprisingly, the screen for creating a Commons account looks very similar to the one for creating an account at the English Wikipedia. That's because the two sites are run by the Wikimedia Foundation, and both use MediaWiki software.

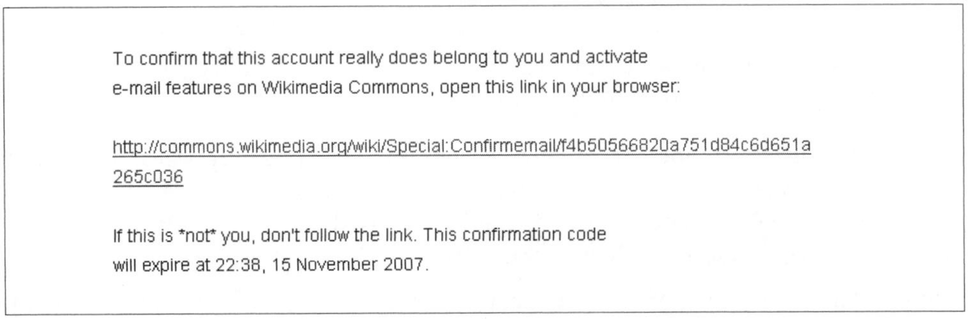

To confirm that this account really does belong to you and activate e-mail features on Wikimedia Commons, open this link in your browser:

http://commons.wikimedia.org/wiki/Special:Confirmemail/f4b50566820a751d84c6d651a 265c036

If this is *not* you, don't follow the link. This confirmation code will expire at 22:38, 15 November 2007.

Figure 15-2. Here's part of the email you'll get at the email address that you provided when you created your account. All you need to do is click the link to confirm.

UP TO SPEED

Quality Counts

Always upload the highest resolution version of your image, keeping within the Commons' 20MB limit. A high-resolution image makes it easier for other editors to crop a photo, if needed. (Or, if you have the tools and time, you can do so before uploading.)

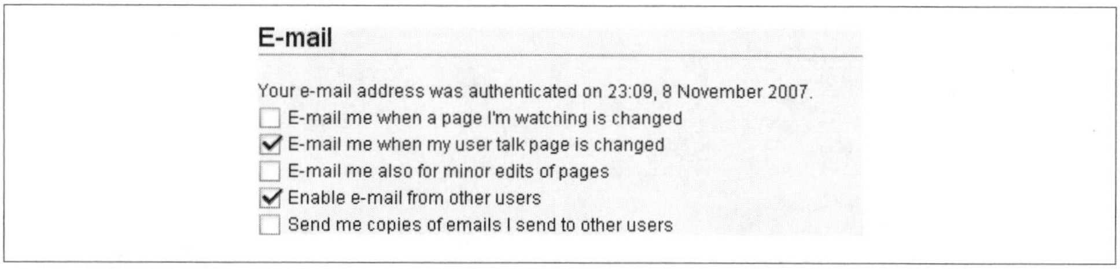

Figure 15-3. The standard email settings in the "User profile" tab of your user account's preferences let the Commons contact you when something changes. The English Wikipedia, by contrast, doesn't offer you the first three options, since the volume of outgoing email could overwhelm Wikipedia's servers.

Plus, as computer screens continue to increase in size, viewing larger images is becoming more common. Don't worry about the space your photo will take up in the article —that's controlled by displaying a smaller, *thumbnail* version and letting readers choose their preferred image sizes.

Images should be free from distortion, watermarks, credits, and anything else that would hamper their free use. If you create an image that contains text that you added, you should also upload a version without any text, so projects in other languages can use the image.

For a number of specific suggestions about image quality, see the page *Wikipedia:How to improve image quality* (shortcut: *WP:HIIQ*). You'll also find JPEG tips in a section of the guideline *Wikipedia:Preparing images for upload* (shortcut: *WP:PIFU*).

Uploading an Image to the Commons

Once you've gone through the checklist on page 272 to determine whether you can use an image in Wikipedia, and you've got your Commons user account, you're ready to upload an image.

These steps assume that you're uploading for the first time, and that it's a photo you took yourself. After you have more experience, you can skip to the upload form (see the bottom of Figure 15-4). Here's the step-by-step process.

1. Once you've logged into your Commons account, click the "Upload file" link on the left side of the screen.

   It's the first link in the "participate" set of links. You'll see the initial screen in the upload process (Figure 15-4).

TIP

That Flickr link is there because so many people post photos at Flickr and release them as free content. That means you can copy those photos to the Commons.

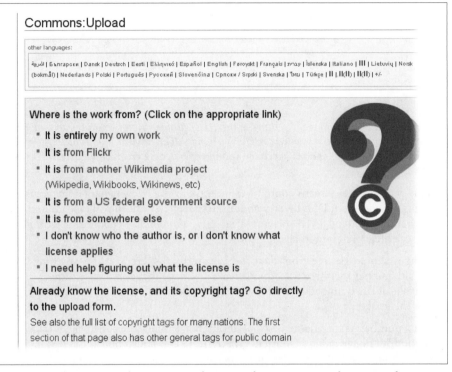

Commons:Upload

other languages:

العربية | Български | Dansk | Deutsch | Eesti | Ελληνικά | Español | English | Føroyskt | Français | עברית | Íslenska | Italiano | ||| | Lietuvių | Norsk (bokmål) | Nederlands | Polski | Português | Русский | Slovenčina | Српски / Srpski | Svenska | ไทย | Türkçe | || | ||(||) | ||(||) | +/-

Where is the work from? (Click on the appropriate link)

* It is entirely my own work
* It is from Flickr
* It is from another Wikimedia project
  (Wikipedia, Wikibooks, Wikinews, etc)
* It is from a US federal government source
* It is from somewhere else
* I don't know who the author is, or I don't know what
  license applies
* I need help figuring out what the license is

**Already know the license, and its copyright tag? Go directly
to the upload form.**

See also the full list of copyright tags for many nations. The first
section of that page also has other general tags for public domain

Figure 15-4. The two critical components, for copyright purposes, are the source of an image, and the license for that image. When you start the upload process to the Commons, the first page is concerned with the source. Which link you click determines which page you'll see next, a page that either helps you figure out the source or moves you to the question of the license.

2. Click the link on the line, "It is entirely my own work".

   The page you see has a number of sections at the top (steps 1 to 3, and "Other tips"). You're welcome to read them, but it's also okay to start at the bottom of the page (Figure 15-5), where you fill out the required information for the upload.

   For copyrights, only two things count: the source and the license. You've already specified a source (you took the photo); next, you need to specify the second. Figure 15-6 shows your choices.

3. Select "Own work, all rights released (Public domain)."

   Whatever you pick, you'll see an explanation immediately below the box with the license choice (Figure 15-7).

   The license you choose doesn't affect the rest of the upload process. If you do want attribution, pick one of the other five options. If you're unsure about licensing, just click each one and read the explanations.

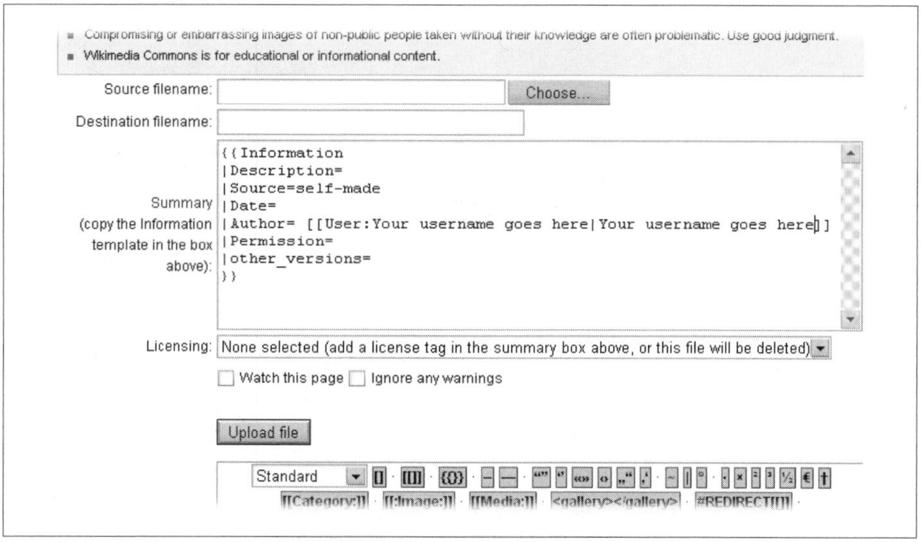

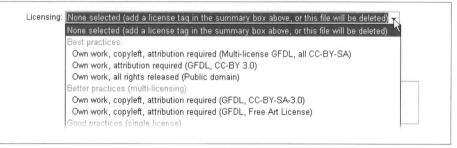

Figure 15-5. *Here's what you need to fill out in order to upload an image to the Commons. The text in the Summary section is preloaded for you, including your user name.*

Figure 15-6. *Once you're specified that what you're uploading is your own work, you have a choice of six different licenses. The top three are categorized as "Best practices," the next two as "Better practices (multi-licensing)," and the last one is in the category "Good practices (single license)." When you select one, you'll see more information about it.*

NOTE

You're doing what Wikipedia calls *adding a copyright tag*. For more information on these tags, including the seven licenses that image creators can choose from, see the page *Wikipedia:Image copyright tags* (shortcut: *WP:ICT*).

---

4. Click the "Choose" button to the right of the "Source filename" field.

Up pops a file selection dialog box for you to navigate to the image on your computer.

5. Double-click the file name.

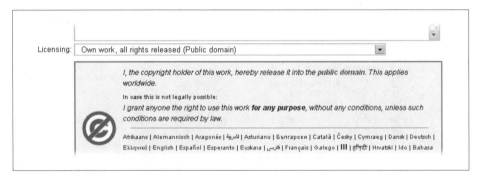

Figure 15-7. When you select the public domain license, the page changes to show what the license actually is. If you decide you don't like what you see, you can choose another license. To get further information about the license you've tentatively selected, you can follow the links in the box that states what the license is.

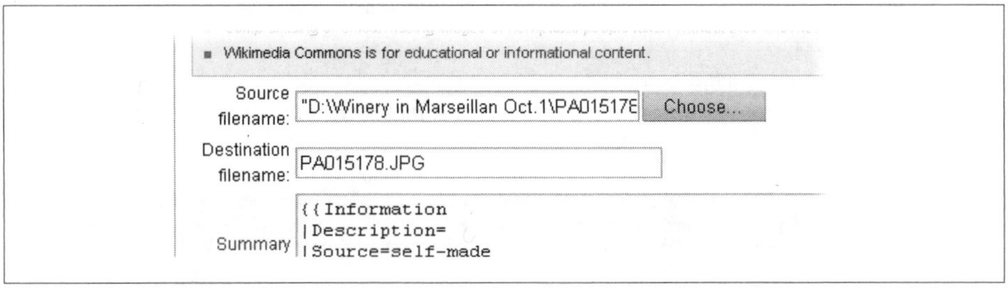

Figure 15-8. When you've selected a file, the "Source filename" field has the full path for that file. The destination filename is automatically given the same name as the source filename, but you can change that.

The text field displays the full path to the file on your computer. Figure 15-8 shows an example.

6. Change the "Destination filename" from whatever was put automatically into the field (see Figure 15-8) to something that describes the image.

7. The name you type becomes the name of the image page after you've finished uploading your photo. Make sure it ends with the correct suffix, such as ".jpg," to match the actual file type. (See the box on page 272 for what file types are acceptable, if you're not uploading a JPEG file.)

WARNING

Get the name right the first time, because you can't rename an image file once it's been uploaded. If you don't get the name right, you'll have to upload the file again, this time specifying a better name.

Getting the Name Right

Short or cryptic names for images make them a lot harder to find and use. If you use a short name, or the default filename from your camera (like DSC123456.jpg), it's much more likely that someone else will later upload an image with exactly the same name, and that will overwrite what you uploaded. Or, if you're uploading to the Commons with the intent to add an image to the English Wikipedia, you'll discover that an image file with the name you picked already exists on Wikipedia, so you can't use the one at the Commons.

The best image name is a fairly long description. A bonus of using such a name is that you can copy and paste it into the Description field for the image, saving yourself some typing. (The maximum file name length is around 250 characters, but you won't need a name that long.)

Finally, the image name you use has to have a three-letter extension, such as .jpg or .svg. The extension must match the actual file type, or the photo won't display correctly. That makes image pages different from regular pages (articles, talk pages, portals, categories, and so on), which don't have a suffix. If you forget the extension, you're going to have to upload the photo again. Lowercase extensions, such as .jpg, are preferred over uppercase, like .JPG, though both work. Note that the Commons (and other MediaWiki websites) considers them two totally different files.

8. Next is the large Summary field, which has already been partially filled out to indicate what is needed. You just add information to two parts.

   For Description, copy what you put into the Destination filename field, since that should have been descriptive, and then elaborate on that a bit, if you want to. You're creating some searchable text here, so don't be reluctant to go into detail. For example, if the photo was taken from another building, or if there is something unusual in the photo, mention that in the description.

   For Date, type the date the photo was actually taken. (The Permission information is for licensing; since you've selected a license using the pull-down menu, leave this field blank.)

   At this point, the page should look something like Figure 15-9.

9. Below the licensing information (scroll down as needed) you'll see the "Upload file" button. Click that.

   You'll see something like Figure 15-10.

At this point, you're done uploading. But it's very helpful to add some categories to the photo, so others can find it more easily. To do so, see the next section.

Figure 15-9. Upload information is complete, with a descriptive filename, and the Summary field filled out. Leave the Permission parameter blank, since you specified a license using the pull-down menu in the Licensing box.

Adding Categories to an Image Page at the Commons

At the Commons, you can add categories to an image page to help other editors find the page (for example, for a different language Wikipedia). These steps continue with the same image from the previous tutorial:

1. Right-click the "find categories" tab at the top of the image page.

    You arrive at a page labeled CommonSense, which is a search tool. It's preloaded with the image page name, and it's already done an initial search on that name. That initial search failed. So you'll want to enter some keywords, as shown in Figure 15-11.

2. With keywords entered, click the Find Categories button.

    The search results appear at the bottom of the page, with text ready to be copied and pasted into an image page to the right of the categories, at the bottom. (Figure 15-12.)

    After expanding categories as needed, and looking for the most applicable subcategories, you're ready to add categories. (For more on finding good categories, see page 328.)

3. Back at the image page (Figure 15-10), click the "edit" tab, scroll down to the bottom of the page, and copy or type the category or categories you've decided fit the photo.

    See Figure 15-13 for an example.

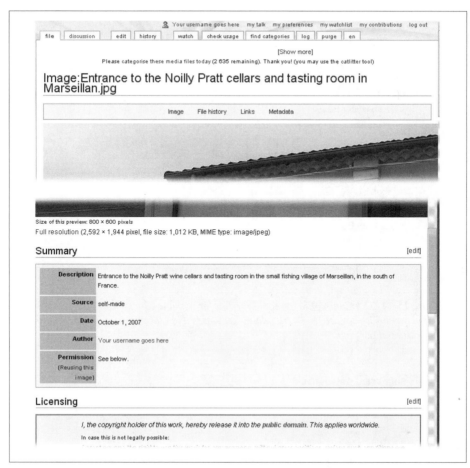

Figure 15-10. *After you click "Upload file," you'll go to the image page for the image you've just uploaded. This figure shows the top and bottom of the page; the image is in the middle. The information you entered in step 6 appears on this page.*

4. Once you've entered the category you want, add an edit summary, like *Adding categories*.

   At the Commons, the box for the edit summary is just labeled Summary.

5. Click the "Show preview" button.

   Go down to the very bottom of the screen to make sure all the category links are blue, not red (if any are red, you mistyped something).

6. When all looks well, click the "Save page" button to make your change take effect.

TIP

For more information, see the guideline *Wikipedia:Commons categories*.

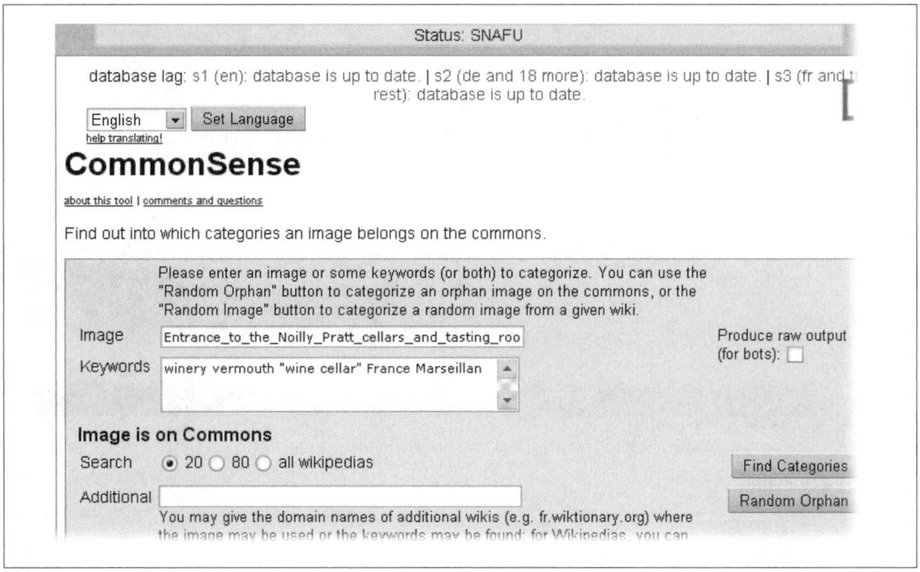

Figure 15-11. The CommonSense tool searches for possible categories. If the initial search fails to find any (as is the case here), try adding keywords and searching again. The results appear at the bottom of the page.

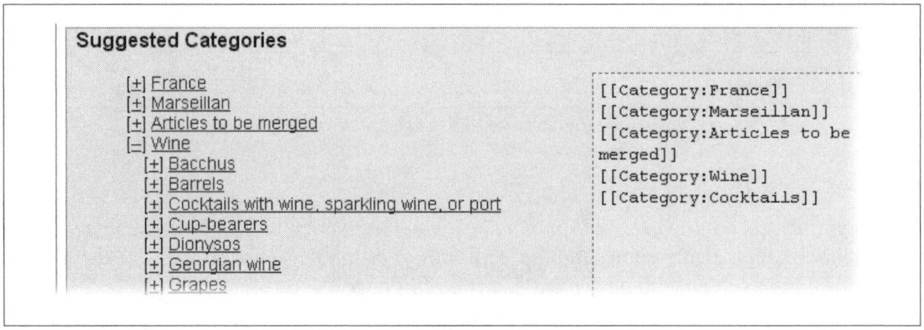

Figure 15-12. The search results, at the bottom of the CommonSense *page, consist of two parts. On the left are categories that can be expanded (for looking at subcategories) by clicking the "[+]" symbol. On the right is some text that's ready to be copied and pasted to the image page.*

Renaming, Replacing, or Moving an Image

You can't change the name of an image page. If you get it wrong—for example, you forgot the extension (like ".jpg"), or you used a non-descriptive name that already existed on Wikipedia (blocking you from using the image you uploaded to the Commons)—then you have to start over. Upload the same image to a page with a new name, and then retype or copy the image description information to the new image page.

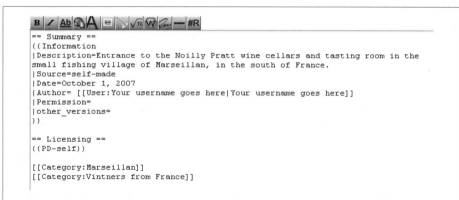

```
B / Ab ⊞A ⊟ √π W — #R
== Summary ==
{{Information
|Description=Entrance to the Noilly Pratt wine cellars and tasting room in the
small fishing village of Marseillan, in the south of France.
|Source=self-made
|Date=October 1, 2007
|Author= [[User:Your username goes here|Your username goes here]]
|Permission=
|other_versions=
}}

== Licensing ==
{{PD-self}}

[[Category:Marseillan]]
[[Category:Vintners from France]]
```

Figure 15-13. Two categories are being added to the wikitext for the image page: Entrance to the Noilly Pratt cellars *and* tasting room in Marseillan.jpg. *The edit toolbar—the row of icons you can click to add text—is different in the Commons. That's because the toolbar is customizable on a project-by-project basis. So, for example, the toolbar for the Spanish Wikipedia is different too.*

If you want to replace an image (you just found another photo of the same thing that's much better than the one you uploaded, for example), simply upload it with the same name as the original image. The system asks if you're sure you want to overwrite the old image; confirm that you do.

NOTE

The ability to upload a new image on top of an old one is restricted a bit: you have to wait until four days after creating an account at the Commons before you can do so.

There's no automatic way to move an image from Wikipedia to the Commons. The standard way is to download the image to your computer (often right-clicking the image gives you this option), and then upload it to the Commons. This procedure gives you a chance to give the image a better (longer, more descriptive) name. If you do change the name, remember to change all links to that image in Wikipedia articles to point to the new image at the Commons, not to the old image.

NOTE

For a full description of the process for this type of move, including a link to the "Move-to-commons assistant" tool, see the page *Wikipedia:Moving images to the Commons* (shortcut: *WP:MITC*).

Finding Images

If you want an image for an article and aren't in a position to take a photo to create that image, you have a number of options:

- Look through the more than two million images and other media files at Wikimedia Commons. Since the Commons is simply a repository for images for various Wikimedia Foundation projects, including Wikipedia, it's not surprising that its category system is displayed on its main page. Or you can search it using the Mayflower tool, at *http://tools.wikimedia.de/~tangotango/mayflower/*.

- Search the Web, including the Commons, Flickr, and other language Wikipedias, using the Free Image Search Tool (FIST), at *http://tools.wikimedia.de/~magnus/ fist.php*. This tool was specifically developed to look for free images for Wikipedia articles. It also lets you replace non-free and placeholder images.

- Review the lists of places that have free or public domain images, to see if one seems like a good candidate for what you're looking for. See the pages *Wikipedia:Free image resources* (shortcut: *WP:FIR*) and *Wikipedia:Public domain image resources* (shortcut: *WP:PDIR*).

- Place a request for an image in the article itself. For details, see the page *Wikipedia:Upload placeholder images* (shortcut *WP:UPPI*). This method adds a generic image of a male or female person to the article.

- You can post a request at the pages *Wikipedia:Requested photos* (shortcut: *WP:RP*) and *Wikipedia:Photo Matching Service* (shortcut: *WP:PMS*).

For even more information, see the page *Wikipedia:Finding images tutorial* (shortcut: *WP:FIT*).

Placing an Image in an Article

Once you've uploaded an image to the Commons, adding it to a Wikipedia article is very simple. You just go to the article, click "edit this page," decide where you want the image to be, and type a link to the image page. It'll look something like this: *[[Image:Nameofimage.ext|some other optional stuff]]*. (More on the "other optional stuff" in a moment.) Add an edit summary, do a quick preview, and save the page.

The software assumes that the image name you add to an article refers to one at the English Wikipedia, if one exists there. If the English Wikipedia doesn't have an image with that name, the software looks at the Commons. That's another good reason to name an image at the Commons in such detail that it's unlikely you'll accidentally choose one that already exists at the English Wikipedia. (No, the software won't warn you.)

Location

When there is more than one image in an article, spread the images evenly within that article. Each image should be relevant to the section it is in, and normally there should be only one image per section.

For accessibility and other reasons, you should put an image inside the section it belongs to, after any "Main" or "See also" template at the top of the section. The more general rule is to put an image immediately above the paragraph of text to which it most closely belongs. It's certainly okay to have text following the image, within the section where it's placed.

Multiple images within a single section, while not forbidden, can cause problems, particularly if the section is short. In particular, don't place an image on the left side of a section and a second image directly opposite, on the right side. For some readers, this squeezes text into a tiny column between the two images. On some computer screens the images may even overlap. (Even if you know how to use special parameters in the image links to force blank space between the images to avoid squeezing the text, don't do it. The blank text looks terrible on larger computer screens.)

Some editors prefer to put all images on the right side of an article, aligned with any info boxes. Other editors prefer them to be evenly alternated between left and right (for example, one image on the left in one section, and the next image, in a following section, on the right). Either approach is acceptable, but don't get into ownership issues over the arrangement of images—aesthetic judgments are inherently subjective, and not worth fighting about.

You control the alignment of images by typing instructions into the wikitext for the link. The next section tells all.

Size, Alignment, and Caption

Once you decide in what section you want an image to appear, and where within that section, you simply place a link to the image within the wikitext. At its simplest, this would be *[[Image:Nameofimage.ext]]*. But you almost never find such a simple image link in an article, because it plops the image, at full size, wherever the image link appears in the wikitext, even if that's in the middle of the screen. Nor, with this simple link, will text flow around the image. So don't create image links like this one, and if you see one, fix it.

The way that you control how an image appears is to specify various options. Here's a common specification: *[[Image:Nameofimage.ext | thumb | 200px | right | caption text]]*. Here's what the details of the options mean:

- **Thumb**. Displays the image as a small thumbnail. The image isn't shown full size (the reader can click the image to get to a full-size version). The image has a gray frame around it and a caption (if you specify one as described in the fourth bullet).

- **200px**. Determines the width of the thumbnail image in pixels. On a screen with 600 by 800 pixel resolution, 200px means that the photo takes up one-quarter of the width of the screen. If you don't specify a size, the default is 180 pixels. *Wikipedia:Extended image syntax* (shortcut *WP:EIS*) recommends *not* specifying a size, so that the reader's preferences determine whether the displayed size is 180 pixels or something larger or smaller.

- **Right, left**. The image appears all the way to the right (left) of the screen. Right is the default setting, so you don't have to type it if you don't want to.

- **Caption text**. The caption should provide useful information. In an article about New York City, for example, an image with the caption "New York City" isn't helpful, while something like "Panorama from the top of the Empire State Building" is much more useful. (You'll find great advice about writing captions at the guideline *Wikipedia:Captions*; the shortcut is *WP:CAP*.)

- Caption text always comes last in an image link. All the other options (thumb or no, size, align right or left) can be in any sequence. And the caption *must start with a capital letter*.

For more image syntax, see the pages *Help:Images and other uploaded files* (shortcut: *H:IOUF*) and *Wikipedia:Photo tutorial* (shortcut: *WP:PIC*).

Galleries

In some articles, a lot of images are useful—for example, the article *Great Wall of China*. But you don't want to put images into sections where they don't really belong just because that's the only place you can think of. Instead, you can put a *gallery* at the end of an article, with lots of images for the reader to see. That way, the images don't get in the way of the content of the article, but they're available to the reader.

The wikicode for creating a standard gallery is very simple; here's an example with three images (and made-up image filenames):

```
<gallery>
Image:Firstphoto.jpg
Image:Secondphoto.jpg | Caption for second image
Image:Thirdphoto.jpg
</gallery>
```

You can have captions on all images, of course, and aren't limited to JPEG images. The page *Wikipedia:Gallery tag* (shortcut: *WP:GALLERY*) has full details.

Questions or Problems with Images

Sometimes you want to mention an image on an article talk page, or at a discussion page such as the Village Pump. If you type *[[Image:imagename.jpg]]*, you insert the image itself onto that talk page, not a link to the image page, as you wanted. Displayed images don't belong on talk pages. To create a link to the image page instead, type a colon just after the first two square brackets, so the link looks like this: *[[:Image:imagename.jpg]]*. Then those interested in actually seeing the image can click the link.

TIP

Using a leading colon works also for links to category pages, when you want to point to them rather than actually add categories to a page.

If you find an image that you think has copyright problems, you should:

- Remove all links to the image from articles, making sure your edit summary mentions copyright issues. (You can find all uses of the image by going to the image page and clicking, in the left margin, "What links here.")

- Post a note at the user talk page of the editor who uploaded the image, mentioning your concerns. You may be able to resolve the issue at that point.

- If the editor who uploaded the image disagrees with your assessment, and you remain convinced there is a copyright problem, list the image at the page *Wikipedia:Copyright problems* (shortcut: *WP:CP*).

- If you get no response from the editor in a reasonable amount of time (say, a week), post the *{{ifd}}* template on the image page, save the change, and then follow the link "How to list a file for deletion" in order to list the file for deletion.

Uploading a Non-free Image

In March 2007, the Board of Trustees of the Wikimedia Foundation passed a policy (see *http://wikimediafoundation.org/wiki/Resolution:Licensing_policy*) banning future uploads of any media unless the media is licensed as free content. *Free content* is any work that doesn't require permission or payment for any use, including commercial. At most, free content requires attribution: crediting the person who created the image. Free content also has no restrictions on redistribution of the image by others.

The Foundation's resolution allows exceptions only as provided by a project-specific exemption policy. That policy for the English Wikipedia is *Wikipedia:Non-free content criteria* (shortcut: *WP:NFCC*). It sets out a list of 10 criteria for copyrighted images and other media files that lack a free content license (see Figure 15-14). You may use such media only where *all ten of the criteria are met*. Otherwise, as explained on page 272, the images you upload must be your own work, or in the public domain, or licensed as free content by its owner.

The Foundation's policy is especially strict about images of living people: An exemption policy must not allow non-free material when freely licensed pictures are readily available, as is almost always the case for celebrities, politicians, and other notable people.

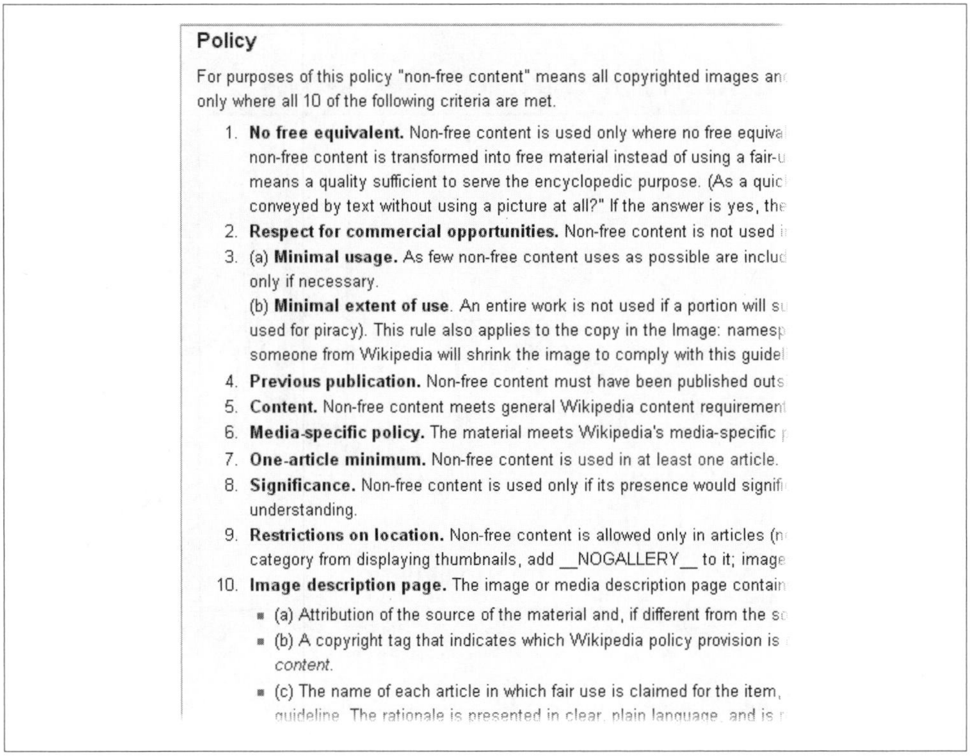

Policy

For purposes of this policy "non-free content" means all copyrighted images an
only where all 10 of the following criteria are met.

1. **No free equivalent.** Non-free content is used only where no free equiva non-free content is transformed into free material instead of using a fair-u means a quality sufficient to serve the encyclopedic purpose. (As a quic conveyed by text without using a picture at all?" If the answer is yes, the
2. **Respect for commercial opportunities.** Non-free content is not used i
3. (a) **Minimal usage.** As few non-free content uses as possible are incluc only if necessary.
   (b) **Minimal extent of use.** An entire work is not used if a portion will su used for piracy). This rule also applies to the copy in the Image: namesp someone from Wikipedia will shrink the image to comply with this guidel
4. **Previous publication.** Non-free content must have been published outs
5. **Content.** Non-free content meets general Wikipedia content requiremen
6. **Media-specific policy.** The material meets Wikipedia's media-specific p
7. **One-article minimum.** Non-free content is used in at least one article.
8. **Significance.** Non-free content is used only if its presence would signifi understanding.
9. **Restrictions on location.** Non-free content is allowed only in articles (n category from displaying thumbnails, add __NOGALLERY__ to it; image
10. **Image description page.** The image or media description page contain
    - (a) Attribution of the source of the material and, if different from the sc
    - (b) A copyright tag that indicates which Wikipedia policy provision is *content*.
    - (c) The name of each article in which fair use is claimed for the item, guideline. The rationale is presented in clear, plain language, and is r

Figure 15-14. Wikipedia doesn't like non-free content. It can be used only if it meets every one of the ten criteria in the policy Wikipedia:Non-free content criteria *(shortcut:* WP:NFCC*). Most of all, note number 8, which specifies that the non-free material must contribute significantly to understanding the article.*

Wikipedia takes copyright issues seriously. Almost every day, at least 1500 images are deleted (see Figure 15-15). Some are deleted because they're orphans—Wikipedia isn't a file-sharing service. Some are deleted because the image was uploaded to the Commons and now isn't needed at Wikipedia. Many, if not the majority, have copyright issues.

The graph shows that beginning in the second half of 2007 there has been essentially no net addition of images to Wikipedia. In other words, as many photos are being removed as added. That's certainly due to the Commons: Either images are being uploaded directly there, or images that were at Wikipedia are being uploaded to the Commons and then deleted at Wikipedia.

Implementation of the Wikipedia policy on non-free content criteria is discussed in the guideline *Wikipedia:Non-free content* (shortcut: *WP:NFC*). If you're thinking about uploading a "fair use" image (one you didn't create, isn't in the public domain, and hasn't been released as free content by the owner), read this guideline first.

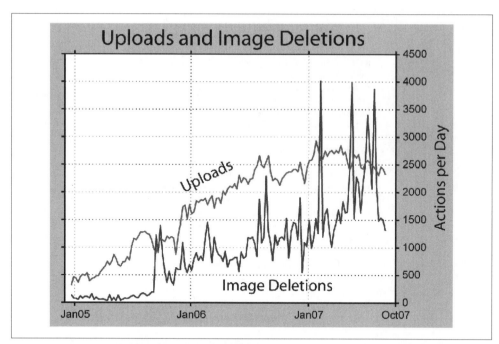

Figure 15-15. While image uploads have been relatively steady at around 2,500 per day throughout the last half of 2006 and well into 2007, deletions have been all over the place, ranging from 1,000 to 4,000 per day. The wide swings are probably due to occasional concentrated efforts to work off backlogs. [This graph is courtesy of editor Dragons Flight (Robert A. Rohde). It's based on a log analysis he did. Points on the graph are plotted weekly, not daily.]

NOTE

Screenshots and similar image captures aren't the same as original photos. They're fair use images, if the original content (being copied) isn't itself free content.

WORD TO THE WISE

Non-photo Images and Other Media

As mentioned at the beginning of this chapter, an image doesn't have to be a photo. It could be a map, an illustration, a graphic, or even an animated gif. The SVG format is preferred for drawings and line-art illustration. The PNG format is preferred for non-vector graphic iconic images, including screenshots. The GIF format is used for animations, but not for static images.

If you're interested in using these file types, here are some places at Wikipedia that you can get more information:

Maps:

- *Wikipedia:WikiProject Maps* (shortcut: *WP:WPMAP*)
- Two pages at Meta: *http://meta.wikimedia.org/wiki/Maps* and *http://meta.wikimedia.org/wiki/Wikimaps*

Graphics and illustrations:

- *Wikipedia:Graphics tutorials*
- *Wikipedia:Preparing images for upload* (shortcut: *WP:PIFU*)
- *Wikipedia:How to create graphs for Wikipedia articles*
- *Wikipedia:Graphic Lab*
- *Wikipedia:WikiProject Illustration*

You can also upload other types of media besides images: audio and video files. Because of licensing issues, the file formats acceptable for uploads are very limited:

- For sound: Ogg (using FLAC, Speex, or Vorbis codecs) or MIDI (with extension .mid). Ogg Vorbis is preferred.
- For video: Ogg (using Theora codec)

If audio or video files interest you, here are some places at Wikipedia where you can get further information:

- *Wikipedia:Media*
- *Wikipedia:Media help* (shortcut: *WP:MH*)
- *Wikipedia:Free sound resources* (shortcut: *WP:FSR*)

PART IV

Building a Stronger Encyclopedia

CHAPTER 16

Getting Readers to the Right Article: Naming, Redirects, and Disambiguation

With more than 2 million articles on the English Wikipedia, how do you get to the one you want? For example, when a reader types "mercury" into the search box, what article does she expect to be displayed? And if she wanted the article "mercury (element)" but put a comma instead of space between "mercury" and "(element)," would Wikipedia's search engine find it? What if someone creates an article called "Mercury (Roman god)" when there already is one called "Mercury (mythology)"?

Wikipedia depends on editors to fix naming errors, to create pages (*redirects*) that automatically correct typing errors, and to set out guideposts to readers to help them find their way (*disambiguation*). The cumulative effort of millions of editors has created web of articles and links that get virtually all readers to the right place within one click.

Naming and Renaming

The best way to deal with an error is to not make it in the first place. That's why Wikipedia has a naming convention for just about any kind of new article. The more you and other editors follow these conventions, the less renaming you'll have to do. But with so many naming conventions (see Figure 16-1 for a sampling), new editors can get confused and name articles incorrectly.

Common Naming Mistakes

This book can't discuss every possible mistake in article names—if it did, you'd need a forklift to carry it. If you have a very specific question about what to name an article for a geographical location in Ireland, for example—whether to use the official Irish name or a former English name—you'll probably find an answer at the policy page

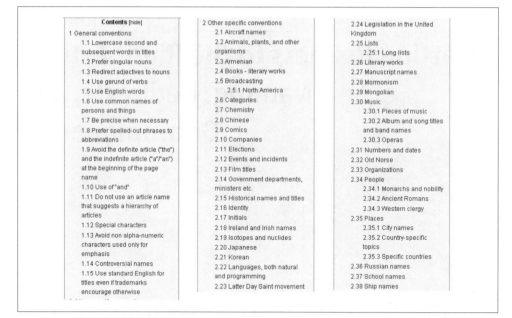

Figure 16-1. The table of contents of the policy Wikipedia:Naming conventions *(shortcut* WP:NAME*), only partly shown here, gives you a sense of how detailed the policy is, including the related pages such as* Wikipedia:Naming conventions (people) *(shortcut:* WP:NCP*). Fortunately, while new articles often get renamed, name changes thereafter are rarely needed.*

Wikipedia:Naming conventions (shortcut *WP:NC*), which links to dozens and dozens of *naming convention* pages. (You can find the whole list at *Category:Wikipedia naming conventions*, shortcut: *CAT:WNC*). You can avoid the vast majority of errors, however, by keeping the following points in mind:

- **Capitalize only the first word of article titles and section titles**. All other words in a title start with lowercase letters unless they're proper nouns and are capitalized anyway. If the title of the article is the title of a work like a book or a song, minor words like "in" are not capitalized, while the rest of the words in the title are; for example, "A Fool in Love."

- **Use the most common name**. Don't use a person's formal first name ("Christopher" rather than "Chris") or add a middle initial to a name if that's not the most common usage. If you're not sure, use a search engine and compare the counts of results for each option.

When several people in Wikipedia articles share the same common name, like George Allen, some editors try to differentiate between them by using a less common version of the name. For example, the article for the politician George Allen was once named "George Felix Allen," then "George F. Allen." The problem with these less common names is that they give you no clue, when you see them in an index or wikilink, as to who the person is. So avoid this approach. Check the disambiguation page (page 313), if there is one, and follow the established pattern there. In this example, George F. Allen became "George Allen (politician)."

NOTE

For foreign names and places, keep in mind that the "most common name" means the most common name in today's English language, not the most common name in the native language. In other language versions of Wikipedia, the article name may well be different. Article names in the English Wikipedia don't affect article names in the other 250-odd language versions of Wikipedia.

- **Organizational titles**. Don't start an article title with "The." It's "Council of Organizational Associations," not "The Council of Organizational Associations," and don't use an acronym (for example, "NATO") even if it's more common than the full name of an organization.

Renaming an Article

Renaming an article is technically easy. The trouble comes when you do something that other editors consider controversial. If you're fixing a clear error, and don't have any particular interest in the topic of an article, then go ahead and rename the article. (That is, do what Wikipedia calls a *page move*, as described on page 299.)

On the other hand, if you have any reason to think the rename (move) might be opposed, then don't make it until you've discussed it on the article talk page. Treat a potentially controversial page move just as you would a controversial rewrite of an article.

GEM IN THE ROUGH

Watching the Action

All page moves are recorded in a move log, which any editor can look at. You get to the log via the page *Special:Log*. Once there, change "All logs" to "Move log," and then click Go. What you'll see is a mix of error fixes and page moves made by administrators based on consensus. Article moves are typically done in pairs: both the article itself and the associated talk page (if one exists).

You also may see vandalism, where an editor deliberately renames a page for malicious purposes. Administrators tend to react sharply to this, since only user accounts that are at least four days old can do page moves; the remedy is usually an indefinite block on the user account.

Discussing a rename

To reach consensus about renaming a page, start a discussion on the article talk page. Focus the discussion on which naming policy and appropriate naming conventions

Move log

From Wikipedia, the free encyclopedia

Below is a list of all page moves. "Title" = old title.

Logs

Move log [v] User: [   ] Title: [   ] [Go]

View (previous 50) (next 50) (20 | 50 | 100 | 250 | 500)

- 22:00, 12 November 2007 GTBacchus (Talk | contribs) moved Los angles schools =D to Los Angeles Recording School *(rv nonsense page move)* (revert)
- 21:58, 12 November 2007 Moonriddengirl (Talk | contribs) moved Talk:UCE Birmingham Faculty of Health to Talk:Birmingham City University Faculty of Health *(Merging page histories)* (revert)
- 21:58, 12 November 2007 Moonriddengirl (Talk | contribs) moved UCE Birmingham Faculty of Health to Birmingham City University Faculty of Health *(Merging page histories)* (revert)
- 21:58, 12 November 2007 GTBacchus (Talk | contribs) moved Talk:A Rush And A Push And The Land Is Ours to Talk:A Rush and a Push and the Land Is Ours *(correcting capitalization per WP:MUSTARD; requested at WP:RM#Uncontroversial proposals)* (revert)
- 21:58, 12 November 2007 GTBacchus (Talk | contribs) moved A Rush And A Push And The Land Is Ours to A Rush and a Push and the Land Is Ours *(correcting capitalization per WP:MUSTARD; requested at WP:RM#Uncontroversial proposals)* (revert)
- 21:56, 12 November 2007 Pixelflash (Talk | contribs) moved Edgell communications to Edgell Communications *(all caps)* (revert)

Figure 16-2. The move log includes moves by administrators (in this case, GTBacchus and Moonriddengirl) and moves by regular editors (Pixelflash). The move shown at the very top is a revert of vandalism.

apply. Avoid arguing, for example, that you like a certain name better, or that you find a name insulting. Stick to citing or interpreting policy and naming conventions.

When debating the name of the page or discussing merging it with another page, always mention the current page name. Otherwise, references to "this page name" become ambiguous after the page is renamed.

If you and the other editors can't reach a rough consensus, or majority rule on the move, then you can move on to one of the methods for resolving content disputes (Chapter 10). In addition, you can list the proposed move at the page *Wikipedia:Requested moves* (shortcut: *WP:RM*). That page lets you request wider community input on your move debate. But if more than just a couple of editors are involved in the discussion and consensus can't be reached, it's probably time for you to move on to other, more productive matters than deleting an article title.

Renaming a page

If there's no controversy about a move, or if you've reached consensus with other interested editors, renaming a page is technically easy. The following steps rename the article *Samuel E. Wyly* to the common, and correct, "Sam Wyly."

To practice along with this tutorial, you need to be logged in (anonymous IP users can't rename pages), and you must have had an account for at least four days. Instead of the

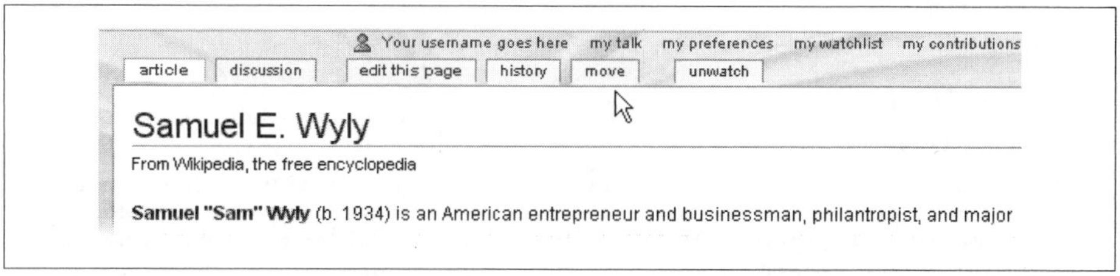

Figure 16-3. To move a page, begin by clicking on the "move" tab at the top of that page. If you don't see the tab, you're not logged in, or you haven't been a registered user for four days. Or, the page may be protected against being moved (typically because of prior vandalism or because of an edit war concerning the name of the page).

Sam Wyly article (or other real article), move a subpage in your user space. (To see how to create such a subpage, see page 56.)

NOTE

You can move pages in user space (normally, your own user subpages), projectspace (pages with a "Wikipedia:" prefix), and page in several other namespaces. But you can't change the name of an image; instead, you must upload the image to a new page, and then copy the image description from the old page to the new page (page 282). You also can't change the name of a category page (page 332).

---

1. Starting at the page you want to move (rename), click the "move" tab near the top of the page (see Figure 16-3).

   You arrive at the *Move page* page, shown in Figure 16-4. It contains a long list of instructions and warnings and, at bottom, a short form for typing the new article name and performing the move.

2. In the "To new title" box at the bottom of the *Move page* page, type a new name for the page. In the Reason box, explain why you're making the move.

   Figure 16-5 shows the form filled in with new name and reason.

NOTE

Leave the "Move associated talk page" box turned on. You want the talk page to be renamed as well, to remain paired with its article.

---

3. Click the "Move page" button.

4. You'll see a new page with "Move succeeded" in small print, at the top of the page (Figure 16-6). You're almost done.

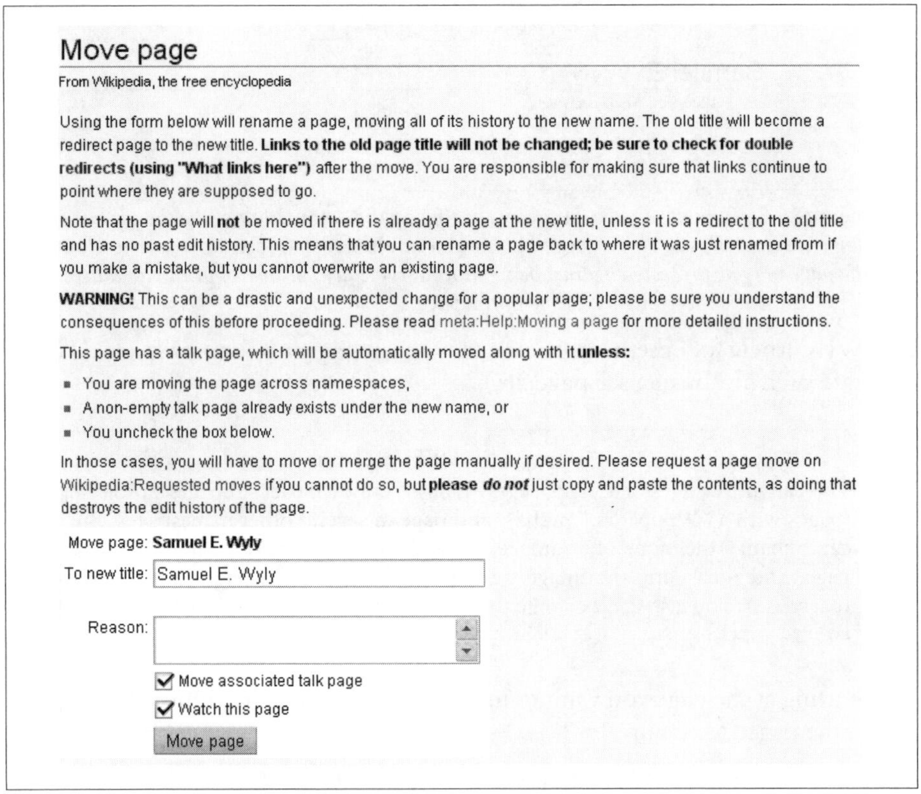

Move page

From Wikipedia, the free encyclopedia

Using the form below will rename a page, moving all of its history to the new name. The old title will become a redirect page to the new title. **Links to the old page title will not be changed; be sure to check for double redirects (using "What links here")** after the move. You are responsible for making sure that links continue to point where they are supposed to go.

Note that the page will **not** be moved if there is already a page at the new title, unless it is a redirect to the old title and has no past edit history. This means that you can rename a page back to where it was just renamed from if you make a mistake, but you cannot overwrite an existing page.

WARNING! This can be a drastic and unexpected change for a popular page; please be sure you understand the consequences of this before proceeding. Please read meta:Help:Moving a page for more detailed instructions.

This page has a talk page, which will be automatically moved along with it **unless:**

- You are moving the page across namespaces,
- A non-empty talk page already exists under the new name, or
- You uncheck the box below.

In those cases, you will have to move or merge the page manually if desired. Please request a page move on Wikipedia:Requested moves if you cannot do so, but **please *do not*** just copy and paste the contents, as doing that destroys the edit history of the page.

Move page: **Samuel E. Wyly**

To new title: Samuel E. Wyly

Reason:

☑ Move associated talk page
☑ Watch this page

Move page

Figure 16-4. Changing the name of an article isn't a trivial matter. If it's your first time, read all the text. You'll find it reinforces what you've learned in this chapter.

NOTE

If instead of the "Move succeeded" page, you see "Error: could not submit form" at the top of the page in small print and, in the middle of the page, rather prominent red wording that begins "The page could not be moved: a page of that name already exists, or the name you have chosen is not valid," then your page move didn't work. See "When administrator assistance is required" (page 303) for advice.

---

5. Click the bolded "check" link to check for double redirects.

   You'll see a page listing all the pages that link to the newly named page (see Figure 16-7). If you don't see any double redirects, as is the case here, you're done.

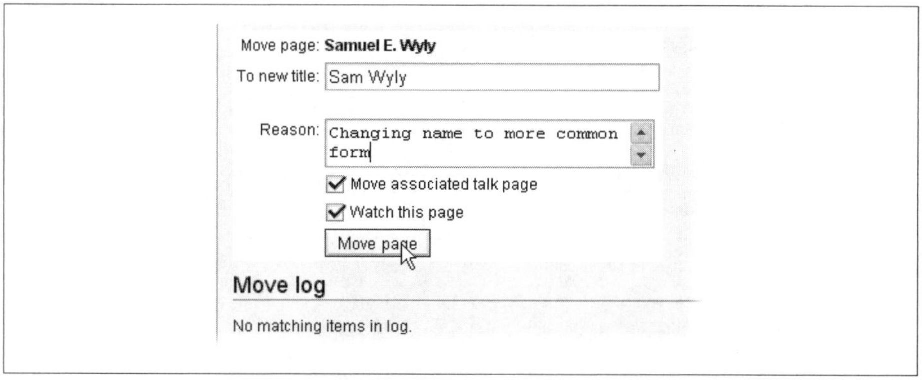

Figure 16-5. Before you click "Move page," double-check the name—is it absolutely correct? Also remember that the text in the Reason box is essentially the edit summary, and will show up in logs, the page history, and other places, so a good explanation is important.

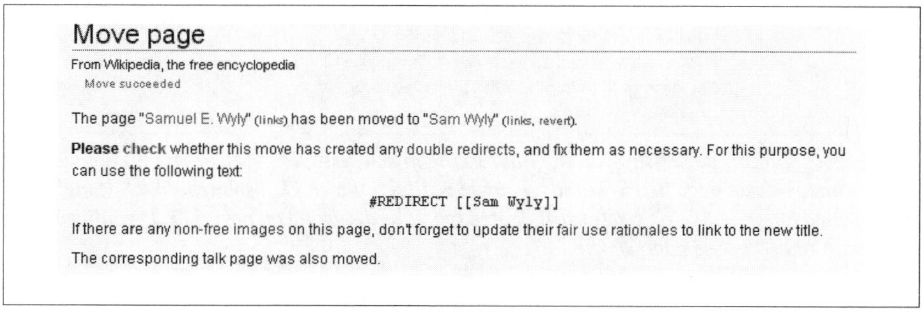

Figure 16-6. You've successfully moved the page. But there's still one more step—to check for double redirects. Double redirects often occur when a page has been moved (renamed) several times. If there are double redirects, you must fix them.

NOTE

Double redirects are when a link on page A goes to redirect page B, which goes to redirect page C, which points to page D. In that case, when you click the link on page A, the Wikipedia software will display the redirect page C; which isn't what the reader needs. The link on page A or the redirect on page B needs to be changed. You'll learn how to fix double redirects later in this chapter (page 310).

WORD TO THE WISE

The Wrong Way to Move a Page

Technically, it's possible to move an entire page by cutting all the text out of that page, and pasting it into a new page. But don't. When you cut and paste, you lose the entire edit history of the page, which is important to anyone editing or examining the article

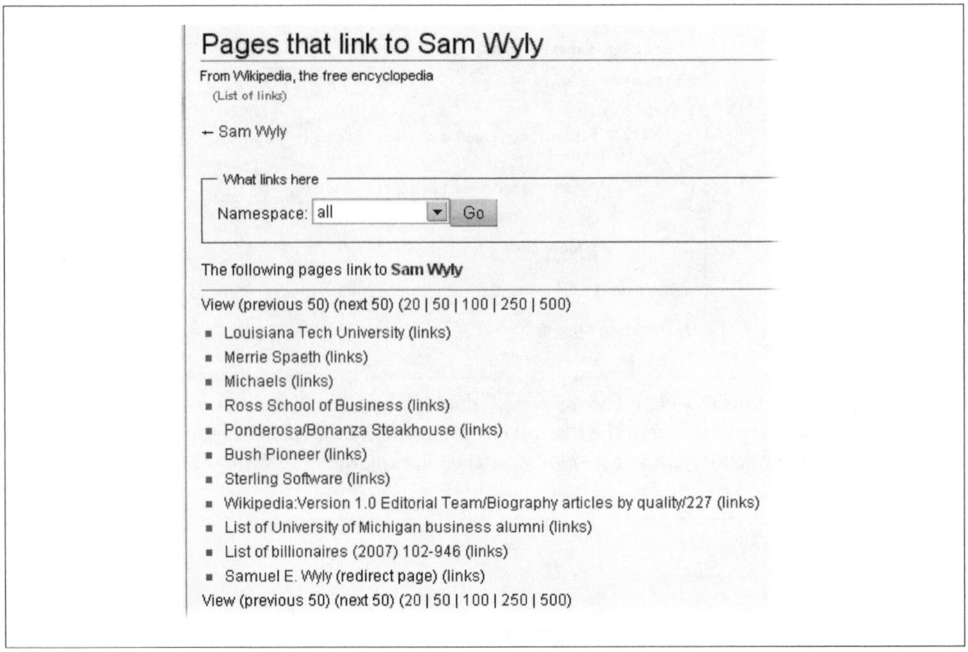

Pages that link to Sam Wyly

From Wikipedia, the free encyclopedia
(List of links)

← Sam Wyly

┌─ What links here ──────────────────────────────
│ Namespace: [all ▾] [Go]
└──

The following pages link to **Sam Wyly**:

View (previous 50) (next 50) (20 | 50 | 100 | 250 | 500)

- Louisiana Tech University (links)
- Merrie Spaeth (links)
- Michaels (links)
- Ross School of Business (links)
- Ponderosa/Bonanza Steakhouse (links)
- Bush Pioneer (links)
- Sterling Software (links)
- Wikipedia:Version 1.0 Editorial Team/Biography articles by quality/227 (links)
- List of University of Michigan business alumni (links)
- List of billionaires (2007) 102-946 (links)
- Samuel E. Wyly (redirect page) (links)

View (previous 50) (next 50) (20 | 50 | 100 | 250 | 500)

Figure 16-7. On this page listing all the links to the article Sam Wyly, *there are no double redirects. There's one redirect page listed—that's a single redirect, which is absolutely okay. (Single redirects are indented once; double redirects are indented twice, as discussed on page 311. If you're not familiar at all with redirects, see page 303.)*

and for legal reasons. Wikipedia's "move page" function preserves the history before and after the move, in one place. If you do make that mistake, you can fix it *if* no one's edited the page. To do so, change the new page to a redirect (so that it points to the original page), as discussed on page 310, and then revert (page 94) the original page to the version just prior to the move.

More likely, someone's already edited the new page at least once after the cut-and-paste. If so, you need an administrator to fix the problem by putting things where they really belong. The page *Wikipedia:How to fix cut-and-paste moves* (shortcut *WP:CPMV*) has the details, including where to request admin help.

If you're splitting an article into multiple topics, then of course you're going to have to cut and paste some of the text to a new article page. But leave the largest chunk of text in the original article, even if that article won't have the same name. When you rename it, all the page history is preserved.

For the other new articles that are being created, make sure that the initial creation (pasting text into a new page) includes an edit summary linking that new article to the original source of the text. Or, put an explanation on the talk pages of the new articles. What you don't want is for it to appear that you're the author of all the text in the new articles. If there are problems with that text, you want to make sure the original authors can be found and notified.

When administrator assistance is required

In general, if you want to rename page A to become page B, but page B already exists, you won't be able to do the renaming yourself. You must ask an administrator to make the move.

NOTE

One exception: You *can* rename page A to page B if page B is a redirect to page A, and page B has only one edit in its history. B might have only one edit if, for example, it was created as a redirect for a less-preferred name for topic A. Or B might have been the original name of the article, and someone moved it to A, creating a redirect at B. (The most common use of this exception is when you move an article and realize you've made a mistake.)

If you can't move a page, list the proposed move at *Wikipedia:Requested moves* (shortcut: *WP:RM*), where administrators and other editors will review it. Requests are generally processed after a five-day review period, although backlogs of a few days develop occasionally. If there's a clear consensus after this time, the request will be closed and acted upon. If not, an administrator may choose to relist the request to allow time for consensus to develop, or to close it as "no consensus," in which case the move isn't going to happen.

For Old Names and Bad Spellers: Redirects

When you or another editor moves a page, the old page name doesn't go away. Instead, it becomes a *redirect page* (or simply a *redirect*). That's good—other pages in Wikipedia are probably linked to the old name, and the redirect means the links on those other pages still work. They take the reader to the page in its new location.

You need to understand how redirects work for two reasons. First, sometimes a page move causes a *double redirect*, which you need to fix. Second, if you want, you can create redirects that will catch common spelling mistakes and get the reader to the right page.

NOTE

Note The editor who moves a page should fix any double redirects the move created (page 310), but sometimes you'll find some that still need to be fixed.

How Redirects Work (and Where They Come From)

To understand why redirects exist, and how they work, consider this generic situation: Article A has a direct wikilink to article B. Say you move article B, changing the title to C. When you do, Wikipedia places a notice to itself—a redirect—at page B, pointing to the new name of page C. A reader clicks the link on page A. The software goes to page B, which still exists, but is now a redirect. The software sees the redirect and takes the reader to page C, where the desired article is now located, and displays that.

Why didn't the Wikipedia software, when you renamed page B to page C, simply change the wikilink at page A, so it points directly to C? One reason—perhaps the most important—is that Wikipedia software never, ever changes a page. Only editors can change pages, and such changes are shown in a page history. Also, the link from A to B could exist in many, many older versions of article A (hundreds, even thousands of prior versions). If B no longer exists, the links on all the older versions of page A become broken. The software would have to change all those hundreds of older versions to point to C as well. Fixing those wikilinks could be a huge load on the Wikipedia hardware, from just a single page move.

Here's an example to illustrate how a redirect caused by a move works, using actual article names. Consider the move of the article about the venture capital firm *Kleiner, Perkins, Caufield & Byers* to a page with a new name: *Kleiner Perkins Caufield & Byers* (the change was the deletion of commas, which aren't in the firm's actual name). At the time of the move, the article *Sand Hill Road* had a link to the old, incorrect name. Figure 16-8 shows what happens when a reader clicks that link.

Adding a Redirect

Redirects are useful for more than when you move a page. You can create redirects when there's an alternative term for a subject, when there's alternative capitalization and/or hyphenation, and when there's an alternative spelling (for example, British versus U.S.).

You can also use redirects to help readers get to the right page when they misspell a word or phrase, or enter incomplete information. For example, if you've just created a new article about a person, and you know that it's common to misspell the name of that person (Arnold Schwarzenegger, for example), you can create a redirect so that when a reader searches for the misspelled name (Schwartznegger), a redirect sends the reader to the article.

If fact, if you attempt to go to an article via the search box, and get "No page with that title exists" because you've misspelled a word, others will probably make exactly the same mistake. If so, you have an opportunity to create a redirect, so you'll be the last person ever to see that search results page rather than the desired article.

Figure 16-8. Top: When an article is renamed, as was Kleiner, Perkins, Caufield & Byers, *links to that article (like the link in the article* Sand Hill Road*) do not change. They continue to point to the old name. Middle: When you click the old link in the* Sand Hill Road *article, the software goes to the article's old name, where it finds a redirect. Instead of displaying this redirect page, the software follows the redirect. Bottom: The redirect points to the new name of the article, so that's what you'll see. Renaming the article didn't break links to it. Instead, the rename just added one brief, intermediate stop at the redirect page. (The "Redirected from" in small print tells you that the original link is incorrect, though it's good enough to get you to where you wanted to go.)*

Creating a new redirect page

The following steps walk you through the process of creating a redirect. First, you need a common misspelling to redirect *from*. If you can't think of one off the top of your head, you can use, say, Microsoft Word's list of commonly misspelled words (see Figure 16-9).

1. Type a misspelled word into Wikipedia's search box, click Go (or press Enter), and see if you get a response of "No page with that title exists."

    If so, you've got your example.

2. Put the correct word into the search box to see where that goes, which is where your redirect page should send the reader when she types the incorrect spelling into the search box.

3. Suppose, for the sake of example, that you type "lisence" into the search box and see a page titled *Search* with bolded words "No page with that title exists" (Figure 16-10.).

4. Leaving open the window shown in Figure 16-10, open another browser window, and, in Wikipedia's search box, type the correct spelling of the word or phrase.

    Wikipedia takes you to the page with the article you wanted. It's "License" in this example, which is what you're going to redirect to. This step is important because

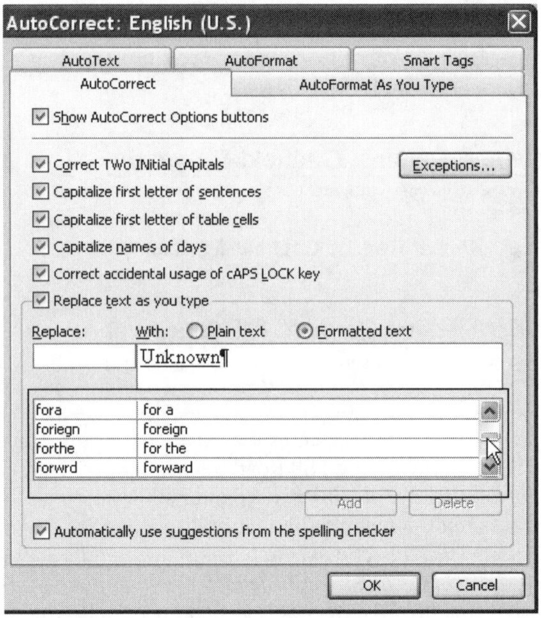

Figure 16-9. Microsoft Word can be a good source if you're looking for a commonly misspelled word for which to create a redirect. You'll find a list of word pairs in the AutoCorrect dialog box. In Word 2007 for Windows, choose Office button→Word options→Proofing. In earlier versions of Word, choose Tools→AutoCorrect.

you need to know the exact title of the page to redirect to (License, Licensing, or whatever).

NOTE

If the correct spelling of a word or phrase still doesn't get you to an article, and if the Wikipedia search results aren't helpful, you'll need to do some further searching to find the best article or disambiguation page (page 61) to send the reader to. When you do find it, create a redirect so others don't have to go through the same process.

---

5. Copy the correct name of the article (press Ctrl+C or ⌘-C). Close this second window when you've done this copying.

   If you copy the name, you don't have to worry about misspelling the article name when you create a redirect, which could be embarrassing.

6. Back at the original window, click the bolded red "create this page" link.

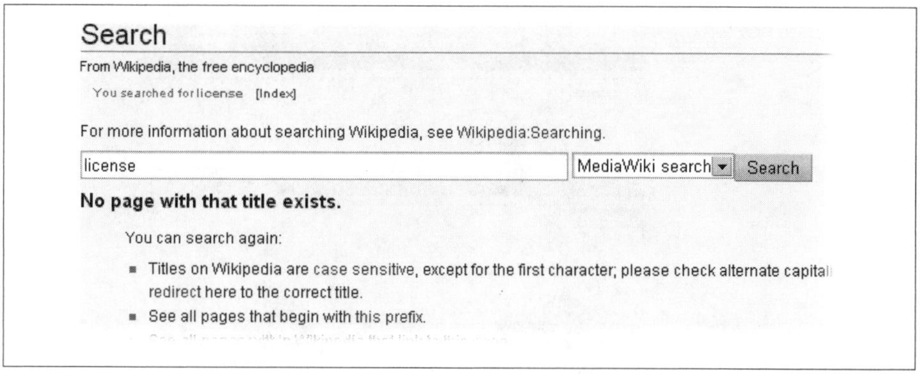

Search

From Wikipedia, the free encyclopedia

You searched for license   [Index]

For more information about searching Wikipedia, see Wikipedia:Searching.

| license | MediaWiki search ▾ | Search |

No page with that title exists.

You can search again:

- Titles on Wikipedia are case sensitive, except for the first character; please check alternate capital redirect here to the correct title.
- See all pages that begin with this prefix.

Figure 16-10. When you're doing a search for a word or a phrase and misspell it, consider that an opportunity to create a redirect for others who might do the same in the future. When you type the misspelling "lisence" instead of "license," you get a search page rather than the article you're looking for.

You'll see a new page, titled *Editing Lisense* (for example), with a bunch of advice about creating an article. Since you're creating a redirect, not an article, ignore the advice and scroll down to the edit box.

7. In the edit box, paste the text of the correct name, highlight this text, and click the "#R" icon.

    You see the text for the new redirect Figure 16-11. Your redirect is almost there.

8. Add an edit summary (*Creating redirect* works well), and do a quick preview.

    The preview shows what your new link will look like, plus the wikitext (Figure 16-12).

9. Click the "Save page" button.

    When you see a page with the misspelled title at the top and the correct link below (Figure 16-13), you're done!

10. For quality control purposes, click the link.

    If that takes you to the wrong page, or even to a different page via a redirect, you need to fix the redirect so it points directly to the page it should. In your browser, click the Back button to get back to the redirect page. Click the "edit this page" tab, and fix the text within the double square brackets (see #4 in Figure 16-11). Then add an edit summary, preview, and save again.

Redirects are handy for more than misspellings. For example, suppose you want to create a redirect for a relatively unknown product, called, say, ObscureProductX. Wikipedia doesn't have an article for ObscureProductX, since it's not notable enough. But the product is manufactured by ObscurbaCorp, about which Wikipedia *does* have an article. You can create a page *ObscureProductX*, and on that page put *#REDIRECT*

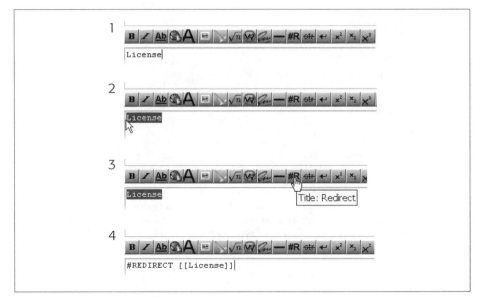

Figure 16-11. 1. In the edit box, copy and paste the correct name of the article you want to redirect to. Pasting the title, rather than typing it yourself, helps prevent typos. 2: Select the text you just pasted so you can apply the Redirect format to it. 3: Clicking the "#R" icon on the edit bar adds the redirect formatting. 4: Voila—the text for the redirect is done. All you have to do is save your work.

[[ObscurbaCorp]]. Someone searching for information about that product will be redirected to the article where it's mentioned.

Enhanced redirects

You can create redirects that take the reader to a section of an article rather than to the top of the page. Continuing the previous example, suppose there's a section of the fictional *ObscurbaCorp* article called "Unusual health products," and that's the only section that mentions ObscureProductX. In this case, create the redirect wikitext like this: *#REDIRECT [[ObscurbaCorp#Unusual health products]]*. The "#" sign tells the Wikipedia software that what follows is the name of the section ("Unusual health products").

NOTE

If you spell the name of the section incorrectly, or another editor subsequently changes the name of the section (or even deletes that section heading), the redirect will continue to function. It will simply take the reader to the top of the ObscurbaCorp article, just as if there were no pointer to a section.

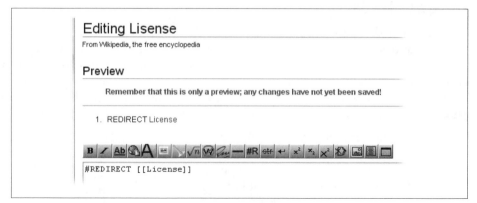

Figure 16-12. *The preview screen for a new redirect, before you save it, shows what the redirect link will look like. Make sure the link is blue; if it's red, your redirect is to a non-existent page, which is what you don't want. Oddly enough, a preview of a redirect doesn't look the same as a saved redirect. Compare this figure to Figure 17-13.*

Figure 16-13. *When you've saved your new redirect, you'll see a page with the misspelled title and a link to the correct page.*

Redirecting to a section, which sends the reader to the middle of an article, has one disadvantage. For example, if the "Unusual health products" section mentions ObscureProductX just briefly near the bottom of a long section, the reader could get confused about why he was sent there. Redirecting to the top of the article, from which a search will find the product, might be better. By contrast, if the redirect in the example had been to a section called "ObscureProductX's evaporation problem," there'd be no confusion.

You can also add a template to a redirect that puts the redirect into a category (page 325)—for example, redirects that deal with misspellings. The guideline *Wikipedia:Redirect* (shortcut: *WP:R*) lists a number of these, although most are likely to be useful only if Wikipedia begins using redirects as a database. You should use *{{R with possibilities}}* for redirects involving topics that might justifiably become an article at some later time. Adding that template puts the redirect page into the "Redirects with possibilities" category, which editors can use to find ideas for new articles. Simply put the template on a redirect page immediately after the ending double square brackets.

Fixing a Bad Redirect

Redirects often don't go bad, so it's rare that you have to change one (except for double redirects, as described in the next section). But sometimes, perhaps due to vandalism, when you click a link on page A, get redirected via page B, and end up on page C, it's clear that page B points to the wrong place. To fix it, you could change the link on page A to point directly to where you want it to go, but if there are other links that go via redirect B, those links are still going to be wrong. Redirect page B needs to be fixed.

The challenge here is that if you type "B" into the search box, the Wikipedia software takes you to page C (that's what redirects do). To edit page B, not C, look for small print near the top of the page that says "Redirected from," followed by a link (see Figure 16-8 for an example). Click that link to go to the redirect page (B) itself.

Once you're at the redirect page, fixing it is straightforward: Click the "edit this page" tab, change the text within the double square brackets (see #4 in Figure 16-11), add an edit summary, preview it (Figure 16-12), and save the change.

Fixing Double Redirects

In the steps starting on page 75, renaming the *Samuel E. Wyly* article didn't cause any problems with *double redirects*. As mentioned there, double redirects are when a link on page A goes to redirect page B, which goes to redirect page C, which points to page D. In such a case, when a reader clicks the link on page A, the Wikipedia software displays the redirect page C, which isn't what the reader needs. The link on page A or the redirect on page B needs to be changed.

Understanding double redirects

Before discussing how to fix a double redirect, consider why the software won't take the reader to page D, even though that's clearly the right place. Or, to be precise, why the software doesn't let two redirects function sequentially. Suppose an editor set up redirect page C so that it pointed *back* to redirect page B? The software would go in circles, processing the same instructions over and over, until a human intervenes or a mechanical failure occurs. (In computer speak, that's called an *infinite loop*.)

Sometimes you stumble upon double redirects, but the best time to find and fix them is when a page move creates them. Using the renaming of *Kleiner Perkins Caufield & Byers* (page 304) as an example again, suppose you had just done that page move and you're at the last step—checking for redirects. When you look at the "Pages that link to" page, in addition to the non-indented links (which point directly to the article as it's currently named) and single-indented links (which are linked by one redirect), you see some double indents. The double indents represent double redirects, like *Brook Byers* in Figure 16-14.

The clue to a double redirect is to look for the black text "(redirect page)" mixed in with the blue links (page names). The first "(redirect page)" you find is okay (that's a

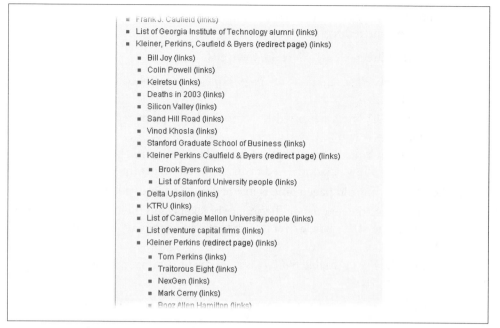

Figure 16-14. The page Pages that link to Kleiner Perkins Caufield & Byers *includes, because of a recent renaming, a number of double redirects. These are the double-indented links, like Brook Byers and List of Stanford University people. Clicking a link in one of those two pages takes you to the redirect page* Kleiner, Perkins, Caufield & Byers *instead of the correct article. (Note the commas in the title; this redirect page has the old title from before the rename.)*

single redirect), but should you find a second redirect page that is *indented under the first*, then you've found a *double redirect that needs to be fixed*.

Fixing double redirects

A number of the links in Figure 16-14 won't work because of double redirects. You have two choices: Fix the links within articles, so they bypass redirects altogether, going directly to the new page name; or, change a redirect. In other words, if article A links to redirect B, which points to redirect C, which points to article D, then you can fix the redirect by changing redirect B so that it points directly to article D. B is now a single redirect, which is okay. Here's how to decide which to do:

- Most of the time, fixing a redirect is better than changing the links to the redirect. In Figure 16-14, notice the large number of links to the redirect *Kleiner Perkins*. Fixing one redirect is faster than fixing a whole bunch of links.

- When there's a spelling mistake or something else where the reader is being mis-informed, it's best to fix *both* the links and the redirect. In the redirect *Kleiner Perkins Caulfield & Byers*, the word "Caulfield" is wrong (it should be "Caufield").

Since there are only two links to this redirect, that's an easy decision—fix the two links plus the one redirect.

Fixing a double redirect is easy. Here are the steps:

1. At the top of the "Pages that link to" page, copy (to the clipboard) the current name of the article.

   Use Ctrl+C, ⌘-C, or whatever works best for you. Copying reduces the likelihood of a typing error.

2. Find a double redirect (for example, *Tom Perkins* in Figure 16-14), and open it in a new tab or window. Click the "edit this page" tab to get into editing mode.

   In the edit box, the old page name is inside double square brackets.

3. Select (highlight) the text inside the square brackets, and then paste (Ctrl+V or ⌘-V) the new name of the article over it. Tab to the edit summary box and type a brief explanation.

   Something like *Fixing double redirect* is a good edit summary. When you're done, click "Show preview."

   NOTE

   If this is starting to sound familiar, that's because the steps are similar to when you're creating a redirect, as shown in Figure 16-11 and Figure 16-12.

   ---

4. Click "Save page."

   You've fixed a double redirect. Close the page or tab you opened (step 2), which brings you back to the "Pages that link to" page, and do the same for all other double redirects.

Once you've fixed all the redirects that didn't point directly to the new name of the article, you can turn to any pages that have a link with a misspelling or other misinformation. Although these links now work, since the double redirects are gone, you may still need to correct other errors.

At the very end, check your work. Refresh the "Pages that link to" page (press Ctrl+R or ⌘-R) to make sure that everything you wanted to fix was fixed.

NOTE

A page that is a redirect can be moved like any other page. *Don't*. You'll break links.

GEM IN THE ROUGH

Bots on Cleanup Patrol

If you or another editor forgets to clean up some double redirects caused when you move a page, a *bot*—a small, automated software program—may fix the double redirects before any human notices. Every three days or so, the Wikipedia software coughs up a list of existing double redirects at the page *Special:DoubleRedirects*. Then one or more bots goes around and fixes them.

So, you don't need to *search* for double redirects, since Wikipedia's software will find them. But if you do encounter one, fix it using the steps on page 311, because it may be days before a bot gets to it. If you've hit the double redirect, others might too.

For Multiple Meanings: Disambiguation

Disambiguation is a fancy word for how Wikipedia handles a single term that's associated with more than one topic. If you type a word or name that pertains to more than one article—Jerry Lewis, for example—disambiguation helps you find the article you're looking for.

You see disambiguation in two places:

- **Disambiguation pages**. These are separate pages where you can pick a link to go to the article you want. Such pages normally begin something like "*Mercury* can refer to the following," followed by a list of several article links to choose from.

- **Disambiguation links**. These are notes at the top of an article that say things like "For other uses of the word *mercury*, go to *mercury (element)*." In this case, the link may go directly to another article, or, if there are several alternative articles, to a disambiguation page—as in *mercury (disambiguation)*.

Figure 16-15 shows both types of disambiguation.

Creating and updating disambiguation pages and disambiguation links at the top of articles are important skills for an editor. This section also shows you how to find and fix links in the body of articles that incorrectly go to a disambiguation page instead of directly to a specific article.

Disambiguation in Wikipedia involves fairly specialized knowledge, so this section starts out by introducing disambiguation concepts and helpful tools for getting readers to the right page. Then, when you end up at a page that isn't where you thought it was going to be, you'll be able to fix the problem.

Disambiguation Pages

Disambiguation pages, as shown at the bottom of Figure 16-15, are easy to use, but creating them involves a bit of complexity. Naming such pages effectively is crucial. It's also important to get the formatting right. A good disambiguation page has enough details so readers can find the article they're looking for, but not so much text that they get muddled.

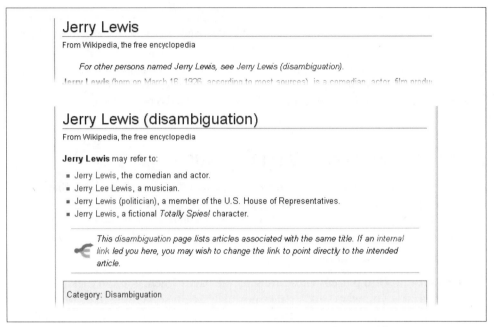

Figure 16-15. Top: If you type Jerry Lewis *in the search box and click Go, you arrive at this article. If you had another Jerry Lewis in mind, simply click the Jerry Lewis (disambiguation) link near the top of the page. Bottom: The Jerry Lewis (disambiguation) page lists four articles that editors think readers might want when they search for the name Jerry Lewis.*

Naming disambiguation pages

Wikipedia has tens of thousands of disambiguation pages, which fit into two groups —those that have *(disambiguation)* as part of their name, and those that don't. Going back to the Jerry Lewis example, since the comedian Jerry Lewis is more well known than, say, a politician named Jerry Lewis, when you type *Jerry Lewis* into the search box, you arrive at the article about the comedian, titled *Jerry Lewis*. The other (not quite as famous) person has an article titled *Jerry Lewis (politician)*.

Now suppose the two Jerrys are equally well known. The previous arrangement wouldn't be fair. Or suppose there are several other famous Jerry Lewises as well. In such cases, the page titled *Jerry Lewis* should be a disambiguation page, listing individual articles called *Jerry Lewis (politician)*, *Jerry Lewis (comedian)*, and so on, exactly as shown in Figure 16-15. Figure 16-16 shows another example.

With disambiguation, Wikipedia aims for the *principle of least astonishment*—that is, to avoid surprising readers. So if there's a predominant article that most readers will expect—like an article about the comedian Jerry Lewis—searches for *Jerry Lewis* go directly to that article. That article has a disambiguation link going to a disambiguation page: *Jerry Lewis (disambiguation)*. If there's no overwhelmingly popular answer, as is the case for Donald Davidson, then searches for *Donald Davidson* go to a disambiguation page of the same name.

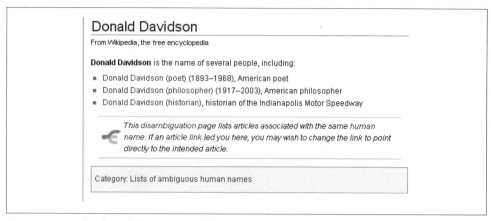

Figure 16-16. This disambiguation page doesn't have the parenthetical (disambiguation) in the title. None of the three Donald Davidsons are famous enough to be the overwhelming choice of someone searching for that name, so readers are sent to the disambiguation page to sort out the matter. Since the disambiguation page now owns the name, the three articles on individuals need to be named something else, such as Donald Davidson (poet).

If you create a disambiguation page without the parenthetical phrase *(disambiguation)* in the title, you should list the page at *Wikipedia:Links to disambiguating pages* (shortcut: *WP:LDP*), so that it doesn't get listed as an orphan page (no incoming links), and so the Wikipedia software can identify it as a problem should there be lots of incoming links.

TIP

If you're a big fan of something that's the subject of an article, say, a band called Upper Crust, don't let your enthusiasm get in the way of your neutrality. If other editors have made *Upper Crust* a disambiguation page, accept the consensus and don't change things. Instead, focus your energy on, say, making the article *Upper Crust (band)* so good that it becomes a featured article on the Main Page, without fighting about the article's title.

Proper formatting and entries

Once a disambiguation page has a title, it needs two more elements—an introductory sentence and the entries. The guideline *Wikipedia:Manual of Style (disambiguation pages)* (shortcut: *MOS:DAB*) goes into great detail about how to format these elements.

NOTE

The prefix for the shortcut for that guideline was "MOS," not "WP." And yes, shortcuts with prefixes like MOS do function correctly when you type them in the search box.

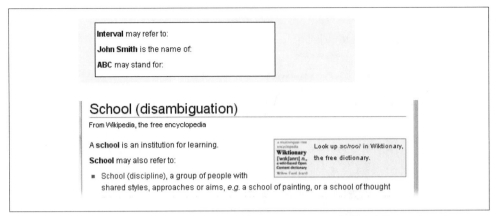

Figure 16-17. Top: Here are the sample opening sentences you might find in different disambiguation pages, using the three standard phrases prescribed at Wikipedia:Manual of Style (disambiguation pages) (shortcut: MOS:DAB). Bottom: If the disambiguation page has (disambiguation) in the title, it starts by defining the primary term first. The link school goes to the most popular article for that term.

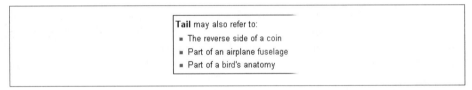

Figure 16-18. The guideline MOS:DAB includes three examples of acceptable piped links that aren't the first words in an entry.

Disambiguation pages get one of three standard opening sentences. After the name of the topics comes "may refer to:," "is the name of:," or "may stand for:," as shown in Figure 16-17 (top). The exception to these three is for pages with *(disambiguation)* in the title, where there's a clear primary meaning. In such cases, a sentence defining that primary meaning, with a link to the article, is recommended.

After the brief opening sentence or sentences, the bulleted entries immediately follow. Make sure entries are in order of usage, with most-used meanings at the top. Here are some more tips:

- **The first word or phrase in each entry normally has one navigable (blue) link**. These links shouldn't be piped; they should show exactly the name of the page that readers will go to when they click.

  One exception is when an entry is only one section in an article. In that case, you can link to that section with a piped link, and the link doesn't have to be at the beginning of the entry (see Figure 16-18.)

- **Keep descriptions in entries minimal**. In general, don't exceed a single line onscreen. For example, for people, include their birth and death years (when

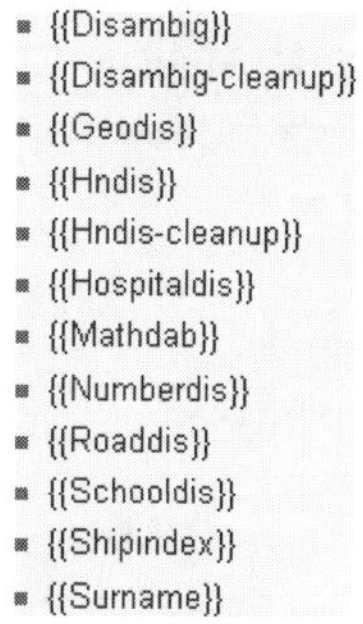

- {{Disambig}}
- {{Disambig-cleanup}}
- {{Geodis}}
- {{Hndis}}
- {{Hndis-cleanup}}
- {{Hospitaldis}}
- {{Mathdab}}
- {{Numberdis}}
- {{Roaddis}}
- {{Schooldis}}
- {{Shipindex}}
- {{Surname}}

Figure 16-19. Every disambiguation page needs one—and only one—of these templates at the bottom (that is, at the very end of the page's wikitext). You'll find the full list at the page Category:Disambiguation and redirection templates *(shortcut:* CAT:DRT*).*

known), plus brief descriptive information to help the reader distinguish between different entries.

- **Don't bold or italicize entries**. If part of an entry should be italicized (for example, the name of a song), then use a piped link—for example, *[[Flower (Liz Phair song)]|"Flower" (Liz Phair song)]]*.

As for what entries should and shouldn't be included, keep in mind the following:

- A disambiguation page isn't a list of all entries that include a given word or phrase, but rather a place for readers who can reasonably be expected to arrive at that page.
- If there is a reasonable chance of reader confusion due to misspelling ("Kington" versus "Kingston"), put the misspellings in a separate "See also" section.
- You should add links to a non-existent article ("redlink") only when you're confident that an encyclopedia article can be written on the subject. (Every entry should have a link, either blue or red; a disambiguation page isn't a directory to the Internet.)

Long disambiguation pages can be broken into sections ("In science," "In music," "In popular culture"). If there are four or more sections, put the template *{{TOCright}}* at the top of the page (see page 249 for details) to float the table of contents to the upper-right corner of the page.

Finally, at the bottom of a page, there must be a disambiguation template telling readers what the page is and reminding them to fix improper links. It also puts the page into a proper category. Figure 16-19 lists the choices for such a template. For example, *{{Geodis}}* is for locations (towns, rivers, and so on) and *{{Hndis}}* for human names. If more than one specialized template would apply to the page, use the general template *{{disambig}}*.

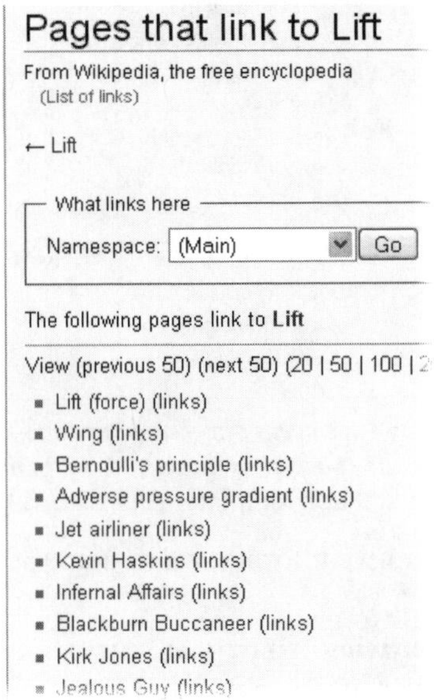

Pages that link to Lift

From Wikipedia, the free encyclopedia
(List of links)

← Lift

┌─ What links here ─────────────────────┐
│ Namespace: (Main)   ▼   Go   │
└───────────────────────────────────────┘

The following pages link to **Lift**

View (previous 50) (next 50) (20 | 50 | 100 | 2

- Lift (force) (links)
- Wing (links)
- Bernoulli's principle (links)
- Adverse pressure gradient (links)
- Jet airliner (links)
- Kevin Haskins (links)
- Infernal Affairs (links)
- Blackburn Buccaneer (links)
- Kirk Jones (links)
- Jealous Guy (links)

Figure 16-20. Links to disambiguation pages come in two flavors—links at the top of pages (as discussed in the next section), which are okay, and links in the body of articles, which are not okay. The pages listed in this figure are all of the second type: The wikilinks of the word "lift" in articles like Jet airliner *and* Kevin Haskins *shouldn't link to a disambiguation page, they should link to a page like "Elevator" or "Lift (force)." These wikilinks need to be changed.*

Fixing incoming links to disambiguation pages

With the exception of clarifying links at the top of articles (page 319), articles should never have a link to a disambiguation page. But editors do make mistakes. For example, a British editor might wikilink the word "lift," unaware that the page *Lift* is a disambiguation page. (The editor should have used the piped wikilink *[[elevator|lift]]*, which would display "lift" to the reader while taking the reader, if she clicks that link, to the article *Elevator*.)

Finding and fixing wikilinks that link to disambiguation pages is easy: At a disambiguation page, in the "toolbox" links at the left side of the screen, click the first one, "What links here." Change the Namespace box to "(Main)," and click Go. You'll see a list of pages with links to the word "lift," as shown in Figure 16-19.

For each article that links to the disambiguation page but shouldn't, go to the article and edit the link so it's correct. For example, in the *Jet airliner* article, you would change *wing [[lift]] performance* to *wing [[lift (force)|lift]] performance*, since the word "lift" should link to the article *Lift (force)*.

These erroneous links accumulate over time, since editors rarely verify wikilinks when editing an article, and readers taken to disambiguation pages rarely see the note on the bottom of such pages about fixing incoming links. So, not surprisingly, there's a

WikiProject (Chapter 9) for those interested in fixing disambiguation links: *Wikipedia:WikiProject Disambiguation*. But you don't have to be a member of that WikiProject to fix problems.

GEM IN THE VERY ROUGH

Programs that Help Fix Links

If you only occasionally fix incoming wikilinks to disambiguation pages, doing it manually is fine. But if you find you enjoy doing these fixes and want to do more of them (and there are a lot of links that need to be fixed), you have a choice of two programs that you can download that create a semi-automated, specialized browser for fixing links to disambiguation pages. Both have limitations:

- *CorHomo*, at the page *Wikipedia:WikiProject Disambiguation/fixer*, as of mid-2007 works only on Linux (version 1.3.3) The Windows version (1.3.2) has not been fixed as of this writing. The user interface is a bit terse, but it takes only four clicks to select and fix a link, once you specify a disambiguation page.

- *Windows Cleaner*, at the page *User:NicoV/Wikipedia Cleaner/Documentation*, is a bit less automated, but still is much faster than fixing links manually. It requires Java (version 6 is recommended).

Both programs were developed at the French Wikipedia. Language choice is built into both, but the English wording can be a bit idiosyncratic.

Disambiguation Links

When a term is ambiguous, like, say, Ally McBeal, readers may not reach the article page they expected (the TV show instead of the character herself). In such cases, the article should contain, at the top, one or more links to alternative articles. You create these links using a disambiguation template, not formatting them by hand. Figure 16-21 shows the simplest example, the *{{for}}* template, in action:

There are a large number of disambiguation templates. The notes at the top of pages created by these templates are often called *hatnotes*. You can find a fairly complete list of these templates at the guideline *Wikipedia:Hatnote* (shortcut: *WP:HAT*). You only need to know the basic concepts, not memorize the list. (A more organized list is found at *Wikipedia:Otheruses templates (example usage)*, shortcut: *WP:OTEU*.)

Hatnotes come in a long form ("This article is about the concept X; for the concept Y, see [[link]]") and a short form ("For the concept Y, see [[link]]"). Don't argue with other editors about which to use—it's not worth the trouble. But if you're adding a hatnote yourself, generally use the short form. Figure 16-22 shows an extreme example of how awkward the long form of a hatnote can be.

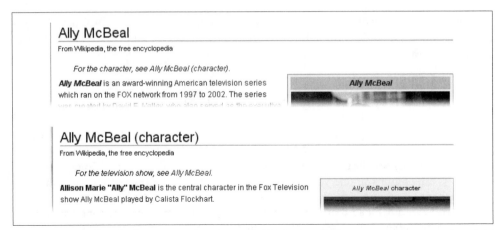

Figure 16-21. *Wikipedia has two articles about Ally McBeal, and it's easy to see that a reader might want one rather than the other (or even both). When there are exactly two articles that can be confused with each other, no disambiguation page is needed—just a link at the top of each page to the other page. These two pages use the {{for}} template for disambiguation. To be specific, in the second article, the wikitext looks like this: {{For|the television show|Ally McBeal}}.*

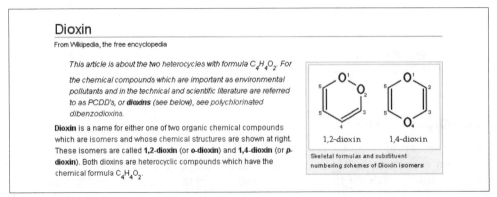

Figure 16-22. *If a reader searches for dioxin, she arrives at this article. The too-long hatnote on this page probably befuddles many readers looking for the Wikipedia article* Polychlorinated dibenzodioxins, *which is about the environmental pollutants known as dioxins. The reader has to get past 37 words, including one wikilink, before finding the desired link.*

NOTE

You get bonus points if you wondered why the article about the more widely known "dioxins" of environmental concern is called *Polychlorinated dibenzodioxins* rather than *Dioxins*. The technical name for the article appears to violate the principle of least surprise. Perhaps consensus will have developed to change the title by the time you read this.

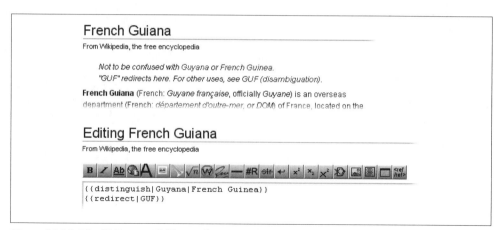

Figure 16-23. The {{distinguish}} template creates text that begins "Not to be confused with." Here, the template has two parameters, "Guyana" and "French Guinea," which become links within the note at the top of the article (top). Also shown here (bottom) is the template {{redirect}}, which explains to a reader who typed "GUF" into the search box why they are looking at this particular article, and not another article, and the page to go to if not where desired.

As a rule, add disambiguation links only when there's a good chance that a confused reader has arrived at the wrong article. Thus, for an article like *Tree (set theory)*, a hatnote pointing to the page *Tree (disambiguation)* isn't needed, because someone reading up on set theory isn't expecting to read about greenery. Don't use disambiguation template links that have nothing to do with disambiguation. So, for example, in the article *Merck & Co.*, it's incorrect to put a note at the top of the article saying "For the controversy over the drug Vioxx, which was manufactured by Merck, see *Rofecoxib*."

In an article's wikitext, disambiguation templates go below cleanup templates (also called *article messages boxes*, *amboxes*, and *message templates*) and should, in turn, be followed by images, navigational and infobox templates, and other article content.

For articles that can be confused with each other but aren't actually related, use the *{{distinguish}}* template. Figure 16-23 shows an example, and the underlying wikicode.

CHAPTER 17

Categorizing Articles

When you look at the bottom of a Wikipedia article, you see category links. For example, the article *Coat of arms of Copenhagen* has two category links: "Copenhagen" and "Danish coats of arms." Category links are a big help for readers looking for articles related to a topic. Those links are there because editors like you added them. Wikipedia's software doesn't do automatic categorization, and Wikipedia employs no professional categorizers.

Adding categories to articles is easy: Just type a few words, add brackets, and save. The trick is figuring out what category links would provide maximum usefulness to readers, and that's what this chapter shows you. It also explains the other half of the categorization picture—the category pages where category links are listed. You can create and improve upon those pages, too.

Fundamentals of Categorization

When you click one of the category links at the bottom of articles and other Wikipedia pages, you go to a category page. For example, in the article *Zolan Acs*, if you click *Category:Economists*, you go the page shown in Figure 17-1.

Categories aren't limited to articles. Portal pages, Wikipedia instructional pages, some user pages, for example, also have categories. Even category pages themselves have categories; in fact, that's a critical part of how the category system works at Wikipedia. (More on that a bit later.)

Category pages are the payoff for category links at the bottom of articles—they help readers find other articles about the same topic as the one they were reading. Without category pages, there'd be little point in adding category links to articles. Without category links in articles, category pages wouldn't have any content other than some introductory text.

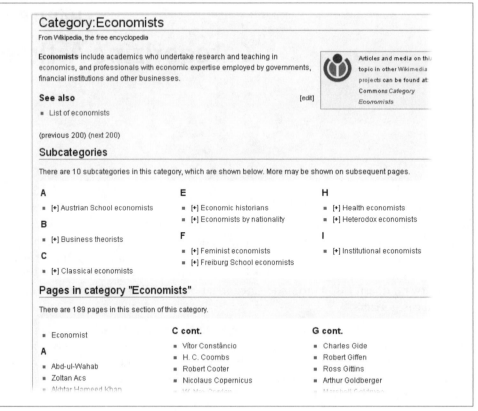

Figure 17-1. When you go to the page Category:Economists, *you see links to 189 articles categorized as being about economists, covering the letters A through K, plus ten subcategories. Every category page looks like this one, with four parts: some introductory text, possibly with a link or two; a list of subcategories; a list of any pages that belong directly to the category rather than one of its subcategories; and finally the categories to which the category page belongs.*

Category Links in Articles

Wikipedia has plenty of category pages, like the one shown in Figure 17-1. These pages become more useful when editors keep adding relevant articles to them. You do that not by editing a category page, but by editing the articles themselves.

Adding Categories to Articles

You can add a category link to the bottom of an article in two ways: by typing the category link into the article's wikitext (in the edit box), or by adding a template to the wikitext. You do the first for the topical categories that interest readers, such as *Category:Australian astronomers.* The second way (with a template) is usually for marking an article as needing cleanup (improvement) work, for example, *Category:Articles lacking sources from September 2007*.

The basic category link

Adding a topical category to an article is easy. To add the category *Toddler sports* to an article, for example, open that article for editing, and type, near the bottom (more on that in a moment), the text *[[Category:Toddler sports]]*. Then do the standard stuff: Add an edit summary, preview your edit, and save the change. The text you typed is exactly how the link appears at the bottom of the article.

There's one twist, however: When you preview, *you won't see the new category above the edit toolbar*, where the rest of the article is displayed. Nor will you see any existing categories for the article above the toolbar. Rather, you have to scroll down, past the edit box, past the insertable wikicode, and past the template list, to the very bottom of the window—that's where you'll see the categories displayed.

NOTE

Where categories show in preview mode is just an oddity of Wikipedia. Bug 10244, which reported this issue in June 2007, doesn't seem to be a priority for the developers, so don't hold your breath that it'll change.

New category links always should be added near the bottom of an article's wikicode. You normally edit (add, delete, change) category links by going to the last section of an article and clicking the "edit" link. If you find any category links anywhere other than in the last section of an article, move them.

NOTE

The only wikitext below the links for categories should be *stub* templates (used for short articles) and *interlanguage links*. Stub templates look like this: *{{text including "stub"}}*. Interlanguage links look like this: *[[fr:Parapsychologie]]*. The latter is a link to the article in the French Wikipedia on the topic of parapsychology, and you'd find the link near the bottom of the wikitext of the English Wikipedia article *Parapsychology*.

Category links from templates, for maintenance and stubbing

You usually create cleanup or maintenance category links with a template. For example, adding the template *{{unreferenced|date=January 2008}}* to an article creates an article message box wherever in the article you placed the template, plus it adds the category *Articles lacking sources from January 2008* to the bottom of the article. To see the many such templates that you can add to articles, go to *Category:Wikipedia maintenance templates*.

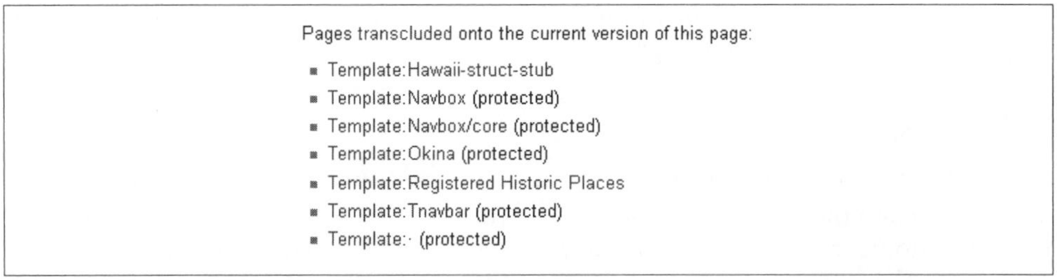
Pages transcluded onto the current version of this page:

- Template:Hawaii-struct-stub
- Template:Navbox (protected)
- Template:Navbox/core (protected)
- Template:Okina (protected)
- Template:Registered Historic Places
- Template:Tnavbar (protected)
- Template:· (protected)

Figure 17-2. These templates are in the article Hulihee Palace. *They're visible only when you click "edit this page," and then scroll to the bottom of the page.*

Stub templates—templates added to very short articles—aren't maintenance templates per se, but they're similar. They similarly change the contents of an article as well as adding one or more categories at the bottom of the article. Consider, for example, the article *Hulihee Palace*, which includes the template *{{Hawaii-struct-stub}}* (see Figure 17-2).

The template *{{Hawaii-struct-stub}}* generates two categories *Western United States building and structure stubs* and *Hawaii stubs*. Those two categories may be of some use to readers, but their main purpose is to signal to editors that this article needs to be expanded.

Fixing Category Links that Come From Templates

Occasionally, when you want to change a category shown at the bottom of an article, you can't find that category link in the article's wikitext, even if it's a topical category that normally wouldn't come from a template. If you can't find the category link in the article's wikitext, it must be coming from a template. Finding that template, and perhaps changing it (for example, to delete the category from the article), is a five-step process:

1. Click the "edit this page" tab.

   Don't click a section edit link; click the tab at the top of the article.

2. Scroll down to the bottom of the page, where you'll see the lists of templates used for the page.

   Figure 17-3 is an example.

3. Check a template (open it in a separate window or tab), starting either at the top or with the most likely suspect.

   You'll arrive at a page with the prefix *Template:*, like *Template:Registered Historic Places*.

4. Click "edit this page" to see the wikitext of the template; see if the category in question is there. If it isn't, try the next template.

   When you do find the category, it will look just like an article wikilink: *[[Category:Whatever]]*.

5. Usually, the problem is that the category is relevant to the template, but not to articles that the template is in. In that case, put *<noinclude>* in front of the category link and *</noinclude>* just after it.

   This code tells the software that when the template is put into an article page, the category link should not be.

When you change a category as described in these steps, the change can take days to show up in the article itself. The reason for the delay is that a given template can be located in thousands of articles. Trying to update all categories immediately could severely affect Wikipedia's servers. So the changes go into a job queue, and the software handles them little by little. Be patient.

Effective Categorization

Every article should have a category, even if it's the *Uncategorized pages* category. That's one reason to add a stub template to an article—it puts it into one or more categories. In fact, articles usually have multiple categories, at least one of which should be the relevant category subject. If you see an article with only one category, you usually can improve things by adding more categories.

A category's relevance should be immediately apparent. For example, if an article has the category *Russian architects*, but there's no indication that the subject of the article is either Russian or an architect, then either the category is wrong or the article needs to be expanded.

Don't add both a category and its subcategory. For example, Golden Gate Bridge is in *Category:Suspension bridges*, so it should not also be in *Category:Bridges*. (If you think you've got a valid exception, check at the guideline *Wikipedia:Categorization and subcategories*—shortcut: *WP:SUBCAT*—to see if you're right.)

> **Pages in category "People"**
>
> There are 6 pages in this section of this category.
>
> - Person
> - People
>
> - Portal:Biography
>
> **A**
> - Altun Bishik
>
> **K**
> - Kailash Singh Parihar
>
> **S**
> - Stranger (person)
>
> Categories: Categories requiring diffusion | Humans | Society

Figure 17-3. The category People *includes a number of subcategories (not shown) plus six individual articles. Two of these are not like the other four—*Altun Bishik *and* Kailash Singh Parihar*. Both should be in a subcategory.*

Finding the Right Category

The real challenge is to find the right categories to add to an article. Some suggestions:

- Go as low as possible in the hierarchy of categories. The more specific, the better. To this end, putting an article into a huge category—like *People*—is better than nothing, but not by very much, as Figure 17-3 shows. It's unlikely that a reader is going to say "Ah, this article is about a person. I'm really interested in reading about people—let's see what other articles Wikipedia has that are also about people."

- If you can think of a similar article (for example, for an article about a ballet star who else is or was a similar star?), check that article to see what category links appear there.

- If you can't think of a similar article, use a wikilink in the lead paragraph to get you to one. For example, if the first sentence of an article begins "Penalty methods are a certain class of algorithms to solve constraint optimization problems," you could click the link to the article *Algorithm* or to the article *Optimization (mathematics)*. Once there, look at the links in the article, links to the article (at the far left, click "What links here"), and categories of the article. All of these could lead you to similar articles; the category links might even be useful as is.

- Be thorough. Think of all the different things a topic may be associated with—geographic area, a historical period, an academic subfield, a certain type of thing (like a food or an ornament), or a special interest topic. The more, the better. Just remember there needs to be some supporting text in the article. For example, the

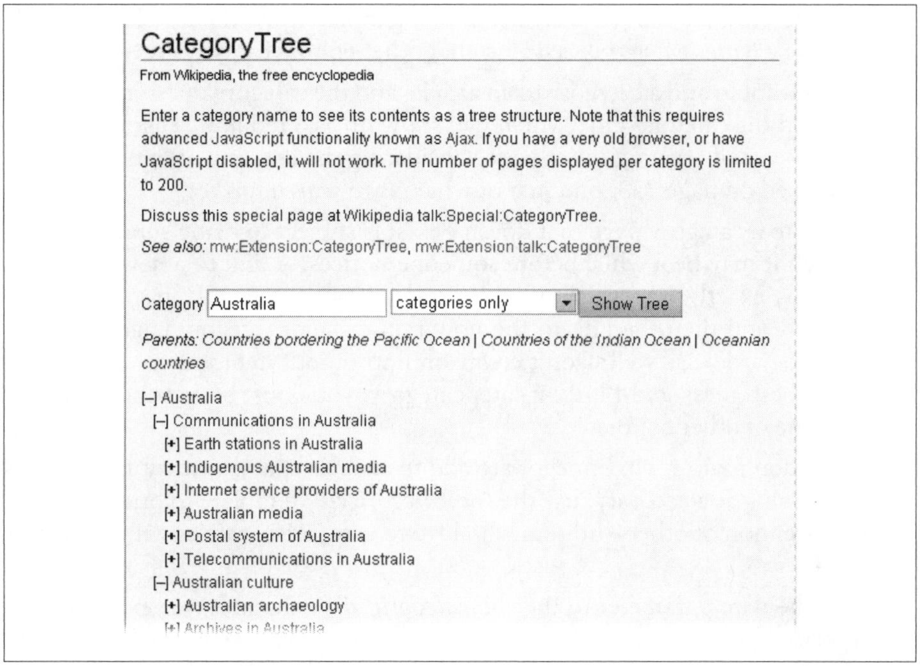

Figure 17-4. *The great thing about the* CategoryTree *Special page is that you don't have to open a bunch of category pages to find good subcategories. You can simply click one here, find (or not find) something you want to add to an article, and then try another category, drilling down as needed—all in one place.*

article *Terra cotta* has links to the following category pages: *Shades of red*, *Ceramics*, *Sculpture materials*, *Building materials*, *Pottery*, and *Construction*.

WORD TO THE WISE

The CategoryTree Special Page

One of the best ways to find a good category for an article is to start at a higher level category and see what subcategories are available. The easiest way to do that is with the *CategoryTree* Special page (Figure 17-4). This special page is a window into Wikipedia's category system, starting wherever you want to.

To get to this page, look in the "toolbox" box on the left side of the screen. Click the "Special pages" link, and click CategoryTree. Then enter a category (for example, *Australia*), and click "Show Tree." You can either pick a subcategory that's visible, or click a "[+]" indicator to see subcategories under any particular line.

- If you're not sure about a category, either be bold and add it, or use a higher level category that you're sure about. In either case, add the template *{{checkcategory}}* to the article *talk* page (not to the article page; articles don't need more banners like the one this template creates). The template puts the article talk page into *Category:Better category needed* so that other editors can see a review is needed.

- If you want to add a category to an article, and the category doesn't exist yet, don't just add the category link (which will show up as a red link). Instead, go through the process of creating (or at least considering the creating of) a new category, as described on page 333, one step of which is to *search further*.

  A link to a category page that doesn't exist is subject to being summarily deleted, though it may be a while before someone notices. A link to a new category page that has exactly one article is likely to lead to the category page being deleted quickly, and then the link to the now non-existent category page being deleted from the article as well. Don't create an impromptu, temporary, spur-of-the-moment, best-guess-and-I'll-fix-it-later category; you'll just be wasting your time and the time of other editors.

- If you don't know what category to add to an article, don't worry about it. Instead of guessing at a category, use the *{{uncategorized}}* template to bring the article to the attention of others. Editors who love to categorize articles will find a category for it.

  Add the date parameter to the *{{uncategorized}}* template—for example, *{{Uncategorized | date=January 2008}}*. (Be careful of the parameter spelling; parameters are *never* capitalized. If you type *Date* instead of *date*, the software will ignore the parameter altogether.) If you don't add this parameter, a bot will do so, adding yet one more edit to Wikipedia and the history of the article. That could obscure other edits, such as vandalism, so don't skip the parameter.

Getting Articles into the Right Place on a Category Page

Suppose you've added a good category to an article page, and you then look at the category page to make sure the new category is there. You find it but in the wrong place: The article is about Jane Doe, and it's in the category page's "J" section, not the "D" section where it belongs. The article is in the wrong place (as far as you're concerned) because the Wikipedia software doesn't understand anything about names of people.

You can fix this problem in one of two ways:

- You can specify, in a category link, where the title of an article is to be listed within a category page. You do this in a way that looks very much like a piped link: *[[Category:Female crime victims | Doe, Jane]]*. (The spaces around the "|" symbol are optional.)

- You can add something that specifies the sorting information ("sort order") for all the categories on the page, rather than doing that link by link. In this example, you just place the following directly above the listed categories in the wikitext: *{{DEFAULTSORT:Doe, Jane}}*.

Neither of these methods of changing where an article appears on a category page changes the name of the article. The article's name will still be *Jane Doe*, but it will now be listed in the "D" section, not the "J" section, of a category page. In the best of worlds, all the editors who add a category to an article will add the same sort order (in this case, lastname, then firstname). If they don't, you should feel free to fix the (hopefully few) category links that don't.

Category Pages

As you work on adding good categories to articles, you'll encounter category pages like the one in Figure 17-1, and as a reader, you'll find them useful for getting to articles you're interested in. But there's more to category pages. They're created and managed by editors, and, like all other pages at Wikipedia, there are times when you, as an editor, can edit them to improve them. This section explains what you need to know.

Hierarchy: The Categorizing of Category Pages

Every category page should have at least one parent—a higher-level category. (The exception, of course, is the category page at the very top of the hierarchy.) Or, to put it differently, every category page but the very highest (shown in Figure 17-5) should be within a subcategory of at least one higher-level category.

Figure 17-6 shows a category page that itself is assigned five categories.

Changing the categories assigned to a category page

Did you spot the error with the five parent categories in Figure 17-6? The problem is that *Algerian culture*, if you check, also has the parent category *Algeria*. A category page shouldn't have two parents where one parent (*Algerian culture*, in this case) is itself a subcategory of the other parent (*Algeria*, in this case). One parent category (*Algerian culture*) is enough, since someone looking at the higher level category (*Algeria*) can always find the page by just drilling down.

Fixing this categorization error is simple: Open the page *Category:Algerian culture* for editing (Figure 17-7), find the line with *[[Category:Algeria|Media]]*, and delete that. Then, following the standard procedure, add an edit summary, do a preview (categories show up at the very bottom of the page), and save the change.

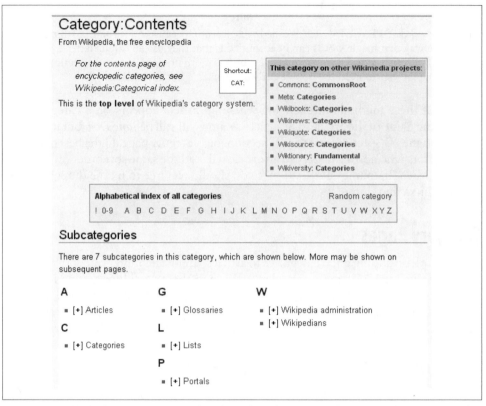

Figure 17-5. The highest category in Wikipedia—the only category that doesn't belong to a higher category—is Category:Contents. *It has seven subcategories and (not shown) one page that belongs to the category but isn't in a subcategory, the page* Wikipedia:Contents.

NOTE

You can find category pages without parents (category pages not themselves in a subcategory) by looking at the page *Special:Uncategorizedcategories*. This page is a specialized report that's not constantly updated, so if you're not looking at a fresh report, you'll probably find that a lot of the listed pages have either been fixed or proposed for deletion. If you find categorization interesting, you may want to help out here: Every category page but one (*Category:Contents*) should have a parent category.

Renaming, merging, or deleting a category page

Changing a category assigned to an article or a category assigned to a category page is easy—just a quick edit. By contrast, if you want to rename a category page, you need to go through a longer process; you can't just click the "move" tab, because there is no move tab.

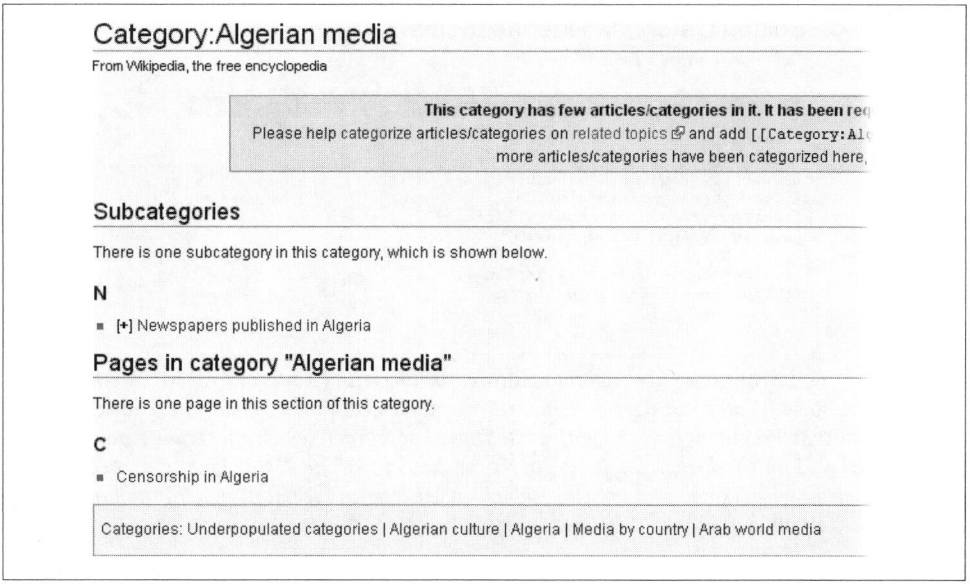

Figure 17-6. The category page Algerian media *has five parent categories—one is a cleanup category; the other four are higher level topical categories. Put differently,* Algerian media *is a subcategory of five categories, four of them topical and one a cleanup category.*

Renaming, merging, and deletion of pages in the Category namespace is discussed at *Wikipedia:Categories for discussion* (shortcut: *WP:CFD*). See Figure 17-8.

If you think this type of action is needed, follow the instructions on the *WP:CFD* page. Note that there are sections for non-controversial actions: "speedy renaming" (after a wait of 48 hours) and "speedy deletion" (for example, because a category is what Wikipedia calls "patent nonsense," defined as something "unsalvageably incoherent").

Creating a new category

If the category doesn't exist, you can create one. Whether you *should* create a new category, however, is another matter. While Wikipedia clearly still needs a lot more articles, it's not clear that it needs a lot more categories for those articles. So, here are some questions to consider before you create a new page:

- **Will the new category have more than a few pages on it?** The more pages you can put that fit the category, the more likely the category will survive. A category with just one article belonging to it is likely to have a short life.

- **Is the category being added to pages that already have adequate categories assigned to them?** As the guideline *Wikipedia:Overcategorization* (shortcut: *WP:OC*) says, "not every verifiable fact (or the intersection of two or more such facts) in an article requires an associated category. For lengthy articles, this could potentially result in hundreds of categories, most of which aren't particularly

```
Editing Category:Algerian media
From Wikipedia, the free encyclopedia

[toolbar]

{{popcat}}

[[Category:Algerian culture|Media]]
[[Category:Algeria|Media]]
[[Category:Media by country|Algeria]]
[[Category:Arab world media]]

[[de:Kategorie:Medien (Algerien)]]
[[fr:Catégorie:Média en Algérie]]
```

Figure 17-7. On the category page Algerian culture, *the line with [[Category:Algeria|Media]] needs to be deleted, since [[Category:Algerian culture]] already leads to that. While you're looking at the wikitext, note that three of the four categories listed have a sort order, which affects where this category page is displayed on the higher level category page (under "A" or "M"). Finally, notice the two interlanguage links—German and French—which create links in the left margin to similar category pages at the German and French versions of Wikipedia.*

relevant." (The essay "Do not write articles using categories"—shortcut *WP:DNWAUC*—is also informative on this mater.)

- **Is the category name neutral and factual?** A category like *Shiftless no-good politicians who should be recalled from office* is hopelessly non-neutral (see *WP:NPOV*), not to mention unverifiable (see *WP:V*).

- **If a category seems obvious, did you thoroughly look for it under a different name?** Particularly when you're adding a category to a new or stubby article, don't just assume that if *Category:People from New Zealand* doesn't exist, and if it fits the article, you should create it. (See page 328 for more detail on finding good categories for articles.)

If you decide to create a new category, you do that by creating a category page, exactly as you would any other page. Just type the name (for example, *Category:Some new article category that Wikipedia needs*) into the search box, and click Go. When the software tells you no such page exists, click the "Create the page" link, type some introductory information about the category, and save the page.

NOTE

Alternatively, you can first add a not-yet-created category to an article, which creates a red link. When you click the red link, you'll see the "Create this page" option. Click it, and then follow the rest of the procedure in the prior paragraph.

There's one clear exception to the general rule that you should always be hesitant to create a new category: when a lot of articles (say, over a hundred) are in a non-cleanup category that has no subcategories, or are in a category when no applicable

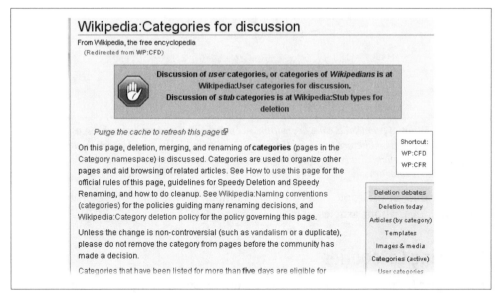

Figure 17-8. The page Wikipedia:Categories for discussion *is for discussion of renaming, merging, or deleting of all types of categories except for two, discussed elsewhere: user categories (as in* Category:Wikipedians *who dislike excessive categorization) and stubs (categories for very short articles). There's a separate page for discussion of user categories probably because they can be particularly controversial, or trivial. The separate page for discussion of stub categories is because this is a very specialized area.*

subcategories for them exist. In such a case, creating additional subcategories, and moving articles out of the category and into a subcategory by editing article pages, is a good thing to do.

Building Out Categories

Suppose you've found a good category for an article you're working on, and when you get to the category page, you're surprised that there aren't many more articles listed there. Consider your surprise an opportunity to improve Wikipedia. You can take up the challenge to make the category page a much better place for readers to go.

WikiProject members do this type of work all the time. They look for articles encompassed by their project, and then add WikiProject templates to article talk pages and categories to articles. You don't have to be a member of a WikiProject, however—just someone who realizes how useful categories are to both readers and editors.

There are significant advantages to working from a category page outward, looking for articles to add. Use existing articles to get clues to similar topics, both by reading the article text and following internal and external links in the articles. If you're fairly

Figure 17-9. Want to mention a category within a comment you're making on a discussion page? If so, either add a colon just before the word Category, or use the {{cl}} template. Both choices display the category name where you typed it, within your comment, and neither will put the discussion page they're on into a category.

knowledgeable on the topic of a category, so much the better; you've probably got a lot of good ideas about articles to look for.

Discussing Categories

Here's a puzzle that new editors often encounter: How do you mention a category on a discussion page? If you type *[[Category:WhatevertheCategoryis]]*, you've just put the discussion page into that category, and the category name itself won't show up where you typed it. It'll show up at the bottom of the page, which isn't very helpful. Wikipedia has two different ways to display the category link where you want it: Add a colon just before the word *Category*, or use the *{{cl}}* template, as shown in Figure 17-9.

If you're looking at a category page for articles, and find talk or user or other pages listed there as well, it's worth taking a quick look at these other pages to see if you can fix the problem with a judicious insertion of a colon. Sometimes you shouldn't (for example, a draft article in user space probably isn't hurting anything if it's being worked on and already has a category), and sometimes you can't easily insert a colon (if the category is embedded in a template, for example). But often the mislisted page is just a simple mistake by an editor that can be easily fixed.

Categories, Lists, and Series Boxes

Categories are not the only way to provide readers with an organized approach that ties a group of articles together. Lists and series boxes (templates) both can do the same thing. For example, Figure 17-10 is a list that essentially does the same thing as the category shown in Figure 17-1 (page 324).

You've probably seen the third option—series boxes—but you may not be familiar with the label. Figure 17-11 shows a series box for winners of the Nobel Memorial Prize in Economics.

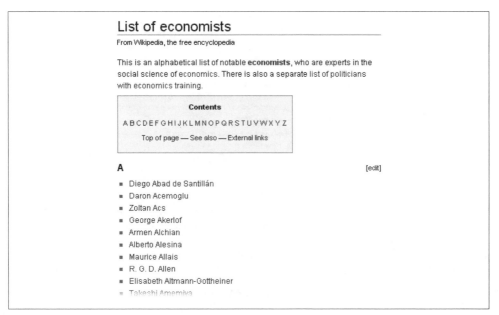

Figure 17-10. If this list of economists looks familiar, it's because it's also Figure 14-6 (page 259), and because Figure 18-1 earlier in this chapter, showing the category page Economists, *has almost the same set of links in it. Lists and categories can overlap considerably, but each has strengths and weaknesses.*

The guideline *Wikipedia:Categories, lists, and series boxes* (shortcut: *WP:CLS*) discusses the advantages and disadvantages of each of these three ways of providing navigation among articles. It also notes that "When developers of these redundant systems compete against each other in a destructive manner, such as by nominating the work of their competitors to be deleted simply because they overlap, they are doing Wikipedia a disservice." In short, there's room on Wikipedia for editors to offer readers multiple ways to get around; no single approach is as good as a mix of all three; and editors who believe their approach is superior should direct their efforts at improving what they favor, to offer something even better to readers, rather than trying to convince other editors that their approach is inferior.

NOTE

Search engines do notice category pages. In Google, for example, the page *Category:Economists* was the fourth result of a search on "economists" (with results limited to pages on the English Wikipedia). The article *List of Economists* was the second result. (*Economist* was first, *Economics* was third).

If categorizing articles intrigues you, one place to start is the page *Category:Underpopulated categories*, a category for categories that contain at least one page, and where

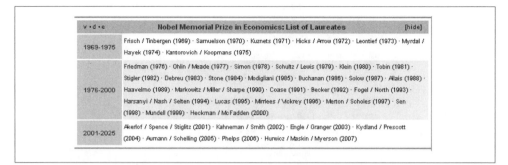

v · d · e	Nobel Memorial Prize in Economics: List of Laureates	[hide]
1969-1975	Frisch / Tinbergen (1969) · Samuelson (1970) · Kuznets (1971) · Hicks / Arrow (1972) · Leontief (1973) · Myrdal / Hayek (1974) · Kantorovich / Koopmans (1975)	
1976-2000	Friedman (1976) · Ohlin / Meade (1977) · Simon (1978) · Schultz / Lewis (1979) · Klein (1980) · Tobin (1981) · Stigler (1982) · Debreu (1983) · Stone (1984) · Modigliani (1985) · Buchanan (1986) · Solow (1987) · Allais (1988) · Haavelmo (1989) · Markowitz / Miller / Sharpe (1990) · Coase (1991) · Becker (1992) · Fogel / North (1993) · Harsanyi / Nash / Selten (1994) · Lucas (1995) · Mirrlees / Vickrey (1996) · Merton / Scholes (1997) · Sen (1998) · Mundell (1999) · Heckman / McFadden (2000)	
2001-2025	Akerlof / Spence / Stiglitz (2001) · Kahneman / Smith (2002) · Engle / Granger (2003) · Kydland / Prescott (2004) · Aumann / Schelling (2005) · Phelps (2006) · Hurwicz / Maskin / Myerson (2007)	

Figure 17-11. Shown is the series box titled Nobel Memorial Prize in Economics: List of Laureates. *This series box appears in an article when the template {{Nobel Prize in Economics}} is added to the article's wikitext. Series boxes are appropriate for relatively short lists (the one shown has about sixty links). Series boxes are also appropriate only when membership in a list is very clear. Prominent British politicians, for example, would not be good for a series box, since "prominence" is on a continuum. Even if everyone agreed on relative prominence, the cut-off point for being in or not in the series box is still arbitrary.*

an editor felt that more pages were needed. Another place is *Category:Category needs checking*.

Also consider joining *WikiProject Categories* (shortcut: *WP:CATP*). And more editors are always welcome at *Wikipedia:Categories for discussion* (shortcut: *WP:CFD*).

CHAPTER 18

Better Articles: A Systematic Approach

Most of the first 17 chapters of this book offered you an assortment of how-to advice on improving Wikipedia articles. Now it's time to tie all that advice together, and to fill in some of the gaps.

If you're a less experienced editor, this chapter can serve as a detailed checklist. When you're looking at an article you want to improve, you have a step-by-step process for going from the top to the bottom of that article. For experienced editors, the section headings in this chapter can serve as a reminder of everything that goes into making a good Wikipedia article.

This chapter is particularly intended for articles that are short and/or relatively unsourced. It also contains a lot of advice about minimizing disagreements with other editors—a good idea even if you're working on an article where other editors are scarce to non-existent. Consider the advice about disagreements as safety insurance, in case a cranky fellow editor comes out of the woodwork.

Avoid Surprises

You don't want to spend time researching and editing an article, and then discover (or be told about) something that sharply reduces the value of much or all of what you've done. Here's a list of questions to ask yourself, to avoid unpleasant surprises:

- **Has the article been vandalized?** Check for both recent edits and for edits in the past that removed a large chunk of good information. If the vandalism is recent, revert it, or use the good information to improve the article.

  Chapter 5 discussed how to use the article history page to analyze what's happened recently. You can check for the second issue—missing material—by looking at whether the size of the article has decreased (a sharp drop in byte count). Vandals and POVers do remove good content and don't always get caught. If you're planning to spend a couple of hours on an article, take a minute or two to glance at older versions of the article. If it's been stable or showing accumulating information, with no signs of vandalism, go right ahead and continue working on it.

- **Is the article a massive copyright infringement?** If so, revert to a version without the copyright problem, or, if it started out life that way, nominate it for speedy deletion (under criterion G12, as shown in Figure 19-3 on page 365).

  If the article links only to the one company or product or Web site most closely associated with the topic, then click that link to see if that's where most of the text was taken from. Warning signs of copyright infringements include: The article was created relatively recently; it has a concentrated number of edits from an editor who has done little else beside this article; it reads like something taken from a company or organization marketing Web page. If any of these apply, go to the page history, find a large chunk of added text, and then do a Web search for that text. Most results will probably be Wikipedia mirror sites, but you may get lucky and find the real Web site with the text on it. Bingo—copyright infringement. (For more information, see the page *Wikipedia:Spotting possible copyright violations*—shortcut *WP:SPCV*.)

- **Does the article have a unsolvable problem with sourcing?** Does it have no sources, or only bad sources (blogs, Web sites that can't be considered reliable sources, and so on), or a mixture of bad and incorrectly used sources? (For example, it cites a newspaper article which mentions the Wikipedia topic only very briefly, because the article is really about something else.) If the article has no sources or poor ones, and you can't find any reliable ones, the topic may not be notable enough for Wikipedia.

  Even if you think the topic is notable, if the article is essentially lacking any reliable source, search the Web. If you can't find anything, you need to dig deeper, or turn to Chapter 19 on deleting articles.

TIP

Also remember *WP:NOT*, that Wikipedia isn't a dictionary. Dictionary definitions, no matter how well cited, are still dictionary definitions. Consider moving the definition to Wiktionary (page 428).

- **Does the article already exist under another name?** The longer an article has been around, the less likely that it's a duplicate, but if it's less than a couple months old, use your favorite search engine to do a quick domain-restricted search (for example, blue-footed booby site:en.wikipedia.org (*http://blue-footed booby site:en.wikipedia.org*)). The search helps you figure out whether it's a duplicate or whether there are other Wikipedia articles that should link to the one you're working on. If so, add the wikilinks.

  If you do find another article that largely duplicates the one you're planning to work on, then you need to read the page *Help:Merging and moving pages* (shortcut: *H:MMP*) and do, or propose, a merger. And if you're bold and actually do the merger, wait a couple of days before starting to edit the merged article, to see if other editors show up to oppose what you've done. (For more on merging, see page 346.)

- **Is the article the center of disagreements?** If you decide to work on a controversial article, you may spend more time negotiating with other editors than editing the article. The article history (lots of reverts, full protection because of an edit dispute, and so on) and the article talk page should make clear how controversial an article is. Also check the history of the article talk page, for any active discussions.

The fact that an article's contents are being vigorously disputed isn't necessarily a reason to work on something else. It just means that you must be extra careful with your edits, and be willing to spend as much time as necessary discussing changes with editors who may have ownership issues; see the guideline *Wikipedia:Ownership of articles* (shortcut *WP:OWN*). If you have doubts, consider working on something else. (There's plenty—see the box below.)

Finding Noncontroversial Articles

With more than two million articles to chose from, you don't have to get stuck working on one that comes with contentious editors. Although Wikipedia needs editors who are willing to work on such articles, constructively working with editors who may not be as open to change as they should be, sometimes you just don't need the stress. You can work on non-controversial articles, avoid frustration and burnout, and still make a valuable contribution to Wikipedia.

Here are some relatively dispute-free zones with plenty of articles that need work:

- Articles listed by WikiProjects and collaborations (Chapter 9). You can find WikiProjects you might be interested in at *Wikipedia:WikiProject Council/Directory* (shortcut *WP:PROJDIR*). You don't have to join (list your name) in order to participate. One nice thing about such projects is you have backup if you run into problems.

- *Category:Stub categories* has stub articles neatly sorted by category. Find something you're interested in—your state or province, a hobby, an area of science, whatever—and jump to that spot in the index. But be selective—many stubs don't have the potential to ever be really good articles.

- A list with more promising articles than the one for stubs (but less well-sorted) is *Category:All articles to be expanded*. Consider using the category intersection tool, at the page *User:Duesentrieb/CatScan*, to find articles that need expanding, in a topical category that interests you.

- At *Special:Newpages* you can watch Wikipedia grow, and see if anything brand-new looks interesting to you. It's best to pick something not highlighted in yellow. Those articles are new and not yet reviewed—marked as *patrolled*—by an editor. If you stick to the non-highlighted articles, you can pick an article that at least one

---

other editor thought was worth keeping. The list also includes a number of articles marked for speedy deletion, as discussed in Chapter 20—don't work on those, of course. And double- and triple-check to make sure the article you work on doesn't already exist under another name.

- Ask *User:SuggestBot* to suggest some articles for you to work on.

Don't Suppress or Separate Controversy

People have different ideas about what they believe is true. That's a good thing. Discussing controversial issues makes articles—and life—more interesting. It's not your job as a Wikipedia editor to decide the truth about a subject: What's fair, what happened, who's responsible, who's to blame, or whatever. It's your job, however, to let the reader know that a point has been publicly debated, if the debate itself was newsworthy.

The issue of reliable sources is more relevant than ever when controversies are involved. You should ignore, for example, a self-published book attacking the theory of gravity. It isn't citable in and of itself, though you might include it in the biographical article of its author, if the author was notable. On the other hand, if there are a number of major newspaper articles about the book, then the controversy (as reported in the newspapers) is worth mentioning. (See *Wikipedia:Fringe theories*—shortcut *WP:FRINGE*— for details.)

When citing controversy or criticism, integrate it into the article. Suppose a politician had a major role in getting a particular controversial policy implemented. If you describe that policy in one section of the article ("Accomplishments") and put criticisms of the policy together with other criticisms of that politician in a separate section, you harm the narrative of the article. It's easy to throw all the negative stuff into one section of an article, or even spin it off as a separate article (see the box below), but it's a disservice to the reader.

UP TO SPEED

Separate "Criticism of" Articles

Wikipedia has about 60 articles whose titles begin "Criticism of." The governing guideline for such articles is *Wikipedia:Content forking* (shortcut: *WP:POVFORK*), which states "There is no consensus whether a 'Criticism of...' article is always a POV fork. At least the 'Criticism of...' article should contain rebuttals if available, and the original article should contain a summary of the 'Criticism of...' article."

The existence of these articles shouldn't be taken as justifying a separate "Criticism of" section in an article. Rather, it shows the relatively few times where criticisms have been numerous and varied, and editors have chosen not to include these in the main articles.

Reorganize and Edit Existing Content

Chapter 10 was entirely about content disagreements among editors—how to minimize them and how to resolve them. When there are other editors very interested in an article, any major change is going to meet with skepticism, if not outright opposition. If you're working on a really bad article that needs a major overhauling, you have three choices:

- Make series of incremental changes to the article.
- Make specific proposals on the article talk page.
- Rewrite the article in your user space, or a subpage of the article talk page, and discuss that rewrite on the article talk page.

This section discusses the first approach, which is generally quicker to implement, and well-suited for articles without active editors who may oppose a major overhauling. It has the advantage of being easier for other editors (who may just be checking the changes to make sure they're not vandalism) to follow what you're doing, and thus to maintain the assumption of good faith (shortcut: *WP:AGF*) that you're not trying to slip something by other editors.

> **WARNING**
>
> Don't reorganize a major, established article (one that has lots of edits in the article history, lots of comments on the talk page, lots of interested editors, and so on) by simply starting to edit it. The organization of such an article represents a consensus, albeit an informal one. You should post advance notice on the talk (discussion) page about anything you'd like to do that's more major than shuffling a few subsections around.

Reorganize

The first step in overhauling an article is to move information around so it's better organized. In this step, don't add or delete any text except headings. If that means a section ends up being lengthy because of a lot of redundant information, that's okay at this stage of changing the article. Some specifics:

- **The goal here is to create a better structure for the article**. By not deleting any information, other editors can focus on whether or not the organization is better, rather than arguing about additions or deletions. Your goal at this point isn't to get sections to read smoothly; just to cut and paste information to get it into the right section or subsection.
- **Don't put or keep controversies and criticisms in a separate section**. Instead, integrate them into the article.
- **Don't forget the lead section**. It should be a short introduction and summary, not long and filled with content not found in the rest of the article. Either move excess information out of the summary, or, if you think editors may be particularly

attached to the lead section as is, copy all excess information to where it should be, and deal with cleaning up the lead section later in the process.

- **Use headings and subheadings to indicate the direction you think the article should go**. Short sections are fine, but you need at least a paragraph to justify a heading. Don't add headings if there's no content for a section, and don't add content in order to justify a heading.

- **In your edit summary, explain what you did**. It's very important to clearly state that you were reorganizing the article, and that nothing was added or deleted.

- **You have missing sections or subsections after you finish your edit, as well as missing citations and added content.** That's okay—this is an incremental process. Each step adds value, but the article isn't finished until all the steps are complete.

On Consensus and Ownership

Among the worst defenders of the status quo are those who believe that consensus needs to be established *before* any change to an article. That's a total misreading of Wikipedia rules, especially *Be bold* (shortcut: *WP:BB*), which encourages editors to make changes whenever there seems to be a good reason to do so.

In one clear case, changing an article without discussion is inappropriate: when the specific change in question has been fought over previously, and there was either no consensus, or rough consensus against the change. In that case, the edit is either out of ignorance (hence the advice on page 341 to read the talk page of an article before starting to overhaul it) or it's disruptive editing.

If you reorganize an article and another editor then reverts the change because consensus was not established, revert it back (just *once*) with *See talk/discussion page* in the edit summary. Then, on the talk/discussion page, restate what you were doing and that you didn't add or delete any text. Point out that the page *Help:Reverting* says, "Do not revert good faith edits", and that you were editing in good faith. Also invite editors who have any specific problems with your reorganization to state them, so that a consensus on the organization of the article can be reached. Then wait a day or two, and, if no one speaks up with anything major, proceed to the next step—rewriting (see below). (If anyone raises objections, see Chapter 10, which discusses content disputes.)

Rewrite

Once you've got a good organization for an article, even if it's incomplete, you want to switch to editing section by section. Section-by-section editing assuages suspicions by letting other others clearly see what you're doing. Moreover, if someone objects to an edit of one section, that objection doesn't impact the improvements you're making to other sections.

---

344 | Chapter 18: Better Articles: A Systematic Approach

The goal in this second step is to make the best of the text that already exists, and to do so in as non-controversial a manner as possible. Fix one section, save the edit, go on to another section, save the edit, and so on—don't do multiple sections in a single edit. Here are some rewriting tips:

- **Remove duplicate information**. You often find the same sentence, or variants of it, in multiple places in the article. You don't need to say something twice, so remove one of them.

NOTE

Don't remove citations at this point. If you end up with two (or more) citations for the same sentence, so be it.

- **Don't add information**. Add bridging or transitional text where needed ("Back in India," or "For example,"), but don't add anything that needs a source, since you're not adding citations at this step. Moreover, since you're deleting information (see the next point), other editors are less likely to object if it's clear that your goal isn't to replace their text with yours.

- **Put the remaining information into a logical sequence, and copyedit for encyclopedic tone**. That may require removing entire unverifiable sentences (for example, "Smith was admired and respected by all his friends and neighbors."). Just don't delete any information that seems plausible, though unsourced. Someone might still find a verifiable source.

  Removing an unverifiable sentence could mean removing an unacceptable source for that sentence, such as a blog. That's fine—the problem and its problem source are really one and the same.

- **Make sure your edit summary explains what you're doing.** When you rewrite a section, your edit summary should explain what you did and, ideally, provide a pointer to policy; for example, *Cleanup per [[WP:NPOV]] and [[WP:V]]; no new content was added.*

After you do rewrites as outlined in this section, you can expect that the only challenges to your edits—other than other editors tinkering with them a bit—is perhaps a complaint or two about removed information. If you were careful to remove only unverifiable, unsourced information, complaints are unlikely. But if other editors object, refer them to *WP:V* and ask them to explain how the information you removed is consistent with those policies, or just ask them for a good source so you can put the information back.

NOTE

Some Wikipedia articles include text, images, or links that many people find objectionable. If these are relevant to the content of the article, then they belong in the article. Nor does Wikipedia use disclaimers. There is no child-safe version of Wikipedia; editors who support such a concept should to try to get a change made to the policy *WP:NOT*, which includes a section called "Wikipedia is not censored".

Don't Take Article Scope as a Given

You've picked an article, started in on it, and discovered that it's getting too long, or one part of it is getting too long. Or, alternatively, you don't believe can build it up into something reasonably good. If so, rethink the article's scope. You don't have to accept what you're found, when you started on the article, as the definitive boundaries of the article's scope.

Too Much Content: Spinoffs

Chapter 13 (page 236) explains how to spin off a section of an article into a new article. That's the way to go when a section become too long and is about a subject notable enough for an article of its own. Keep this concept in mind as you work on any article: If a section becomes so long that it unbalances an article, if it's truly notable and not a collection of minor facts—spin it off.

Overlapping Content: Merging

Say that you've starting working on the article *Thingabobbery*, and you notice that another article, *Thingabboberists* (about the professionals who do thingabobbery for a living), has a lot of overlap in content. Moreover, there aren't a lot of articles about one that don't discuss the other.

Wikipedia has a standard solution for overlapping articles—merge them. Merging is a normal editing action, something any editor can do. You're not required to propose it to other editors, and you don't have to ask an administrator to help you do it. If you think merging something improves Wikipedia, you can be bold and just do it. Still, if you think the merger is going to be controversial, then you should propose it (see page 347) rather than risk starting a fight (and wasting your time) by just going ahead.

Doing a merge

Merging is straightforward:

1. Pick one of the two articles to be the survivor.

   In general, choose the better known of the two words or phrases. Using a search engine to see the number of results is a good way to find out.

2. Cut and paste material from the doomed article to the surviving article. In the edit summary, put *Moving content from [[Name of other article]], in preparation for merger*.

   Only add content that isn't already in the surviving article. Don't worry much about getting the wording right—just bring any new material across. When in doubt, copy more rather than less.

3. Now that you've copied what you need, delete all text from the article that isn't going to survive, and change it to a redirect. Save it with an edit summary like *Changing to a redirect; article merged into [[Name of surviving article]]*.

   See Figure 16-11 on page 308 for instructions on doing redirects.

4. Check the talk (discussion) page of the article that's now a redirect. If any sections have active discussions (say, ones with a posting in the past week), copy those sections to the talk page of the surviving article.

   Include a note at the top of each section, just below the heading, mentioning the merger and the name of the page from which the section was copied.

NOTE

While you could make the talk (discussion) page of the non-surviving article into a redirect, there's no harm in leaving it as is. Any editor thinking about posting there is going to notice that the related article page is a redirect.

After the merger's done, clean up the surviving article. See "Reorganize and Edit Existing Content" (page 343) for tips.

Proposing a merger

If you don't want to merge two or more articles yourself, propose a merger by placing a merger template at the top of each article. There are different templates depending on whether you propose to:

- Merge articles A and B, survivor to be determined (*{{merge}}*).
- Merge article A into article B, with A becoming a redirect (*{{mergeto}}*, *{{mergefrom}}*).
- Merge many pages into one page (*{{mergeto}}*, *{{mergefrom-multiple}}*).

The page *Help:Merging and moving pages* (shortcut: *H:MMP*) has details.

Any merge templates you add must link to a section of a single article talk page, where you'll start a discussion of the proposed merger. Before you post the templates, start that new section on that talk page, explaining your reasons for suggesting a merger. Also add a listing to the page *Wikipedia:Proposed mergers* (shortcut: *WP:PM*).

After that, you wait. If you want to speed up the process, you can post a note on the user talk pages of the major or recent contributors to the articles, noting that a merger has been proposed to an article they've contributed to, with a link to the article talk page where you posted your reasons.

If there's clear agreement with the proposal by consensus or silence, then you can proceed with the merger. *Consensus* means that no one, or a small minority, has opposed the merger; *silence* means you've waited a week and no one has responded. If you get a limited response, with no clear consensus, then consider following the process for content disagreements as laid out in Chapter 10.

Too Little Content: Merging

Sometimes you just can't find much information about a topic, or you find a topic that's only mentioned in the context of a larger grouping. One example would be an article about a small island that's part of a large, notable chain of islands. If you can find only a couple of newsworthy paragraphs about the small island, or isolated incidents that you really can't tie together, then consider merging the information about this small island into the article on the chain. Moreover, look at any articles about other small islands in the chain, and consider those for merging as well. And where a small island in the chain doesn't have an article, consider creating a redirect for it so that editors, in the future, go to the article on the chain.

Of course, in the future there may be a large, newsworthy resort on the small island, and content about it may be spun off from the article about the chain, into a separate article. In the meantime, however, it does readers no good to have a bunch of short articles scattered throughout Wikipedia, when collecting them together could make a reasonable article. Go where available sources of information lead you—don't create or keep an article just because, sometime in the future, someone may write a book about it and provide content to make it larger.

Improve the Citation of Sources

Chapter 2, starting at page 25, discusses how to properly cite sources, as well as what sources are acceptable. For each existing source in the article, go through a three-step process to determine if it's salvageable and, if so, improve it. This section goes through the three options in detail:

- If there's a bad URL, try to fix it.
- Determine whether the source is verifiable and reliable (see *WP:V* and *WP:RS*). If not, determine if it can be easily replaced. If not, delete it.
- If the source is reliable but not formatted properly, convert it into a correctly formatted footnote with full information.

NOTE

While your goal is to convert all embedded links (the ones that look like this: "[1]")
to footnotes, you might want to avoid the temptation of starting by putting <ref>
tags around them to immediately convert them to footnotes. It's easier to work with
sources section by section, and if you create footnotes, the URLs go down to the
bottom of the page, where you can't see them when previewing a section.

Fixing Bad URLs

Links go bad: A link that worked on the day it was added to an article may not work a
month or a year later. That's why full citations are so critical: If the URL stops working,
the citation—to a magazine, newspaper, or other source available offline—is still acceptable, because it's still verifiable.

Unfortunately, you're often looking at a source that consists *only* of a URL. So your
challenge is to find where the content moved to, or to get a copy. Here's a step-by-step
process:

- **If the URL were working, would the source be acceptable?** For example, if the
  link is to a page at BloggersOnFire.com (*http://bloggersonfire.com*) or at
  ExtremistRant.net, you can probably use it only if the article is about the Web site
  or the organization behind it, or a notable author of posts at the site. Most of the
  time, you have to discard it.

  As discussed in the next section, a link to an unacceptable source can sometimes
  lead you to an acceptable source. But here, if the source is unacceptable, you're
  facing a double problem: First you've got to figure out a fix for the bad URL, and
  then you've got to get lucky and have that lead you to another, acceptable source.
  In such a case, you're justified in only doing a few, not particularly time-consuming
  things to try to fix the URL. You need not invest a lot of time in something that
  probably has no payoff.

- **Can I find a substitute source?** For example, Reuters stories are removed from
  the Web after 30 days, but if the subject was a national story, you're likely to find
  it at the *New York Times*, which provides full access to the last 20 years of its
  archives at no cost. Select some key words from the sentence just before the URL,
  and do a Web search, if the facts involve recent events. Or just head for NY-
  Times.com (*http://nytimes.com*) for a replacement URL and a full citation.

- **Does the bad link go to a newspaper site?** If that's the case, it typically gets
  redirected to the front page. The story of interest has probably been archived and
  now simply has a different URL. Search the archives, even if you know you have
  to pay to see the full story. You goal is to get a URL that's the free abstract or free
  initial paragraph of the news story, to replace the old URL and create a full citation.

- **Does the bad link go to an existing Web site?** If the site doesn't hide its old
  content behind an internal search engine, as many newspaper sites do, then the

content you're looking for may still exist at a different URL, and you can find it using a search engine. For example, if you're working on an article about "Joe Bfystlat" and the site is NukesForPeace.org (*http://nukesforpeace.org*), try a domain-restricted search like *"Joe Bfystlat" site:* NukesForPeace.org (*http://nukesforpeace.org*) to turn up any existing pages.

- **Does the bad link go to a now-defunct Web site?** If so, or if it's to a missing page on a Web site that still exists, try the Internet Archive (also known as the Wayback Machine), at www.archive.org (*http://www.archive.org*).

- **If entering the full URL doesn't yield any results, try trimming it.** (For example, trim www.example.com/Level1/Level2/detail.htm (*http://www.example.com/level1/level2/detail.htm*) to be www.example.com/Level1/Level2/ (*http://www.example.com/level1/level2/*); if that doesn't work, try www.example/.com/Level1/ (*http://www.example/.com/level1/*).) If you do find a copy, see the page *Wikipedia:Using the Wayback Machine* (shortcut: *WP:WBM*) on how to cite the page.

Replacing or Deleting Unacceptable Sources

You're improving citations to make sure all remaining ones are acceptable per *WP:V* and *WP:RS*. So you need to replace each bad source with a good one. If you can't find a good one, you should still delete the bad source. Here are three approaches to finding a replacement:

- If you've got a functioning URL to a source isn't acceptable (a blog, forum, or personal Web page, for example), see if that Web page has a link to an acceptable source. For example, a blog often has a link to the news story the blogger's writing about, a link you can follow. Then simply replace the unacceptable URL with the better one, and finish fixing the citation.

- Blogs often quote part of a news story or document without providing a link. If that story or document is what you're looking for, then search the Web for part of the quoted text. Pick a group of five or six consecutive words that's a bit unusual in some way, and search that, putting quotation marks around the words so the search engine looks for them in exactly that sequence.

- Finally, as mentioned previously, if the unacceptable source is discussing a news story that got national coverage, look up the story on the *New York Times* or search Google News (*http://news.google.com*), and then use that as a replacement.

NOTE

Remember, an acceptable source doesn't have to be online. If you have easy access to a microfiche copy of old newspapers in your home town, for example, you can use that information for a citation. Wikipedia prefers online sources when available, but there's no exclusionary rule.

If you've made a good faith effort to find a replacement for an unacceptable source, and weren't successful, then delete the source, with a brief explanation in the edit summary about what you tried.

Converting Embedded Links to Footnotes

Once you have an acceptable source, change whatever was in the article (typically just a URL) to a fully formatted citation—a footnote. Chapter 2 discusses citations in depth, with instructions on formatting footnotes on page 33.

TIP

If you cite a source more than once in an article, or if the source looks like a promising place to get information for the article later, then make the footnote for that source into a *named* footnote. As the leading tag, use, for example, *<ref name="AJJones">*, where the author is A. J. Jones, rather than just *<ref>*.

Build the Web

Since Wikipedia is an online encyclopedia, articles don't exist in isolation. By building links into and out of the article you're working on, you not only do a service for readers, but you also increase the chances that other editors will come across the article you're working on, and add their contributions. Wikipedia editors call adding wikilinks *building the web*.

Here are specific ways for you to build the web:

- **Link words in the article to other articles**. For example, link jargon and technical terms to articles that explain them. Link words that lead to related articles, especially about organizations, people, and places. Link common words used in a technical or uncommon way. But don't overlink, as discussed in the box on page 15.

  When you add links, check to make sure they don't end up at disambiguation pages (page 313). While someone will eventually fix them, they defeat most of the purpose of linking in the first place. (You can also link to just a single section of an article, as described on page 244.)

- **Red links are an opportunity, not a problem**. If you think there should be an article about something, but there isn't, create the wikilink anyway. If the wikilink turns red, showing that such an article doesn't exist, then check the spelling (a Google search is good) and recheck the capitalization (except for the very first letter, it matters in Wikipedia page names).

  If you find there's a relevant article in Wikipedia but under a different name, click the red link so you can create a redirect (page 304), and then change the wikilink in your article so it points directly to the new article.

Don't delete red links if you can't find an existing Wikipedia article for the wikilink. A red link is an invitation for an editor to create the article. The page *Wikipedia:Most wanted articles* (shortcut *WP:MWA*) lists nonexistent pages with more than 20 wikilinks pointing to them.

- **Check incoming links**. You find these by going to the toolbox at the left side of the screen, and clicking the "What links here" link. Treat this list as possible outgoing wikilinks to add to your article, although you're not required to do so. These articles are also places to check for good sources that you might use in the article you're working on.

- **Consider linking to this article by editing other articles**. If the article you're working on has an outgoing wikilink to another article, and that other article doesn't link back (as shown in the list of incoming links), then perhaps it should. You may be able to expand that other article slightly, with a sentence or so, and an additional wikilink. (You can link the article to WikiProjects by editing the article talk page; see the box below.)

- **Add categories**. Categories tie articles together in a way that readers find useful. See page 324 for details.

- **Create or add to the "See also" section**. Per the guideline *Wikipedia:Layout* (shortcut: *WP:GTL*), the "See also" section "provides an additional list of internal links to other articles in Wikipedia that are related to this one as a navigational aid." The "See also" section shouldn't duplicate links already in the article. It's for linking to subjects closely related to the article.

UP TO SPEED

Linking to Wikiprojects

One of the purposes of building the web is to increase the chances that other editors will come across the article you're working on, and add their contributions. You can also further increase such chances if you make sure that the article talk page has templates that mark the article as of interest to the relevant WikiProjects.

If you find one or more WikiProject templates already on the talk page, no problem— look to see if you can add another. If you see none at all, then go to the page *Wikipedia:WikiProject Council/Directory* (shortcut: *WP:PROJDIR*), find one or more relevant projects (often both a geographical WikiProject and non-geographical one), and add their templates to the article talk page.

Look for Guidance and Examples

Before you start adding sourced content, look for roadmaps to help you decide where to put citations and format text. There are several possibilities:

- Check the *Manual of Style* (shortcut: *WP:MOS*) for topical guidelines. For example, the guideline *Wikipedia:Manual of Style (Japan-related articles)* might apply to your article.

- Check the relevant WikiProjects (see the box on page 352). Sometimes they have guidelines for articles.

- Look for a featured article (FA) on a similar topic. You might find a Featured Article or a Good Article close to your topic listed at the WikiProjects you've checked for guidelines. Or select one of the two dozen grouping of FAs at the page *Wikipedia:Featured articles* (*WP:FA*), and see if it includes a useful article. (If nothing else, you'll probably get an appropriate listbox template to use.)

Add Sourced Content

If an article doesn't have sources, it's pointless to spend a lot of time working on the organization or writing. The article may get deleted for lack of reliable sources, so you may be just rearranging junk in a garage so it looks aesthetically pleasing. Instead, devote your time to finding sources. If an article has little content, you need sources that provide more content. If an article has lots of unsourced statements, you need to find sources to do one of three things:

- Support those statements, so you can keep them in.

- Contradict those statements, so you have justification to delete them (by adding cited information that says the opposite).

- Provide enough new content to supplant those statements, so you can move them to the article talk page, and invite others to add them back when they find sources.

Chapter 2 discussed *how* to add content, and listed a number of places on Wikipedia that can help you find it. Here are some additional considerations to think about as you look for and add content:

- **Don't just use a search engine**. There are lots of places to find sources. Chapter 4, on new articles, has a comprehensive list (page 78). Most good articles aren't built just by using a search engine like Google. Among the most valuable sources are online databases of articles available through schools and libraries.

- **Edit one section at a time, not the entire article, if you anticipate objections**. If there's any possibility that other editors who have worked on the article in the past few months may have concerns about your edits, you'll make their lives much easier if you edit section by section. They'll also be less inclined to object if they see what you're doing, which means taking an organized, methodical approach. It's also easier if editors can discuss objections in the context of a section, not the whole article.

Alternatively, you can copy the information in one section to another place (a subpage of yours, or totally off Wikipedia), edit it there, and then bring it in as a new chunk of information.

NOTE

For articles with lots of editing ongoing by other editors, working on a copy of a section usually isn't a good approach. When you plop down your new version of that section, you overwrite anything that happened since you made your copy. So restrict this approach to articles that are relatively orphaned, where you're not competing with other editors who are constantly changing information.

- **Stay on topic**. The most readable articles contain no irrelevant or only loosely relevant information. While writing an article, you might find yourself digressing into a side subject. If you find yourself wandering off-topic, consider placing the additional information into a different article, where it fits more closely with the topic. If you provide a link to the other article, readers who are interested in the side topic have the option of digging into it, but readers who are not interested won't be distracted by it.

- **Don't use a huge percentage of material from a single source as content for an article**. For example, don't add more than five to 15 percent of the information in a single source (like a newspaper article) to a Wikipedia article. Don't have 90 percent of the information in a Wikipedia article come from a single book.

  If you find yourself struggling with this issue, reconsider how notable the subject is, and whether a really long article is appropriate. For some subjects, you can say everything important in less than 10 or 15 paragraphs. Or you may decide that you're going to have to dig deeper into the resources available to you—ask your local library to order for you some books not in its collection, or go online at the library to get to specialized collections.

- **Keep length and balance in mind**. If a section gets too long, split it into subsections. If it becomes clear from the sources you're using that a particular aspect of the article is notable in its own right (because you keep finding good content), spin that off as its own article (see "Don't Take Article Scope as a Given" on page 346), rather than bulking out a section or pruning it back severely to fit with the rest of the article.

- **If you're an expert, avoid temptations**. You know this stuff cold, so you don't really need sources, right? Wrong. Yes, it's tedious to look up things you learned 20 years ago, but things may have changed since then. In any case, remember that the goal of Wikipedia isn't to contain all human knowledge—it's to provide a starting point for readers, to get them interested enough in the topic that they'll consider reading the cited sources as well. They can't go get more information if you don't tell them where they can do so. And, as a bonus, if you cite your sources, other editors don't have to rely on your word that you're an expert.

A second temptation is to cite your published writings as a source. That's considered by many editors to be a violation of Wikipedia's conflict of interest guideline (see *WP:COI* for details). It puts you into the awkward position of having to judge whether your own work is a reliable source. (Is the publication peer-reviewed? Is that small publisher really anything other than a vanity press?)

If a section, when you're done with it, is clearly superior in terms of the amount of information and the number of sources cited, you're much less likely to run into opposition. Well-documented information is the nirvana of Wikipedia. It's also wonderful point-of-view-repellent when other editors have strong opinions about a subject.

Remove Cruft and Duplication

Once you've added a bunch of good stuff—content and sources—then you're in a much better position to remove content that doesn't add materially to the article. Some editors call such useless information *cruft*, and most readers hate it. Furthermore, per *WP:NPOV*, giving undue space to any particular aspect of a topic is a violation of the neutral point of view. It may be worth mentioning that someone has eight honorary degrees, but a list of them all is pure cruft.

- **Remove trivia**. Trivia, by definition, is not encyclopedic. Editors frequently remove trivia sections, sometimes pasting the content to the article talk page, and you should do the same. If a trivia sections happens to contain any important facts, you can work them into the rest of the article. Sometimes trivia sections masquerade under the names "Other facts", "Miscellaneous", and "In popular culture." For details, see the guideline *Wikipedia:Trivia sections* (shortcut *WP:TRIVIA*).

- **Remove unnecessary links in the "See also" section**. As mentioned on page 241, this section should "ideally not repeat links already present in the article". At minimum, you should make sure it has no links to articles that are only vaguely related to the topic, or articles that don't exist yet.

- **Remove unnecessary duplication among sections that list sources**. A "Further reading" section, if there is one, shouldn't contain any sources used as citations—those are already in the "References" section. Nor should it include anything also in the "External links" section, or the body of the article (for example, books written by the article's subject).

  There should be minimal duplication between the "External links" section and the "References" section. In general, if something is cited as a source, it shouldn't also be listed in "External links". (The reader can figure out, if there's a blue link in a footnote with an icon indicating it's not a wikilink, that it's an external link.) The exception to the "no duplication" rule is Web sites identified with the subject of the article—an organization's Web site, a politician's campaign Web site, a celebrity's official publicity page, and so on. Readers expect to find these things at the top of the "External links" section, so they don't have to search through footnotes for them. Other than that, however, duplication is not only pointless, but gives undue weight to links listed twice over those only listed once.

- **Remove linkspam, if you've not already done so**. The "External links" section should be limited to official Web sites and similar closely related links, along with links to sources that could have been used for footnotes but weren't (due to lack of time, for example). For details, see page 241 and the guideline *Wikipedia:Spam* (shortcut: *WP:SPAM*), and the guideline *Wikipedia:External links* (*WP:EL*).

Get the Wording Right

Wikipedia has a very large number of rules about wording, including spelling. Here's the quick summary:

- **All the standard rules about good writing apply**. If you didn't do well in English classes, don't worry, since other editors will edit (and, generally, improve) what you write. You can consider working on parts of Wikipedia that put less emphasis on writing skills. Good writing—smoothly flowing, interesting, and informative— is one of Wikipedia's goals, so it's always appreciated. So is good copyediting (see *WP:COPYEDIT*).

- **Wikipedia is an encyclopedia, not a soapbox**. Opinions—even yours—come from knowing the facts, so the best thing you can do is let readers see those facts, and decide for themselves. If making a particular statement is really important to you, find an acceptable source that says it (that's a fact), rather than saying it yourself (that's a point of view). *Neutral point of view WP:NPOV* is a core content policy because Wikipedia is impossible without it. Content decisions can only be resolved by looking at documented facts, not by evaluating the rightness and wrongness of an editor's point of view.

- **Avoid words that subtly push a point of view**. Wikipedia frowns upon using certain words to slant an article towards a particular point of view. If you're unfamiliar with them, read the guidelines on *peacock terms*, words like "immensely" and "legendary" (*WP:PEA*); *weasel words*, phrases like "some people say" and "many would argue that" (*WP:AWW*); *words to avoid*, such as the verb "reveal" and the adjective "so-called" (*WP:WTA*); and *rhetoric*, wording intended to be persuasive rather than factual (*WP:RHT*).

- **Avoid jargon and other reader-unfriendly terms**. As an encyclopedia, Wikipedia has a bias against words that are reader-unfriendly: jargon (*WP:MOSDEF*), neologisms (*WP:NEO*), statements that will soon sound dated (*WP:DATED*), and references in articles that assume the article is being read at Wikipedia, online (*WP:SELF*).

- **Don't trust your spell checker implicitly**. Words aren't always spelled the same in all English-speaking countries. (See the box on page 23 for details.)

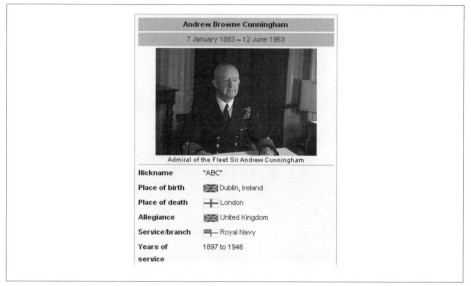

Figure 18-1. Here's the top of the infobox for the Andrew Browne Cunningham *article, which was the Featured Article on the* Main Page *on November 28, 2007. The* Infobox Military Person *template created this infobox and others like it. Infoboxes normally appear in the upper-right corner of an article. The right-alignment is built into the template, so you don't need to specify it.*

Make the Article Look Appealing

Looks count. They don't count nearly as much as good text, but readers do notice when an article looks boring or has odd formatting. Here are some suggestions for making an article look better, keeping in mind that looks are no more important than the content issues discussed in the rest of this chapter.

- **Get the lead section right—it's what people read first**. Sometimes it's the only thing people read, if they're just looking to find out what a word or phrase refers to. Lead sections are discussed in detail in Chapter 13 (page 234).

- **Add an image**. Chapter 15 is all about adding images to articles. If you can't find an image yourself, submit a request (see page 284) for someone else to help out.

- **Add an infobox**. These template-based boxes, normally found in the upper-right of an article, summarize information for the reader to see at a glance (Figure 18-1 is an example). The guideline *Wikipedia:Manual of Style (infoboxes)* (shortcut: *WP:IBX*) has details. You almost always see infoboxes in articles about celebrities, important politicians, animals and plants, and countries.

- **Make sure headings conform to Wikipedia standards**. For example, headings should not contain wikilinks or footnotes. Headings are discussed in detail in Chapter 13 (page 242).

- **Tweak the table of contents**. Avoid a lengthy table of contents, and long headings. If there isn't an image or infobox on the right, use a floating TOC (page 249) on the left.

Getting Help: Article Reviews

When you've spent time improving an article, and aren't sure what to focus on next, one option is to submit the article for review by other editors. Chapter 12 has an entire section, "Reviewing Articles and Images" (page 219), which lists places at Wikipedia where you can do so. Read the instructions to see what articles are appropriate for submission. Don't start, for example, by asking for it to be considered for a Featured Article designation. And don't submit an article to more than one place simultaneously, which causes more work for other editors. Fix the problems identified by one set of reviewers before you ask others to look at it.

If you're comfortable with JavaScript (see Chapter 21), then you have another option —an automated review of an article you've worked on. The page *User:AndyZ/peerreviewer* provides the details of how to install the user script that generates such a review.

CHAPTER 19

Deleting Existing Articles

One of Wikipedia's strengths is how easily editors create new Wikipedia articles—quick, efficient, no bureaucracy to get permission from. But some editors abuse the privilege, creating nonsense articles, attack articles, or promotional articles, for instance. Others just make mistakes because they don't understand Wikipedia's rules and purpose: They create an article about a non-notable topic, or a subject already covered by an article of a different name, or containing a definition—not an encyclopedic topic, for example.

In order to keep Wikipedia the useful encyclopedia that it is, articles with all these problems need to be removed. For Wikipedia, the challenge is to have processes that delete inappropriate articles (more than a thousand a day) while keeping potentially good articles and avoiding offending well-intentioned editors. In this chapter, you'll learn the different ways to deal with problem articles, often without resorting to one of the three deletion processes. You'll also learn what recourse you and other editors have if you feel that an article was deleted inappropriately.

Responding to Problem Articles

You can stumble across a problem article in a number of ways—doing a search, reviewing the User Contributions page of an editor, or just clicking "Random article" to see what you see. When your first reaction is, "You're kidding!" or "I can't believe this is a Wikipedia article," your second reaction should be to analyze the article, systematically. There may be grounds for a quick deletion, or you may have to do some further research.

First Analysis

Here's a systematic approach to dealing with an article that you think may not belong in Wikipedia. Ask yourself the following questions in order:

- **Is this vandalism?** What you see may be the result of someone deliberately damaging a perfectly good article. You should look at the article history (as discussed in detail in Chapter 5) to see what the article looked like in previous versions.

  Obviously, any major decrease in the size of the article is grounds for suspicion. If the article was created recently, check the similarity of the first version to the current one. If it's been around for a while, then check the versions from 3 and 6 months ago. If you do find vandalism, revert the article to its last good version.

- **Is this article worth trying to salvage?** Some articles are just junk, not worth the time it would take to fix them. Wikipedia has a *Criteria for Speedy Deletion* policy (shortcut: *WP:CSD*). The candidates for immediate deletion include patent nonsense and gibberish; test pages ("Can I really create an article?"); attack pages, including entirely negative, entirely unsourced biographical articles (don't attempt to salvage these); no evidence that the subject is notable enough to belong in an encyclopedia; and no content (only links or chat-like comments about the subject). If the article is any of these things, then nominate it for speedy deletion, as discussed on page 363.

NOTE

If the problem is no content, the easiest course of action may be simply to change the page to a redirect, assuming you can figure out a relevant article to redirect to. See page 303 for more detail on redirects.

- **Does the article look like** *blatant advertising*, **or does it appear to be copied and pasted from a Web site (***blatant copyright violation***)?** These criteria both call for speedy deletion, though for the second you'll need to find the source of the text before nominating the article for speedy deletion. But also ask yourself: Is there something salvageable here, something worth an article? If you think there might be, read the next section.

Notability and Verifiability

At Wikipedia, notability (page 64) is an important criterion for creating a new article. Since Wikipedia contains no original research, notability is determined by coverage of the topic in upstanding, independent sources, like books, newspapers, and sometimes Web sites. (For full details, check out the guideline *Wikipedia:Notability*; shortcut: *WP:N*.)

At its heart, deleting an article—other than by speedy deletion—is the Wikipedia community's way of saying that reliable sources of information simply don't exist out there in the world to make the article lengthy enough to stand on its own. Of course, it's impossible for you, or other editors, individually or collectively, to know if that's really true. You simply have to make your best guess, because it's impossible to prove something's non-existence.

The challenge of notability and acceptable sources

Consider, for example, an article about a high school teacher, describing her classroom manner, the names of her pets, and how much her students like her. Is that ever going to be acceptable as an article? Is it likely that a number of newspaper articles have been solely about this teacher? While it's possible (if, say, the article's about the National Teacher of the Year), it's also unlikely. If a quick search turns up nothing, then the article should be tossed.

Compare, by contrast, an article about a 19th century Portuguese poet. If the article makes no claims about notability (says nothing about "famous", or "well-known", then it's a candidate for speedy deletion. But you're probably not an expert on 19th century poets, of any nationality, so for you it's probably a sheer guess as to whether you're looking at a vanity—someone's great-great-great-grandfather—or someone once famous who's faded into obscurity, but whose life and accomplishments are well-documented in books published more than a hundred years ago.

Possible responses

You have three options when faced with a problematical article that you decide you don't want to nominate for a speedy deletion until you evaluate notability:

- If you're inclined toward non-notability, do a quick search or two to see if you're mistaken. Spend, say, 3 minutes on the matter, and then take a look at the alternatives to deletion in the next section.

- If you're inclined toward notability, but don't have time (or inclination) to spend much time fixing the article, still do a quick search or two (again, just a couple of minutes), add anything you find to the article (as an external link), and then add a cleanup message box to the article if it's lacking one. (You'll find nicely organized ones at the page *Wikipedia:Template messages*, shortcut *WP:TM*.)

- Finally, and best of all, if you have the time, you can fix the article. If the topic is notable but the article is missing sources, put in some citations (page 31). Chapter 18 also discusses a general approach for improving articles, though it's tailored more for long articles than for stubby ones without any sources.

Copyright Violations

The hardest articles to fix are massive copyright violations, when you believe there's an article in there somewhere, one that Wikipedia doesn't have. You need to trim these to the bone—keep in only the verifiable facts. When the text is lengthy, you need to remove most of it, because minor rewording isn't going to cure the problem.

If you trim the article to the most important facts (facts can't be copyrighted), then the legal liability issue goes away. (Yes, older versions of the page are still available, but search engines ignore them, as do sites that take large amounts of Wikipedia and reuse

---

it.) Also, you can draw on the text in the older version as you look for acceptable sources, without keeping it in the current version.

If you're not going to fix the article, you need to delete the information that's a copyright violation, and put a template on the top of the page about the problem. (See the "Instructions" section of the page *Wikipedia:Copyright problems*, shortcut *WP:CP*.) If you can't find a salvageable article—the topic is non-notable—then recommend the article for speedy deletion to get rid of the article immediately (page 363). (Using both may seem like overkill, but copyright violations are dangerous to Wikipedia, and need to be dealt with promptly.)

Alternatives to Deletion

If you find a problem with an article, consider some alternatives that might make the author of the article feel better, while protecting the quality of Wikipedia. These alternatives also have the advantage of not requiring an administrator's help:

- If there's nothing on the page worth keeping, try to identify a related page that's useful to readers, and create a redirect (page 303). Redirects work particularly well when the editor who created the page has lost interest and stopped editing, and that would be the only person objecting.

- Move the page to a new subpage in the user space of the editor who created it. This approach (called *userification*) is particularly good for articles where it's unclear that notability can ever be established. It challenges the editor to find sources, or let the page languish. Make sure that you put a note on the user talk page about what you've done, with a link to the new subpage, and offer to help explain policies and guidelines further if the editor would like. (For further information, see *Wikipedia:Userfication*, shortcut *WP:UFY*.)

> **NOTE**
> Userificiation is excellent for a page that's well-meant but has little hope of ever becoming a valid article. After you move the page to userspace, your note should also mention that there are other places where the writing might really belong (WikiInfo.org (*http://WikiInfo.org*) and *WP:TRY* are particularly good things to include). Also ask that the editor delete the contents of the moved page within a week or so, because Wikipedia isn't a hosting service.

- Where there's a bit of useful information, but only a smidgen, and you have doubts that the article can be easily expanded (or ever expanded into a real article), *merge* the information into another article on a broader topic, and put a redirect in place. In the best of worlds, you can create a new section in the article on the broader topic, and link to that. In any case, try to link to a section of the article, to encourage the editor to expand that.

Here too, leave a note on the user talk page for the author of the article, saying that you've merged the information from that article into another article, and that you hope the editor can expand what's in that larger topic.

- You can also copy the information to a sister project such as Wiktionary (most commonly), or at least put a template on it suggesting that it be copied, and hope that someone else will do so. Once the information is copied across, the page can be made into a redirect, or deleted.

Obviously, this final option is limited to things that really do belong elsewhere, such as a dictionary definition, and only when such an entry doesn't exist at all in the other wiki. (If it does exist, then copying the article in its entirety isn't really an option.) But if you can move the material, it may make the editors feel that's he's contributed to something, even if not Wikipedia. (For more information, see the Meta page *Help:Transwiki* and the guideline *Wikipedia:Wikimedia sister projects*; shortcut: *WP:SIS*.)

Three Ways to Delete an Article

Only administrators can delete articles outright. Your job is to ask for deletion using one of three methods:

- **Speedy**. If the article meets any of the criteria in the Criteria for Speedy Deletion policy, then go for it.
- **Proposed deletion**. If the article doesn't quite qualify for a speedy deletion, then use the *Proposed Deletion* template, which starts a 5-day countdown.
- **Articles for Deletion (AfD)**. If you're in doubt, start a discussion at the Articles for Deletion page about whether or not the article is worth keeping.

Each of the three methods follows a different procedure, discussed next.

NOTE

An article should have only one type of deletion being considered at any time: CSD, proposed deletion (prod), or AfD. If you see an AfD messagebox on an article, you should remove any CSD or prod templates on the same article; if you see a prod messagebox, you should remove any CSD template.

Speedy Deletion

Speedy deletions are based on specific criteria, listed in the policy *Wikipedia:Criteria for speedy deletion* (shortcut: *WP:CSD*). (See Figure 19-2.)

If you want to propose a speedy deletion for an article, you need to cite a specific criteria found on this page, either from the "G" (general) series (which applies to all types of

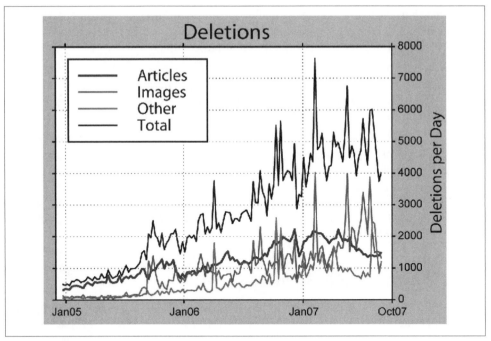

Figure 19-1. During 2006 and 2007, about half the articles that were created were subsequently deleted; an unknown number were also essentially deleted by being made into redirects. Between late 2006 and mid-2007, article deletions averaged about 2,000 per day. Since then, the trend has been downward, with the average in late 2007 being about 1,500 articles per day deleted. [This graph is from editor Dragons Flight (Robert A. Rohde), based on a log analysis he did in late 2007.]

pages, not just articles), or the "A" (article) series. For example, criteria G2 applies to test page (pages created by a new editor, just exploring possibilities).

You use the criteria to determine the template to post on the article; once you've done that, an admin shows up fairly quickly, reviews your nomination for deletion, and decides whether to remove the template (as an error) or accept it and delete the article. If you've made a particularly egregious error in placing the template on the page, you'll also probably get a note to that effect from the admin.

Initial review

Take, for example, an article called *Timberwilde Elementary School*. The first step in any speedy deletion is to figure out whether the article in fact meets any specific CSD criteria. The entire article under consideration in this example reads, "Timberwilde Elementary School, Built In 1980, Is A School In The Texas District Northside Independent School District." That's better than the original posting, which read, in its entirety, "Timberwilde Elementary School Is The School Of Awesomeness! It Has A Graet Varitey Of Students Teachers And Staff! Visit Us At NISD.NET/TIMBERWILDE Click On Campus Webpage."

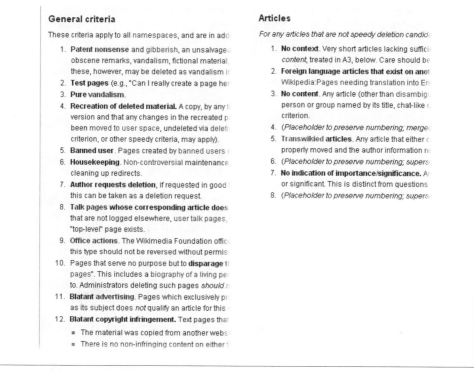

General criteria

These criteria apply to all namespaces, and are in add[...]

1. **Patent nonsense** and gibberish, an unsalvage[...] obscene remarks, vandalism, fictional material[...] these, however, may be deleted as vandalism i[...]
2. **Test pages** (e.g., "Can I really create a page he[...]
3. **Pure vandalism.**
4. **Recreation of deleted material.** A copy, by any [...] version and that any changes in the recreated p[...] been moved to user space, undeleted via delet[...] criterion, or other speedy criteria, may apply).
5. **Banned user.** Pages created by banned users [...]
6. **Housekeeping.** Non-controversial maintenance [...] cleaning up redirects.
7. **Author requests deletion,** if requested in good [...] this can be taken as a deletion request.
8. **Talk pages whose corresponding article does** [...] that are not logged elsewhere, user talk pages, "top-level" page exists.
9. **Office actions.** The Wikimedia Foundation offic[...] this type should not be reversed without permis[...]
10. Pages that serve no purpose but to **disparage** t[...] pages". This includes a biography of a living pe[...] to. Administrators deleting such pages *should* [...]
11. **Blatant advertising.** Pages which exclusively p[...] as its subject does *not* qualify an article for this [...]
12. **Blatant copyright infringement.** Text pages tha[...]
    - The material was copied from another webs[...]
    - There is no non-infringing content on either [...]

Articles

For any articles that are not speedy deletion candid[...]

1. **No context.** Very short articles lacking suffici[...] *content,* treated in A3, below. Care should be [...]
2. **Foreign language articles that exist on** ano[...] Wikipedia:Pages needing translation into En[...]
3. **No content.** Any article (other than disambig[...] person or group named by its title, chat-like c[...] criterion.
4. *(Placeholder to preserve numbering; merge[...]*
5. **Transwikied articles.** Any article that either c[...] properly moved and the author information r[...]
6. *(Placeholder to preserve numbering; supers[...]*
7. **No indication of importance/significance.** A[...] or significant. This is distinct from questions [...]
8. *(Placeholder to preserve numbering; supers[...]*

Figure 19-2. You can nominate an article for speedy deletion using criteria from either the general ("G") list or the article ("A") list. There are also separate lists, not shown, for redirects, images, media, categories, user pages, templates, and portals.

This article looks like it fits CSD number A7, "No indication of importance/significance." But before you pull the trigger, you should check five other things:

- **The article talk page.** In this case, it has a template for *WikiProject Texas*, and the history of the page shows no postings relating to the contents of the article. So, there's no indication of importance/significance. (The article being marked as within the scope of a WikiProject proves absolutely nothing about notability—in this case, it's because the article included the word "Texas.")

- **The article history page.** In this case, there were basically two editors—one who created the article (and never came back to expand it) and one who did a tiny bit of cleanup. That's further evidence of non-notability. If the school were notable, a bunch of editors would have contributed at least a little bit each (assuming an article isn't brand-new).

- **The *What links here* special page.** Click the link in the left margin to see it. In this case, no other articles link to this article.

- **The *User contributions* page for the editor who created the article**. In this case, it shows only two edits, both on the same day (more than a month ago). The second edit was of a regular article. So there really isn't any reason to assume that the author of the article understands Wikipedia rules.
- **A Google or Yahoo or other search of the topic**. In this case it shows nothing significant.

So, from the review, it seems fair to say that this article looks like an A7.

NOTE

At this point, stop and consider if the solution to this problem article is to create a *redirect*, as discussed in "Alternatives to Deletion" on page 362. Redirects are quicker, and don't require an administrator. In this case, you'd redirect to the school district in which the elementary school is located. In this case, though, you can make a good argument for deleting the page altogether. That way, if the author creates it again, it shows up in the new page log, and gets more review than if an editor simply changes the redirect back to an article.

Making the nomination

Once you've completed your initial review and found a criterion for deletion that fits, you can turn to the second step: actually nominating the article for deletion. Here's the process:

1. Further down the CSD page, in the "Deletion templates" section, look for the templates that match the specific criteria you've found.

   In this case, the choices are *{{db-bio}}*, *{{db-band}}*, *{{db-club}}*, *{{db-corp}}*, *{{db-group}}*, and *{{db-web}}*. All rather specific, and none quite on point. The topic here is an organization. That's OK under criteria A7, but there isn't a specific template for it.

2. When the specific templates for a criterion don't fit the situation exactly, use a general criterion.

   You'll find them at the top of the "Deletion templates" section, as shown in Figure 19-3. In this case, a good template is *{{db|reason}}*.

3. Edit the article page, adding the template at the top of the edit box.

   Paste it all the way at the very beginning of the wikitext, as shown in Figure 19-4.

4. Add an edit summary, being sure to mention both "speedy delete" and the specific CSD (in this case, "A7"). Preview the page, and then save it.

   You see your request for deletion in a message box at the top of the article, as in Figure 19-5.

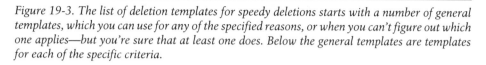

- **Reasons derived from essays**, such as WP:DENY, WP:LC, or the like.

Deletion templates   [edit]

In order to alert administrators that a page meets one of the criteria for speedy deletion, place one of the following relevant templates at the top of the page. Please be sure to supply an edit summary that mentions that the article is being nominated for speedy deletion.

What to type	Criteria	Used for
The following templates add pages to Category:Candidates for speedy deletion:		
{{db-reason|*reason*}} {{db|*reason*}} {{deletebecause|*reason*}} {{delbecause|*reason*}} {{delete|*reason*}} {{d|*reason*}}		Replace *reason* with a specific reason for speedy deletion. **Please try to write out a reason that will be comprehensible to non-Wikipedians.**
Or, you can use a specific reason template:		
{{db-nonsense}}	CSD G1	Patent nonsense. You can put {{subst:Nonsensepages|*page name*}} ~~~~ on the user's talk page.
{{db-test}}	CSD G2	Test page. You can put {{subst:uw-creation1|*page name*}} on the user's talk page.
{{db-vandalism}}	CSD G3	Vandalism. You can put {{subst:uw-creation2|*page name*}} on the user's talk page.

Figure 19-3. The list of deletion templates for speedy deletions starts with a number of general templates, which you can use for any of the specified reasons, or when you can't figure out which one applies—but you're sure that at least one does. Below the general templates are templates for each of the specific criteria.

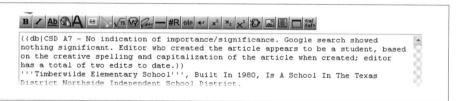

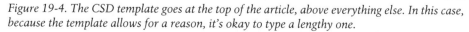

```
{{db|CSD A7 - No indication of importance/significance. Google search showed
nothing significant. Editor who created the article appears to be a student, based
on the creative spelling and capitalization of the article when created; editor
has a total of two edits to date.}}
'''Timberwilde Elementary School''', Built In 1980, Is A School In The Texas
District Northside Independent School District.
```

Figure 19-4. The CSD template goes at the top of the article, above everything else. In this case, because the template allows for a reason, it's okay to type a lengthy one.

5. Post a notice on the user talk page of the editor who created the article.

   Doing so isn't just being nice (although it is nice). It also creates a record of the fact that this editor created this article. If the article does get deleted, the edit that created it will no longer be visible on the editor's *User contribution* page, so this user talk page posting will be the only notice to other editors, useful if the pattern persists.

Once you complete these steps, you're done for now. Check back in a day or so. What you do next depends on what's happened to the article.

- Most of the time the article's gone, deleted by an admin.

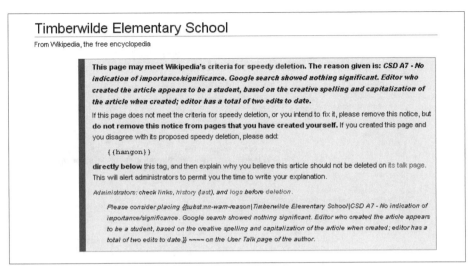

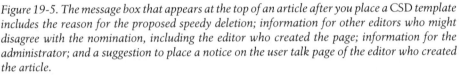

Figure 19-5. The message box that appears at the top of an article after you place a CSD template includes the reason for the proposed speedy deletion; information for other editors who might disagree with the nomination, including the editor who created the page; information for the administrator; and a suggestion to place a notice on the user talk page of the editor who created the article.

- If the admin reviewing the action rejected the nomination, then you usually want to move to the next step—deletion via proposed deletion (nicknamed *prod*), as discussed in the next section.

  Maybe the reason for rejection is a persuasive argument against any type of deletion. If so, then it's time to move on to something else. But usually rejection is because the admin decided that the CSD criterion really didn't apply. That's fine —there's more than one way to get an article deleted.

- If the editor who created the article deleted the CSD template (which is against the rules, but it happens), put it back up. You can just revert to your version. Also, post a warning on that editor's talk page about violating the rules.

- If another editor (besides the one who created the article) deleted the CSD template, look at the stated reason. Hopefully there's one in the edit summary. Try to discuss the matter with that other editor, with the goal of arriving at consensus (you both agree whether the article should stay or go). Or try to get a commitment by the other editor to fix the article by a certain date, or let it get deleted.

  If you can't reach a consensus or find a way to fix the article, then go straight to the third type of deletion, an AfD (page 373).

Proposed Deletions

Proposed deletion (shortcut: *WP:PROD*) is a way to nominate an article for deletion, used when you think the deletion won't be controversial. If the deletion meets the more stringent criteria for speedy deletion (page 363), then use that. But often you can't; for example, when an article contains a bit of reasonable content, or indicates that the topic is notable.

Nominating an article as a proposed deletion starts a 5-day clock. If no other editor objects, then an administrator shows up after 5 days, reviews the nomination, and, if it looks okay, deletes the article.

When you can't use the proposed deletion process

As convenient as the proposed deletion process it, you can't use it on the article if any of the following are true:

- **The article has previously been proposed for deletion**. If one editor puts a *{{prod}}* template on an article and another editor removes it (and the removal isn't part of a vandalizing edit), then the proposed deletion is contested.

- **The article has previously been undeleted**. To be undeleted, an editor has to make a case that the article was deleted by mistake. That makes deleting it again at least somewhat controversial.

- **The article has been previously nominated for deletion using the AfD process**. Presumably, the editor wouldn't have gone to AfD unless deletion at that time was considered potentially controversial. So deletion may still be controversial.

You can check for these three situations by looking at the article history. Normally it's not very long; if it is, you should rethink the prod (consider an AfD instead).

If you can't do a proposed deletion because of one of these three circumstances, your choices are to drop the matter or use the AfD process (page 373) to nominate the article for deletion.

Initial review

Take as an example the article *SQL-I*. SQL-I, the article says, is a programming language, "a tool anyone with basic knowledge of SQL syntax can learn in one day." It "provides system administrators, advanced users and independent developers the option to write their own plug-ins." You could argue that this article's a candidate for speedy deletion, either as an A7 (no claim to notability) or a G11 (blatant advertising). But there's a bit of meat to the article (the total text is about three times what's quoted here), and a prod is just as efficient as a CSD (it just takes longer), so you decide to do a prod instead.

When you're considering a proposed deletion, first you appropriately research the article. Researching is critical because an incorrect prod is worse than an incorrect CSD.

Articles that meet the CSD usually don't contain much useful material, so if the deletion's in error, very little is lost. With a prod, there's normally more information in the article—more of a potential foundation for other editors—as in this case. So if it's deleted by mistake, more is lost.

Since SQL-I is a current software product, a Google or Yahoo search seems reasonable. In Google, searching for both the product name and the company that sells it, and restricting results to English, yields a total of seven results, none of which are of citable quality. Apparently, SQL-I is not notable.

NOTE

If you search the Internet and find something useful indicating notability, add that to the article, as an external link. Ideally, take a bit of time to expand the text in article as well, so that other editors don't spend time duplicating exactly what you just did. And of course drop the idea of proposing deletion.

Next, you want to look at the same four other things that you do for potential CSDs:

- **The article talk page**. In this case, it doesn't exist, so check it off the list.

  If there *is* a talk page, see if it has anything helpful, like some suggested sources. You also want to see if there's any indication that the article's been through the AfD process (page 373); if so, you can't do a proposed deletion. (You can still nominate the article via the AfD process *again* if you want.)

- **The article history page**. In the SQL-I case, one editor created the article, made six more edits on the same day (almost a year previously), and never came back. There are no other contributors. A bot tagged the article as uncategorized, and another editor added a category, but that doesn't count as people actually interested enough in the article to come across it on their own and expand it. So the history page has further evidence of non-notability. Also, there's no indication anyone's ever proposed deletion.

- **The *What links here* special page**. In this case, one other article links to this one. And, as you'll find out next, it turns out that other article was created by the same editor.

- **The *User contributions* page for the editor who created the article**. Reviewing this page is the most important step before doing a prod. If the editor turns out to be an active contributor to a variety of articles, then you want to ask that editor about the article, not nominate it for deletion.

  In this case, the editor created three articles—this one, one about another product of the same company (this product seems a bit more notable, though the article is similarly unsourced), and a third about a mountain resort (which seems the most notable article of all). There are no other contributions, and the last edit was more

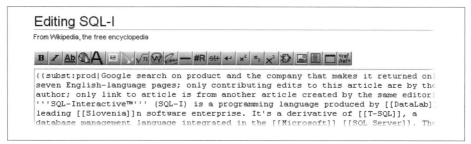

Figure 19-6. *Place the {{prod}} template at the top of the article, above everything else. It's important to explain what you did to come to the conclusion that an article isn't salvageable, for both the reviewing administrator (in 5 days) and other editors.*

than 10 months ago. So, there's no compelling reason to start a dialog before proposing a deletion—it's likely that no one's home.

Making the nomination

Once you've completed the initial review, move on to the second step: actually nominating the article for deletion. Here's the process:

1. Edit the article, placing the *{{subst:prod|reason}}* template at the top, and then change the word "reason" to explain your rationale.

   Place it at the very beginning of the wikitext, as shown in Figure 19-6.

NOTE

There's a WikiProject for editors who want to systematically check proposed deletions for possible mistakes, so there's a good chance that another editor will take a look at the article after you've saved your edit.

---

2. Add an edit summary, being sure to mention *proposed delete*.

   If you want to add some information on your reasoning, that might save an editor time going to the article to see if the "prod" is justified.

3. Preview the page, and then save it.

   You see a message box asking for deletion, like the one in Figure 19-7.

WARNING

The typical way to use the prod template is *{{subst:prod|Give your reason}}*. But if the text of your reason contains an equal sign (for example, in a URL), then the entire explanation won't show up when you preview or after you save. To fix the problem, you need to add the *concern=* parameter, so the template looks like this: *{{subst:prod| concern= Give your reason, which can include an equal sign}}*.

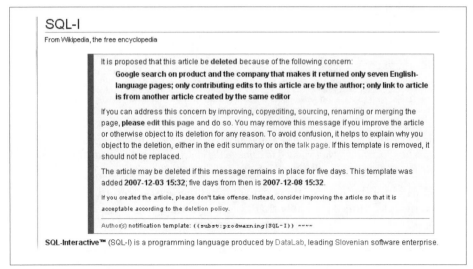

Figure 19-7. The article message box that appears at the top of an article after you place a prod template includes the reason for the proposed deletion; information for other editors who might disagree with the nomination, including the editor who created the page; the date and time the message was posted, and when the 5 days will be up; a comment for the editor who created the article; and a suggestion to place a notice on the user talk page of the article's creator and major contributors.

4. Post a notice on the user talk page of the editor who created the article, and anyone else who was a major contributor.

    The notification is more than a courtesy. Ideally those editors will come back and fix the article before it's deleted. On the other hand, if you're notifying more than two or three people, you're either over-notifying or you shouldn't have proposed the article for deletion in the first place.

After you're done, check back every day or two. What you do next depends on what other editors do:

*   If no one removes the prod template, then in 5 or so days an admin will probably delete the article.

*   If the admin reviewing the proposed deletion rejected it, then consider the next (and final) step—nominating the article for deletion via AfD, as discussed in the next section.

*   The reason for rejection might be a persuasive argument against any type of deletion. If so, then you're done here. But it's more likely that you missed one of the three reasons why prodding wasn't allowed (see page 369). Fortunately, you can still turn to the AfD process.

*   If another editor has removed the prod template, he should have explained why. But even if he didn't, you should still consider the deletion to be contested. If that

> **Wikipedia:Articles for deletion**
>
> From Wikipedia, the free encyclopedia
>   (Redirected from WP:AFD)
>
> Before listing an article for deletion here, consider whether a more efficient alternative is appropriate:
>
> - For problems that do not require deletion, including duplicate articles, articles needing improvement, pages needing redirects, or POV problems, be bold and fix the problem or tag the article appropriately.
> - If an article is a copyright violation, please list it at Wikipedia:Copyright problems.
> - Some articles may qualify for speedy deletion; please refer to the speedy deletion criteria and process.
> - For non-controversial deletions, please refer to the proposed deletion process.
> - For a potentially controversial merger, consider listing it at proposed mergers.

Figure 19-8. Don't bring articles to AfD if you can handle them another way. That's the clear message at the top of the page Wikipedia:Articles for deletion. *For example, first make sure you can't use the speedy deletion or proposed deletion processes, which make less work for administrators.*

editor or others get busy improving the article, then you need to reassess your intent to get the article deleted. If nothing has changed, however, turn to the AfD process. Don't repost the prod template after another editor removes it; removal alone is considered enough to make the deletion controversial.

NOTE

You have one reason to put the prod template back after removal—vandalism. But you can only assume vandalism if the editor who removed the template damaged other parts of the article. Otherwise, you should assume that even if the edit summary gives no reason, and even if the editor removing the prod template has no prior editing history, the removal was done in good faith, and your only recourse is to escalate to the AfD process.

Articles for Deletion (AfD)

When you nominate an article for deletion in the *AfD* process, you must have a good reason. You're asking other editors to spend their time reviewing the article and commenting on the reasons given for the nomination, so don't waste their time. The CSD and proposed deletion processes are preferable, but they don't apply to some articles. Before initiating AfD, explore alternatives to deletion (page 362). AfD is a last resort, when an article is unsalvageable and there are no alternatives. *Wikipedia:Articles for deletion (WP:AFD)* lists measures you should consider first, like improving the article or making it a redirect (Figure 19-8).

Justification for an AfD nomination

When you nominate an article for deletion using the AfD process, you get to a point in the process where you have to give a reason. Don't make the mistake of reaching that point only to realize that you don't actually have a good reason. Or worse, don't make the mistake of completing the AfD process and discovering, when discussion starts, that what you thought was an acceptable reason was not.

Reading two policies will keep you from making such mistakes:

- The section "Before nominating an AfD", at *WP:AFD*, is a quick, step-by-step summary of everything from alternatives (tagging for cleanup, doing a redirect, and so on) to guidelines you should know (*WP:BIO*, *WP:CORP*, and so on) to some suggestions on the technical aspects of an AfD nomination.

- The section "Reasons for deletion" at *Wikipedia:Deletion policy* (shortcut: *WP:DEL*) is a list of 15 reasons (some not pertaining to articles) that probably cover almost all successful AfDs.

You need just a couple of minutes to read each of these. Once you read them, you're well-prepared to do an AfD nomination if that is, in fact, appropriate. You may have to follow some links and do some more reading. If so, what you read will be useful in your normal editing work as well, so consider it an investment, not drudgery.

Nominating an article at AfD

The following steps walk you through the AfD process using the article *Salmon fishing with the Dry Fly* as an example. An editor had proposed the article for deletion (with a "prod" template, as discussed above). The editor who created the article removed that template, without any explanation.

This example assumes that you've already tried, unproductively, to discuss with the author the unacceptability of such a "how-to" article. You also did a redirect to the article *Fly fishing*, but it was reverted, leaving no choice but AfD.

1. Review the "Reasons for deletion" section of *Wikipedia:Deletion policy* (shortcut: *WP:DEL*) and prepare your argument as to why the article should be reviewed.

   If you can't point to one of the reasons here in that policy, like "All attempts to find reliable sources in which article information can be verified have failed", it's more than likely that the nomination won't result in a "delete" decision.

TIP

If you're basing your argument on the lack of reliable sources, make sure that you've done some research to confirm that there are no such sources. The purpose of AfD isn't to goad other editors into finding sources, it's to weed out problem articles. Or, to put it differently, AfD is a way of trying to find consensus. If you're not willing to do some research yourself, don't do an AfD.

Salmon fishing with the Dry Fly

From Wikipedia, the free encyclopedia

This article is being considered for deletion in accordance with Wikipedia's deletion policy.
Please share your thoughts on the matter at this article's entry on the Articles for deletion page.
Feel free to edit the article, but the article must not be blanked, and this notice must not be
removed, until the discussion is closed. For more information, particularly on merging or moving
the article during the discussion, read the guide to deletion.

Steps to list an article for deletion: 1. {{subst:afd}} 2. Preloaded debate OR {{subst:afd2|pg=Salmon fishing with the Dry Fly|
cat=text=}} ~~~~ (categories) 3. {{subst:afd3|pg=Salmon fishing with the Dry Fly}} (add to top of list) 4. Please consider
notifying the author(s) by placing {{subst:adw|Salmon fishing with the Dry Fly}} ~~~~ on their talk page(s).

Unregistered users placing this tag on an article cannot complete the deletion nomination and should leave detailed reasons
for deletion on Talk:Salmon fishing with the Dry Fly. If the nomination is not completed and no message is left on the
talkpage, this tag may be removed.

Normally one-handed rod[[1] 🔗] is used; the class [[2] 🔗] ranging from 6-8 would be the best. The tip could range from
25 mm; it all depends on the size of the Salmon[[3] 🔗] in the river. Normally a tip of 25 mm is a good start — with this, y

Figure 19-9. After you've put the {{subst:afd1}} template at the top of the article, you see a large message box. The link to the discussion page is red, because you have yet to create it. The notice contains a link for the next step, in small print: "Preloaded debate".

2. Open the article for editing. Add the template *{{subst:afd1}}* at the top of the text in the edit box, and add the recommended text to your edit summary, changing "PageName" to the article's actual name.

   Preview the page; if you see an article message box that starts, "This article is being considered for deletion ...", as shown in Figure 19-9, then save the edit. (Otherwise, fix the template.)

3. In the AfD message box at the top of the article, click the "Preloaded debate" link (it's in small print, in the second grouping of text).

   That link takes you to a page with a five-step set of instructions (Figure 19-10). These five steps take you through the process of creating a discussion page for this specific AfD, and adding that page to the daily log of AfDs so that other editors can find the page. Each is discussed below.

4. Do the first two steps—select the article's category, and add a reason to the standard template.

   The edit box for the page should look like Figure 19-11.

TIP

Don't be casual about picking the category—a lot of editors use AfD categories to decide what AfD discussions to participate in. That's because the daily volume is so high (well over 100 per day or so) that many editors want to be selective, focusing on what interests them.

---

5. Copy (Ctrl-C or ⌘-C) the text listed in step 3 of the instructions (in this case, *{{subst:afd3|pg=Salmon fishing with the Dry Fly}}*). Then open a new tab or window for the link "today's AfD log", which is also in step 3 of the instructions.

Editing Wikipedia:Articles for deletion/Salmon fishing with the Dry Fly

From Wikipedia, the free encyclopedia

Remaining steps to list Salmon fishing with the Dry Fly for deletion:

1. Replace "*cat=U*" in the box below with an appropriate category for the article being deleted:

cat=M Media and music

cat=O Organisation, corporation, or product

cat=B Biographical

cat=S Society topics

cat=W Web or internet

cat=G Games or sports

cat=T Science and technology

cat=F Fiction and the arts

Figure 19-10. The instructions on this page, five steps in all (only part of the first step is shown) get you through the rest of the AfD nomination process.

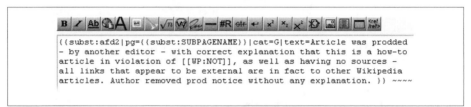

```
{{subst:afd2|pg={{subst:SUBPAGENAME}}}|cat=G|text=Article was prodded
- by another editor - with correct explanation that this is a how-to
article in violation of [[WP:NOT]], as well as having no sources -
all links that appear to be external are in fact to other Wikipedia
articles. Author removed prod notice without any explanation. }} ~~~~
```

Figure 19-11. The text you add as a reason, in the {{subst:afd1}} template, shows up as a sort of "opening statement for the prosecution" on the AfD discussion page. So things like logic and spelling do count.

You arrive at the log page for the current date, in edit mode. In the edit box, scroll down until you see the place where you want to paste this text (see Figure 19-12).

6. Flip back to the window where you were editing the discussion page, as shown in Figure 19-11 (this is the page with the five steps on it). Copy the text in step 4 to the clipboard. Now flip back to the log page (Figure 19-12), paste this text into the edit summary, and then save the page.

   Don't bother with a preview, or with looking at the log page after you've saved your edit—until you finish creating the discussion page, the log page doesn't show the discussion page correctly. Next, you'll finish the discussion page.

7. Tab to the edit summary box. The box should already be filled in. If not, paste (again) the text from step 4 into that edit summary box. Turn on the "Watch this page" checkbox, if you use your watchlist regularly, since you'll want to watch the discussion. Do a preview, and then save the page.

   What you see should be similar to Figure 19-13. You're almost done.

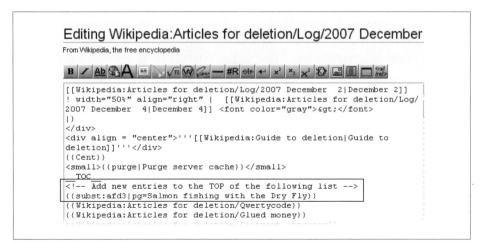

Figure 19-12. In the edit box of the deletion log page, scroll down to where you want to add an entry for your deletion, and then paste it. Your entry in the edit box looks different from the others, but it won't after you save the edit.

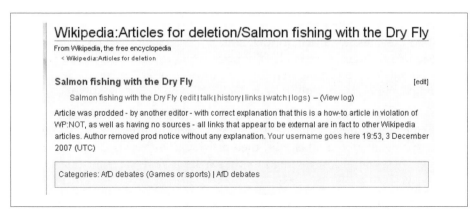

Figure 19-13. Other editors will comment on this discussion page as to whether they agree or disagree with deleting the nominated article. It includes your reason, your signature, and the category you chose for the article.

8. Go back to the log page and check that it shows your discussion page (it should be at the top). If it does, close it.

   If there's a problem on the log page, then fix it. Looking at the wikitext, figure out what's different about your listing, and change that.

   The final step is to notify the editor who created the article that it's being considered for deletion.

9. Go to the discussion page, and then click the link to the article. Copy the small print at the very bottom of the message box (in this case, *{{subst:adw|Salmon fishing with the Dry Fly}}* ~~~~ and paste it to a new section on that editor's user talk page. Leave the "Subject/headline" box blank—the template will take care of that.

You're done—except for the actual discussion, of course.

NOTE

If you found these complicated, you're not alone. Perhaps at some point Wikipedia will have a bot to take care of the entry of an AfD in the daily log, and the notification to the article creator. Until then, you need to do it yourself when you nominate an article for deletion via the AfD process.

Participating in AfD discussions

An AfD discussion normally runs for 5 days, though it can be closed earlier if the discussion is clearly, massively one-sided. (The page *Wikipedia:Snowball clause*, shortcut: *WP:SNOW*, explains the concept of not letting a process continue when continuing makes no sense. The guideline *Wikipedia:Speedy keep*, shortcut *WP:SK*, explains when and how to close an AfD as a "keep" before the full five days are up.)

If you've nominated an article for deletion, be judicious in adding comments to the discussion. You should have made your point when you gave the reason for the nomination. If you keep repeating that, or variants of it, or argumentatively question the reasoning of editors who want to keep the article, you'll lose credibility.

As nominator, think of your role as a facilitator. You've created the agenda, now let the Wikipedia community decide. If you have additional information to offer in response to a posting of another edit, then provide it. Otherwise, let the conversation flow. It's not a win or lose competition; it's a discussion about making Wikipedia a better encyclopedia.

If you want to participate in AfD discussions you didn't start, here are some suggestions:

- Start by participating in discussion about topics that you know. Use the "Categorized discussions" section at *WP:AFD* to narrow the range of articles on which you focus. As you get more familiar with AfDs, you can contribute to discussions about topics you know less about, because you'll know more about relevant policies and guidelines.

- Read the essay *Wikipedia:Arguments to avoid in deletion discussion* (shortcut: *WP:AADD)*, which is a collection of unpersuasive arguments that experienced AfDers have heard over and over: "Delete as unencyclopedic", "Keep—it's clearly notable", "Delete because *WP:RELEVANT* is only a guideline"; "Keep because I like it", and so on.

- The best way to win the argument for keeping an article is to improve it with good citations, and text from good sources, while the discussion's going on. If you can fix the problems that lead to the deletion nomination, even the editor proposing the deletion should be happy to see the article kept.

Deletionism versus Inclusionism

Some Wikipedians think the best way to handle unsourced or poorly sourced articles is to delete them on sight. Ideally, there should be rigorous standards for new articles, to raise the average quality of Wikipedia articles. Conversely, some Wikipedians think Wikipedia ought to have an article on almost any topic, and that a start to an article, no matter how poor, is better than nothing.

Those are extreme positions—almost caricatures. In fact, there's broad agreement in Wikipedia about whether to delete or keep most articles. Most debates are mostly about inherent notability (should all high schools automatically have an article?) rather than about standards that apply to all articles. Still, editors differ, and occasionally name calling erupts—"Inclusionist!" "Deletionist!" Avoid getting caught up in unproductive bickering.

Some editors do care a lot about what they see as excess deletions. If you're interested, take a look at *Wikipedia:Article Rescue Squadron* (shortcut: *WP:ARS*); "Only articles about non-encyclopedic topics should be deleted, not articles that need improvement" and *Wikipedia:WikiProject proposed deletion patrolling* (shortcut: *WP:WPPDP*); "responsible patrolling of proposed deletion on Wikipedia".

After an Article is Deleted

Someday, an article you created or worked on may be deleted, and you won't know or won't agree with the reason for the deletion. If so, remember that very little is actually deleted in Wikipedia—it's still visible to admins, just not to regular readers. And Wikipedia's processes are not infallible, so you have some options.

First, read *Wikipedia:Why was my page deleted?* (shortcut: *WP:WWMPD*). Among other things, this page explains how to find out why an article was deleted. If an article was deleted as a result of a proposed deletion, any administrator will usually restore it upon reasonable request. Follow the link at *WP:WWMPD* to post such a request.

A second option is to try to persuade the admin who made the deletion that it was in error. This option is worth trying only for CSD deletions, since prods can be reversed on request, and AfDs won't be reversed just because you ask nicely. Before you make such a request, do your homework—does the CSD deletion really seem unreasonable? Don't, for example, argue that the deletion was wrong because the article could have been fixed. CSDs are based on what was actually in the article, not the article's potential.

Another option is simply to start over. If the article was short, you've really not lost much if it was deleted. (You might even find a copy at Google—click the Cached link rather than the main link.) Just be sure that you start the article in your own user space, and don't move it to mainspace (where all regular articles are) until you're sure it can survive on its own. CSD criteria G4 allows the speedy deletion of a "substantially identical" copy of any article deleted via AfD, particularly where the problems identified in the AfD discussion have not been addressed.

Sometimes you might acknowledge that the deletion was probably right, given the shape the article was in, but you think you could fix it. If so, it would help to have a copy of what was deleted. Check the page *Category:Wikipedia administrators who will provide copies of deleted articles*, and make your case to one of the admins (check his User contributions page first, to make sure he's still active). Ask that a copy of the article be put into your user space, as a subpage. If the article wasn't libelous, a massive copyright infringement, or an attack page, you're likely to succeed.

Finally, you can initiate a deletion review process, at the page *Wikipedia:Deletion review* (shortcut: *WP:DRV*). This page is for appeals to restore deleted pages (and also for appeals to delete pages which were closed as "keep'" in an AfD discussion). Before you do so, read the section, "What is this page for?", which explains that DRV is for cases where you believe the process was wrong, or where "significant new information has come to light." DRV is not a place to say that you didn't like the outcome, or a place to go in the hopes that a new discussion can occur that'll lead to a different result.

NOTE

As of September 2007, 1.2 million articles and redirects had been deleted. Of these, the most frequently deleted articles were *The weather in London* (70 times), *Userboxes* (43 times), and *Brian Peppers* (34 times). (For the longer list, see the page *User:Emijrp/Statistics*.) Administrators can now protect pages from being re-created; this is called "salting the earth." If you're interested, you can check out the technical details at *WP:SALT*.

PART V

Customizing Wikipedia

CHAPTER 20

Customizing with Preferences

What you see in the Wikipedia window in front of you isn't fixed in concrete. Wikipedia has a surprising number of ways that you can modify its appearance when you view it. If you're a registered editor, you have a My Preferences page, where you can change a number of settings that control how Wikipedia's pages look on your screen. The link to My Preferences is in your screen's upper-right corner, when you're logged in.

The My Preferences page has 11 tabs, as shown in Figure 20-1. This chapter walks you through each of them, showing you what each tab can do for you.

My preferences
From Wikipedia, the free encyclopedia

| **User profile** | Skin | Math | Files | Date and time | Editing | Recent changes | Watchlist | Search | Misc | Gadgets |

Figure 20-1. The preferences page has 11 tabs. When you click the My Preferences page at the upper right of any Wikipedia page, it opens to the first tab, "User profile".

User Profile

At the very top of the user profile tab are three non-changeable fields: your user name, your user ID (if it's 5000000, for example, then you're the five millionth registered user name at the English Wikipedia), and the number of edits you've done.

NOTE

In various nooks and crannies of Wikipedia, you can find a number of *edit counters*, programs that sort and count your edits (so many to articles, so many to user talk pages, and so on). These edit counters don't include edits to deleted pages, because they use your User contributions page, which doesn't list such edits. But the edit count in your user profile *does* list all your edits, regardless, so for editors with lots of edits, it's higher.

Figure 20-2. This page is the same as in Figure 21-1, but with the French language chosen. You're still at the English Wikipedia, so the titles and content of regular pages are still in English, as are URLs. But all the top and side links are in your chosen language, as are all special pages, and the standard text at the bottom of all pages.

The rest of the tab involves things that you can actually change: language, email address, signature, whether you need to log in each time you edit, and your password.

Language

Interestingly, you can change the language through which you read and interact with Wikipedia. If you change to something other than the normal setting (English), your Wikipedia experience is very different (Figure 20-2).

So if English isn't your primary language, you can edit pages in English, while navigating Wikipedia (and seeing the introductory text for special pages) in a language you're more comfortable with.

Email Address

If you didn't set up an email address when you registered, or want to change that address, you can always do so (Figure 20-3). Having email set up has one big advantage —if you forget your password, email's the only way you can get a replacement. (If you forget your password and don't have email turned on, plan on starting a new user account.)

If you do turn on email for getting a temporary password, you may someday get an unsolicited email from Wikipedia with a new, temporary password. You get such an email if someone else tries to log in under your user name, fails, and then clicks the "E-mail my password" link (see Figure 20-4). Unfortunately, the software has no way of knowing when someone other than the real user clicks this button. If you do get a temporary password from Wikipedia, don't worry. Your old password doesn't get changed automatically. Your old password will continue to work, and you can safely

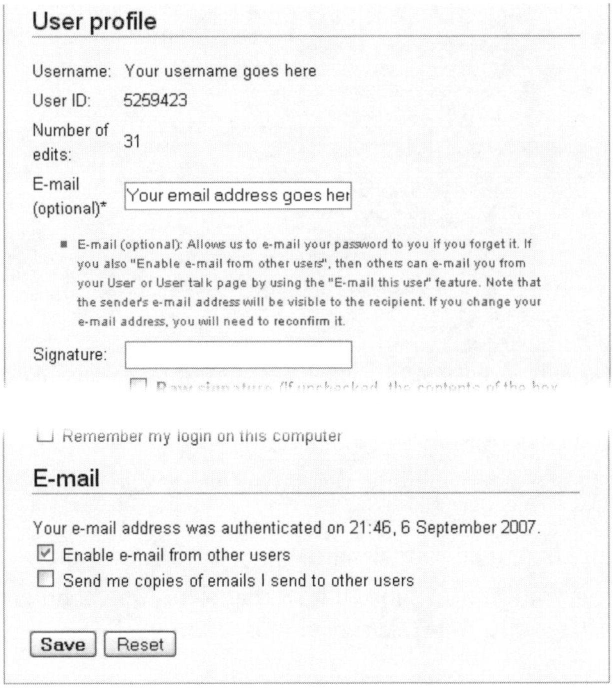

Figure 20-3. To set up or change your email address at Wikipedia, enter the email address (new or changed) at the top of this tab. Unless you want email only in case you forget your password, turn on the "Enable e-mail from other users" box, and then click Save.

ignore the email. Also, any would-be hacker can't get into your account, because the temporary password goes to *your* email address.

Signature Change

When you type four tildes at the end of a posting on a talk page (page 144), Wikipedia adds your *default signature*. Until late 2007, this default signature included only a link to the user page. Many editors changed their default signature, using the options here, to add a second link in their signatures, a link to their user talk page.

As of late 2007, the default signature now includes that user talk page link, so the need to change the default is much less. But if you want to change your signature, follow these steps:

1. On the User Profile tab, turn on the "Raw signature" checkbox.

   This option tells Wikipedia to treat what you enter in step 2 as instructions. If you leave this checkbox turned off, the software places the text in the signature box in

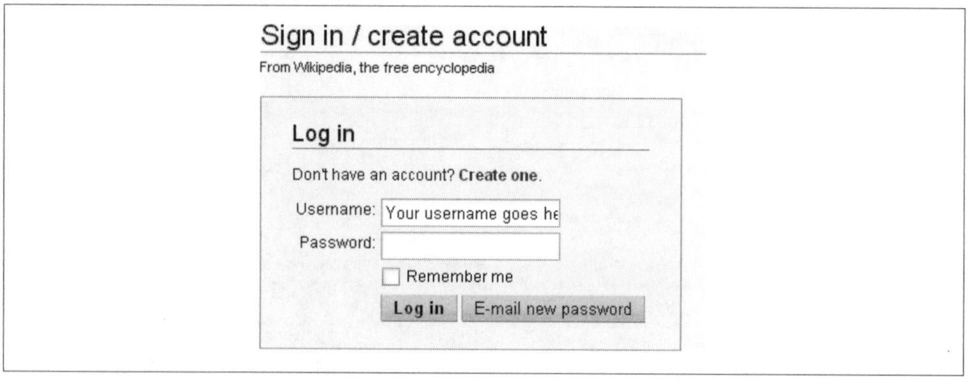

Figure 20-4. The "Log in" screen has an "E-mail new password" button. When you click this button, Wikipedia sends you an email with a new, temporary password. You can then change the temporary password to something more memorable.

the second half of a piped wikilink, displaying what Wikipedia thinks is your nickname.

2. In the signature box, type your signature as you want it to appear.

   For example, if you want to shorten it so that it has only a link to your user talk page, enter: *[[User talk:Your Username|Your Username]]*.

TIP

If the text for your signature is long, you may find it easier to type it elsewhere, then copy and paste it into the raw signature box, since the signature box isn't very large.

---

3. Click Save.

   If you don't see the Save button, scroll down.

4. Test your new signature by going into edit mode on a page *other than* your user page or user talk page (the sandbox, for example, via *WP:SAND*), adding four tildes, and clicking the "Show preview" button.

   If what you see looks okay, then just exit the page without saving.

Wikipedia software doesn't enforce any relationship between the displayed link for your signature and your actual user name. For example, in step 2 you could have entered *[[User talk:Your Username|Totally different name]]*. But according to *Wikipedia:Signatures* (shortcut: *WP:SIG*), your signature should accurately reflect your user name. If you create a signature that's totally different from your user name, another editor will probably drop you a polite note about changing it. If you ignore the first note, a less polite note may follow. If you persist in your position, you'll eventually get warning from an administrator that you're being disruptive. In short, if you don't like your user name, don't change your signature, change your user name (*Wikipedia:Changing username*, shortcut *WP:CHU*). (For more detail on what's appropriate in a signature, see the box below.)

Fancy Signatures

You can customize your signature using any of Wikipedia's text formatting tools. You can mix and match fonts, font sizes, font and background colors, and so on. But before you pursue such changes, remember that Wikipedia's purpose is to build an encyclopedia, not to provide a creative playground.

If you're interested in exploring signature changes, start at *User:Smurrayinchester/Tutorial/Signature*.

From there, take a look at *User:Athaenara/Gallery* (although signatures that include images, like flags, are no longer permitted). You can look at the underlying code by going into edit mode. Unfortunately, some of the sections contain tables (page 262) and are a bit difficult to read in that mode. Finally, at *User:NikoSilver/Signature shop*, you'll find more examples (again, in edit mode you can see the underlying code), and a link where you can ask for further customization.

If you break something, see *Wikipedia:How to fix your signature* (shortcut: *WP:SIGHELP*).

WARNING

If you're inclined towards a very fancy signature, be aware that, as of June 2007, Wikipedia administrators can restrict the maximum length of all signatures. The original limit, set by the Wikimedia developers, is 255 characters. Fancy signatures are inevitably long signatures because of all of the included formatting instructions. If you have a very long signature, and community consensus shortens the maximum length of signatures to less than what you have, you could have a broken signature.

Password

The usual password advice applies at Wikipedia: Don't use your user name or a variant of it as your password. Don't use something obvious like "password," "password 1," "letmein," or "123456." Don't use an obscenity (that may seem original and unique, but it's not). Don't use "qwerty," "monkey," or "myspace 1" (these are numbers 3, 6, and 7 respectively in a 2007 survey of the most commonly used passwords).

The good news is that your Wikipedia password probably isn't that important to others Unless you're an admin, you don't need an industrial strength password, nor do you need to change it every month. Just avoid the obvious. Wikipedia suggests you read the article *Password strength*. (Just remember that that article, like every other article on Wikipedia, can be edited by anyone.)

Login

If you don't want to have to log in each time you visit or edit Wikipedia, you can turn on "Remember my login on this computer". Once you've done so and saved this change, the software places a cookie in your browser's cache, so Wikipedia recognizes you each time you visit the page. This checkbox is also available each time you manually log in, so you can turn it on any time you want.

> **NOTE**
>
> If you forgot your password and had a temporary, software-generated one emailed to you, you have to change your password in order for the "Remember my login on this computer" feature to work. It's a security measure.

As convenient as this feature is, don't use it if you think anyone else in your household —or anyone with access to your computer—might edit using your account. If you've set up Windows so multiple people share a single user account, or if you have no password on your account, then leave the box unchecked. (And don't tell your browser to remember your password, either.)

Even if you're not worried about anyone using your account, Wikipedia is. Wikipedia doesn't allow sharing of user account, not even by spouses, for legal (accountability) reasons. You don't want to have your account blocked because your teenage son vandalized Wikipedia repeatedly using your login, or because someone with whom you used to have a special relationship decided to ruin your reputation at Wikipedia by doing some "special" editing. You won't get much sympathy from Wikipedia's administrators.

> **NOTE**
>
> If you log out of Wikipedia, you have to enter your password the next time, and—if you want continue to use this feature—to recheck the "Remember me" box when logging in. Wikipedia figures that if you log out, you really don't want Wikipedia to automatically sign you in again.

Skin

Think of skins as putting on colored sunglasses—red, yellow, blue, or whatever. The world looks very different, but only to you. You can chose from one of seven separate skins, each of which creates a distinct look using different fonts, colors, and even positioning of links and images.

You have a choice of seven different skins, including the standard Monobook. All the figures in this book were taken with the standard Monobook screen. Figure 20-5 shows

Figure 20-5. Here's the top of the Main Page *in the Nostalgia skin rather than the usual Monobook. The Wikipedia logo appears on the right side of the page rather than the left, and the six standard links (username, "my talk", My Preferences, and so on), normally in the upper-right corner, aren't visible at all. You find them, along with a multitude of other links, in a drop-down menu.*

Figure 20-6. In the Skin tab of your My Preferences page, you'll see Monobook plus your six other choices: Chick, Classic, Cologne Blue, MySkin, Nostalgia, and Simple. You can click on a link to see a preview.

a different skin, Nostalgia, to give you get a sense of how dramatic a change a skin can make.

Figure 20-6 shows the seven different skins that you can choose from.

If you pick either the Classic or Cologne Blue skin, you also get another tab in your My Preferences page, called Quickbar (Figure 20-7), which gives you even more flexibility in layout.

WARNING

If you select "None" for the Quickbar, only a small subset of editing links remains available, at the bottom the page. There's no My Preferences link, so there's no obvious way to change back if you decide you've made a mistake. To change this setting back to what it was, at the bottom of the page, type *Special:Preferences* in the Find box, and then click Go. Alternatively, at the upper right, click SPECIAL PAGES, and then My Preferences.

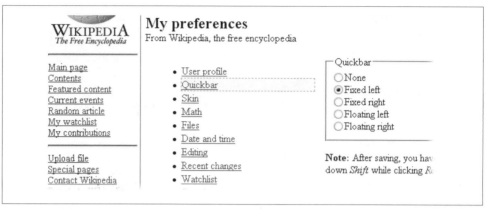

Figure 20-7. In the Classic and Cologne Blue skins, you can use the Quickbar tab to customize the links that usually appear on the left—you can put them on the right, have them always visible when you scroll down a long page, or hide them altogether. (The screenshot here is with the Classic skin; the Cologne Blue skin offers the same five options.)

Which skin should you use? If you really like one of the skins other than Monobook, consider that JavaScript-based changes to your Wikipedia page, mentioned in the Power Users Clinic boxes in this book, mostly assume that you're using Monobook. They may still work if you're using another skin, but they may not. (See page 401 for full instructions on using JavaScript with Wikipedia.)

If you're not using JavaScript, then there's no disadvantage in picking a skin that you really like. Or just stay with the Monobook, the skin that almost all editors use.

NOTE

If you change to a skin other than Monobook, decide to change back to Monobook, and run into a problem trying to do so, you've run into a known bug. The workaround is: Click "my preferences"; add *?useskin=monobook* to the end of the URL; and then press Enter. Now you're temporarily back to Monobook, and can go to the Skins tab and make the change permanent.

Math

If you often read articles with mathematical formulas, you might want to play with settings here, but the standard setting ("HTML if very simple or else PNG") usually works fine. It shows complex formulas as an image, which may make them more readable than the usual text display. But check out the alternative, "Recommended for modern browsers", which you may like better. For text-based browsers like Lynx, there is the "Leave it as TeX (for text browsers)" option. ("TeX" is a typesetting system that works very well for complex mathematical formulas.)

Files

The two options here control how Wikipedia displays separate image files.

- **Limit images on image description pages**. This option affects you only if you go to the page that stores an image (a page like *Image:Picture used in the article.jpg*). Such pages are where you get more details about a picture—copyright, where it came from, upload date, and so on. If you have a very small screen and want to look at an image page (just click on the image), you may need to adjust this setting down from the initial setting of 800 by 600 pixels. Similarly, you may want to reduce image size if you have a very slow connection.

NOTE

You don't need to change this setting to see images larger than the setting; it simply controls what you see initially when you arrive at an image page. When you're there, clicking on an image that has a higher resolution shows that image in the higher resolution.

- **Thumbnail size**. As mentioned on page 286, if you've got a particularly big or particularly small screen, you can tell Wikipedia how you want to see thumbnails displayed on your screen: Select from one of the six sizes (120px to 300px). After you click Save, you see all thumbnailed pictures in Wikipedia in that size.

Date and Time

Wikipedia shows the time for each edit on the *Special:Contributions* page, your Watchlist report, and on every other page that has date and time information for edits, is Coordinated Universal Time (UTC), which means the same thing as Greenwich Mean Time. Unless you live in the Western European Time zone, UTC is not your local time. Fortunately, you can change the time displayed for edits to your local time.

Changing to your local time for edits on special pages and in page histories saves you from constantly making the mental correction from UTC. But here's the rub: Date and time stamps on *talk* pages are still in UTC.

Suppose you're trying to figure out whether an editor did a vandalizing edit before or after a final warning. If the vandalism came after the final warning, you'll ask for the editor to be blocked. The date and time of the warning, on the user talk page, will always be UTC. If you've changed the times on the *User contributions* page to your local time, then you'll need to convert your local time back to UTC to figure out whether the edit truly came after the warning. (Or switch back to UTC, as described in the Tip on page 392.)

If you want to switch to local time, here are the steps:

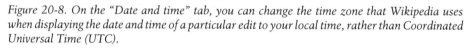

My preferences

From Wikipedia, the free encyclopedia

| User profile | Skin | Math | Files | **Date and time** | Editing | Recent changes | Watchlist |

Date format

- ● No preference
- ○ 16:12, January 15, 2001
- ○ 16:12, 15 January 2001
- ○ 16:12, 2001 January 15
- ○ 2001-01-15T16:12:34

Time zone

Server time 21:57

Local time 21:57

Offset¹ [   ]

[Fill in from browser]

¹The number of hours your local time differs from server time (UTC).

This will adjust the times shown on your watchlist and recent changes, but not in signatures on talk pages which will always be in UTC.

Figure 20-8. On the "Date and time" tab, you can change the time zone that Wikipedia uses when displaying the date and time of a particular edit to your local time, rather than Coordinated Universal Time (UTC).

1. On the "Date and time" tab (Figure 20-9), click the "Fill in from the browser" button.

   The difference in hours between your local time and UTC appears in the Offset box. It's an hour off if daylight savings time is in effect in your locality; if so, you'll fix it in a later step.

2. Click Save. Then follow the instructions at the bottom of the page for bypassing your browser's cache.

   This step ensures that you see the effect of the setting you just changed. (If you're using Firefox, follow the instructions for Mozilla.)

3. On the left side of your screen, in the "interaction" box, click the "Recent changes" link to make sure your local time now shows up on special pages.

   If the time shown on the *Special:Recent changes* page is off by an hour, adjust the time in the Offset field accordingly, and then repeat the previous step.

TIP

If you want to go back to UTC everywhere, simply delete the number in the Offset field, and then click Save.

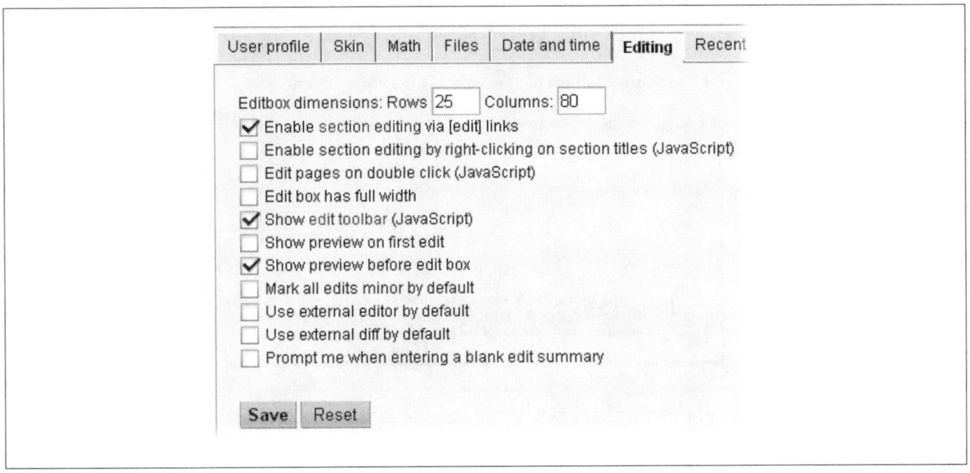

Figure 20-9. These three editing options start out turned on, and most editors leave them that way. For example, it's very handy to be able to click a link to edit an individual article section (page 18). So are the editing toolbar, and the preview feature.

Editing

The Editing tab (Figure 20-9) lets you select from among 11 options that let you tweak how edit mode looks and feels. In general, you'll rack up several dozen hours of editing before you feel the need to play with these settings.

This tab also lets you resize the edit box. Resizing the edit box makes sense if you have an extra-wide or extra-deep screen. On the other hand, if you're constantly having to tab down to enter an edit summary and click "Show preview" and "Save page", you might be willing to live with fewer rows visible and a bit more scrolling to get to the text you want.

Three of the editing tab options are initially turned on, and it's good to leave them that way: "Enable section editing via [edit] links", "Show edit toolbar (JavaScript)", and "Show preview before edit box".

The eight other options start out turned off. Whether you want to use them is up to you:

- **Enable section editing by right-clicking on section titles (JavaScript)**. If you're one of those Windows fans who expect everything to be right-clickable, this one's for you.

- **Edit pages on double click (JavaScript)**. This option is probably not a good idea, since it's better to edit individual sections, not whole pages, as explained on page 18. Besides, clicking "edit this page" isn't so hard when you want to edit an entire page.

- **Edit box has full width**. This item doesn't really make the edit box the full width of the screen, because the boxes and links on the left side remain in place.

Figure 20-10. If you set up your preferences to use an external editor instead of Wikipedia's edit box, then the first time you start to edit a file, Wikipedia sends the file to your browser. The browser opens a dialog box for you to specify actual editing program. The dialog box varies by browser—this picture shows Internet Explorer 7.

- **Show preview on first edit**. When you go into edit mode, you see not only the edit box but also a preview of the section or page as it was before you started editing. (In other words, this option is like clicking the "Show preview" button immediately after going into edit mode, before you actually do any editing.) Mostly useful if you do a lot of work with template pages.

- **Mark all edits minor by default**. This setting saves you from having to turn on the "This is a minor edit" box every time you edit a page. If you do lots of copyediting work—for example, correcting punctuation errors or fixing disambiguation links—it's good to mark such edits as "minor", so that other editors can screen them out of various lists if they want to.

  If you set this option, you must remember to turn off the "This is a minor edit" box if you're making a non-minor edit.

- **Use external editor by default**. With this option, when you click "edit this page", or an edit link for a section, Wikipedia doesn't go into editing mode. Instead, it calls up your browser, which offers you the chance to choose a different program in which to do your editing (Figure 20-10).

  If you have a text editor that you really like to use (BBEdit, emacs, Kedit or vi for example), read more about this option at *Help:External editors* and *Wikipedia:Text editor support*.

- **Use external diff by default**. Does the same as the previous option, but for diffs.

- **Prompt me when entering a blank edit summary**. Once you set this option, you never have to worry about inadvertently forgetting to fill in the edit summary field. Edit summaries are very helpful to other editors reviewing a page history, as page 9 explains.

Recent Changes

This tab lets you control what appears on the *Special:Recentchanges* page and its sibling, the *Special:Recentchangeslinked* page (also known as "Related changes." The first of these two is used in vandal-fighting (page 122); the second for monitoring pages (page 118).

This tab has four things you can change:

- **Days to show in recent changes**. Shortens or lengthens the total number of edits that you can see when you go to one of the two report pages. Since just one day's worth of edits at the *Recent changes* page is more than 100,000, changing the limit here (from the default of "7") affects only what you see when you click the "Related changes" link.

- **Titles in recent changes**. Affects how many edits you see on each page, not the total number of edits that a special page shows you (you just change the number of edits to show on the page itself). Think of this option as setting a soft limit on the number of edits displayed per page, while the first setting, "days to show", sets a hard limit on the total report length.

- **Hide minor edits in recent changes**. Hiding minor edits screens out inconsequential edits so you can focus on important ones. On the other hand, depending on your paranoia level (and how important you consider the pages you're monitoring), if you hide minor edits and a very sneaky editor improperly classifies a damaging edit as "minor", then you'll probably miss something you'd like to have seen. (On the other hand, there are other editors out there looking for vandalism too.)

  In any case, you can change this option on the report itself, whether it's turned on in this tab or not.

- **Enhanced recent changes (JavaScript)**. Changes the format of these two special report pages. See Chapter 6 (page 111) for illustrations of the enhanced formats.

Watchlist

Your watchlist lets you monitor changes to pages. The settings in this tab let you customize your watchlist report, which shows recent edits to pages on your watchlist, including changing to an expanded version of the watchlist report. The expanded version shows *all* changes to all watched pages during a period, not just the most recent. The settings in this tab are discussed extensively in Chapter 6, starting on page 108.

Search

This tab has four settings, counting that last set of checkboxes as one setting, as seen in Figure 20-11. These settings affect what happens when you use Wikipedia's internal

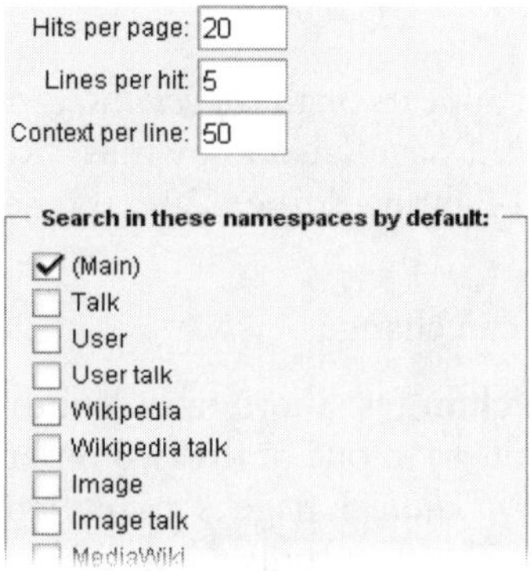

Figure 20-11. The Search tab lets you tailor the results from Wikipedia's internal search engine. The fourth of these settings, not completely shown, is a listing of all namespaces that you want to include in all your searches.

search engine. (For why you may not want to use that engine for searches, see page 431.)

- **Hits per page** isn't as useful as it sounds. Only the top handful of hits are normally worth looking at anyway.

- If you fill in **Lines per hit** with, say, 5 lines, Wikipedia won't show the context of the search term if it occurs after line 5 on the page. But testing shows that this option makes no difference: Whether set to 5 or 5000, the results are the same. (See the Meta page *Help:Preferences* for more information.)

- **Context per line** means the amount of text the search engine shows you when it finds the word you're looking for. Figure 20-12 shows the difference between the initial setting of 50 and a setting of 200, which shows you a lot more of the surrounding text. This context helps you decide whether it's worth visiting the result page.

- **Search in these namespaces by default**. You might want, for example, to expand your routine searches to include article talk pages, but it's difficult to think of any circumstances where you'd routinely want search results from the many other namespaces.

TIP

For the occasional search of a namespace other than mainspace, where articles are, just do a search, and then, at the bottom of the page of search results, indicate, using the checkboxes there, the other namespaces you're interested in.

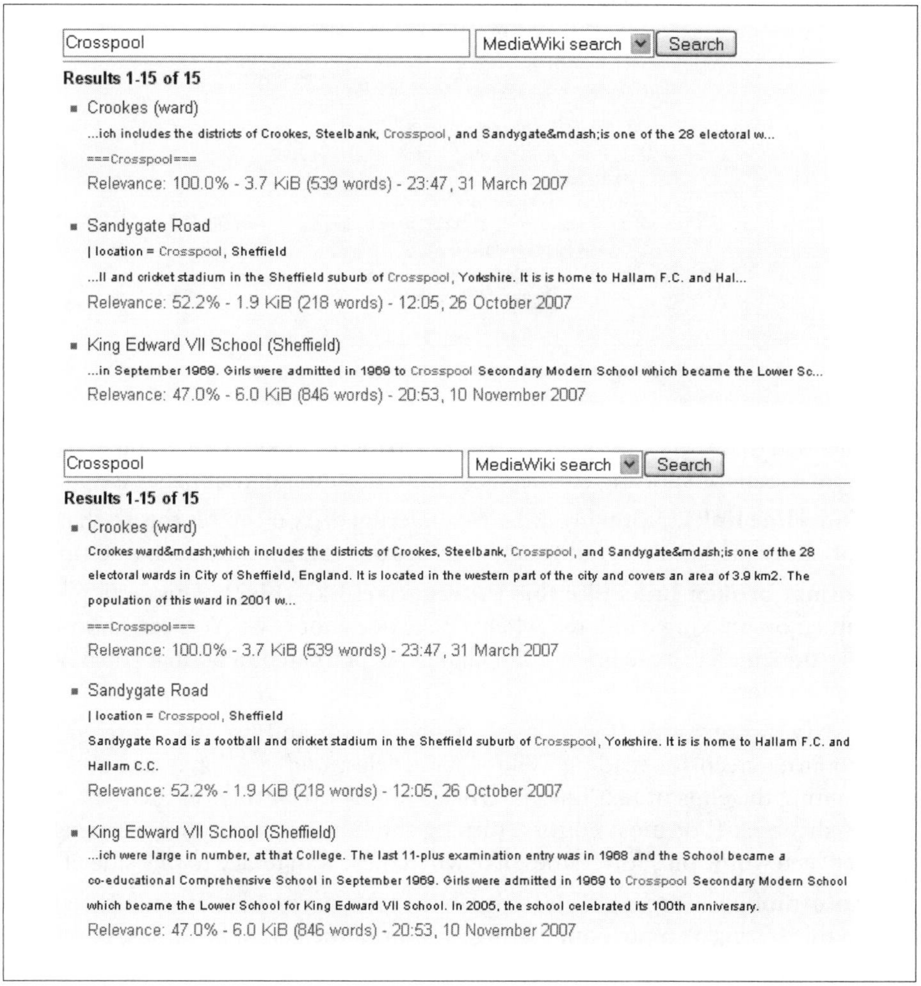

Figure 20-12. On the top is a search on the word "Crosspool," with the "Context per line" set to 50 (which means 50 characters). (Only the first three results are shown). On the bottom is the same search, with this option set to 200. (Again, only the top three results are shown.)

Misc

The next-to-last tab in My Preferences is the miscellaneous tab (Figure 20-13). True to its name, it contains settings that don't quite fit anywhere else.

Here's what each of the settings does:

• **Threshold for stub link formatting (bytes)**. Changes the color of links to articles that are smaller than the specified size. Such links are shown in dark brown.

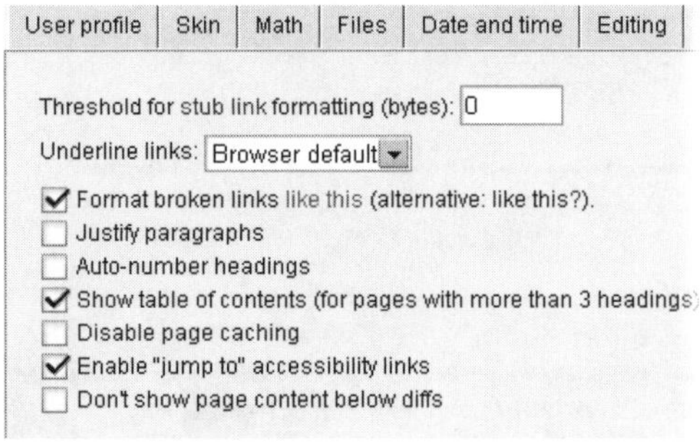

Figure 20-13. The Miscellaneous tab has a varied assortment of nine options, three of which are turned on initially.

Intended (in theory) to encourage editors to follow links to stubs and expand them; more useful for spotting erroneous links to disambiguation pages (see page 313).

- **Underline links**. Normally links are underlined. You can set this so that links are not underlined (Never), although your browser may ignore such a setting.

- **Format broken links like this (alternative: like this?)**. This setting is initially turned on, making a link red when a page does not exist. You can choose to use a question mark instead of the color change, which can be a boon if you have trouble seeing colors.

- **Justify paragraphs**. If you have a huge monitor and use the entire width of the monitor screen for reading Wikipedia articles, *and* you have an obsession with wanting the ends of text lines in articles to line up cleanly on the right, then turn on this box. (For most editors, turning the box results in disconcerting spacing between words on shorter lines, like when there's an image to one side of the text.)

- **Auto-number headings**. Headings in the table of contents are numbered; turning on this setting also puts numbering in front of the actual headings, in the body of the article.

- **Show table of contents (for pages with more than 3 headings)**. Tables of contents are useful; they let you see what's in an article without reading all the way down. It's not clear why you'd want to uncheck this option.

- **Disable page caching**. Prevents you from ever seeing outdated versions of pages, at the cost of longer loading times for all pages.

- **Enable "jump to" accessibility links**. According to *Help:Preferences*, this option "provides or hides the two links (*Jump to: navigation* and *search*) at the top of each page, to the navigation bar and the search box." In reality, turning this option on and off seems to make no difference.

- **Don't show page content below diffs**. When you look at what editors did in specific edits (a diff, as described on page 88), the page has two parts: At the top,

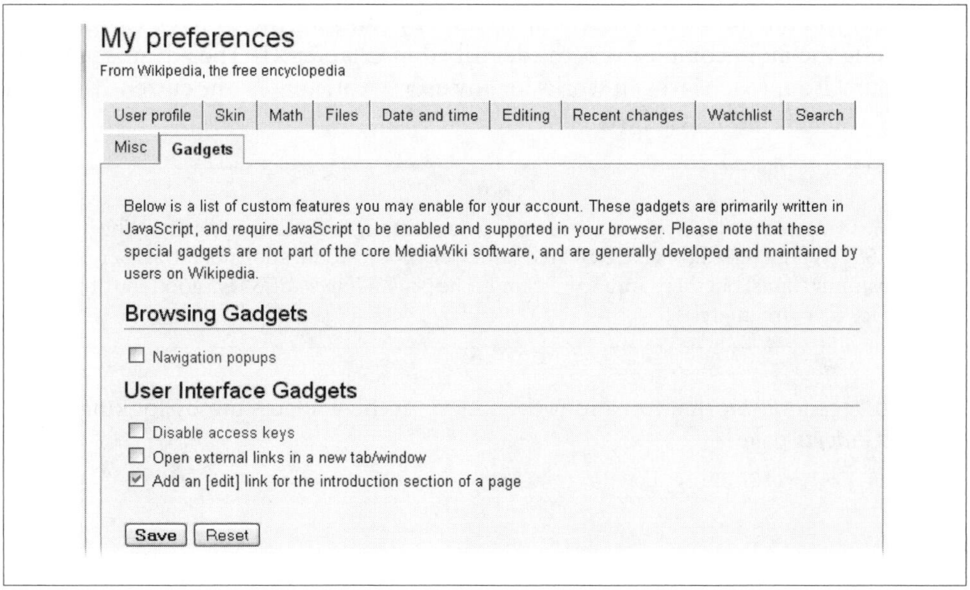

Figure 20-14. At this writing, the Gadgets tab only includes four JavaScript user scripts. But its potential is limited only by editors' time and imagination.

you see the before-and-after text for what was changed (and only what was changed). At the bottom, you see the article as it was after the edit. With this box turned on, you see only the top part. You probably want to leave this box turned off, since the article text can provide additional context. Besides, the article text is on the bottom, so you can ignore it when you don't need it.

Gadgets

In late 2007, Wikipedia added a new, eleventh tab to the My Preferences page—the Gadgets tab. Its contents are still being developed, so by the time you read this, the tab may offer more options than in Figure 20-14. The Gadgets tab lets you quickly implement JavaScript user scripts developed by other editors to add cool new features to Wikipedia.

Chapter 21 (page 403) describes how to implement JavaScript user scripts by copying them to a page in your userspace. Using the Gadgets tab is much easier; just select a gadget, and then click Save. Then, as the instructions at the bottom of the tab say, bypass your browser cache to see the gadget's effects.

NOTE

Page 401 describes how to make sure that you have JavaScript turned on in your browser. If you add a gadget and it doesn't seem to be taking effect, check your browser.

Currently, you can implement user scripts either by choosing them on the Gadgets tab, or by using the more complex process described in Chapter 21. The advantage of the do-it-yourself approach is that it works for any user script, not just the currently limited number available on the Gadgets tab.

NOTE

The Gadgets tab also works for personal customization using Cascading Style Sheets (CSS). Wikipedia editors have created far fewer CSS customizations than JavaScript customizations, but there are a few around. The page *Wikipedia:CSS* is a good starting place if you're interested.

You can get more information about each item on the Gadgets tab by looking at the *Special:Gadgets* page.

Easier Editing with JavaScript

You can customize Wikipedia in ways that make your editing easier with *user scripts*, which are written in JavaScript code. As you've seen in Power Users' Clinic boxes in this book, user scripts let you do things like color code your User contributions page, or remove pages from your watchlist by just clicking a box on your watchlist report, or adding additional links on the left side of the screen. As you explore Wikipedia, you'll find many more user scripts that editors have created to make editing work easier.

Here's how it works: When the Wikipedia server builds a page to send to your browser, it includes any JavaScript code stored in your personal JavaScript page at Wikipedia. Your browser follows the JavaScript instructions when it shows you the page, controlling how the Wikipedia page looks and works.

Best of all, you don't have to understand JavaScript to use it. You just need to know the process for cutting and pasting chunks of code to your personal JavaScript file. This chapter shows you how.

Setting Up Your Browser

User scripts don't work if JavaScript isn't turned on. JavaScript is automatically turned on in most every Web browser, so you don't have to change the standard settings. If user scripts aren't working for you (you're just seeing the regular Wikipedia screen after you implement some JavaScript), this section shows you how to check your settings.

How you check the settings depends on your browser:

- **Internet Explorer**. The setting is called "Active scripting". Go to Tools→Internet Options→Security tab. Select Internet for the zone, and then click the Custom level button. Scroll down to the Scripting section, and then, in the Active scripting subsection, make sure that Enable is already selected. If not, click to turn it on, and then click the Okay button. When the Change settings dialog box appears, click Yes. (In Internet Explorer 6, this dialog box is labeled Warning.)
- **Firefox**. In Windows, go to Tools→Options; on a Mac, go to Firefox→Preferences. At the top of the Options box, click Content (if it's not already highlighted), and

make sure the "Enable JavaScript" checkbox is turned on. If not, click to turn it on, and then click OK.

TIP

If you have security concerns about globally turning on JavaScript for all Web sites, the Firefox add-on *NoScript* lets you turn on JavaScript on a site-by-site basis.

- **Opera**. Go to Tools→Preferences→Advanced tab. On the left, select Content, and make sure the Enable JavaScript checkbox is turned on. If not, turn it on, and then click OK.

- **Safari**. Go to Safari Preferences→Security, and, under Web Content, make sure the Enable JavaScript checkbox is turned on. Close the Preferences window when you're done.

Adding and Deleting Scripts

To use user scripts, you create a personal JavaScript page, which only you and Wikipedia administrators can edit. On this page, you put the user scripts that you want to use, or pointers to other pages where JavaScript code is stored (which Wikipedia uses to add code to your page).

When you want to stop using a script, you edit that personal page, deleting the JavaScript code or pointer, or marking it as non-executable information. That's called *commenting it out*, and it just means you're telling the Wikipedia software not to follow those instructions.

NOTE

In late 2007, Wikipedia added a new feature that lets you implement user scripts with just a couple of clicks. On the My Preferences page, check the Gadgets tab to see if the script you want to add is listed on that tab. If so, you can save time by turning it on that tab, rather than following the instructions in this section. (For details, see page 399.)

Your Personal JavaScript Page

Creating your JavaScript page is as easy as creating a subpage in your own user space, as described in Chapter 3. See page 56 if you need a refresher on subpages. This chapter assumes that you're using the standard Monobook skin for your Wikipedia window (page 388), and so you'll name your personal page *monobook.js*. (If you use a different skin, see the box on page 408.)

When you're ready to do the JavaScript jive, go to your user page, and follow these steps:

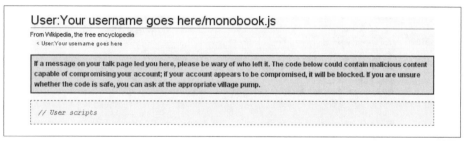

User:Your username goes here/monobook.js

From Wikipedia, the free encyclopedia
< User:Your username goes here

If a message on your talk page led you here, please be wary of who left it. The code below could contain malicious content capable of compromising your account; if your account appears to be compromised, it will be blocked. If you are unsure whether the code is safe, you can ask at the appropriate village pump.

```
// User scripts
```

Figure 21-1. All monobook.js *pages have the same warning at the top – don't copy a script just because someone else leaves a note on your user talk page about what a neato-cool tool they've created. (Leaving uninvited, non-personal postings on user talk pages is considered spam, and fortunately it doesn't happen very often.) If you use JavaScript code someone else wrote, make sure it's someone you trust.*

1. On your user page, click "edit this page". In the edit box, type either *[[User:Your-UsernameGoesHere/monobook.js]]* or simply *[[/monobook.js]]*. Then add an edit summary like *Creating link to new monobook.js page*, do a preview, and then save your edit.

   You've just added a link to your soon-to-be-created JavaScript page. The link to the new page is red, since it doesn't yet exist.

2. Click the red link to the *monobook.js* page, and, at the top of the edit box, add the following: *// User scripts*. (In JavaScript code, anything that begins with double slashes is a comment. You'll see the "User scripts" comment, as shown in Figure 21-1.) Add an edit summary (like *Creating initial page*), preview the page (to reinforce the habit), and then save the page.

   By saving the page with only a comment, initially, you're creating a version of the page that you can revert to if something goes wrong. That's extremely unlikely, but it doesn't hurt to have the option.

Adding a Script

As discussed in Chapter 7 (page 124), when you're evaluating a user account to determine whether it's a vandalism-only account, it's helpful to look at more than the user talk page of the editor. You'll often want to look at individual edits (the *User contributions* page) and the block log, for instance. This tutorial will show you how to implement some JavaScript that add tabs, making that research easier.

1. Go to the page *Wikipedia:WikiProject User scripts/Scripts/User tabs* (Figure 21-2), and copy all the text within the dotted box.

   This page has no "edit this page" tab, meaning it's protected. Don't copy JavaScript or any other code from an unprotected page, since someone may have tampered with it.

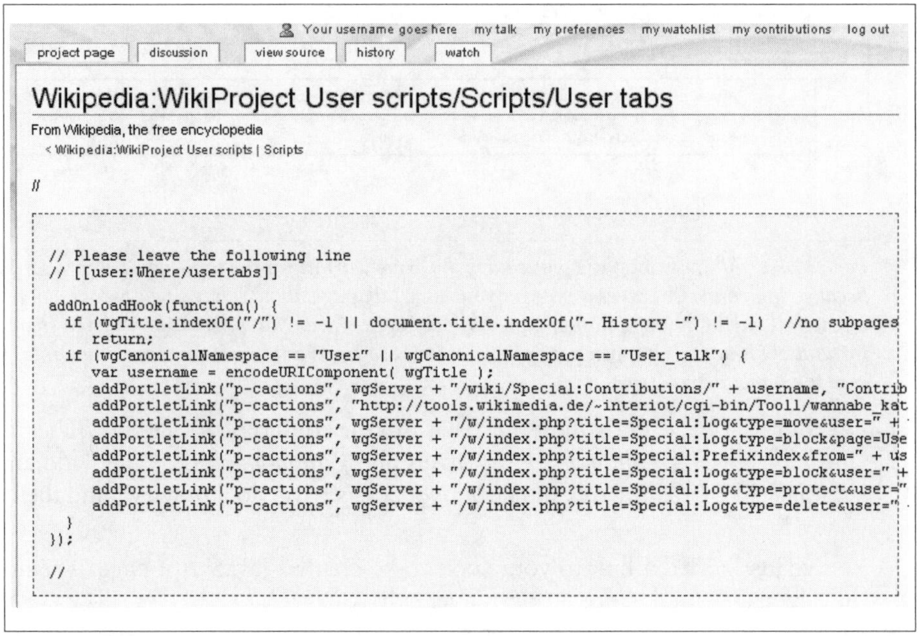

Figure 21-2. The script at the page Wikipedia:WikiProject User scripts/Scripts/User tabs *has three full lines of comment (two at the top, one at the bottom); these have two slashes at the beginning. The actual code that will be executed is the middle fifteen lines. The blanks spaces at the beginning of any line are optional—they're there to make the script easier for humans to read. Computers don't care one way or another. (The blank spaces at the beginnings of lines are why the text goes off-screen on the right; that's normal for Wikipedia wikitext.)*

2. Open your own *monobook.js* page, and then, in the edit box, paste the text that you copied in step 1.

   If you haven't created a *monobook.js* page yet, see page 402.

3. Change *[[User:Where/usertabs]]* to *[[Wikipedia:WikiProject User scripts/Scripts/ User tabs]]*, to show where you got the script.

   Your edit box should look like Figure 21-3.

4. Add an edit summary (Adding JavaScript for user tabs, for example) and then click the "Show preview" button.

   The preview should look like Figure 21-4. If everything looks as you expect (as is the case here, there's no visible change), save the page. If something looks wrong, recheck the code that you added to the page.

5. After you save the change, you should bypass your cache so that Wikipedia isn't using an old version of your monobook.js (see page 409). Then go to a page where you expect the change to appear—for example, click on the "my talk" link on the upper right, and check if the change has happened.

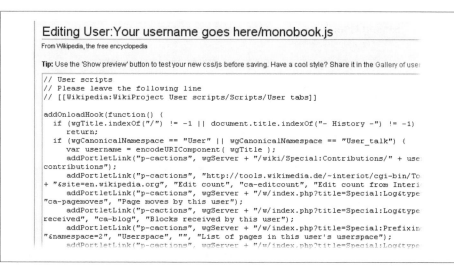

Figure 21-3. In editing mode, monobook.js *pages look different from regular pages. There's no edit toolbar, because there's no need for buttons for inserting a signature, or a table, or other text. There's also a message about using the "Show preview" button to test the added JavaScript before saving the page.*

As shown in Figure 21-5, it indeed has.

If you still can't see what you expect after bypassing your cache, then ask for assistance at the Help desk (shortcut: WP:HD).

Preventing Code Overload

It's good practice to put anything other than a very short script into a separate page, with a name ending in .js, so that only you—and administrators—can edit it. That way, you don't end up with a very long, difficult-to-understand and difficult-to-edit *monobook.js* page.

Suppose, for example, you put the "User tabs" JavaScript from the previous steps, into a new page called *User:Your username goes here/UserTabs.js*. That keeps it out of your *monobook.js* page, but it also means that Wikipedia doesn't recognize it as JavaScript you actually want to use. In fact, when you go into edit mode at a new page, to paste in the code, you see a warning message (Figure 21-7) that tells you that Wikipedia can't match the file name against any of the skins you could have chosen (see page 388), and therefore won't automatically execute the script when you're logged on.

To actually use the JavaScript at your new *User:Your username goes here/UserTabs.js* page, you have to tell Wikipedia to *import* into your *monobook.js* page. When the Wikipedia software reads your *monobook.js* page, it reads the import script, and learns

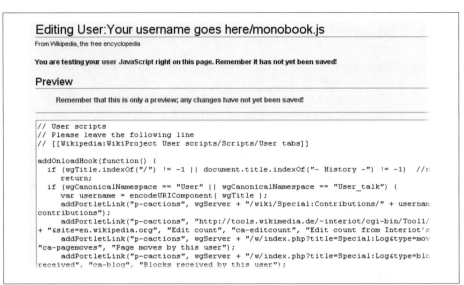

```
Editing User:Your username goes here/monobook.js
From Wikipedia, the free encyclopedia

You are testing your user JavaScript right on this page. Remember it has not yet been saved!

Preview

    Remember that this is only a preview; any changes have not yet been saved!

// User scripts
// Please leave the following line
// [[Wikipedia:WikiProject User scripts/Scripts/User tabs]]

addOnloadHook(function() {
  if (wgTitle.indexOf("/") != -1 || document.title.indexOf("- History -") != -1)  //n
    return;
  if (wgCanonicalNamespace == "User" || wgCanonicalNamespace == "User_talk") {
    var username = encodeURIComponent( wgTitle );
    addPortletLink("p-cactions", wgServer + "/wiki/Special:Contributions/" + usernam
contributions");
    addPortletLink("p-cactions", "http://tools.wikimedia.de/~interiot/cgi-bin/Tool1/
+ "&site=en.wikipedia.org", "Edit count", "ca-editcount", "Edit count from Interiot's
    addPortletLink("p-cactions", wgServer + "/w/index.php?title=Special:Log&type=mov
"ca-pagemoves", "Page moves by this user");
    addPortletLink("p-cactions", wgServer + "/w/index.php?title=Special:Log&type=blo
received", "ca-blog", "Blocks received by this user");
```

Figure 21-4. The nice thing about previewing a change to your personal JavaScript page is that the JavaScript is implemented immediately. If it should change the monobook.js page, you see that. In this case, the new tabs will only show on a user page, so the preview doesn't tell you how you're doing.

where to go to get the actual JavaScript. Figure 21-7 shows a bunch of import scripts on an editor's *monobook.js* page.

NOTE

In Figure 21-7, the line second from the bottom has two slash marks in front, making the line into a comment. In geekspeak, the line is *commented out*, so the script won't run. To reverse that in the future, making it functional again, just delete the slashes.

Importing Multi-Function Scripts of Other Editors

Several Wikipedia editors have created big, fabulously useful, multi-function scripts. You absolutely don't want to cut and paste these scripts, even to a separate page of your own, because you need the editor who created it to maintain it. You want to get enhancements to the code as they occur. By using the import function, you get the benefit of those updates (as do the hundreds of other editors using the same script).

WARNING

As always, don't trust any page that isn't protected from editing by regular editors. Don't ever import from an unprotected page.

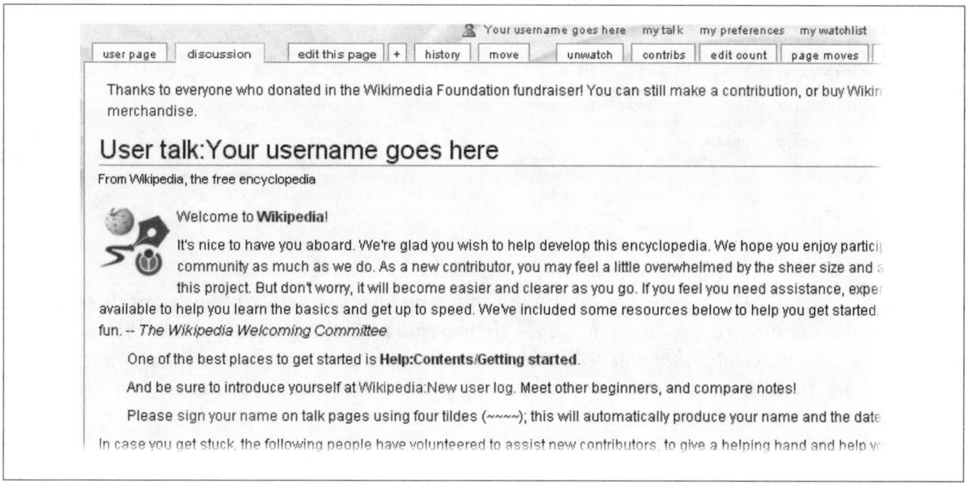

Figure 21-5. Now a number of additional tabs appear whenever you go to a user or user talk page. If you decide you don't want one or more of these, all you need to do is comment out the corresponding line on your monobook.js page (put two slashes at the very beginning), and that tab won't appear any more.

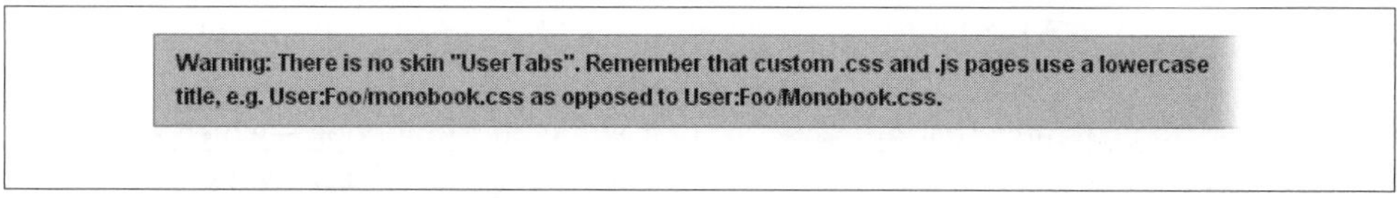

Warning: There is no skin "UserTabs". Remember that custom .css and .js pages use a lowercase title, e.g. User:Foo/monobook.css as opposed to User:Foo/Monobook.css.

Figure 21-6. When you create a page whose name ends with .js or .css, Wikipedia checks to see if that's the name of a skin (see page 388). If not, it gives you this warning. In this case, you can ignore the warning. But if you typed (for example) MonoBook.js *rather than* monobook.js, *earlier in the chapter, the misspelling would be critical and the warning would be relevant.*

Removing Scripts

As you can see from reading this chapter, editing your *monobook.js* page is no big deal. It's no harder than cutting and pasting text to any Wikipedia article. You can remove a function by deleting it, or by commenting it out (putting a pair of slashes at the beginning of each line). Commenting out works best for cases where you're importing a function (see Figure 21-7) and there's just one line to comment out. If you have 10 or 15 lines of code that you copied to your *monobook.js* page that you don't want any more, the page will be a lot neater if you delete it all, perhaps leaving a single comment line about where you found the code, in case you want to copy it back in at some later point.

```
importScript('User:Ais523/votesymbols.js'); //[[User:Ais523/votesymbols.js]]
importScript('User:Ais523/topcontrib.js'); //[[User:Ais523/topcontrib.js]]
importScript('User:Ais523/formatedit.js'); //[[User:Ais523/formatedit.js]]
importScript('User:Ais523/contribcalendar.js'); //[[User:Ais523/contribcalendar.js]]
importScript('User:Ais523/highlightmyname2.js'); //[[User:Ais523/highlightmyname2.js]]
importScript('User:Ais523/catwatch.js'); //[[User:Ais523/catwatch.js]]
importScript('User:Ais523/sandbox.js'); //[[User:Ais523/sandbox.js]]
importScript('User:Ais523/watchlistnotifier.js'); //[[User:Ais523/watchlistnotifier.js]]
importScript('User:Ais523/adminrights.js'); //[[User:Ais523/adminrights.js]]
//importScript('User:Ais523/watchlistei.js'); //[[User:Ais523/watchlistei.js]]
importScript('User:Ais523/editsection0tab.js'); //[[User:Ais523/editsection0tab.js]]
```

Figure 21-7. The page User:Ais523/monobook.js *has a number of JavaScript functions (user scripts) added via the importScript command, rather than pasting all the JavaScript into the page. One advantage of importScript is that you get a neat list of all your user scripts, rather than a mass of code. Separating functions by putting them on separate pages also makes it easier to share scripts with other editors.*

POWER USERS' CLINIC

If You Don't Use the Monobook Skin

As discussed in the previous chapter (page 388), in your My Preferences page, on the Skin tab, you have an option of selecting one of seven skins, which rearrange the elements and formatting on each Wikipedia page that you view. The tab has buttons to click to see a preview of each skin, so you can get a clear sense of what a change of skins can do.

You have no guarantee that a user script that works in Monobook—which is what almost all editors use, and the norm for testing user scripts—will also work if you use another skin. But if you want to try using a different skin, understand that each skin looks for a specific, and different, personal file when it implements your personal Java-Script. Just create that page for your user scripts instead of or in addition to *monobook.js*.

The files used by the other six skins are:

- Chick: *chick.js*
- Classic skin: *standard.js*
- Cologne Blue: *cologneblue.js*
- MySkin: *myskin.js*
- Nostalgia: *nostalgia.js*
- Simple: *simple.js*

Fixing Problems

If you run into a problem with JavaScript, use this tried-and-true procedure to deal with it. Perform the fixes in the following order, so you're starting with the simplest fix, and working your way up to the most complex:

- If you're not sure whether JavaScript is turned on in the browser you're using, follow the procedures on page 401 to make sure that it is.
- You may need to bypass your browser's cache (the copy of pages that it keeps, to speed up the process of showing you want you want to see):
  - **Internet Explorer**. Press Ctrl+F5.
  - **Mozilla Firefox**. Press the Shift key while clicking the Reload button (or press Ctrl+Shift+R).
  - **Opera/Konqueror**. Press F5.
  - **Safari**. Press ⌘-Option-E.
- Sometimes bypassing the cache doesn't work, but purging it does. As discussed at the *Wikipedia:Purge*, page, follow this procedure: Click the "edit this page" tab. In your browser's address bar, at the end of the URL, where you see *&action=edit*, replace *edit* with *purge*, so it reads *&action=purge*. Then press Enter to tell your browser to go to that revised URL.
- Finally, if you're using Firefox 2 as your browser, you can use its browser console to track down errors one by one. Go to Tools→Error Console. You'll probably see a lot of warnings, but you want to see errors, so click the red stop sign icon, the one with Errors next to it.

  The next page lists any scripts with problems. Clicking an entry in the list takes you to the page with the code on it, with the error highlighted. Now recheck the source of the code (that's why you put comments in the code about where you got it). If you didn't make a mistake in copying, then you probably want to comment out the script (by placing double slash marks at the beginning of each line) if it's interfering with other scripts. Then either post a talk page note for whoever created the script, or a note at the Village Pump technical page (*WP:VPT*). (The second choice is better if you think the script is a popular one.)

NOTE

The Opera browser has a similar feature: Go to Tools→Advanced→Error console.

- One error in a JavaScript file is enough to disable all scripts. The error won't damage anything; it just has the effect of commenting out the entire *monobook.js* page, making it inactive. And of course it's irritating. If you can't identify the problem script via the browser error console, revert to the last version of the page that worked (see page 94 for more on reverting). Then add back, one by one, whatever scripts were lost by reverting, being extra careful as you copy or import, to see at what point the problem occurs.

Resources

You'll find technical information about JavaScript (user scripts) here:

- *Wikipedia:WikiProject User scripts* (shortcut: *WP:US*)
- *Help:User style* (shortcut: *H:US*)

User scripts are scattered throughout Wikipedia. You may find one just because someone mentioned it, or because you came across it in the index (shortcut: *WP:EIW*). The largest collection of scripts (or links to scripts) is at *Wikipedia:WikiProject User scripts/Scripts* (shortcut: *WP:JS*). Other places to check are:

- *User:Voice of All/UsefulJS*
- *User:GeorgeMoney/UserScripts*

PART VI

Appendixes

A Tour of the Wikipedia Page

When you're registered (page 45), and logged into Wikipedia, you'll see links in a number of places: at the screen's top right; across the top in tabs; on the left side in boxes, and at the bottom of the page in disclaimers and other boilerplate text.

These features are discussed in detail where they come up throughout this book. This appendix serves as a quick reference when you have a question about what an onscreen element does.

NOTE

The placement of the links and tabs described in this appendix are based on the use of the *Monobook* skin, the standard way that all new editors see Wikipedia. If you're using one of the other six skins that you can choose from, some of these elements will be in a different place on your screen, and some may not be visible at all. (If you're not sure which skin you're using, see page 388.)

The Six Upper-Right Links

The upper-right corner of your screen contains six links when you're logged in. If you're not logged in, it says, "Sign in / create account". Each of these links takes you to one of your personal account pages.

NOTE

If you have windows open to multiple Wikipedia pages, logging out on one page logs you out completely. Each of the other open pages continues to *display* the six links in the upper-right corner until you refresh the page. Beware: If you edit one of those pages—whether you refresh the page or not—you're editing anonymously (page 47), since you're not logged in.

[Your Username]

Opens your user page; *User:Your username goes here*. If the page doesn't yet exist, the link is red. Page 54 describes how to create and use this page.

My Talk

Opens your user talk page; *User talk:Your username goes here*. If the page doesn't yet exist, the link is red. Page 156 discusses user talk pages.

My Preferences

Opens a page with 11 tabs. Starts out showing the contents of the first tab, User Profile. The options listed on these 11 tabs let you customize how you experience Wikipedia, as both a reader and an editor. Chapter 20 discusses this customization in detail (page 383).

My Watchlist

Shows the *Special:Watchlist* report, used for monitoring edits by other editors to pages you're interested in. A lengthy discussion of the use of this report begins on page 101.

My Contributions

Shows the *Special:Contributions* report, preloaded with your user name in the "IP Address or username" field. The report lists all your edits in reverse chronological order, going back to the first edit you ever did. Page 100 shows what the report looks like.

NOTE

If you edited a page that was subsequently deleted, you don't see the edit listed in this report. Only administrators get to see such edits.

Log Out

Clicking this link logs you out of Wikipedia immediately. If you continue editing while logged out, Wikipedia records the edits under the IP address of the computer you're using, rather than under your user name. (Page 47 discusses implications of editing using an IP address.)

The Top Tabs

At the top of every page in Wikipedia, you can expect to see six tabs (seven tabs if it's a talk page). These tabs let you switch between the main article page, the talk (discussion) page, the page history, and so on.

NOTE

Pages with the "Special:" prefix, such as the *Special:Watchlist* page, don't have tabs. Special pages, which Wikipedia's software automatically generates, don't have a history, and you can't edit them. Think of them as one-time reports.

Article, Category, or Project Page

The name of the leftmost tab indicates the *namespace* you're in. For example, if you're looking at an article, it says "article". If you're looking at a WikiProject page, it says "project page". (All WikiProject pages have the have the prefix "Wikipedia:".) if you're looking at a Category page (Chapter 17), it says "category", and so on.

NOTE

You may hear other editors use the term *projectspace*. That just means all WikiProject pages. If the leftmost tab says, "project page", you're in projectspace. If you want to get the terminology right, articles are in *mainspace*, not "articlespace" (though if you slip up and use the latter word, other editors will understand what you're talking about).

Discussion

Displays the talk page associated with an article, Wikipedia instructional page, category, or whatever. The tab probably should say "talk page", since that's what everyone calls them. Maybe someday there'll be consensus to change this tab to "talk". (See page 145 for details on how to properly use talk pages.)

Edit This Page (or View Source)

Clicking this tab takes you to the page's editing screen (page 5). The vast majority of Wikipedia pages have an "edit this page" tab, and you're free to do so.

If you see "view source" rather than "edit this page", the page is protected against editing. If you click that tab, you see the page's wikicode (with a shaded background, not the usual white background). You can see how the page was created, even though you can't edit it, and you can even copy the wikitext.

NOTE

Don't confuse "view source" with your Web browser's Source or Page Source command (which is usually under the View menu). That command shows you the page's HTML code, not the wikisource.

"+" (on Talk Pages Only)

The "+" tab is found only on talk pages and a few project pages, such as noticeboards and the Help desk. When you click the tab, Wikipedia starts a new section at the bottom of a page. As discussed on page 149, use this tab when starting a discussion of a new topic (rather than clicking "edit this page" or editing the existing bottom section, and adding a new heading).

History

Shows all edits of the page, going back to the first edit that created the page. (In Wikipedia, an edit is simply the difference between one version of a page and the previous version.) You can also use this page to see all previous versions of the page, with the most recent listed at the top, going back to the very first version. Chapter 5 explains in detail how to interpret the history pages of articles.

Two things to keep in mind when you're looking at a history page:

- As a regular editor, you don't see any versions of a page that an administrator (page 82) or Oversight (page 164) deleted. Pages are very rarely deleted in this way —it only happens in cases such as libel, copyright violations, or violations of personal privacy—but Wikipedia takes such problems very seriously.
- The "edit this page", "move", and "watch" tabs don't apply to history pages—you can't edit them, rename them, or put them on your watchlist. If you click one of these three tabs, you're really acting on the page whose history you were looking at, not the history page itself. That's why when you select the "history" tab, the "article" or "discussion" tab is selected as well, so you can tell what the history page pertains to. Also, that selected tab shows you what page is affected when you click, say, the "move" tab.

Move

Starts the process of renaming a page. Renaming is extensively discussed in Chapter 16.

If you don't see a "move" tab, the page is protected against being renamed. For example, you can't rename Wikipedia's Main Page. Move protection normally happens when pages have been vandalized by renaming, or where there's been a big controversy over the name.

Watch/Unwatch

Watching a page means adding it to the list of pages in your *Special:Watchlist* report. Chapter 6 explains how to monitor pages using your watchlist.

Left Boxes and Links

The left side of every Wikipedia page has four boxes, three containing a number of links, and one search box. The links in some of the boxes change depending on what type of page you're looking at (article, user, and so on). If you come across technical documentation, you'll find that these boxes and links are referred to, collectively, as the Quickbar or the sidebar.

NOTE

This section describes the state of the links on the left side in late 2007. Wikipedia is quite configurable, and that includes the left-side links. The links are likely to stay the same for a while, unless Wikipedia adds any big new features that require new links.

Navigation Box Links

These five links take you to various Wikipedia entry points. They're intended more for readers than for editors.

Main Page

Takes you to Wikipedia's Main Page, which changes daily. You see the day's featured article and picture, lists of new articles and hot news topics, a "this day in history" section, and links to other parts of Wikipedia.

NOTE

Although the page's left tab says "Main Page", not "article", the Main Page is in mainspace, where all articles reside. (Occasionally editors propose that the Main Page be moved to portalspace, since it has portal-like aspects.)

Contents

This page describes all the reference lists (overviews, lists, glossaries, and so on) and indices available to browse Wikipedia. It's lengthy, comprehensive, and fairly boring.

Featured content

Here's where you can see a randomly chosen selection of featured content—a featured article, picture, list, portal, topic, and sound. The page also has links to the six pages with compete lists of such featured items, a list of new featured content, a section on feature content procedures (criteria, candidates, and so on). For good measure, there's a navigational template at the bottom ("Content listings") that, while useful, has absolutely nothing to do with featured content.

Current events

Shows the "Current events" portal, which has links to new or updated Wikipedia stories about headline news and other current events.

Wikipedia's mission isn't to supply breaking news, so there's a link to a separate project, Wikinews, for those who want to write news stories. The news coverage at Wikinews is much less than at Wikipedia, though, due to the relatively few active editors at Wikinews.

Random article

Takes you to a completely random article among the two million-odd articles on Wikipedia. Clicking the link 20 or so times will give you a pretty good idea of the range of Wikipedia articles, in terms of both topic and quality.

Interaction Box Links

This box has a grab bag of links, all loosely related to different ways you can interact with Wikipedia, from reading about it to editing it.

About Wikipedia

This page has all the facts and figures about Wikipedia. This information may interest readers and potential editors, but it's especially good if you want to use Wikipedia for research or citation, or if you're just curious about Wikipedia's history and ownership. You can learn more about these topics in this book's Introduction, and Appendix C and D.

Community portal

Clicking this link is like going backstage at Wikipedia. Just as if you wander backstage at a busy theater, someone's sure to put a prop in your hand or ask you to help raise the curtain, the *Community portal* page is buzzing with gobs of links to projects that need a hand, groups that want help with articles, and more. There are also links to Wikipedia's internal newsletter—The Wikipedia Signpost—and weekly podcast.

Recent changes

The *Recent changes* page (*Special:Recentchanges*) takes a dip into the stream of Wikipedia edits—the more than 100,000 daily changes to Wikipedia. You can change the namespace to limit what you see; for example, you can choose "(Main)" to see just edits to articles. You can narrow which edits you see; for example, showing only edits by IP (anonymous) editors, in case you're on the prowl for vandals. In fact, the *Recent changes* page is primarily for vandal-fighting, as discussed on page 122.

Contact Wikipedia

A wide range of links for the press, readers, and editors. (No, Wikipedia doesn't have an 800 number to call with complaints. Neither does the Wikimedia Foundation.)

Donate to Wikipedia

Wikipedia runs solely on donations. Credit cards and other forms of payment are gladly accepted.

Help

Goes to the *Help:Contents* page, an organized overview of Wikipedia for editors. This page is discussed extensively in Appendix C (page 448).

Search Box

Wikipedia's search box is handy for the shortcuts mentioned throughout this book, but, frankly, the underlying search engine isn't very good for general searches. If you don't get to the page you want when you click Go, and don't see what you're looking for in the search results, it's time for plan B—using an external search engine—as described in the box on page 432.

Toolbox Links

The first four links in the Toolbox are for primarily for editors, the last three for readers.

What links here

Lists all the *incoming* links to the page where you are. As an editor, you'll find this useful in several ways:

- When you're improving an article (page 352), you can identify potential *outgoing* links that would improve the article.
- When looking at a disambiguation page, you can identify incoming links that need to be fixed (page 318).

- When you're trying to figure out how a template works by looking at pages that use it. (All pages that use a template link to the template page.)
- When you're trying to figure out whether a Wikipedia instructional page is often cited or virtually ignored.

Related changes

Shows the page *Special:Recentchangeslinked*. Here's an example of how it works: Suppose you're looking at article A, which has wikilinks to articles X, Y, and Z. Clicking the "Related changes" link displays a report showing recent edits to those three articles. Page 116 describes using this page as part of an additional watchlist.

NOTE

If you type *Special:Recentchangeslinked* into the search box on the left, then you get a "No target" error page. The search box doesn't know what page you're looking at in the window.

Upload file

Starts the process of uploading an image to Wikipedia. Also has link to uploading to the commons (page 271).

Special pages

Lists about 60 of these pages, essentially one-time reports, which are like snapshots and can't be edited. Among the most common that you'll use as an editor are the *Special:Contributions* report (page 100) and the *Special:Watchlist* report (page 101), both of which are also available from the links on the upper right.

Printable version

Generates a page without all of the tabs, boxes, and links described in this Appendix, which is more suitable for printing.

Permanent link

Equivalent to clicking the most recent version of a page in the page's history tab. The URL points to that version, so you can use it as a permanent link.

Cite this article

Appears only when a page is an article. It provides a cut-and-paste citation for that article in a wide variety of formats (APA style, MLA style, BibTeX entry, and so on).

NOTE

When you use "Cite this article", you see a disclaimer advising you not to use Wikipedia (or any encyclopedia) as your only source for information in professional or academic settings, like published articles and term papers. As the disclaimer says, "Citing an encyclopedia as an important reference in footnotes or bibliographies may result in censure or a failing grade."

Languages

This link appears only when an editor has included at least one link within the English Wikipedia page to a comparable page in another language version of Wikipedia. Such links are called *interlanguage* links, and they're at the bottom of the page's wikicode. Most articles in the English Wikipedia don't have a link to a comparable page on another language Wikipedia. Most of the larger articles, such as featured articles, do have such links.

Links in the Body of the Page

The body of a Wikipedia page is where the content goes. It's a blank page Wikipedia provides for editors to fill in. On regular Wikipedia pages, category links always appear at the very bottom of a page's body. All other types of links, including the table of contents, can show up wherever the editor wants to put them.

However, as discussed in Chapter 13, there are standards for article pages: which sections go where, and how sections should be named, and where the table of contents goes. Still, these are human-monitored standards, not software-determined formats, so if you see something unusual, take a look—it may be something that needs fixing.

There are two kinds of pages where human editors can't add or edit links:

- **Special pages**. Special pages are automatically generated one-time reports. Since you can't edit these pages, you can't add links to them.
- **Category pages**. The body of a Category page is essentially a bunch of links that the software has kept track of.

Bottom Links

At the bottom of every Wikipedia page you'll find a standard set of links, as shown in Figure A-1. These links take you to Wikipedia's five disclaimers—general, risk, medical, legal, and content.

Figure A-1. The standard links at the bottom of each Wikipedia page include ones to the license (GNDL) under which content can be legally copied, to the home page of the Wikimedia Foundation, which owns Wikipedia, and to Wikipedia's privacy policy and disclaimers.

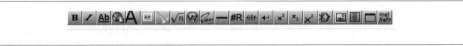

Figure A-2. The edit toolbar is always just above the edit box, near the top of the page. If you're not sure what an icon does, just move your mouse pointer to one of the icons and see what the tooltip says.

Additional Features in Edit Mode

When you click "edit this page" or the "edit" link for a section, the page's format changes.

Edit Toolbar

At the top of the page when you're in editing mode, you see the edit toolbar (Figure A-2).

Most icons on the toolbar work in either of two ways:

- If you select text and then click an icon, then you format the selected text.
- If you don't select any text, then when you click on an icon, the software adds and formats some sample text for you, highlighting it so you can be replace it with your own text.

Exceptions to this are the signature icon, the horizontal line, the line break, and the table insertion icon, which aren't formatting actions. Instead, they insert specific text into the edit box, wherever the cursor is.

NOTE

Don't highlight text before clicking the table icon, because the resulting table is probably going to be too simple for your needs. See page 265 for more detail on creating tables.

One preference lets you hide the edit toolbar if you never use it. If you haven't turned the toolbar off, but you don't see it, or it doesn't function correctly, then you may not have JavaScript turned on (see page 401).

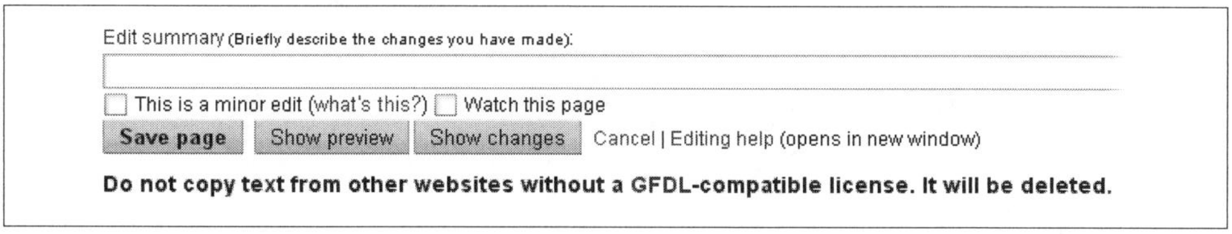

Figure A-3. Below the edit box is a box to enter the edit summary for the change you're making to the page you're editing, plus two checkboxes, three buttons, and three links.

Edit Box

The edit box is where you find (or enter) the wikicode that creates content for a Wikipedia page. If you're creating a page, it starts out as a big, empty box. You can specify the size of the edit box in your preferences (see page 393).

Below the Edit Box

A number of essential things are located just below the edit box (Figure A-3).

- **Cancel**. Cancels your edit and goes back to reading mode.
- **Editing help**. Opens the page *Wikipedia:Cheatsheet*, which has some fairly basic editing information. (The shortcut is *WP:CHEAT*, if you want to get there via the search box.)
- **GFDL**. Goes to *GNU Free Documentation License*, which explains the "copyleft" license used by Wikipedia to release its pages as free content.

NOTE

In December 2007, the Wikimedia Foundation requested that this license be modified to allow the Foundation to move all its projects, including Wikipedia, to a different free content license, Creative Commons CC-BY-SA. If that happens, you'll see a different link, which explains whatever new licensing scheme is in place.

- **Edit summary**. As discussed on page 9, always explain your edit by putting something into the edit summary box.
- **"This is a minor edit" checkbox**. Turn on this box if you're making an edit that's so tiny it could never be the subject of dispute—like changing a misspelling or punctuation. Page 108 has more details about edits marked as minor.

TIP

You can change a setting so this box is always checked by default (and you uncheck it only as needed). See page 394.

- **"Watch this page" checkbox**. Adds a page to your watchlist (page 103).

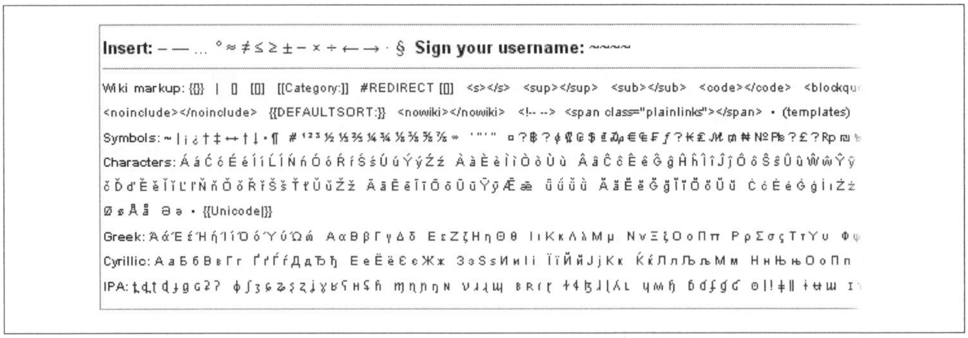

Figure A-4. There are hundreds of symbols and other text below the edit summary box, which appear in the edit box when you click them. These include wiki markup, symbols, special characters, the Greek and Cyrillic alphabets, International Phonetic Alphabet (IPA) symbols, and so on.

- **"Save page" button**. Click here when you've finished your edit. (Don't forget to enter an edit summary and preview the page first.)

- **"Show preview" button**. It's always a good idea to check your work before saving it (page 8).

- **"Show changes" button**. Shows the difference, above the edit box, between the current version of the section or page you're editing and the section or page as you've changed it. (In other words, it's a diff of your yet-to-be-saved edit.) It's useful if you've forgotten what you've done; or to check whether you've deleted some text by mistake; or to recover some deleted text without having to go back to the article, in another window, and copy from there.

Insertable Text

Moving further down the page, you find a large amount of text in blue, as shown in Figure A-4. Clicking one of these items inserts something into the edit box—something that would otherwise require a lot of typing or cryptic codes.

Notes

Below the insertable text is a link to the Sandbox, for risk-free editing. (There's more on the sandbox on page 4.) Then there are several notes directed to you as an editor, including one that's often quoted when ownership issues arise concerning an edit: "If you don't want your writing to be edited mercilessly or redistributed for profit by others, *do not submit it*."

List of Transcluded Pages

Finally, at the very bottom of the edit window is a list of *transcluded pages*—generally, but not always, these are templates (page 17). This list is extremely helpful in figuring

---

out, on the rare occasions that page displays are odd, whether the problem might be in the wikicode that a template adds to a page.

Additional Options on User Pages

When you're viewing a user page or user talk page, you'll see three more links in the middle of the toolbox.

User Contributions

Shows all edits by the editor whose user or user talk page you're looking at. Page 100 shows what the report looks like. This report lets you check for unreverted vandalism or spam by someone who just vandalized or spammed an article. It also help you get a more general sense of whether an editor is doing constructive edits or not.

Chapter 7 discusses a "revert, review, report or warn" process for vandalism; this report is one of the major parts of the review step. It also has a link to a page that shows whether the editor has been previously blocked.

Logs

Shows a combined display of a number of different logs: upload, patrol, page move, user creation, deletion, protection, user block, user renaming, and user rights. (The last five are logs of actions that normal editors can't do.)

You can narrow the list of edits in three ways:

- By selecting a log type
- By selecting the user name for a user of interest
- By selecting a page name ("Article", or "User talk:Username", for example)

Normal edits aren't in any of those logs; for those, see the *Recent changes* special page (filterable by namespace), or use the *User contributions* special page, or use a page history.

E-mail This User

If an editor has enabled email from other users (Figure 20-3, page 385) and you have a confirmed email address (page 52), then you can email that editor. Details on this email process are on page 162.

Keyboard Shortcuts

If you like to keep your hands on your keyboard, typing key combinations to save time rather than using the mouse, you may be surprised not to find many keyboard shortcuts sprinkled throughout this book. Wikipedia does have such shortcuts, but the exact key combinations depend not only on your operating system (Mac or Windows) and your Web browser, but even the version of the Web browser you're using.

The page *Wikipedia:Keyboard shortcuts* (shortcut: *WP:K*) tells you what special keys to press in combination letter or number keys to do something. For example, in Internet Explorer for Windows, Shift+Alt+Z takes you to the Main Page. A number of the keystrokes work for administrators (sysops) only. But you'll find keyboard shortcuts for the Wikipedia features in the following locations:

- The search box
- Buttons below the edit box, like "Show preview" and Save
- The standard tabs along the top of the page
- The six links at the upper-right of the screen

Reader's Guide to Wikipedia

Most of this book is aimed at folks who want to edit Wikipedia articles and become more active in the Wikipedia community. But this appendix is all about appreciating Wikipedia as a *reader*. It gives you some background on what Wikipedia is and how to get the most out of it even if you have no intention of editing an article.

Some Basics

Wikipedia is a collaboratively written encyclopedia. It's a *wiki*, which means that the underlying software (in this case, a system called *MediaWiki*) tracks every change to every page. That change-tracking system makes it easy to remove (*revert*) inappropriate edits, and to identify repeat offenders who can be blocked from future editing.

Wikipedia is run by the not-for-profit *Wikimedia Foundation*; that's why you don't see advertising on any of its pages, or on any of Wikipedia's sister projects that the Foundation runs (more on those later). To date, almost all the money to run Wikipedia and its smaller sister projects has come from donations. Once a year or so, for a month or so, you may see a fundraising banner instead of the standard small-print request for donations at the top of each page, but, so far, that's about as intrusive as the foundation's fundraising gets.

What Wikipedia is Not

To understand what Wikipedia *is*, you may find it very helpful to understand what Wikipedia is *not*. Wikipedia's goal is not, as some people think, to become the repository of all knowledge. It has always defined itself as an *encyclopedia*—a reference work with articles on all types of subjects, but not as a final destination, and not as something that encompasses every detail in the world. (The U.S. Library of Congress has roughly 30 million *books* in its collection, not to mention tens of millions of other items, by comparison to about two million *articles* in Wikipedia). Still, there's much confusion about Wikipedia's scope.

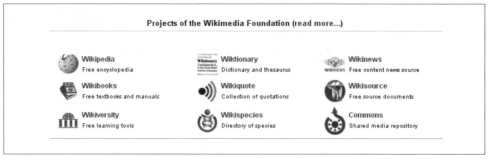

Figure B-1. The Wikimedia Foundation has eight parallel projects, the oldest of which is Wikipedia, plus the Commons, a central repository of pictures and other media.

Wikipedia has a well-known policy (to experienced editors, at least) stating what kinds of information belong in the encyclopedia. The sister projects that the Wikimedia Foundation supports, such as Wiktionary, fulfill some of the roles that Wikipedia does not.

Wikipedia's Sister Projects

The Wikimedia Foundation has seven projects that are parallel to Wikipedia, plus a project called the Commons, where pictures and other freely-usable media are stored for use by all projects in all languages (Figure B-1).

Several of the projects listed in Figure B-1 overlap (or potentially overlap) with Wikipedia:

- **Wiktionary** is a free, multilingual dictionary with definitions, etymologies, pronunciations, sample quotations, synonyms, antonyms and translations. It's the "lexical companion" to Wikipedia. It's common at Wikipedia to move (*transwiki*) articles to Wiktionary because they're essentially definitions.

- **Wikinews** and Wikipedia clearly overlap. A story in the national news (Hurricane Katrina, for example) is likely to show up on both. Unlike Wikipedia, Wikinews includes articles that are original writing, but the vast majority are sourced. Because of the overlap between the two, Wikinews has struggled to attract editors. Given a choice, most editors chose to work with Wikipedia articles, which are more widely viewed.

- **Wikisource** is an archive of "free artistic and intellectual works created throughout history." Except for annotation and translation, these are essentially historical documents (fiction as well as nonfiction) that are in the public domain or whose copyright has expired.

Policy: What Wikipedia is Not

Wikipedia's policy, *What Wikipedia is Not*, is lengthy, so this section just hits the highlights. Aside from the what seem obvious to more experienced editors at Wikipedia ("Wikipedia is not a blog, Web space provider, social networking, or memorial site", "Wikipedia is not a mirror or a repository of links, images, or media files") and ones that follow from sister projects ("Wikipedia is not a dictionary", "Wikipedia is not a textbook"), here are several that readers and contributors frequently misunderstand:

- **Wikipedia is not a publisher of original thought**. You won't find groundbreaking analysis, original reporting, or anything else in Wikipedia that hasn't been published elsewhere first. (If you do find any of these, it's a violation of the rules and likely to be removed when other editors discover it.) Thousands of wikis do welcome original research and original writing, but Wikipedia isn't one of them. (You'll find hundreds listed at WikiIndex.org (*http://WikiIndex.org*), a site not associated with Wikipedia.)

- **Wikipedia is not a directory**. Articles aren't intended to help you navigate a local bureaucracy, find the nearest Italian restaurant, or otherwise include information that other Web pages do a perfectly fine job of maintaining.

- **Wikipedia is not a manual or guidebook**. Wikipedia articles aren't intended to offer advice, or to include, tutorials, walk-throughs, instruction manuals, game guides, recipes, or travel or other guides.

- There actually are wikis for how-to stuff (wikiHow.com (*http://wikiHow.com*)) and for travel (Wikitravel.org (*http://Wikitravel.org*)), but neither is affiliated with the Wikimedia Foundation and its projects.

- **Wikipedia is not an indiscriminate collection of information**. It's not the place for frequently asked question (FAQ) lists, collections of lyrics, long lists of statistics, routine news coverage, and "matters lacking encyclopedic substance, such as announcements, sports, gossip, and tabloid journalism."

How Good is Wikipedia?

The best answer may be "Compared to what?" Wikipedia wouldn't be one of the world's top 10 most visited Web sites (that includes all 250-plus language versions, not just the English Wikipedia) if readers didn't find it better than available alternatives. To be sure, Wikipedia is an encyclopedia under construction. As the general disclaimer (see the Disclaimers link at the bottom of every page) says, "WIKIPEDIA MAKES NO GUARANTEE OF VALIDITY. Please be advised that nothing found here has necessarily been reviewed by people with the expertise required to provide you with complete, accurate or reliable information."

On the other hand, Wikipedia has been reviewed by a number of outside experts, most famously in an article published in *Nature* in December 2005. In that article, a group

Figure B-2. Featured articles (articles with the highest assessed quality in Wikipedia) have a star in the upper right corner. You can click the star to learn how articles get their featured status (page 221).

of experts compared 42 articles in Wikipedia to the corresponding articles in Encyclopaedia Britannica. Their conclusion: "The number of errors in a typical Wikipedia science article is not substantially more than in Encyclopaedia Britannica." (The actual count was 162 errors vs. 123.) That comparison is now more than 2 years old, and editors have continued to improve those 42 articles as well as all the others that were in the encyclopedia back then. (For a full list of outside reviews of Wikipedia, see the page *Wikipedia:External peer review*.)

None of which is to say that Wikipedia editors are wildly happy about the quality of many, if not most articles. Those most knowledgeable about Wikipedia have repeatedly talked about the need to improve quality, and that quality is now more important than quantity. The challenge is whether Wikipedia can implement a combination of technological and procedural changes that'll make a difference, because so far relatively incremental changes haven't made much of a dent in the problem of accuracy.

So, should you trust Wikipedia? That should depend somewhat on the article. If you see a star in the upper right corner (see Figure B-2), indicating a featured article, you can be virtually certain that what you'll read is correct, and that the cited sources back up what's in the article.

You'll find that each article contains clues to its reliability. If you see a well-written article with at least a reasonable number of footnotes, then you should be reasonably confident that almost all the information in the article is correct. If you see a lot of run-on sentences and templates noting a lack of sources, point of view problems, and so on, then you should be skeptical.

You can get more clues from the article talk (discussion) page; just click the "discussion" tab. At the top, see if a Wikipedia WikiProject (a group of editors working on articles of common interest) has rated the article. Also at the top, look for links to archived talk pages, indicating that a lot of editors have talked a lot about the article, and have therefore edited it a lot.

If there are no archive pages, and not much indication of activity on the talk page you're looking at, then the opposite is true—few editors have been interested in editing the article. That doesn't mean it's not good—some excellent good editors toil in relative backwaters, producing gems without much discussion with other editors. Still, absence of editor activity should make you more doubtful that you've found an example of Wikipedia's best.

Bottom line: Think of Wikipedia as a starting place. If you're just interested in a quick overview of a topic, it may be an ending place as well. But Wikipedia's ideal is for articles to cite the sources from which their content was created, so that really interested readers can use those sources to get more information. If the editors at Wikipedia are doing things right, *those sources* are the ones that readers can absolutely depend upon to be informative and accurate.

Navigating Within Wikipedia

There are two basic ways to find interesting articles in Wikipedia: Do a search, or browse, starting from the Main Page. Wikipedia has lots of organizing features depending on how you want to browse, like overviews, portals, lists, indexes, and categories. But for a bit of amusement, you can also try a couple of unusual ways to go from article to article, as discussed in this section.

Searching Wikipedia

On the left side of each Wikipedia page, you'll find a box labeled "search", with two buttons—Go and Search. Wikipedia's search engine is widely acknowledged to be not particularly good. Your best bet to find what you want is to type the title you're looking for into the search box, and then click Go (or press Enter). If you're right, and Wikipedia finds an *exact* match, you'll be at that article. If it doesn't find an exact match, Wikipedia provides you with a link to "create this page", which you should ignore if you're searching only for reading purposes. It also provides you some search results. Figure B-3 shows the result of a failed search for the title *Institute of Institutional Research*, including the start of some best guess results).

NOTE

If you click "Search", for curiosity's sake, you'll just get some so-so search results. For example, if you search for *Reagan wife*, the article *Nancy Reagan* shows up 6th and *Jane Wyman* shows up 16th. Worse, the context Wikipedia's result page shows is terrible. With a Google search, by contrast, you can get these two names from the context shown for the first result without even having to click a link.

If you don't arrive at an article page when you click Go, and you don't find what you're looking for in the search results toward the bottom of the page, your next best move is to switch to another search engine. Wikipedia makes this very easy for you—just change "MediaWiki search" to another menu choice, as shown in Figure B-4.

Figure B-5 shows the search done again using Google. To those familiar with the Wikipedia search engine, it's not surprising that the top results are completely different.

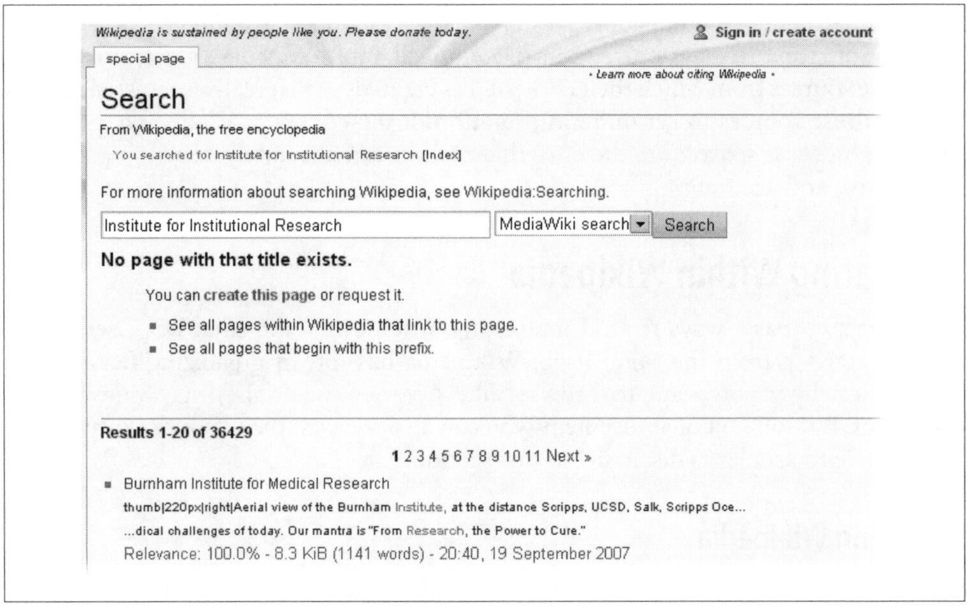

Figure B-3. When Wikipedia can't find an exact match to a Go request, it provides search results, but it also offers a link to create an article with the same name as the word or phrase you entered.

POWER USERS' CLINIC

Searching from Outside Wikipedia

Figure B-4 shows how to use an outside search engine to search Wikipedia, once your initial attempt to find an article has failed. You can do the same thing (get the same results as Figure B-4, for example) without using a Wikipedia page initially, which may be easier.

To do so, type *site:en.wikipedia.org* into the search engine's search box, along with whatever word or phrase you were looking for. (The "en" prefix restricts results to the English Wikipedia, otherwise you could get results from a version in the other 250 or so languages.) This technique works for the big three: Google, Yahoo, and MSN searches. If you use another search engine, look at the "advanced search" option (often available only after you do a search) for how to specify that the results should come only from one domain.

You generally *don't* want to initiate an internal Wikipedia search via your browser. If you see a pull-down menu that lets you pick Wikipedia as your search engine, ignore that choice. It just gets you to Wikipedia's internal search engine, which, as discussed earlier, just isn't very good.

The single exception to all the above is if what you're searching has been added to Wikipedia in the last day or two. If so, only the Wikipedia search engine is likely to give you a successful search, because that engine is the only one using the live database

---

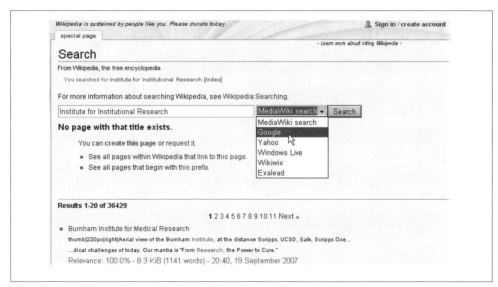

Figure B-4. Wikipedia makes it easy to pick another search engine. Here Google's being selected, but other search engines are available. Take advantage of this option if your initial Go attempt doesn't succeed.

for its searches. Everyone else has a not quite up-to-date *list* of Wikipedia pages, and not-quite up-to-date *versions* of Wikipedia pages.

Navigating from the Main Page

You can also navigate Wikipedia via a number of different starting points. The best way to get to them is via the links near the top of the Main Page, as shown in Figure B-6. Every Wikipedia page has a link to the Main Page, on the left side, in the navigation box below the Wikipedia globe. From the Main Page, you can see the vastness of Wikipedia via three different approaches: categories, portals, and the A-Z index.

Categories

Any article may belong to one or more categories (Chapter 17), which you'll find listed at the bottom of the article. Like everything else in an article, editors add the categories, so categories are only as accurate as the people who enter them; like everything else, if someone sees a mistake, she can fix it. When you click the Categories link shown in Figure B-6, you'll see the master index (see Figure B-7).

The text in Figure B-7 is hand-crafted, not computer-generated, but once you leave the page via a link on it, the lists you'll see will be computer-generated and thus completely current. For example, when you click Geography at the top of the index, that takes you

Figure B-5. The same search for "Institute for Institutional Research" as in Figure C-1, but this time searching with Google. The search results are completely different.

Figure B-6. Wikipedia's Main Page is accessible via a single click from any other page in Wikipedia. At the top are three links to starting points within Wikipedia that provide different top-down views.

to a section of the page called "Geography and places", with the main category Geography. Click that word, and you'll see Figure B-8. If you're interested in Geography, you can drill down in whatever subcategory you want until you reach actual links to articles, and then follow them.

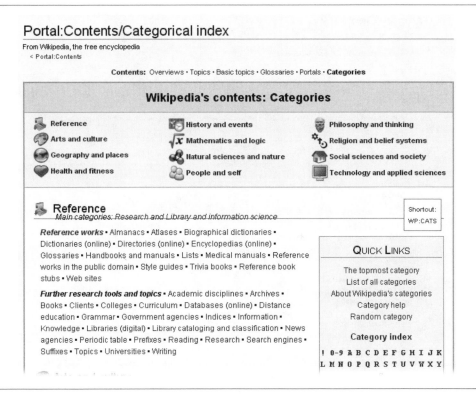

Figure B-7. Here's the top-level list of categories. It's the starting point for drilling down to find all articles in any particular subcategory.

NOTE

Not every article in Wikipedia is intricately categorized. For example, at the bottom of the *Category:Geography* page, you see articles in that category which are *not* in any subcategory (you can't see them in Figure B-8). Those may be truly unique articles, or articles just waiting for further categorization work.

Portals

From the Main Page, you can also follow the bolded link "All portals" to the main page for portals (Figure B-9). Like categories, portals can be a great way to narrow down the number of articles you're particularly interested in reading, or to lead you to articles that you otherwise might never have known existed.

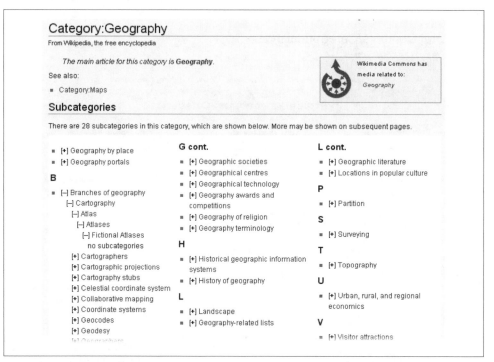

Figure B-8. The category Geography *had 28 subcategories when this screenshot was taken. In the "B" section, you see an expansion of one of those subcategories, Branches of Geography, displaying all the sub-subcategories until there are no further ones, along one line of that subcategory.*

The A-Z index

The third entry point link on the Main Page is the A-Z index. It's equivalent to browsing the shelves of a library, with the books in alphabetical order on the shelves. Figure B-10 shows what you'll see if you click the "A-Z index" link at the top of the Main Page.

If you were trying, for example, to find the name of an article that began with an unusual pair of letters (say, *Cg*), then the A-Z index may be helpful (see Figure B-11).

The alphabetical index to articles is actually more useful after you've drilled down one level. Now you have the option of searching for articles that start with three or four or even more characters.

Other entry points

You may have noticed, in Figure B-7 and Figure B-9, a top-level row of links: Contents, Overviews, Academia, Topics, Basic Topics, and so on. Three of these (Overviews, Topics, Basic Topics) are also high-level entry points into Wikipedia that you might want to check out to see if one or more are interesting.

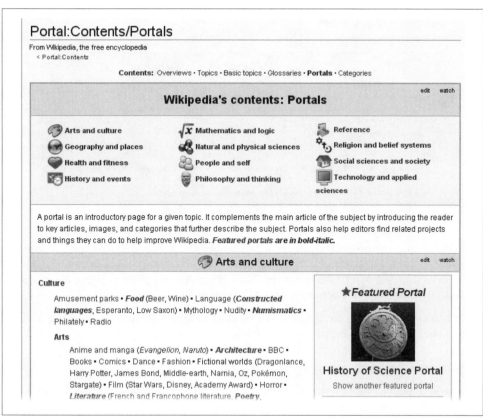

Figure B-9. Portals are probably one of the least known ways to find articles on Wikipedia. If you're particularly interested in a topic, one of the 500 or so existing portals can be a great page to bookmark.

Categories

You can view Wikipedia's entire hierarchy of categories by clicking the Categories link near the top of the Main Page, as shown in Figure B-7. But you can also use the category system to browse Wikipedia in a number of other ways, using tools both inside and outside of Wikipedia. For example, there are links at the bottom of each article that let you find articles in related categories. You can also find articles that fall into two different categories. You can even narrow your search by category when you're using an external search engine.

Category links at the bottom of articles

At the bottom of virtually every article, you'll find the categories that Wikipedia editors have assigned to that article. Figure B-12 shows an example.

Wikipedia:Quick index

From Wikipedia, the free encyclopedia

A–Z Index

The MediaWiki software is case sensitive: Pages under **AA** will correspond to different pages compared with **Aa**. On each index page, *italics* indicate redirects. To view the index at the precise starting point of your choosing, *use **Prefix index***.

Shortcut:
WP:QI

See also: ***Wikipedia:Contents***.

No. :		0	1	2	3	4	5	6	7	8	9				
	-a	-b	-c	-d	-e	-f	-g	-h	-i	-j	-k	-l	-m	-n	-o	-p	-q	-r	-s	-t	-u	-v	-w	-x	-y	-z
	-A	-B	-C	-D	-E	-F	-G	-H	-I	-J	-K	-L	-M	-N	-O	-P	-Q	-R	-S	-T	-U	-V	-W	-X	-Y	-Z
A	Aa	Ab	Ac	Ad	Ae	Af	Ag	Ah	Ai	Aj	Ak	Al	Am	An	Ao	Ap	Aq	Ar	As	At	Au	Av	Aw	Ax	Ay	Az
	AA	AB	AC	AD	AE	AF	AG	AH	AI	AJ	AK	AL	AM	AN	AO	AP	AQ	AR	AS	AT	AU	AV	AW	AX	AY	AZ
B	Ba	Bb	Bc	Bd	Be	Bf	Bg	Bh	Bi	Bj	Bk	Bl	Bm	Bn	Bo	Bp	Bq	Br	Bs	Bt	Bu	Bv	Bw	Bx	By	Bz
	BA	BB	BC	BD	BE	BF	BG	BH	BI	BJ	BK	BL	BM	BN	BO	BP	BQ	BR	BS	BT	BU	BV	BW	BX	BY	BZ
C	Ca	Cb	Cc	Cd	Ce	Cf	Cg	Ch	Ci	Cj	Ck	Cl	Cm	Cn	Co	Cp	Cq	Cr	Cs	Ct	Cu	Cv	Cw	Cx	Cy	Cz

Figure B-10. The A-Z index (also called the Quick Index) lets you go directly to a list of articles beginning with any two characters: El or Na or Tr or whatever.

Click any of these categories, and you'll be on a category page similar to Figure B-8. With a click, you can jump to another article in the same category.

Articles in two different categories

One of Wikipedia's most requested features is "category intersection"—the ability to get a list of all articles that fall into two or more categories. Wikipedia still lacks that ability, but you can find it at an off-Wikipedia page called CatScan at http://tools.wikimedia.de/~daniel/WikiSense/CategoryIntersect.php. Figure B-13 shows how to use it to find, for example, baseball players that have been members of both the Seattle Mariners and the Washington Nationals.

WARNING

When using CatScan, capitalization—except for the very first letter—is critical. For example, in Figure B-13, if you had search on the category "Seattle Mariners Players" instead of "Seattle Mariners players," you'd have gotten no matches.

Searching for Categories

External search engines are generally better than Wikipedia's search feature lacks, as discussed on page 431. When you use an external search engine, you simply restrain your search results to Wikipedia pages and apply any other options you like. If you use Google, for example, you can search just Wikipedia category pages by typing

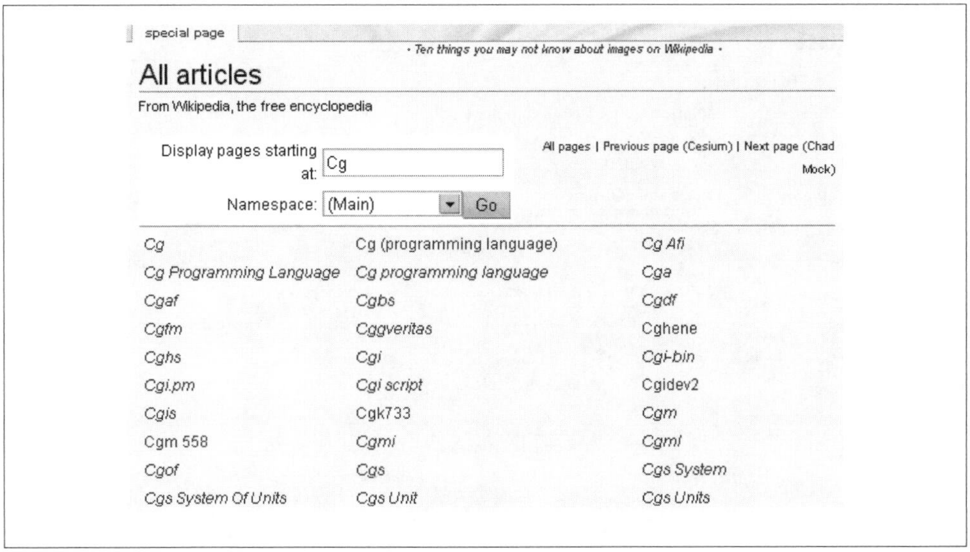

| special page | · Ten things you may not know about images on Wikipedia · |

All articles

From Wikipedia, the free encyclopedia

Display pages starting at: `Cg`

All pages | Previous page (Cesium) | Next page (Chad Mock)

Namespace: (Main) ▼ Go

Cg	Cg (programming language)	*Cg Afi*
Cg Programming Language	*Cg programming language*	*Cga*
Cgaf	*Cgbs*	*Cgdf*
Cgfm	*Cggveritas*	Cghene
Cghs	*Cgi*	*Cgi-bin*
Cgi.pm	*Cgi script*	Cgidev2
Cgis	*Cgk733*	*Cgm*
Cgm 558	*Cgmi*	*Cgml*
Cgof	*Cgs*	Cgs System
Cgs System Of Units	*Cgs Unit*	*Cgs Units*

Figure B-11. If you pick a two-letter starting pair, in Figure B-10, and click that link, here's what you see. The links in regular text are articles; the links in italics (the majority) are redirects, which take you to an article with a different name. Redirects are used for misspellings, for less common variants of a particular name, and for subjects that don't (yet) have their own articles, and are related to an existing article to which the reader will be directed.

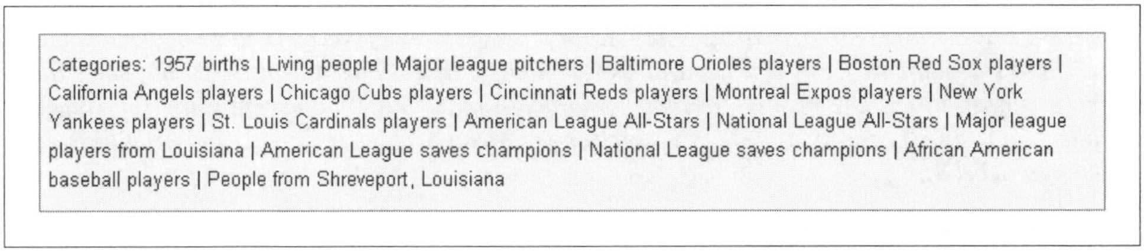

Categories: 1957 births | Living people | Major league pitchers | Baltimore Orioles players | Boston Red Sox players | California Angels players | Chicago Cubs players | Cincinnati Reds players | Montreal Expos players | New York Yankees players | St. Louis Cardinals players | American League All-Stars | National League All-Stars | Major league players from Louisiana | American League saves champions | National League saves champions | African American baseball players | People from Shreveport, Louisiana

Figure B-12. The article on major league baseball player Lee Smith has, at the bottom, a larger than usual number of categories. In this case, it's mostly because Smith was a member of eight different teams.

site:en.wikipedia.org/wiki/Category in the search box. Figure B-14 shows an example of using this domain restriction in Google.

TIP

You can also use the technique shown in Figure B-14—finding category pages of interest—before you use the category intersection tool CatScan, to avoid having to guess the exact names of categories that you want to use in CatScan.

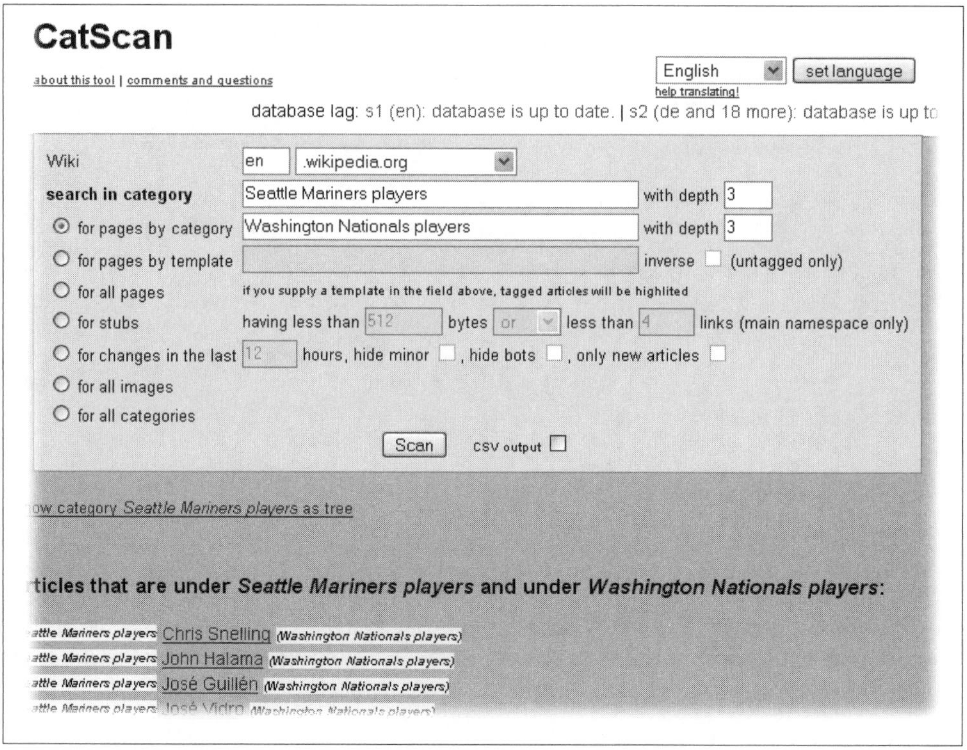

CatScan

about this tool | comments and questions

English ▼ | set language

help translating!

database lag: s1 (en): database is up to date. | s2 (de and 18 more): database is up to

Wiki	en	.wikipedia.org ▼	
search in category	Seattle Mariners players		with depth 3
⦿ for pages by category	Washington Nationals players		with depth 3
○ for pages by template			inverse ☐ (untagged only)
○ for all pages	if you supply a template in the field above, tagged articles will be highlited		
○ for stubs	having less than 512 bytes or ▼ less than 4 links (main namespace only)		
○ for changes in the last 12	hours, hide minor ☐ , hide bots ☐ , only new articles ☐		
○ for all images			
○ for all categories			

Scan   CSV output ☐

ow category *Seattle Mariners players* as tree

ticles that are under *Seattle Mariners players* and under *Washington Nationals players*:

attle Mariners players Chris Snelling *(Washington Nationals players)*
attle Mariners players John Halama *(Washington Nationals players)*
attle Mariners players José Guillén *(Washington Nationals players)*
attle Mariners players José Vidro *(Washington Nationals players)*

Figure B-13. When you search for articles by category using CatScan, you can choose how many levels of sub- and sub-sub-categories you want to search. This search shows a depth of 3, but since there were no subcategories, the results are only for a depth of 1. But if you were using the category Architects, you'd see results in subcategories such as American Architects (level 2) and Architects from Cincinnati (level 3).

Other Ways of Navigating

When you're not on the Main Page, every Wikipedia page offers ways of browsing around. Most of them are in the list of links at the left.

Random article

If you want to get a sense of the more than two million articles in the English language, a good way is to use the *Random article* feature. On any page on the *http://en.wikipe dia.org* Web site, you find this link at upper-left (Figure B-15) that you can click to ask the Wikipedia software to select one of those two million articles for you.

What links here

When you're on an article page, you may find that another link on the left side of the screen, the first in the box labeled *toolbox* (see Figure B-16) can also be fun to play with.

Figure B-14. This Google search restricts results to category pages, since "site:en.wikipedia.org/wiki/Category" was typed into the search box. It furthermore requires that the title of the category page contain the word "spy"; note "intitle:spy" at the beginning of the search term. There are 16 categories with "spy" in the title. Searching for "spy" instead of "intitle:spy" would turn up category pages with "spy" anywhere on the page (of which there are about 500).

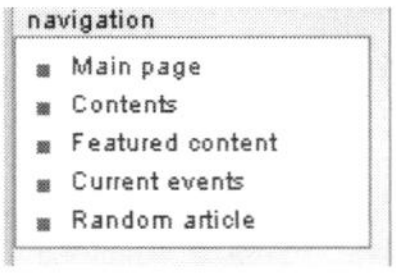

Figure B-15. On the left side of any Wikipedia page, the navigation box has a "Random article" link. Click again to go elsewhere. Click it 20 or 30 times, and you have a pretty good idea of Wikipedia's wide range of articles.

Click *What links here,* and you're now looking at a list of incoming links to the article you were just reading.

The list of links may seem random, but it's not—the oldest page (based on when the page was created) is listed first, the youngest page is listed last (and may very well not show on the screen, which normally lists just 50).

Figure B-16. The toolbox on the left of the screen includes a "What links here" link. Click it to see all the Wikipedia pages that link into the page you're on.

Six degrees of Wikipedia

It can also be fun to just follow links from one article to another: For example, start at *Kevin Bacon*, then to *Circle in the Square Theatre*, to *Theodore Mann*, to *Drama Desk Award*, to *New York Post*, and end up at *Alexander Hamilton*. You can also do the same with the "What links here" links mentioned in the previous section.

Images

Wikipedia aims to distribute free content worldwide in any and all media—including the images used in its articles, and even articles uploaded to its repository for potential use in articles. What does that mean to you? It means you can download almost all of these images to your computer, free of charge.

Images in Wikipedia Articles

If you see an image in a Wikipedia article that you'd like to have, just click it. You'll see a new page showing a larger image, as shown in Figure B-17.

The vast majority of images on Wikipedia are free content—they're in the public domain or have Creative Commons licenses, for example. If you come across an image labeled as a "fair use" image (a screenshot of a commercial software program, for example), don't treat it as free content. Don't download it unless you're sure you're not infringing a copyright by doing so.

The Commons

Several years ago, the Wikimedia Foundation realized that it didn't make sense to have images stored on language-specific Wikipedias, so it created the Commons (*http://commons.wikimedia.org*) as a central storage area available to all language Wikipedias. Think of it as a stock media site for Wikipedia and other Wikimedia Foundation projects (it has sounds and other media files as well as images). In fact, the image in Figure B-17 is actually in the Commons, not the English Wikipedia.

Figure B-17. The file Image:Fujisan from Motohakone.jpg is used in the article Tokyo. Clicking the thumbnail image in the article shows you this larger image, though not necessarily a full-sized image. Click "full resolution" to see the full-sized version. Right-click the full-sized image to save it to your computer. You can also save the image as your new desktop background image.

Finding pictures in the Commons

Because the Commons is a media storage site, you'll find a table of contents right on its Main Page (Figure B-18). With more than 2 million images, you may find something you really like—and it's all free content.

Picture of the Day

If you'd like a free, high-quality picture emailed to you each day (or, to be technical, a link to such a picture), you can subscribe to the Commons' Picture of the Day mailing list. Sign up at *http://lists.wikimedia.org/mailman/listinfo/daily-image*.

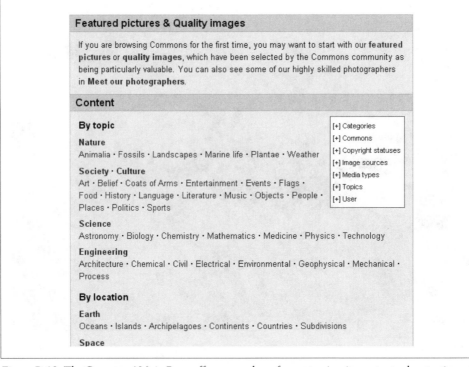

Figure B-18. The Commons' Main Page offers a number of ways to view its content—by starting with featured pictures, by drilling down through categories, or by choosing a topic area. If you choose a topic, you'll arrive at a category page similar to Figure B-5 with one interesting difference—the page has a tab labeled CatScan. Yep—that's the category intersection tool mentioned on page 438, and it works for the Commons as well as Wikipedia.

You Can Help

Wikipedia calls itself "the free encyclopedia that anyone can edit." If you don't think you have anything to add to it, you're wrong—Wikipedia is still far from complete. But you as a reader can help when you see an article with a problem, or if you search for an article and don't find it.

TIP

When you're thinking about fixing or adding to a Wikipedia article, make sure you have reliable sources at your fingertips first, as described on page 65.

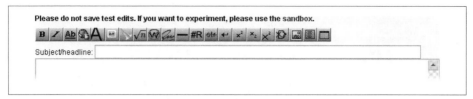

Figure B-19. Here's what the page should look like after step 3: It's ready for you to enter a brief summary ("Possible vandalism" or "Birthplace seems wrong" or whatever) and then, below the summary line, to type in your full comment or question.

Articles with Problems

If you see vandalism in a Wikipedia article, it could easily have just happened, and an editor's in the process of fixing it. Wait 5 minutes or so, and then refresh your browser window (or leave the page and return). If it's still not gone, you can ask editors to help. Similarly, when you see something in an article that's incorrect or obviously missing (perhaps you had a question that you expected the article to answer), you can always ask about the problem, which makes it much more likely that active editors will fix it.

Asking about something in (or missing from) an article is an easy six-step process:

1. At the top of the article, you'll see a tab called "discussion". Click it.

   The article's talk (discussion) page opens.

2. Do a quick scan of the talk (discussion) page to see if your issue or question has already been asked.

   If so, you don't need to post anything; you're done.

   But if you're looking at something that looks like an error message, which starts, "Wikipedia does not have a talk page with this exact title. Before creating this page, please verify that an article called ... ", *don't worry*—this message means that your question couldn't possibly have been previously asked, because the talk page didn't even exist. You can go on to step 3.

3. Assuming your issue or question is new, click the "+" tab at the top of the talk page to start a new comment.

   You're in edit mode, with two boxes where you can type information.

4. Type a brief summary of the issue or question into the "Subject/headline" box at the top of the screen (Figure B-19).

   Up to 10 words should be enough.

5. In the main edit box (see Figure B-19 again), explain the issue/question. At the end of the last line of your comment, add a couple of spaces and then put four tildes, next to each other (like this: ~~~~).

   The four tildes tell the Wikipedia software to put a signature and date-stamp there. Figure B-20 shows an example of a comment after being typed in.

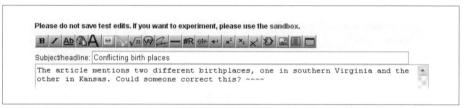

Figure B-20. Here's what the input screen shown in Figure C-14 looks like after someone has entered a section heading (summary) and a comment. It's now ready to be saved.

NOTE

The Wikipedia software records, in the page history, exactly the same information that displays when you add four tildes. So you're not revealing anything by "signing" your comment. If you don't, an automated editor (a *bot*) does it for you. You get more credit if you do the signing yourself. (See page 144 for more on signatures.)

---

6. Click the "Save page" button (you may have to tab down or scroll down or page down to see it).

Voilá! You've posted a comment to Wikipedia, thereby contributing to the improvement of an article (or bringing missed vandalism to the attention of other editors).

Missing Articles

You've searched for an article and didn't find it, even using an outside search engine (page 431). Now what? Wikipedia has created a page where you can check to see if someone has already suggested that Wikipedia needs such an article. And that page, *Wikipedia:Requested articles*, has associated pages where you can add the name of the article as a suggestion if no one else already has.

Unfortunately, this page, and its associated pages, isn't particularly user-friendly for someone unfamiliar with Wikipedia editing. You have to pick the correct general topic area from a list of 10, then a topic area from what can be a long list, and then maybe even go down yet one more level just to see the area of a page where you're supposed to post.

Finally, when you're at the right area of the page, you have to figure out how to post your suggestion. If all the sections of all the associated pages were consistently formatted, you'd find instructions here on how to post to them—but they're not.

An easier way to suggest to the Wikipedia community that an article is needed is to find a relatively close *existing* article, and then, following the steps on page 445, post a note on the article's talk page. When you post, describe the topic that you looked for and couldn't find, and that you'd appreciate it if a more experienced editor added the subject at the *Wikipedia:Requested articles* page.

Learning More

No book, not even the one you're holding, can tell you everything you'll ever need to know about Wikipedia, especially since Wikipedia is a work in progress, always changing and growing in the hands of a changing and growing community of editors. Being a Wikipedia editor is like being an eternal student, acquiring as well as transmitting new knowledge all the time.

Think of this appendix as a campus map. It shows you the myriad places you can go, both inside and outside Wikipedia, to learn what you need to know when you're ready. It focuses on three main areas of learning:

- **Finding exactly the right information**. Wikipedia has many hundreds of pages of detailed policies, guidelines, technical advice, and essays, not to mention specialized pages that simply list other pages. You're more likely to find what you're looking for, among all these instructional pages, if you choose one of several good starting points.

- **Getting personalized help**. An unspoken assumption about editing in Wikipedia, as you may have noticed, is that you're supposed to figure out things mostly by yourself. Still, you can get personal help, if you know where and how to ask.

- **Understanding Wikipedia as a community**. You may be curious about what's going on in the Wikipedia community. This appendix shows you how to get the news (and the gossip) about Wikipedia, and even how to meet other Wikipedians face-to-face if you so desire.

Information Pages

Wikipedia has help pages, FAQs, and other kinds pages offering information about editing and using Wikipedia. If you had to choose one place to go to first in your quest to find specifics about editing Wikipedia, a good candidate would be *Help:Contents* (shortcut: *WP:HELP*). It does a nice job of organizing information you might need into a dozen subtopics (most are shown in Figure C-1), plus links to a lot of other useful pages.

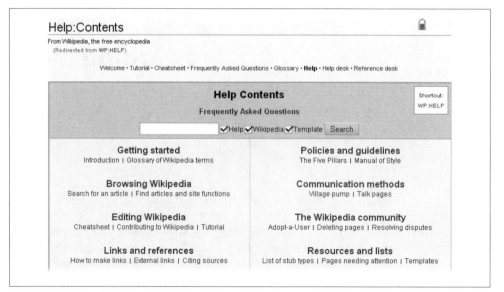

Help:Contents
From Wikipedia, the free encyclopedia
(Redirected from WP:HELP)

Welcome · Tutorial · Cheatsheet · Frequently Asked Questions · Glossary · **Help** · Help desk · Reference desk

Help Contents
Frequently Asked Questions

Shortout:
WP:HELP

☑Help ☑Wikipedia ☑Template Search

Getting started
Introduction | Glossary of Wikipedia terms

Policies and guidelines
The Five Pillars | Manual of Style

Browsing Wikipedia
Search for an article | Find articles and site functions

Communication methods
Village pump | Talk pages

Editing Wikipedia
Cheatsheet | Contributing to Wikipedia | Tutorial

The Wikipedia community
Adopt-a-User | Deleting pages | Resolving disputes

Links and references
How to make links | External links | Citing sources

Resources and lists
List of stub types | Pages needing attention | Templates

Figure C-1. From the Help:Contents *page, you can go in one of four directions if you're looking for useful information about editing. From the top bar, you can go to two somewhat similar pages:* Wikipedia:Tutorial *and* Wikipedia:FAQ. *Secondly, you can use the search box. A third option is to select one of the subpages, each of which contain a list of specific pages for a particular area. The fourth option is to go directly to an individual page; the top bar includes two particularly detailed individual pages,* Wikipedia:Cheatsheet *(editing markup) and* Wikipedia:Glossary.

The *Help:Contents* page contains two separate links to the *Frequently Asked Questions (FAQs)* page. If you click either link, then you go to a page that lists available FAQs (Figure C-2).

FREQUENTLY ASKED QUESTION

Editing Instructional Pages

If I see an "edit" tab at the top of an instructional page, can I really edit it?

Yes. If you're logged in, you can edit pretty much every instructional page. (Figure C-1 is an example of an instructional page that's semi-protected, so that only editors who are logged in can edit it—note the small padlock at the upper right.) As for whether you *should*, the answer is generally not, until you're a more experienced editor. Until then, the most productive use of your time is probably helping improve articles.

Still, if you see a typo or something that you're absolutely sure isn't right (probably because it hasn't been updated), you may want to do an edit and fix the page. Given that there are thousands of such pages (this book only mentions a hundred or two), you'll probably find errors if you look. These pages are maintained in exactly the same way as Wikipedia articles—by editors like you; no editors "own" any page or are assigned to maintain any pages.

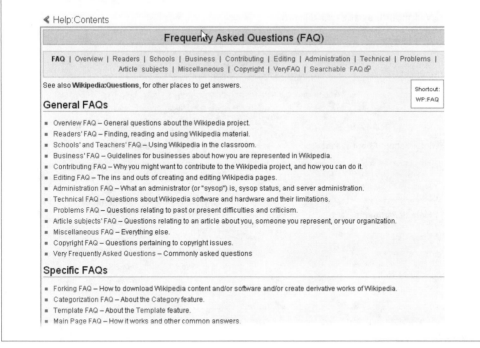

Figure C-2. Wikipedia has a number of compilations of frequently asked questions. If you're looking for information in one of these areas, you can probably get it, and also learn other useful things.

Another option, if you see anything in an instructional page that doesn't make sense, is to leave a question about the matter on the related talk page. Normally, experienced editors respond to your question, and often reword the instructional information for errors, clarity, or both. For a faster response, you can ask for clarification on the Help desk (*WP:HD*) rather than the talk page; just don't do both at the same time.

You should also fix instructional pages if you see vandalism or spam edits, as discussed in Chapter 7. Unfortunately, registration isn't a guarantee of good behavior, so even semi-protected pages aren't vandalism-free 100 percent of the time.

Directories and Indexes

The *Help:Contents* page and its FAQ brethren provide fairly tightly organized information. By contrast, two directories offer a jumping-off point for a much larger number of instructional pages. One, the *Wikipedia:Department directory* (shortcut: *WP:DIR*), with more than 150 links to specific pages, is organized by categories of general Wikipedia functions (Figure C-3).

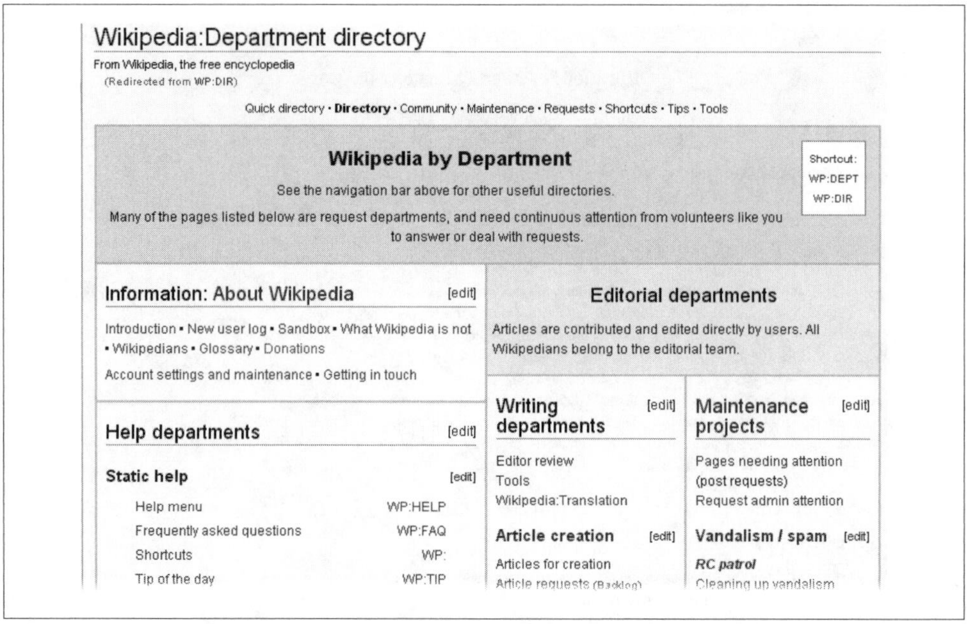

Figure C-3. The Department directory page organizes more than 150 links to specific pages (more than two dozen links are shown here, at the top of the directory) into rough categories called departments. While there's no such thing as a department in Wikipedia (even informally), the groupings are a handy way to find your way around.

Figure C-3 also has a top bar, similar to the one in Figure C-1. One of the links listed there is to *Wikipedia:Quick directory* (shortcut: *WP:QUICK*). Figure C-4 shows the Quick Directory.

The newest addition tool within Wikipedia for finding information is the *Editor's Index to Wikipedia* (shortcut: *WP:EIW*). Figure C-5 is a snapshot of part of this index, which has over 2,000 entries.

Places to Ask Questions

Despite the many thousands of instructional pages with information for editors (some would say *because* of the thousands of pages), you may want to ask other editors how to do something, or why something is the way it is. Before listing the places where you can ask questions, here are two caveats:

- If you have a question about a specific article, it's best to start by asking at the article's talk/discussion page (see page 145). If you don't get any response within a day or two, then ask at one of the pages listed below.

Figure C-4. The Quick Directory *gives you a good overview of the ecology of Wikipedia, with relatively few links to follow.*

- If you have a question about a specific policy or guideline, ask at the talk page for that policy or guideline. For example, if you have a question about articles that are lists, and the relevant guideline is *Wikipedia:Lists*, then ask on the page *Wikipedia talk:Lists*.

Here are four places for editors to ask (more or less) general questions:

- *New contributors' help page* (shortcut: *WP:NCHP*)
- *Help desk* (shortcut: *WP:HD*)
- *Village pump (assistance)* (shortcut: *WP:VPA*)
- *Village pump (technical)* (shortcut: *WP:VPT*)

In addition, for specialized questions about images and other uploaded media that Wikipedia can use:

- *Wikipedia:Media copyright questions* (shortcut: *WP:MCQ*)

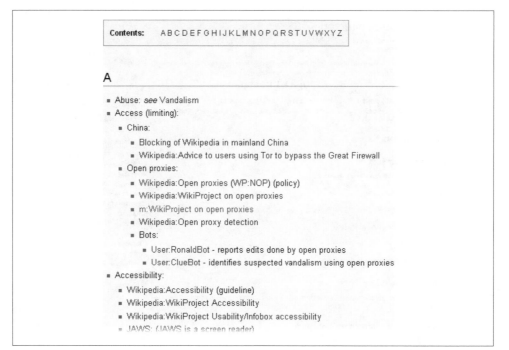

Figure C-5. The beginning of section "A" of the Editor's Index to Wikipedia. *In addition to the links to specific pages, the index also has links from one major topic (like Administration) to others (in this case, Enforcement). All major topics also have shortcuts (not shown here) for easy linking from other pages.*

WORD TO THE WISE

Frequently Asked Errors

When you post a question at one of the five general help pages listed here, you can make things easier for yourself and the editors who answer questions by doing the following:

- Read the information at the top of the page. There may be a link there that's more useful than asking a question. Or a good suggestion about asking your question somewhere else.

- Start a new section for your question, using the "+" tab.

- If you have a question about a specific page, wikilink to it (put paired square brackets on either side of the page name).

- Don't post your email address or any other kind of personal information.

- Don't put spaces at the beginning of a line. You don't need any indentation when you ask your question.

- Sign your question by adding a couple of spaces and then four tildes (~~~~) at the end of your last line of text. (Don't start a new line for your signature; just put it at the end of the last line of text.)

    If you do all those things, you'll come across as an editor who knows enough to ask questions right. And when you've gotten a good answer (or need to clarify your question), come back to the section and acknowledge the answer (click on the "edit" link for the section). Editors who answer questions particularly like to hear that their answers have been useful—or that you want to clarify so they can really give you the answer you need.

You can also post your question on your own user talk page (page 156). When you do, add the following template to the section of the page where the question is: *{{helpme}}*. That template adds the category *Wikipedians looking for help* to your user talk page, and then one or more editors who monitor that category will show up to answer your question.

Finally, if you're an IRC user, you can connect at *irc://irc.freenode.net/wikipedia-en-help*, the help channel for Wikipedians.

Coaching and Classes

If you learn better in a one-on-one situation, you're not alone. Wikipedia has three pages where an editor can go for personalized advising. Consider one of these services if you're serious about honing your skills:

- *Wikipedia:Adopt-a-User* (shortcut: *WP:ADOPT*). A program where experienced editors pair up with and help new, inexperienced editors.
- *Wikipedia:Editor review* (shortcut: *WP:ER*). Lets an editor have several peers evaluate his edits and provide tips and pointers on areas for improvement.
- *Wikipedia:Admin coaching* (shortcut: *WP:ADCO*). This program is for editors who know the basics of editing articles, but need help learning new roles like vandal-fighting.

In addition, *Wikipedia:IRC channels* (shortcut: *WP:IRC*) has information about the freenode network's dedicated chat rooms. These are online meeting places, open 24 hours a day, in which Wikipedians can engage in real-time discussions with each other.

Wikipedia News and Gossip

Like any place with lots of action (Hollywood and Washington, D.C. come to mind), Wikipedia generates a body of news and gossip. When people are interested in something, they crave reading and talking about it. If you've been bitten by the Wikipedia bug, you'll be glad to know there's plenty of official news and unofficial gossip to satisfy your craving to know more.

News

If you expect to continue editing at Wikipedia for any length of time, by all means subscribe to the weekly internal newsletter, the *Wikipedia Signpost*. You can get it in any of three ways:

- If you want to read the newsletter at your user talk page (page 156), go to the *Signpost's* main page (shortcut:*WP:POST*), click "About the Signpost", then "Tools", and then "Spamlist".

- If you want the latest issue displayed on your user page (see page 53), go to the *Signpost's* main page, click "About the Signpost", then "Tools", and then "Story template".

- If you want the newsletter delivered by email, go to *http://wikipediasignpost.com/signup.php*.

Another way to keep up with what's happening with Wikipedia is to read the page within Wikipedia that tracks news stories, *Wikipedia:Press coverage* (shortcut *WP:PC*).

Gossip

You can also get information about Wikipedia-related goings-on from the following sources (which Wikipedia's guidelines define as *not* reliable sources).

- *Planet Wikimedia* (*http://en.planet.wikimedia.org*) is a Web log (blog) aggregator operated by the Wikimedia Foundation. Some of the posts are about wikis in general, and some are on topics peripheral to Wikipedia, but the quality is quite high, and interesting things are likely to show up here at least as quickly as anywhere else.

- *Wikipedia:Mailing lists* (shortcut: *WP:ML*) provides links to subscribe to any one of a number of mailing lists. For the English Wikipedia, *WikiEN-l* is the most subscribed to (roughly 1,000 subscribers as of mid-2007). Before you sign up, read the threaded archives at *http://lists.wikimedia.org/pipermail/wikien-l/*. You may decide that the signal to noise ratio is lower than you want (Figure C-6).

If you want to talk about Wikipedia face to face, your best opportunities are regional meet-ups. Future (planned) events are listed on the *Wikipedia:Meetup* page (shortcut: *WP:MU*). Wikipedians have roughly five to ten meet-ups per month, which may sound like a lot, but that figure is for all meet-ups across the entire world. Meet-ups that are not in North America, the UK, or Oceania are likely to focus on a non-English language edition of Wikipedia.

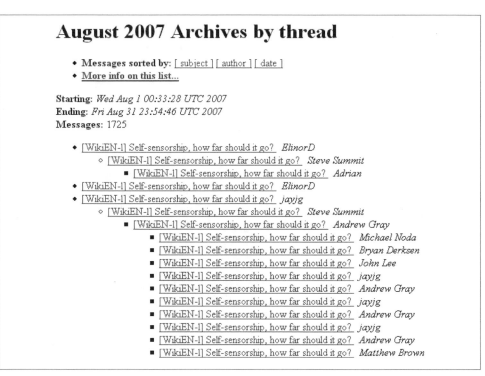

Figure C-6. The archived messages of the WikiEN-1 newsletter offer a good preview, before subscribing, as well as a way to look back through old messages to see what topics were hotly discussed.

Index

Symbols

! (exclamation points)
  invisible comments and, 15
  table headings and, 267
" (quotation marks), source names and, 39
(pound signs)
  numbered lists and, 15, 255
  wikilinks and, 149, 245
' (apostrophes), text formatting and, 8
* (asterisks)
  as wildcards, 128
  bulleted lists and, 15, 255
  indenting using, 148
+ tab, 131, 149, 416
/ (slash), in paired tags, 14
3RR warnings, 182
: (colons)
  indenting using, 148
  links and, 288
; (semicolons), pseudo-headings and, 247
<> (pointy brackets), in tags, 14
= (equal signs), section headings and, 7
[] (square brackets), links and, 14, 31
^ (carets), footnotes and, 39
{} (curly brackets), templates and, 7, 14
| (vertical lines)
  as parameter separators, 18
  tables and, 15
~ (tildes), in signatures, 144

A

A-Z index, 436
About Wikipedia page, 418
abuse, reporting, 132
acceptable sources, 361
accessibility
  shortcut (WP:ACCESS), 235
  voice browsers, 268
accounts (see user accounts)
added characters (WP:AORC), 110
adding text, 5
  edit conflicts and, 12
administrators
  admin coaching (WP:ADCO), 228, 453
  conduct violations and, 197
  intervention against vandalism (WP: AIV),
    137
  moves and (WP:RM), 303
  noticeboard/incidents (WP:AN/I), 159,
    206, 228
  requests for selective deletion
    (WP:SELDEL), 82
  role of, 199
  selection of, 197
  vandalism assistance, 133–137
Adopt-a-User (WP:ADOPT), 227, 453
advertising, 360
  internal (WP:BANNER), 172
AfD (Articles for Deletion), 373
AGF (see assume good faith policy (WP:AGF))
aggregators (see feed readers)
alerts
  user talk page postings, 157
  wikiquette, 226
alternative websites for content (WP:OUT),
    54
amboxes, 177
annotated articles (WP:ANAR), 73
annotated lists, 259

distinguish template, 321
documenting sources, 25–42
   content disputes and, 185
   guidelines, 25
domains, Wikipedia, xvi
Donate to Wikipedia link, 419
double redirects, 76, 301, 303, 310
Drawing board (WP:DRAW), 78, 218
duplicate articles, 340

E

edit box, 5, 423
   creating wikilinks in, 15
   formatting text in, 6
   preferences, 393
edit conflicts, 11–13
   on WP:AIV, 137
   reverting and, 92
   undoing and, 93
edit counters, 383
edit mode, 5, 422–425
   confirming, 30
   features of, 422
   moving text in, 158
   signing comments and, 144
Edit raw watchlist, 105
edit summaries, 9
   blank, bug, 94
   character limit on, 93
   for reversions, 95
   for undos, 93
   in page histories, 84
   legend (WP:ESL), 9
   prompt to enter, 10
   vandalism and, 124
   vandalism reports, 136
Edit summary box, 9
edit this page tab, 5, 415
edit toolbar, 6, 422
edit wars (WP:EW), 182
editing, 3–23
   adding text, 5
      edit conflicts and, 12
   archive pages, 156
   article sections, 18
   comments, 154, 158
   conflicts, 11–13
   edit box, 5
   edit toolbar, 6

footnotes, 36
in sandbox, 4
instructional pages, 448
inuse template and, 13
JavaScript and, 401–410
lead sections, 20, 74
pages, watchlists and, 110
preferences, 393
previewing changes, 8–10, 424
saving changes, 10, 424
sections, 41
spelling guidelines, 23
tables, 262
tables of contents, 245
editor assistance (WP:EA), 64, 226
editor review (WP:ER), 223
editor-focused WikiProjects, 167
editors
   anonymous, 124, 298
   awards for (WP:Award), 219
   backgrounds of, 179
   behavior of, 195–211
   block logs, 124
   coaching, 223
   combining edits in page histories, 96
   editor assistance (WP:EA), 192, 204
   emailing, 162, 425
   evaluating, 202
   identifying, 84, 96
   motivations of, 180
   new, 219
   problem, 123
   User contributions page, 126
Editor's Index to Wikipedia (WP:EIW), 183, 213
editor's notes, 245
edits
   bad faith, 129
   by bots, removing from watchlists, 108
   counting, 97
   diffs and, 87
   edit summaries, 93
   evaluating for vandalism, 124–125
   explaining, 126, 181
   interior, 91
   minor (m), 84, 423
      removing from watchlists, 108
   name of editor, finding, 84
   previewing, 8, 424

Freenode IRC network, 164
fringe theories (WP:FRINGE), 342
further reading section, 241

G

Gadgets tab, 399
galleries, 287
geographical WikiProjects, 166
GNU Free Documentation License (GFDL), 68, 423
Go button, 431
good article nominations (WP:GAN), 221
Google Scholar, 40
gossip, 454
Graphic Lab (WP:GL), 218
graphics (see images)

H

Harvard referencing (WP:HARV), 32
Harvard-style footnotes, 33
hatnotes, 319
headings, for a table, 268
headings, section (see section headings)
help
    Adopt-a-User (WP:ADOPT), 227, 453
    asking questions, 450
    Editing help link, 423
    editor assistance (WP:EA), 64
    FAQs, 215
    for sections (WP:SEC), 250
    Help desk (WP:HD), 128, 214–215
    Help talk pages, 145, 215
    Help:Contents page, 419
    Help:Contents page (WP:HELP), 447
    information pages, 447
    Nubio, 215
    Reference desk (WP:RD), 216
    Village Pump (WP:VP), 145
    with images, 287
highlighting text, 150
histories (see page histories)
history tab, 416
    edit conflicts and, 13
history WikiProjects, 166
hits (search results), preferences, 396

I

images, 271–289
acceptable formats, 272
alignment of, 285
captions, 287
categorizing, 280
description preferences, 391
finding, 284
Flickr, 275
galleries, 287
help with, 287
inserting in articles, 284
maps, 290
moving, 282
naming, 279
policies, 288
quality of, 274
renaming, 282
replacing, 282
requesting, 284
reviewing, 222
screenshots, 272
sections and, 285
thumbnails, 286, 391
uploading, 271
watchlists and, 107
importing
    tables, 269
    user scripts, 406
improving articles, 339–358
incidents (WP:AN/I), 159
incivility, 153, 183, 195–211
    dealing with, 200
    requests for comment (WP:RFC) and, 207
    vs. personal attacks, 196
    warnings and, 197
inclusionism, 379
indentation
    in discussions, 148
    in lists, 259
index to Wikipedia (WP:EIW), 213, 450
infoboxes (WP:IBX), 357
informal dispute resolution, 188–191
insertable text, 424
interaction box, 418
interior edits, 91
internal links (see wikilinks)
Internet Explorer
    cache, bypassing, 112
    JavaScript and, 401
Internet Protocol address (see IP addresses)

Internet relay chat (IRC), 164
inuse template, 13
invisible comments, 15
IP addresses
    bad behavior and, 202
    privacy and, 47
    problems with using, 47
    semi-protection and, 134
    shared, 132
    vandalism and, 124, 128
IRC (Internet relay chat), 164, 453
ISBNs, in Rp template, 42
italic text, 8
    headings and, 243
    quotations and (talk pages), 151

J

JavaScript (see user scripts)
joining WikiProjects, 170

K

keyboard shortcuts (WP:K), xix, 426
Kindness Campaign (WP:KC), 219

L

language links, 421
language preferences, 384
(last), in page histories, 83, 90
layout of articles (WP:GTL), 73
lead sections
    citations and, 27
    editing, 20, 74
    sequence of items in, 234
    shortcut (WP:LS), 234
least astonishment principle, 314
length of articles, 236
levels, warning, 130
links, 440
    About Wikipedia, 418
    and colons (:), 288
    blue, 75, 160
    category, 15, 324
    Cite this article, 420
    Community portal, 418
    Contact Wikipedia, 419
    Content, 417
    Current events, 418
    disambiguation, 313, 319

Donate to Wikipedia, 419
embedded, 31, 351
external, 14, 241
    adding, 30
    fixing bad, 349
    numbering of, 31, 36
    shortcut (WP:EL), 73
Featured content, 418
guidelines for linking, 15
headings and, 243
Help, 419
internal (see wikilinks)
link rot, 31
linkspam, 90
log out, 414
Main Page, 417
my contributions, 414
my preferences, 414
my talk, 414
my watchlist, 414
Permanent, 420
piped links, 15
preferences, 398
Printable version, 420
Random article, 418
Recent changes, 419
red, 71, 75, 86, 124, 125, 256, 351
Related changes, 420
Special pages, 420
square brackets ([]) and, 14, 31
to article sections, 244
to disambiguation pages, 318
to WikiProjects, 352
Upload file, 420
What links here, 419
wikilinks, 14, 15, 28, 351
Linksearch page, 128
linkspam, 90, 121, 128, 356
Liquid Threads, 147
list of bibliographies (WP:LOB), 79
lists, 253–262, 336
    annotated, 259
    as articles, 256
    asterisks (*) and, 255
    bulleted, 259
        markup for, 15
    creating, 254
    editing, 253
    embedded vs. standalone, 253

Colophon

Our look is the result of reader comments, our own experimentation, and feedback from distribution channels. Distinctive covers complement our distinctive approach to technical topics, breathing personality and life into potentially dry subjects.

The cover design of this book is based on a series design originally created by David Freedman and modified by Mike Kohnke, Karen Montgomery, and Fitch (*http://www.fitch.com*). Back cover design, dog illustration, and color selection by Fitch.

The illustrations that appear in *Wikipedia: The Missing Manual* were produced by Robert Romano and Jessamyn Read using Macromedia FreeHand MX and Adobe Photoshop CS.

70502